DISCARDED

THE ENGLISH SERMON 1750-1850

General editors

C. H. Sisson
Val Warner
Michael Schmidt

THE ENGLISH SERMON

volume III: 1750 - 1850

an anthology

ROBERT NYE

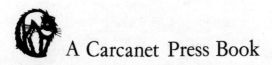 A Carcanet Press Book

SBN 85635 095 8

First published in 1976
by Carcanet Press Limited
266 Councillor Lane
Cheadle Hulme, Cheadle
Cheshire SK8 5PN

Printed in Great Britain
by Unwin Brothers Limited
The Gresham Press, Old Woking, Surrey.

Contents

FOREWORD

IT IS a pleasure to thank Mr C. H. Sisson, first for suggesting this book, then for putting me right in a general way during its making, lastly for specific criticisms of a draft of the introduction and the biographies and notes. I have also to thank Fr Marcus Lefébure, O. P., who read the same draft of the introduction so closely that I was able to come at it again with new eyes. Neither of these friends is of course responsible for any errors of fact or emphasis which may remain; their service to the book is precisely that they did not try to influence it, but required me to clarify my own mind. I am also grateful to Fr W. Gordon Reid, Rector of St Michael and All Saints, Edinburgh, for reading the original introduction and indicating ways in which it could be improved, and to Mr Michael Schmidt for encouragement at all stages beyond the bounds of what an author commonly enjoys at the hands of his publisher. In the choice of matter for the book I received helpful guidance from Fr Brocard Sewell, O. Carm., who introduced me to James Archer and Samuel Ogden, and I record my indebtedness to Canon Charles Smyth, in whose book *The Art of Preaching* I first met Charles Augustus Hare. I have also to thank Mrs Ida Matthews, Miss Marion Lochhead, Fr Christopher Bryant, S. S. J. E., Mr James Douglas, Mr Victor Young, and again Fr Marcus Lefébure, for the gift or loan of books. I am especially grateful to Mrs Anne Tibble for out-of-the-way information about Thomas Sikes of Guilsborough. Finally, my thanks to Mr John L. Howard and the staff of New College Library, Edinburgh, who provided unfailing assistance in the recovery of scarce texts, and more than thanks to my wife Aileen for generally sharing her natural gifts of insight and intuition, and through whom I met Fr Marcus Lefébure.

1750	Death of Bach
1751	Voltaire, d'Alembert, Diderot, Rousseau,etc: first volume of *Encyclopédie*
1753	Birth of Chatterton
1755	Johnson: *Dictionary of the English Language*
	Rousseau: *Discours*
	Lisbon earthquake
1756	Lisbon Cathedral rebuilt
	Birth of Mozart
1757	Hume: *Natural History of Religion*
	Birth of Blake
1759	Voltaire: *Candide*
	Burke begins *Annual Register*
1760	Accession of George III
1761	Death of Law
1762	Rousseau: *Du Contrat social*
	Suppression of the Jesuits in France
1763	Smart: *Song to David*
1765	d'Alembert: *Sur la Déstruction des Jésuites en France*
1770	Death of Chatterton
	Birth of Beethoven
	Birth of Wordsworth
1772	Birth of Coleridge
1774	Accession of Louis XVI
1776	American Declaration of Independence
1778	Roman Catholic Relief Act
1780	'No Popery' riots in London
	Encyclopédie completed, 35 vols.
1783	American Independence
1786	Mozart: *Le Nozze di Figaro*
1788	Kant: *Critique of Pure Reason*
1789	Blake: *Songs of Innocence*
	French Revolution
1790	Kant: *Critique of Judgement*
	Burke: *Reflections on the French Revolution*
	Mozart: *Cosi fan tutte*
1791	Massacres in Paris
	Paine: *Rights of Man*
	Blake: *The French Revolution*
	Mozart: *Die Zauberflöte*

1791	Mozart: *Requiem*
	Death of Mozart
	Death of Wesley
1792	France declared a republic — Reign of Terror lasting fifteen months — the Catholic religion abolished in France — churches become Temples of Reason — execution of Louis XVI
	Birth of Dominic Barberi
1793	Kant: *Religion within the Boundaries of Pure Reason*
	Blake: *The Marriage of Heaven and Hell*
1794	Paine: *The Age of Reason*
	Cult of the Supreme Being substituted for the Cult of Reason — Robespierre executed
	Blake: *Songs of Experience*
1796	Haydn: Holy Mass in B flat
1797	Coleridge: 'Ancient Mariner' and 'Kubla Khan'
1798	Coleridge and Wordsworth: *Lyrical Ballads*
	Haydn: *The Creation*
	French troops loot Rome — Pius VI taken prisoner, dies in exile
1799	Bonaparte master of France
1800	Pius VII comes to Rome
1801	Birth of Newman
1802	Concordat between France and Roman Catholic Church
	Chateaubriand: *Le Génie du Christianisme*
1803	Wars between Britain and France until 1815
1804	Bonaparte proclaims himself Emperor of France
	Preparations along English coast for expected French invasion
	Blake: *Jerusalem*
1805	Trafalgar
	Wordsworth: *The Prelude*
1806	Death of Haydn
	Beethoven: Mass in C
1809	Bonaparte excommunicated by Pius VII
1812	Bonaparte retreats from Moscow
	Hegel: *Logik*
1814	Bonaparte exiled to Elba
	The Bourbon Restoration: Louis XVIII
1815	Waterloo
1816	Coleridge: *Lay Sermons*

1818	Birth of Emily Brontë
1819	Agitation for reform in England — Six Acts passed to prevent riot and sedition
1820	Accession of George IV
1822	Civil War in Spain between Liberal and Royalist forces
1824	Accession of Charles X
	Beethoven: *Missa Solemnis*
1827	Death of Blake
1829	Roman Catholic Emancipation
1830	Accession of William IV
	July Revolution in France — Charles X overthrown — Louis-Philippe elected king
	Coleridge: *On the Constitution of the Church and State, according to the Idea of Each*
	Apparition of the Blessed Virgin Mary to Katherine Labouré in the rue du Bac, Paris
1831	Struggle for Reform Bill in the Commons — it is rejected by the Lords — riots in Bristol, Nottingham and Derby
1832	Reform Bill passed by Parliament
	Republican rising in Paris — suppressed
1833	First session of reformed Commons — Whigs in power, supported by Roman Catholics and Protestant Dissenters — Whigs reduce Irish bishoprics from 22 to 12
	Tracts for the Times begin
1834	Death of Coleridge
	Faraday enunciates laws of electrolysis
1837	Accession of Queen Victoria
	Carlyle: *The French Revolution*
1839	Publication of Peoples' Charter at Glasgow — riots in Newport and Birmingham
1841	Dominic Barberi comes to England
1842	Second Chartist Petition rejected by Commons — riots in Staffordshire and Lancashire
1845	Newman: *An Essay on the Development of Christian Doctrine*
	Newman received into the Roman Catholic Church by Dominic Barberi
1846	Election of Pius IX
1847	Emily Brontë: *Wuthering Heights*
	Marx and Engels: *The Communist Manifesto*
1848	Third Chartist Petition exposed as fraudulent by

Commons
Revolution in France — Louis-Philippe deposed
Clausius and Kelvin expound second law of thermo-
dynamics
Revolutions in Berlin, Vienna, Venice, Milan, Naples,
Prague and Budapest
Revolution in Rome — Pius IX driven to Gaeta
Death of Emily Brontë

1849   Fizeau measures speed of light
Restoration of Pius IX
Death of Dominic Barberi

1850   Death of Wordsworth
Establishing of Roman Catholic Hierarchy in Britain

THE HUNDRED years from 1750 to 1850 consist of the usual war between the *ecclesia* and the gates of hell, between the Church as the divine society praying for its promised ending, 'Thy kingdom come', and those forces which would like to prevail against it to prevent that coming if they could. This century's particular conflict may be better seen first by looking back at it through the eyes of an author who refers to himself only as 'an hereditary High Churchman', and then by looking forward through the eyes of Samuel Taylor Coleridge.

The author of *Reminiscences of Forty Years* (1868) says that his mother came of a Non-Juring and Jacobite family, and that from his father, a clergyman, he had learned to believe in the Real Presence, to defend the Catholicity of the English Church, and to value the importance of her Apostolic Succession.* What Lancelot Andrewes and Thomas Ken celebrated and made, this anonymous member of the Church of England insists, was what his father had celebrated and made. Obviously, then, in the latter half of the eighteenth century the Church was not everywhere regarded as a mere department of State, the Tory party at prayer.

Yet having made the point for Catholic continuity it must be conceded that those who preserved a serious sense of the *ecclesia* through this period stood often to one side of the mainstream of Anglicanism. It is the Non-Jurors such as Ken, William Law, George Hickes, John Kettlewell and Robert Nelson who give us a link between the Caroline divines of the seventeenth century and the Tractarians of the nineteenth, although High Church principles lived on also in the interstices of power, as well as in that unobtrusive piety which has usually found a home in one English village or another. When Keble heard the teaching of the Tractarians spoken of as new, he remarked, 'It seems to me to be the same as what my father always taught me.'

A link can be found, also, between the Wesleys and the Oxford Movement. This exists in Alexander Knox, born in 1757 of the family which gave Scotland its reformer, friendly in youth

---

* As did Samuel Johnson a hundred years earlier, when he shocked Boswell by declaring that he preferred Papal to Presbyterian religion. Boswell: 'How so, Sir?' Johnson: 'Why, Sir, the Presbyterians have no Church, no apostolical ordination.' Boswell: 'And do you think that absolutely essential, Sir?' Johnson: 'Why, Sir, as it was an apostolical institution, I think it is dangerous to be without it.'

with John Wesley, who was his spiritual adviser, living on to entertain a small circle with his talk and his letters. Knox is significant in the stress which he puts upon the Liturgy, in his observation of a possibly providential role which the English Church might have as a *via media*, and in his respect for the Fathers. On the first matter, he writes, in a letter dated 1812, 'I know nothing more settled, in the whole reformed body, than the Liturgy of the Church of England . . .'[1] And again,

> To the Liturgy, therefore, I adhere, as the golden chain, which binds us, or rather as the silver cord (for so Solomon calls the spinal marrow) which unites us to the great mystical body; other parts of our constitution (such as super-added prayers and the Thirty-Nine Articles) were no doubt seen to be expedient, especially considering the middle point we were to occupy; and (I trust) the conciliatory function to be one day exercised by us. But our vitality as a Church consists in our identity of organisation, and of mental character with the Church Catholic: and as our unbroken episcopacy implies the first, our Liturgy—and that alone—contains the other.[2]

Knox was a visionary of a kind. Who else then would have seen in Wesley what several see now — that he was a forerunner of the Catholic renaissance of the English Church? 'I consider John Wesley,' Knox wrote towards the end of his life,

> as promulgating in his latter days, above all uninspired men who had gone before him, Christianity in all its efficacy, and yet in all its amiability. On this ground he appears to me the first competent unveiler of that concentration of the evangelic rays, which has been so wonderfully (and I would almost venture to say exclusively) insphered in our established Liturgy. And I trust the time will yet come, and that it is not at any very great distance (though I confess as yet I see no sign of its approach), when the providential deposit which distinguishes the Church of England will be appreciated; and Mr Wesley's designation, as the precursive announcer of its hitherto undeveloped excellences, will be fully understood and adequately recognised.[3]

Knox died in 1831, having lived a hermit's life in Dublin, erudite, dishevelled, his usual garb a dressing-gown, skull-cap and slippers, his mind seldom coming awake before ten o'clock at night. A year before, a similar but greater spirit, the poet who wrote 'The Ancient Mariner', had published his final book, *On the Constitution of the Church and State, according to the Idea of Each*.

This work is a statement of Coleridge's grasp of the values given in national history by the development of that divine society which is the Church, and more unusually it is also what amounts to a vision of the *ecclesia* in its spiritual and supernatural aspect. Coleridge makes a distinction between the historical *ecclesia*, as it penetrates and informs the English Constitution, and the universal *ecclesia*, the Catholic Church of Christ. Hooker's treatise *Of the Laws of Ecclesiastical Polity* (1594) had set forth the ideal for the relations of Church and State — that they are identical, the one society seen from different points of view. Coleridge's thinking is more complex, no less Catholic. He speaks of a twofold conception of the Church and a twofold conception of the State. The State comprehends the *ecclesia* in its national aspect, which gives the State such glory as it might be thought to have, but at the same time the State is an historical organism, outside the *ecclesia*, which gives it its limits. The Church also has two faces in Coleridge's vision — the national *ecclesia*, which penetrates the body of the State, and the *ecclesia* proper, the universal Christian Church, which is itself a kingdom, though not of this world. Coleridge's thoughts on the national *ecclesia* are chiefly of interest for his insistence that statesmen should know and acknowledge that 'a permanent, nationalized, learned order, a national clerisy or Church, is an essential element of a rightly constituted nation.'[4] His thoughts on the *ecclesia* as the kingdom which is not of this world can hardly be over-valued. To his eye, this divine society founded by Christ appears with four distinguishing marks by which it may be recognized: one, it is the antithesis of the world, which it criticizes by its existence, contributing to the stability of the State by going about its own business without asking for 'wages or dignities', requiring only protection and *to be let alone*; two, it is no secret community, but 'most observable', a city built on a hill, 'visible and militant under Christ'; three, it exists in different countries and societies, enabled to avoid opposition to them by reason of its head being Christ, to whom it owes sole allegiance; four, it is Catholic and everywhere.

15

It is neither Anglican, Gallican, nor Roman, neither Latin nor Greek. Even the Catholic and Apostolic Church *of* England is a less safe expression than the Churches of Christ in England: though the Catholic Church *in* England, or (what would be still better), the Catholic Church under Christ throughout Great Britain and Ireland, is justifiable and appropriate: for through the presence of its only head and sovereign, entire in each and one in all, the Church universal is spiritually perfect in every true Church . . . The true Church *of* England is the National Church or Clerisy. There exists, God be thanked! a Catholic and Apostolic Church *in* England: and I thank God also for the Constitutional and Ancestral Church of England.[5]

Coleridge's version of the supernatural *ecclesia* would have been recognized by Newman, Froude, Keble or Pusey. He refrains, however, from relating the English branch of Christ's universal Church to the hierarchic structure of the national Church as boldly as the young Manning does (see page 245 below). F. D. Maurice admitted his debt to Coleridge, but it is hard to say to what extent ideas in the *Idea* were consciously or otherwise developed by the Tractarians themselves. (Newman once expressed surprise, on looking into Coleridge, to find how much of the poet's work anticipated his own.)

Theological considerations apart, Coleridge provides us with a link between the Tractarians and the Romantic Movement. As the previous volumes in this series have shown it is impossible to separate the sermon literature of a period from its other literary and philosophical manifestations. The sermons in the present book react against the tyranny of reason in much the same way as the Romantic poets reacted against the neo-Augustans. There is a danger of seeing the Oxford Movement as the Romantic Movement in a surplice. It would be crude to reduce the century to a quarrel between reason and revelation. But if we keep in mind the usefulness of some such definition as reason being no more than the intellectual power of man's understanding, while revelation might be no less than *God's reason* shown to us, then we may have some grip of the shift from Wesley and Ogden to Newman and Robert Wilberforce, as from Pope and Charles Churchill to Blake and Emily Brontë. The movement in both cases is from rationalism to mystery. In Christian terms, it is a movement away from the pulpit and towards the altar.

It is a paradox that the same movement gave to the Church

in England its greatest preacher, John Henry Newman. This, also, despite the fact that Newman did not care much for sermons. When James Stephen complained that from the point of view of 'touching other men's hearts and influencing their conduct ... Charles Simeon is worth a legion of Newmans,' Newman replied courteously that,

> Doubtless Mr. Simeon is ten thousand times more attractive than I, but not than the Church I serve . . . . It is as a Priest that I should have influence — i. e., in the Sacraments, ordinances etc. of the Church — and since the divinely ordered system is (alas!) but poorly developed among us, no wonder I seem cold and uninfluential. The single ordinance of the Lord's Supper, rightly taught and administered, is full of persuasion. But that is a large subject.

It will be seen that it is also a subject much visited in the sermons selected for this book, for the Tractarians aimed at nothing less than the restoration of the principle of symbolism in Christian worship, the revival of the sacramental character of religion, and the showing forth to men of a mystery—'that which is beyond human knowledge unless revealed, and beyond complete human comprehension even when revealed.' The Mass — the great action, 'the greatest action that can be on earth', as Newman calls it in his novel *Loss and Gain* (1848) — looks likely to be the symbol round which Christendom will unite, when it unites, since it is the Meal of the Christian family. It is the Mass that matters, and it is towards the mattering of the Mass that the Oxford Movement moved.

II

Now the Christian faith claims to be an eternal revelation of God to man. It is therefore in one sense incapable of change. None the less, that sense does not often coincide with what we see with our eyes or hear with our ears, and little evidence for it will be found in our calendar of what was happening while these sermons were being preached on Sundays and other holy days between 1750 and 1850. History cannot tell us what goes on in the mind of God — yet the *ecclesia* is there, always the same and always changing, deepening itself, defining its deposit of truth more faithfully, modifying its language to the ways of the human mind as that entity struggles to understand and

17

interpret the world. The century with which we deal is the site for what looked like major battles between revelation and reason, battles fought first in books and then in the streets. The only victory which emerges from these battles is something in the way of a commentary upon them, Newman's *Essay in Aid of a Grammar of Assent* (1870). In it a first-rate intellect looks harder and more critically at reason than had reason's enthusiasts.

Newman examines the phenomenon of thought by analysing the mental acts involved in holding propositions of any kind. There are, he suggests, three such acts: doubt, inference and assent. Doubt asks questions. Inference jumps to conclusions — but lands, as it were, on ground already taken for granted. Assent says yes, assertively, like Molly Bloom, or amen, categorically, like Christians receiving the Body and Blood of Christ. Even so, there are degrees of assent, and Newman distinguishes between one yes or amen and another. There is what he calls *notional* assent, the yes given to propositions which remain abstract and general. There is also what he calls *real* assent, the yes given to propositions which are singular and specific. Real assent asks more of us than notional assent. It is bound up with man's capacity to make metaphors, to find connections between things considered disparate, to celebrate a *kindness* — or kinship, or relatedness — which the logical mind neglects or ignores. If you give *notional* assent, say, to the Real Presence of Christ in the Blessed Sacrament, you are making a theological act, difficult enough, but not demanding suspension of anything more vital than your disbelief; if you give *real* assent to the same proposition, however, you will in all probability be making a religious act, and on your knees, for your yes, your amen, will have taken you beyond the area of propositions and you will be responding to a *fact*.

Aldous Huxley called the *Grammar* an 'analysis of the psychology of thought' which 'remains one of the most acute, as it is certainly the most elegant, which has ever been made.' For Christians, the book is chiefly of value for what comes out of Newman's final distinction between acts of assent and acts of inference. Inference is conditional — Thomas believing in the Risen Christ because he can put his fingers in the wounds. Assent is not only independent of inference, it is also unconditional, so that the mind can make an act of assent to something infinitely complex (for example, the Holy Trinity)[6] as easily as to something infinitely simple (for example, that God, having

18

made the world, permitted man to have free will in it). The question arises: how does the mind pass from inference to assent? *Non in dialectica complacuit Deo salvum facere populum suum*. Newman set these words of St Ambrose on his title page, knowing that in the end it is the heart which is granted revelation, when the head has done reasoning. All the same, he does not dodge the intellectual issue. The very act of assent, he implies, requires a quickening of heart, mind and soul, which makes them as one while they retain their separate faculties. The action of this little trinity of human consciousness he christens the *illative sense* — 'an *organon* more delicate, versatile, and elastic' than anything we use in doubting and inferring and the usual processes of verbal argumentation.[7] It is by means of the illative sense — an uncommon name for a common thing — that Christians have certitude in matters of faith, and can speak of Christianity as a *Revelatio revelata* or

> definite message from God to man distinctly conveyed by His chosen instruments, and to be received as such a message; and therefore to be positively acknowledged, embraced, and maintained as true, on the ground of its being divine, not as true on intrinsic grounds, not as probably true, or partially true, but as absolutely certain knowledge, certain in a sense in which nothing else can be certain, because it comes from Him who neither can deceive nor be deceived.[8]

Newman spent all his life, first in the English Communion, then in the Roman, trying to match man's logic and God's grace, the human will and the divine — 'Thy will be done'. In one of his University sermons, *The Usurpation of Reason*, dating from 1831, he observes in the history of revelation the human conscience triumphing over its intellect, or thinking part — what he calls 'the triumph of holiness over ability'. That faith should have primacy over reason was a conviction Newman reached long before the writing of the *Grammar*, indeed long before that stormy night in October 1845 when he knelt before a rain-soaked traveller dressed in shabby black, St Dominic Barberi, and asked to be received into the Roman Catholic Church. He has been criticized on the grounds that his is an all-or-nothing attitude, sceptical in that it denies the possibility of justifying faith by intellectual processes. This is less than fair. Newman wrote the *Grammar* to show by those intellectual processes, that thinking

19

part, how conscience is not dishonoured by believing where we cannot prove. He wrote to insist that we are religious animals and that far from living by bread alone, we needs must live by bread and wine which have become the Body and Blood of Christ, a foretaste of eternity.

A deepening sense of the reason for the Eucharist, and a richer understanding of the revelation of the Eucharist, seem, looking over the sermons I have selected, to be the dogmatic drift of the century. The *Grammar*, of course, lies twenty years beyond our time limit, but since it is sweet with the full blossom of Newman's thinking on the relation of reason and revelation, and since prejudice regarding that relation was responsible for much of the century's distress, it may be recommended as relevant, despite the probability that A.D. 1976 will find any reference to Revealed Religion far-fetched and oldfashioned. A.D. 1876 found it far-fetched and oldfashioned, too — Matthew Arnold soothed himself with admiring the Cardinal's literary style while believing that what that style consisted of was 'impossible'. The first 76 years A.D. found it equally far-fetched and oldfashioned, when the not particularly talented apostles came speaking to its intellectuals on the same matter. The far-fetched nature of the Christian faith has always bothered the wise. Call to mind the *certum est, quia impossibile* of Tertullian.

III

The *Idea* and the *Grammar* provide a syntax for reflections on such things as the Lisbon earthquake, the ethos of the *Encyclo-pédie*, and the benighted face of the Church of England in the first eighty years of our period.

The first, the earthquake in Lisbon, killed between thirty and forty thousand persons, and caused the ground to shiver from Scotland to Asia Minor. For Christians it was an appalling test of faith. For Voltaire it provided an opportunity for ridiculing the belief that God is infinitely good and omnipotent — although the best professional sceptics no longer claim that he succeeded in showing any absolute contradiction of those divine attributes. What Voltaire did show, without doubt, was the incapacity of the human intellect, even such a marvellously developed speci-men as his own, to make sense of an appalling 'act of God' with-out recourse to the Christian faith. Give notional or real assent to the proposition that on a hill called the skull, just outside Jerusalem, another appalling Act of God made sense of the pain

20

of our self-wounded world, and that on the third day after that another Act of God promised us that there is a sense beyond the pain of sense, death's senselessness being not the death of us, and the Lisbon earthquake, while awful, is not the end of the world of meaning. Reason may be applied to our reaction to those events in Jerusalem, but the events themselves could never have been arrived at by reason. The disciples were being reasonable when they thought the death of Christ the end of him, and ran away, and hid. Revelation brought them out of their holes and made them do one or two unreasonable things. (See Ogden's sermon, page 91 below.)

The *Encyclopédie*, on the other hand, recommends nothing that is not reasonable, being, as its subtitle declares, a *Dictionnaire raisonné, des sciences, des arts et des métiers*. In fact, as Desnoiresterres says, this remarkable work is 'a war machine',[9] to be deployed by a revolutionary army in the name of free thought. Whether you see it as a useful invention will depend upon your view of that day in November 1793 when the Catholic Religion was officially abolished in France, and the National Convention proclaimed the cult of the Goddess of Reason. (A quick-witted cleric in the cathedral at Chartres put a red cap on the image of the Virgin; the mob went home happy.) Less than a year later, Robespierre watered down the cult of reason by replacing it with the cult of the Supreme Being, for which he even composed a creed: 'The French nation acknowledges the Supreme Being and the Immortality of the Soul.'

Compared with these antics, the spiritual defects of the Church of England in the eighteenth century are dull to recount. To explain them it is necessary to refer back to that day in 1688 when William Sancroft, Archbishop of Canterbury, found that his conscience forbade him to break the oath of allegiance he had sworn to James II. The obscurity of the Non-Jurors tells you why the Church of England all but lost consciousness of her heritage at this point in history — her Catholics were cut off from the main body of Anglicans, and in their absence not just sermons but the whole theology of the sacraments was neglected.

Then, in the middle and later decades of the eighteenth century, the Church had Wesley to contend with. This proved tricky, partly because the Methodist Revival had roots in High Church sacramentalism crossed with the mystical piety of William Law (see note on Wesley, page 31 below), partly because Wesley's eloquent appeal to the working classes coincided with a widespread decay of faith in western Europe which left men hungry for 'personal' religious experience of an enthusiastic kind. The bishops did their best to ignore Wesley, and on the whole succeeded. This was a mercy. If they had pushed him as they pushed Newman a century later it is possible that Wesley would have been driven into schism. As it was, their reluctance to appoint a bishop in the newly independent America drove him to the momentary schismatic aberration of 'ordaining' some of his followers for service there. His brother Charles protested, John had second thoughts and managed to die as he had lived, an itinerant priest of the Church of England. You could call it a tribute to the apostolic ethos of the English Church, rather than to the bishops as the actual heirs of those apostles, that it never occurred to either Wesley to look otherwhere than to the Church of their baptism for the continuance in these islands of the divine society founded by Christ.

IV

The eighteen sermons in this volume, so far as they have a doctrinal common denominator, reflect the way the century recovered a consciousness of the mystery of Christian worship, to be mentioned at first behind locked doors at the Ship Inn (see note on Archer, p. 96), then by Newman to parties of English tourists in Rome, finally from the pulpits of the University city on the Isis and in many an ordinary village church up and down the country.

This sacramental development is indeed glorious, but the two views from which we started — that of the anonymous hereditary High Churchman and that of Coleridge — should enable us to consider the Oxford Movement without the perfervid glamour often attached to it by Evangelicals on their way to Rome. There are those who imagine that the whole history of the Church in these islands is tedious, and who light upon the Tractarians as at least something 'different', outrageous, colourful or newsy. The facts are less dramatic, the mood more complicated. The Church of England had lost her memory under the Georges. In the years from 1833 to 1845, Newman and others helped to call it back. The *Tracts for the Times*, it might be as well to stress, were not concerned with ritual but with rite. The issue was not whether the English Church should be 'High' or 'Low', but whether she had gone out of her mind — which is to say, parted company with dogma. A similar struggle was going on elsewhere, only abroad the battle seemed to be between the

22

Church and the forces of rationalism outside the Church. In England the enemy, so to speak, was already outwith the gates of hell and almost prevailing in the one place where he had no business to prevail. The tracts stood to remind the English Church of her supernatural origin. Newman's opponents seem sincerely to have held that Christianity was a bracing and beautiful *philosophy*. He believed that it was true.

V

There were others who spoke of truth, who did not care for the *ecclesia* on earth or as it is in heaven, and who were not philosophers:

> We hold these truths to be self-evident: that all men are created equal, that they are endowed by their Creator with certain inalienable Rights, that among these are Life, Liberty and the pursuit of Happiness. That to secure these rights, Governments are instituted among men, deriving their just power from the consent of the governed. That whenever any Form of Government becomes destructive of these ends, it is the Right of the People to alter or abolish it, and to institute new Government, laying its foundations on such principles and organizing its powers in such form, as to them shall seem most likely to effect their Safety and Happiness.

Modern ears find nothing shocking in this, the 1776 Declaration by the American Congress, except perhaps its *naïveté*. But at the time such 'truths' were only 'self-evident' to a generation of dissenting emigrants reared in the wide open spaces of the Age of Reason and fed on a diet of Locke and Newton. If you value any of the basic differences between the English mind and Constitution and their American counterparts, your valuation, although you may not be aware of it, rests in some degree on the accident that the Methodists — when they drifted into schism after Wesley's death in 1791 — did not adopt the republican sympathies of the older non-conformist sects. Wesley's followers who remained loyal to the national *ecclesia*, known soon as Evangelicals, contributed most of the energy which went to the movement for the suppression of slavery, and eventually secured its abolition in 1833. The Evangelical party had a strong heart, but proved a little weak in the head — it possessed no theologians. Hence, by the 1820s, there was a generation to whom indifference was a problem. (See Froude's sermon on this subject, page 131 below.)

Events in America and France brought out the Erastian streak in England — there was an identification of the Church with order. Coleridge's national *ecclesia* was appreciated, his supernatural *ecclesia* all but lost to the eyes of men. Threatened as they were by the State's power to interfere with the rights of the Church, as in the case of the Whig suppression of the Irish bishops (see note on Keble, page 170 below), as well as sensitive to an industrial revolution beginning to pollute and deface not just the countryside but the human spirit, it is easy to imagine many a churchman who was not necessarily a fool referring to Hooker's *Ecclesiastical Polity* because, as a member of what Coleridge had called the *clerisy*, he considered himself as standing *pro causa Dei* against that innocent shout for 'Reform' which now sounded from all sides. Behind that shout could be heard the babble of Bentham and the Utilitarians, and behind them again the iconoclastic and jeering rationalism which had executed first the King, then Robespierre, all in the name of enlightenment. We should not too piously condemn those who looked to the national *ecclesia* as the house of order. These men were not Erastians in any careerist sense. They associated what was good in the English Church with what was good in the English tradition, and they wanted the *ecclesia anglicana* because they thought that the *ecclesia anglicana* alone could hold the times together.

Despite appeals to common sense and divine order, however, republican sentiment spread. But for the passing of the Reform Bill in 1832, it is possible that there would have been a revolution in England. The Bill itself seemed to imply further constitutional conflict. Few foreign observers thought that either the Church or the monarchy could survive. The Russian ambassador in London, for example, reported that the English king had 'cast his crown into the gutter', and said that while the throne might last for his lifetime, his heir, the young princess Victoria, was sure to be swept away by the rising tide of democracy. Now it is true that the Bill effectively transferred political power from those who generally supported the Church and the crown to those amongst whom dissent was rife, but the Russian ambassador underestimated the English hold on something other than reason, and must have forgotten that the Church is guided in the last instance, and whatever men may wish, by powers which are not political. Others than Russians made the same mistake. 'The Church of England as it now stands no human power can save,' wrote Dr Arnold to a friend in the same year.

Dr Arnold was right. Dr Arnold was reasonable. Dr Arnold also had a human plan to save us. In a pamphlet entitled *Principles of Church Reform* (1833) he proposed the union of the Church of England with all Dissenters save Roman Catholics, Unitarians, Quakers and Jews. The idea was for a kind of Benthamite social club in every parish church, since the main object for which the Church had been instituted, according to Arnold, was 'the production of man's highest possible perfection and happiness'. Membership of his happy band would be offered to all who could promise perfection by subscribing to the first and second articles of the Apostles' Creed, and who fancied in place of the third a vague definition of Holy Scripture as inspired. There was, naturally, to be no more talk of the old nonsense of the Catholic Church, with her divine origin and her ministry reaching back to the apostles. There was to be no suggestion that the *ecclesia* was anything other than a God-given umbrella under which everyone — save Jews, Quakers, Unitarians and Roman Catholics — could shelter when it rained. Not that Dr Arnold believed that it had ever rained, in that sense, or would ever rain. With the abolition of the Holy Catholic Church, that divine society founded by Christ, Dr Arnold would abolish rain, along with miracles, priests, the Eucharist and all other Romish tricks. These proposals for the Body of Christ on earth sounded no doubt to the Oxford men like Rugby School transmogrified. You can suppose that they sounded even more promising to the gates of hell and their keeper.

Meanwhile, at about the same date, a friend of Dr Arnold's, the godfather indeed of his son Matthew, was making a few unreasonable remarks which proved more to the point. This man was Thomas Sikes, rector of Guilsborough, a little parish not many miles from the home of the poet John Clare. Sikes was a student of Non-Juring theology and of the Anglo-Catholic divines who predated it. He was forty-seven. He was dying. He was walking in a garden, talking to a younger priest, just *after* Dr Arnold's wonderful undenominational Umbrella Plan, just *before* Keble's Assize sermon:

> I seem to think, I can tell you something, which you who are young may probably live to see, but which I, who shall soon

be called away off the stage, shall not. Wherever I go all about the country, I see amongst the Clergy a number of very amiable and estimable men, many of them much in earnest, and wishing to do good. But I have observed one universal want in their teaching: the uniform suppression of one great truth. There is no account given anywhere, so far as I see, of the one Holy Catholic Church. I think that the causes of this suppression have been mainly two. The Church has been kept out of sight, partly in consequence of the civil establishment of the branch of it which is in this country, and partly out of false charity to Dissent. Now this great truth is an article of the creed; and if so, to teach the rest of the creed to its exclusion must be to destroy 'the analogy or proportion of the faith' . . . This cannot be done, without the most serious consequences. The doctrine is of the last importance; and the principle it involves, of immense power; and some day, not far distant, it will judicially have its reprisals. And whereas the other articles of the creed seem now to have thrown it into the shade, it will seem, when it is brought forward, to swallow up the rest. We now hear not a breath about the Church; by and bye, those who live to see it, will hear of nothing else; and, just in proportion perhaps to its present suppression, will be its future development. Our confusion now-a-days is chiefly owing to the want of it; and there will be yet more confusion attending its revival. The effects of it I even dread to betide, especially if it come suddenly. And woe betide those, whoever they are, who shall, in the course of Providence, have to bring it forward. It ought especially of all others to be matter of catechetical teaching and training. The doctrine of the Church Catholic and the privileges of Church-membership cannot be explained from pulpits; and those who will have to explain it will hardly know where they are, or which way they are to turn themselves. There will be one great outcry of Popery, from one end of the land to the other. It will be thrust upon minds unprepared, and on an uncatechized Church. Some will take it up and admire it as a beautiful picture; others will be frightened and run away and reject it; and all will want a guidance which one hardly knows where they shall find. How the doctrine may be first thrown forward we know not; but the powers of the world may any day turn their backs upon us, and this will probably lead to those effects I have described.[10]

Sikes was a friend of Wordsworth, who visited him at Guils-borough and is supposed to have planted the (rarish) lesser balsam flowers which still blossom there. He wrote a few pamphlets, it appears, very High Church and anti-Evangelical in tone — for instance, he refers to Wesley's *Journal* as 'disgusting'—but little else has survived save this remarkable bit of prophecy. As for Dr Arnold, he lived on to join in the cry of Popery, a reasonable development.

VI

A word remains to be said concerning Newman's secession. I prefer it to be Pusey's word, not mine. In a letter to the *English Churchman*, a mere week after Newman had been received into the Church of Rome by Father Dominic Barberi, now canonized, Pusey wrote:

Our Church has not known how to employ him. And since this was so, it seemed as if a sharp sword were lying in its scabbard, or hung up in the sanctuary, because there was no one to wield it. . . . He is gone, unconscious (as all great instruments of God are) what he himself is. He has gone as a simple act of duty, with no view for himself, placing himself entirely in God's hands. And such are they whom God employs. He seems then to me not so much gone from us as transplanted into another part of the Vineyard, where the full energies of his powerful mind can be employed, which here they were not. And who knows what, in the mysterious purpose of God's good Providence, may be the effect of such a person among them? You too have felt that it is what is unholy on both sides which keeps us apart. It is not what is true in the Roman system, against which the strong feeling of ordinary religious people among us is directed, but against what is unholy in her practice. It is not anything in our Church which keeps Rome from acknowledging us, but heresy existing more or less within us. As each, by God's grace, grows in holiness, the Churches will recognize more and more the presence of God's Holy Spirit in the other; and what now hinders the union of the Western Church will fall off. As the contest with unbelief increases, the Churches, which have received and transmitted the substance of the faith as deposited in our common creeds, must be on the same side. If one member suffers, the other members suffer with it; and so, in the

27

increasing health of one, others too will benefit. It is not as we would have had it, but God's will be done. He brings about His own ends, as, in His sovereign wisdom, He sees to be the best. One can see great ends to be brought about by this present sorrow, and the more so, because he, the chosen instrument of them, sees them not for himself. It is perhaps the greatest event which has happened, since the communion of the Churches has been interrupted, that such an one, so formed in our Church, and the work of God's Spirit as dwelling within her, should be transplanted to theirs. If anything could open their eyes to what is good in us, or soften in us any wrong prejudices against them, one should think it would be the presence of such an one nurtured and grown to such ripeness in our Church, and now removed to theirs.

ROBERT NYE
Edinburgh
St George's Day, 1975

N.B. Unless otherwise indicated, place of publication of books in all Notes and Bibliographies is London.

1. *Remains of Alexander Knox, Esq.*, 1837, III, p. 61.

2. ibid., p. 69.

3. ibid., p. 489.

4. *On the Constitution of the Church and State, according to the Idea of Each*, 2nd ed., 1830, p. 81.

5. ibid., pp. 150 ff. and 160-1.

6. See J. H. Newman, *Essay in Aid of a Grammar of Assent*, 1870, pp. 118-37.

7. Newman, op. cit., p. 264.

8. ibid., pp. 380-1.

9. Desnoiresterres, *Voltaire et la société française au XVIIIe siècle*, Paris, 1867-76. The phrase comes in vol. V, p. 164.

10. Quoted by E. B. Pusey, in *A Letter to his Grace the Archbishop of Canterbury, on Some Circumstances Connected with the Present Crisis in the English Church*, 2nd ed., Oxford, 1842.

JOHN WESLEY

JOHN WESLEY was born at Epworth in Lincolnshire in 1703, the fifteenth of the nineteen children of the Rev. Samuel Wesley (1662-1735), rector of that parish. Through his father he was descended from Adam Loftus (1533?-1605), Archbishop of Armagh and Dublin.

When Wesley was five, Epworth Rectory was burnt down by parishioners who disliked his father's High Church ways. John had a narrow escape—hence his fondness for alluding to himself in later life as 'a brand plucked from the burning'. After receiving the rudiments of education from his mother, at the age of eleven he proceeded to Charterhouse, and then went up to Christ Church, Oxford, at seventeen. Tyerman, his biographer, says, 'John Wesley entered the Charterhouse a saint and left it a sinner,'[1] and implies an immoral life at Oxford, but there is no evidence.

In 1726 he was elected to a fellowship at Lincoln College, Oxford, where he lectured in Greek. He was ordained deacon in 1725, priest in 1728. At Oxford he became the leader of a group of Christians known for their scholarship and for the application which made them realize the Christian faith as something one *did*, insisting upon regular prayer lives, the practice of fasting and the frequent reception of the Blessed Sacrament. Because of this, Wesley and his friends were nicknamed 'Sacramentalists', and the group was also known variously as the 'Holy Club', the 'Bible Moths', and the 'Methodists'—the last title being the one that stuck.

Looking back on early hopes in 1777, Wesley wrote that 'the Methodists at Oxford were all one body, and, as it were, one soul; zealous for the religion of the Bible, of the Primitive Church, and, in consequence, of the Church of England; as they believed it to come nearer the scriptural and primitive plan than any other national church upon earth.' At this time Wesley also came under the influence of William Law's *Christian Perfection* (1726) and *Serious Call* (1729). He met Law in 1732.

Following the death of his father in 1735, John set out with his younger brother Charles on a missionary visit to Georgia— but a combination of High Church services and impassioned preaching against the slave trade did not recommend him to the colonists. He returned to England in 1738. Friendship with a Moravian, Peter Bohler, convinced him that he lacked 'that faith

31

whereby alone we are saved'. At a Moravian meeting in Aldersgate Street, during a reading of Luther's preface to the Epistle to the Romans, Wesley underwent the experience which he sometimes referred to as his conversion—'about a quarter before nine', on 24 May 1738. 'While he was describing the change which God works in the heart through faith in Christ, I felt my heart strangely warmed. I felt I did trust in Christ, Christ alone for salvation; and an assurance was given me that He had taken away *my* sins, even *mine*, and saved *me* from the law of sin and death,' he recorded in his *Journal*, volume I, pages 475-6.

Wesley's mind was less than warmed by some of the heresies it had now to entertain. Within a year he objected to the Moravian doctrine of justification by faith alone. (He was always opposed to Calvinist predestinarianism and Zwinglian anti-sacramentarian views.) 'I am a High Churchman,' he wrote in a letter, 'the son of a High Churchman, bred from my childhood in the highest notions of passive obedience and non-resistance.'

In 1739 he began that unparalleled career as an itinerant priest which took him on long preaching tours, addressing vast concourses of people wherever they would assemble to hear him. It has been estimated that he travelled about 250,000 miles on horseback and delivered upwards of 40,000 sermons during the sixty years of his ministry.

Wesley had no desire to create a sect. 'I believe I shall not separate from the Church of England till my soul separates from my body,' he declared in a letter in 1784. Three years later he was saying 'when the Methodists leave the Church, God will leave them,' and in 1788 advising all his followers 'to keep close to the Church and Sacrament.' A modern Roman Catholic writer has observed that John and Charles Wesley were both 'determined to remain loyal members of the Church of England, which they regarded as a national Church, part of the universal catholic Church.'[2]

Despite this, Wesley's skill as an organizer—at the time of his death there were 294 preachers holding 'the Methodist connection' within the Church of England—made it possible for the Protestant-minded among his followers to break away from the Church after his death. As for Wesley himself, far from being the democratic preacher of hellfire, and other lusciousness, which he is often assumed to have been, he was a royalist in politics and was accused by his enemies of being in effect a Roman instrument for subverting the English Church. Of one such, who had accused him of being half a Papist, he said: 'What if he had proved that I was a *whole* Papist? . . . Is Thomas à Kempis, Mr. De Renty, Gregory Lopez gone to hell? Believe it who can.'

John Wesley died in London on 2 March 1791, having preached a few days before at Leatherhead, and then written his last letter—urging William Wilberforce to carry on his crusade against the slave trade. His body lies buried in the graveyard behind City Road Chapel. There is a monumental memorial to him in Westminster Abbey.

NOTES

1. L. Tyerman, *Life and Times of the Rev. John Wesley*, 1870-1, I.

2. John M. Todd, *John Wesley and the Catholic Church*, 1958, p. 78. Todd also says, p. 166: 'He simply accepted the Anglican Church as the established Christian authority, the one handed down to him from history, one which seemed to him to have the only valid claim to represent in England the divine society founded by Jesus Christ.'

BIBLIOGRAPHY

Sermons on Several Occasions, 3 vols, 1750.
Works, ed. himself, 32 vols, Bristol, 1771-4.
Collected Works, ed. Rev. Thomas Jackson, 14 vols, 1829-31.
Life and Times of the Rev. John Wesley, M.A., L. Tyerman, 3 vols, 1870-1.
The Works of John and Charles Wesley: A Bibliography, Rev. Richard Green, 1896.
Journal, ed. N. Curnock, 8 vols, 1909.
Letters, ed. J. Telford, 8 vols, 1931.

THE ALMOST CHRISTIAN
Acts 26: 28.
Almost thou persuadest me to be a Christian.

All my Wesley texts are taken from Jackson's fourteen volume *Collected Works* of 1829-31. As his bibliographer Green observes: 'This edition is far more correct and complete than either of the others, Jackson having the advantage of access to Wesley's own corrected copy of the first edition.'

This sermon is number ii in volume V of Jackson. It was first preached in the church of St Mary the Virgin, Oxford, before the university, on 25 July 1741. Because of these circumstances, Wesley is able to assume sufficient intelligence in his audience to save him from having to explain his context. His exordium is brief in the extreme: 'Almost . . . And many there are who go thus far.' For a general audience nowadays, I must be more pedestrian and explain that the words of the text are those of the pagan Agrippa[1] to St Paul. The sermon thereafter is by no means haphazard. It must have pleased its first audience by reason of its conformity to the traditional sermon structure of division into subjects, development of those subjects under heads, and then application of the considerations drawn out. Wesley himself wrote in his *Journal* on that day:

> It being my turn (which comes about once in three years) I preached at St. Mary's, before the University. The harvest truly is plenteous. So numerous a congregation (from whatever motives they came) I have seldom seen at Oxford. My text was the confession of poor Agrippa, 'Almost thou persuadest me to be a Christian.' I have 'cast my bread upon the waters', let me 'find it again after many days'.

The title uses the word 'almost' as an adjective. This is not the last nor the least of Wesley's stylistic peculiarities—although to say this is not to deny him simplicity. Many of the sophisticated audience on this occasion may have felt, as one John Nelson felt on another, that every word was addressed personally and directly to themselves. Nelson, a stonemason, has left a recollection of Wesley preaching in the Upper Moorfields: 'As soon as he got upon the stand he stroked back his hair and turned his eyes upon me. His countenance struck such an awful dread upon me, before I heard him speak, that it made my heart beat like the pendulum of a clock; and, when he did speak, I thought his whole discourse was aimed at me.' Yet, when Wesley had done, Nelson continues, 'I said, "This man can tell the secrets of my heart: he hath not left me there; for he hath showed the remedy, even the blood of Jesus." '[2]

Tyerman, in the *Life and Times*, suggests that *The Almost Christian* was probably *not* the sermon which Wesley *meant* to preach at St Mary's in 1741. After his death, a mutilated manuscript in English was found among his papers, dated 24 June 1741 (a month before he preached at Oxford) and also a copy of the same sermon in Latin. It was a discourse on the text, 'How is the faithful city become an harlot!' Tyerman suggests that this sermon was written with the design of being delivered before the university but that Wesley thought better of it. 'The sermon, if preached, must inevitably have brought upon the preacher the ire of his hearers.'

NOTES

1. King Agrippa II, born A.D. 27; died *c*. 93. In A.D. 60 the newly appointed Roman procurator in Palestine, Porcius Festus, asked Agrippa to help him assess the case of Paul. See Acts, chaps. 25 and 26.

2. Quoted by James Downey, in *The Eighteenth-Century Pulpit: A Study of the Sermons of Butler, Berkeley, Secker, Sterne, Whitefield and Wesley*, Oxford, 1969, p.211.

AND MANY there are who go thus far: Ever since the Christian Religion was in the world, there have been many in every age and nation, who were almost persuaded to be Christians. But seeing it avails nothing before God, to go *only thus far*, it highly imports us to consider,

First, What is implied in being *almost*,

Secondly, What in being *altogether, a Christian*.

I. (I.) 1. Now, in the being *almost a Christian* is implied, first, heathen honesty. No one, I suppose, will make any question of this; especially, since by heathen honesty here, I mean, not that which is recommended in the writings of their philosophers only, but such as the common Heathens expected one of another, and many of them actually practised. By the rules of this they were taught, that they ought not to be unjust; not to take away their neighbour's goods, either by robbery or theft; not to oppress the poor, neither to use extortion toward any; not to cheat or over-reach either the poor or rich, in whatsoever commerce they had with them; to defraud no man of his right; and, if it were possible, to owe no man any thing.

2. Again, the common Heathens allowed, that some regard was to be paid to truth, as well as to justice. And, accordingly, they not only held him in abomination who was forsworn, who called God to witness to a lie; but him also who was known to be a slanderer of his neighbour, who falsely accused any man. And, indeed, little better did they esteem wilful liars of any sort; accounting them the disgrace of human kind, and the pests of society.

3. Yet, again, there was a sort of love and assistance which they expected one from another. They expected whatever assistance any one could give another, without prejudice to himself. And this they extended not only to those little offices of humanity which are performed without any expense or labour, but likewise to the feeding the hungry, if they had food to spare; the clothing the naked with their own superfluous raiment; and, in general, the giving, to any that needed, such things as they needed not themselves. Thus far, in the lowest account of it, heathen honesty went; the first thing implied in the being *almost a Christian*.

(II.) 4. A Second thing implied in the being *almost a Christian*, is, the having a form of godliness; of that godliness which is prescribed in the gospel of Christ; the having the *outside of a real Christian*. Accordingly, the *Almost Christian* does nothing which the gospel forbids. He taketh not the name of God in vain; he blesseth and curseth not; he sweareth not at all, but his communication is yea, yea; nay, nay. He profanes not the day of the Lord, nor suffers it to be profaned, even by the stranger that is within his gates. He not only avoids all actual adultery, fornication, and uncleanness, but every word, or look, that either directly or indirectly tends thereto; nay, and all idle words, abstaining both from detraction, backbiting, tale-bearing, evil-speaking, and from 'all foolish talking and jesting,' — εὐτραπελια , a kind of virtue in the heathen moralist's account;—briefly, from all conversation that is not 'good to the use of edifying,' and that, consequently, 'grieves the Holy Spirit of God, whereby we are sealed to the day of redemption.'

5. He abstains from 'wine wherein is excess;' from revellings and gluttony. He avoids, as much as in him lies, all strife and contention, continually endeavouring to live peaceably with all men. And, if he suffer wrong, he avengeth not himself, neither returns evil for evil. He is no railer, no brawler, no scoffer, either at the faults or infirmities of his neighbour. He does not willingly wrong, hurt, or grieve any man; but in all things acts and speaks by that plain rule, 'Whatsoever thou wouldest not he should do unto thee, that do not thou to another.'

6. And in doing good, he does not confine himself to cheap and easy offices of kindness, but labours and suffers for the profit of many, that by all means he may help some. In spite of toil or pain, 'Whatsoever his hand findeth to do, he doeth it with his might;' whether it be for his friends, or for his enemies; for the evil or for the good. For, being 'not slothful' in this, or in any 'business,' as he 'hath opportunity' he doeth 'good,' all manner of good 'to all men;' and to their souls as well as their bodies. He reproves the wicked, instructs the ignorant, confirms the wavering, quickens the good, and comforts the afflicted. He labours to awaken those that sleep; to lead those whom God hath already awakened to the 'fountain opened for sin and for uncleanness,' that they may wash therein and be clean; and to stir up those who are saved, through faith, to adorn the gospel of Christ in all things.

7. He that hath the form of godliness, uses also the means of grace; yea, all of them, and at all opportunities. He constantly frequents the house of God; and that, not as the manner of some is, who come into the presence of the Most High, either loaded with gold and costly apparel, or in all the gaudy vanity of dress,

and either by their unseasonable civilities to each other, or the impertinent gaiety of their behaviour, disclaim all pretensions to the form as well as to the power of godliness. Would to God there were none even among ourselves who fall under the same condemnation: Who come into this house, it may be, gazing about, or with all the signs of the most listless, careless indifference, though sometimes they may *seem* to use a prayer to God for his blessing on what they are entering upon; who, during that awful service, are either asleep, or reclined in the most convenient posture for it; or, as though they supposed God was asleep, talking with one another, or looking round, as utterly void of employment. Neither let these be accused of the form of godliness. No; he who has even this, behaves with seriousness and attention, in every part of that solemn service. More especially when he approaches the table of the Lord, it is not with a light or careless behaviour, but with an air, gesture, and deportment, which speaks nothing else but, 'God be merciful to me, a sinner.'

8. To this, if we add the constant use of family prayer, by those who are masters of families, and the setting times apart for private addresses to God, with a daily seriousness of behaviour; he who uniformly practices this outward religion, has the form of godliness. There needs but one thing more in order to his being *almost a Christian*, and that is, sincerity.

(III.) 9. By sincerity I mean, a real, inward principle of religion, from whence these outward actions flow. And, indeed, if we have not this, we have not heathen honesty; no, not so much of it as will answer the demand of a heathen Epicurean poet. Even this poor wretch, in his sober intervals, is able to testify,

> *Oderunt peccare boni, virtutis amore;*
> *Oderunt peccare mali, formidine poenae.* *

So that, if a man only abstains from doing evil in order to avoid punishment, *Non pasces in cruce corvos*,† saith the Pagan; there, 'thou hast thy reward.' But even he will not allow such a harmless man as this to be so much as a *good Heathen*. If then, any man, from the same motive, viz., to avoid punishment, to avoid the loss of his friends, or his gain, or his reputation, should not only abstain from doing evil, but also do ever so much good;

---

* Good men avoid sin from the love of virtue;
   Wicked men avoid sin from a fear of punishment.
† Thou shalt not be hanged.

yea, and use all the means of grace; yet we could not, with any propriety, say, this man is even *almost a Christian*. If he has no better principle in his heart, he is only a hypocrite altogether.

10. Sincerity, therefore, is necessarily implied in the being *almost a Christian*; a real design to serve God, a hearty desire to do his will. It is necessarily implied, that a man have a sincere view of pleasing God in all things; in all his conversation; in all his actions; in all he does, or leaves undone. This design, if any man be *almost a Christian*, runs through the whole tenor of his life. This is the moving principle, both in his doing good, his abstaining from evil, and his using the ordinances of God.

11. But here it will probably be inquired, 'Is it possible that any man living should go so far as this, and, nevertheless, be *only almost a Christian*? What more than this can be implied, in the being *a Christian altogether*?' I answer, First, that it is possible to go thus far, and yet be but *almost a Christian*, I learn, not only from the Oracles of God, but also from the sure testimony of experience.

12. Brethren, great is 'my boldness towards you in this behalf.' And 'forgive me this wrong,' if I declare my own folly upon the house-top, for yours and the gospel's sake.—Suffer me, then, to speak freely of myself, even as of another man. I am content to be abased, so ye may be exalted, and to be yet more vile for the glory of my Lord.

13. I did go thus far for many years, as many of this place can testify; using diligence to eschew all evil, and to have a conscience void of offence; redeeming the time; buying up every opportunity of doing all good to all men; constantly and carefully using all the public and all the private means of grace; endeavouring after a steady seriousness of behaviour, at all times, and in all places; and, God is my record, before whom I stand, doing all this in sincerity; having a real design to serve God; a hearty desire to do his will in all things; to please him who had called me to 'fight the good fight,' and to 'lay hold of eternal life.' Yet my own conscience beareth me witness in the Holy Ghost, that all this time I was but *almost a Christian*.

II. If it be inquired, 'What more than this is implied in the being *altogether a Christian*?' I answer,

(I.) 1. First, The love of God. For thus saith his word, 'Thou shalt love the Lord thy God, with all thy heart, and with all thy soul, and with all thy mind, and with all thy strength.' Such a love is this, as engrosses the whole heart, as takes up all the affections, as fills the entire capacity of the soul, and employs the utmost extent of all its faculties. He that thus loves the Lord his God, his spirit continually 'rejoiceth in God his Saviour.' His delight is in the Lord, his Lord and his All, to whom 'in everything he giveth thanks. All his desire is unto God, and to the remembrance of his name.' His heart is ever crying out, 'Whom have I in heaven but thee? and there is none upon earth that I desire beside thee.' Indeed, what can he desire beside God? Not the world, or the things of the world: For he is 'crucified to the world, and the world crucified to him.' He is crucified to 'the desire of the flesh, the desire of the eye, and the pride of life.' Yea, he is dead to pride of every kind: For 'love is not puffed up;' but 'he that, dwelling in love, dwelleth in God, and God in him,' is less than nothing in his own eyes.

(II.) 2. The Second thing implied in the being *altogether a Christian*, is, the love of our neighbour. For thus said our Lord, in the following words, 'Thou shalt love thy neighbour as thyself.' If any man ask, 'Who is my neighbour?' we reply, Every man in the world; every child of His, who is the Father of the spirits of all flesh. Nor may we in anywise except our enemies or the enemies of God and their own souls. But every Christian loveth these also as himself, yea, 'as Christ loved us.' He that would more fully understand what manner of love this is, may consider St. Paul's description of it. It is 'long-suffering and kind.' It 'envieth not.' It is not rash or hasty in judging. It 'is not puffed up;' but maketh him that loves, the least, the servant of all. Love 'doth not behave itself unseemly;' but becometh 'all things to all men.' She 'seeketh not her own;' but only the good of others, that they may be saved. 'Love is not provoked.' It casteth out wrath, which he who hath, is wanting in love. 'It thinketh no evil. It rejoiceth not in iniquity, but rejoiceth in the truth. It covereth all things, believeth all things, hopeth all things, endureth all things.'

(III.) 3. There is yet one thing more that may be separately considered, though it cannot actually be separate from the preceding, which is implied in the being *altogether a Christian*; and that is the ground of all, even faith. Very excellent things are spoken of this throughout the Oracles of God. 'Every one,' saith the beloved disciple, 'that believeth, is born of God.' 'To as many as received him, gave he power to become the sons of God, even to them that believe on his name.' And, 'this is the victory that overcometh the world, even our faith.' Yea, our Lord himself declares, 'He that believeth in the Son hath everlasting life; and cometh not into condemnation, but is passed from death unto life.'

4. But here let no man deceive his own soul. 'It is diligently to be noted, the faith which bringeth not forth repentance, and love, and all good works, is not that right living faith, but a dead and devilish one. For, even the devils believe that Christ was born of a virgin; that he wrought all kinds of miracles, declaring himself very God; that, for our sakes, he suffered a most painful death, to redeem us from death everlasting; that he rose again the third day; that he ascended into heaven; and sitteth at the right hand of the Father, and at the end of the world shall come again to judge both the quick and dead. These articles of our faith the devils believe, and so they believe all that is written in the Old and New Testament. And yet for all this faith, they be but devils. They remain still in their damnable estate, lacking the very true Christian faith.'*

5. 'The right and true Christian faith is,' (to go on in the words of our own Church,) 'not only to believe that Holy Scripture and the Articles of our Faith are true, but also to have a sure trust and confidence to be saved from everlasting damnation by Christ. It is a sure trust and confidence which a man hath in God, that, by the merits of Christ, his sins are forgiven, and he reconciled to the favour of God; whereof doth follow a loving heart, to obey his commandments.'

6. Now, whosoever has this faith, which 'purifies the heart,' (by the power of God, who dwelleth therein,) from pride, anger, desire, 'from all unrighteousness,' from 'all filthiness of flesh and spirit;' which fills it with love stronger than death, both to God and to all mankind; love that doeth the works of God, glorying to spend and to be spent for all men, and that endureth with joy, not only the reproach of Christ, the being mocked, despised, and hated of all men, but whatsoever the wisdom of God permits the malice of men or devils to inflict; whosoever has this faith, thus working by love, is not almost only, but altogether, a Christian.

7. But who are the living witnesses of these things? I beseech you, brethren, as in the presence of that God before whom 'hell and destruction are without a covering,—how much more the hearts of the children of men,'—that each of you would ask his own heart, 'Am I of that number? Do I so far practise justice,

* Homily on the Salvation of Man.

mercy, and truth, as even the rules of heathen honesty require? If so, have I the very *outside* of a Christian? the form of godliness? Do I abstain from evil,—from whatsoever is forbidden in the written word of God? Do I, whatever good my hand findeth to do, do it with my might? Do I seriously use all the ordinances of God at all opportunities? And, is all this done with a sincere design and desire to please God in all things?'

8. Are not many of you conscious, that you never came thus far; that you have not been even *almost a Christian*; that you have not come up to the standard of heathen honesty; at least, not to the form of Christian godliness?—much less hath God seen sincerity in you, a real design of pleasing him in all things. You never so much as intended to devote all your words and works, your business, studies, diversions, to his glory. You never even designed or desired, that whatsoever you did should be done 'in the name of the Lord Jesus,' and as such should be 'a spiritual sacrifice, acceptable to God through Christ.'

9. But, supposing you had, do good designs and good desires make a Christian? By no means, unless they are brought to good effect. 'Hell is paved,' saith one, 'with good intentions.' The great question of all, then, still remains. Is the love of God shed abroad in your heart? Can you cry out, 'My God, and my All?' Do you desire nothing but him? Are you happy in God? Is he your glory, your delight, your crown of rejoicing? And is this commandment written in your heart, That he who loveth God love his brother also? Do you then love your neighbour as yourself? Do you love every man, even your enemies, even the enemies of God, as your own soul? As Christ loved you? Yea, dost thou believe that Christ loved thee, and gave himself for thee? Hast thou faith in his blood? Believest thou the Lamb of God hath taken away thy sins, and cast them as a stone into the depth of the sea? That he hath blotted out the handwriting that was against thee, taking it out of the way, nailing it to his cross? Hast thou indeed redemption through his blood, even the remission of thy sins? And doth his Spirit bear witness with thy spirit, that thou art a child of God?

10. The God and Father of our Lord Jesus Christ, who now standeth in the midst of us, knoweth, that if any man die without this faith and this love, good it were for him that he had never been born. Awake, then, thou that sleepest, and call upon thy God: Call in the day when he may be found. Let him not rest, till he make his 'his goodness to pass before thee,' till he

proclaim unto thee the name of the Lord; 'the Lord, the Lord God, merciful and gracious, long-suffering, and abundant in goodness and truth, keeping mercy for thousands, forgiving iniquity, and transgression, and sin.' Let no man persuade thee, by vain words, to rest short of this prize of thy high calling. But cry unto him day and night, who, 'while we were without strength, died for the ungodly,' until thou knowest in whom thou hast believed, and canst say, 'My Lord, and my God!' Remember, 'always to pray, and not to faint,' till thou also canst lift up thy hand unto heaven, and declare to him that liveth for ever and ever, 'Lord, thou knowest all things, thou knowest that I love thee.'

11. May we all thus experience what it is to be, not almost only, but altogether Christians; being justified freely by his grace, through the redemption that is in Jesus; knowing we have peace with God through Jesus Christ; rejoicing in hope of the glory of God; and having the love of God shed abroad in our hearts, by the Holy Ghost given unto us!

CATHOLIC SPIRIT

2 Kings 10:15.

And when he was departed thence, he lighted on Jehonadab the son of Rechab coming to meet him: And he saluted him, and said to him, Is thine heart right, as my heart is with thy heart? And Jehonadab answered, It is. If it be, give me thine hand.

This sermon (xxxix in volume V of Jackson's edition of the *Collected Works*) was thought worthy of separate publication by its author, and first issued 'printed by H. Cock, in Bloomsbury Market; and sold at the Foundery, near Upper Moorfields, by T. Try, near Gray's-Inn-Gate, Holburn' in 1755. It was twice reprinted in this form, accompanied by a hymn of seven six-line stanzas entitled 'Catholic Love', and signed at the end C. W. [Charles Wesley]. Wesley's bibliographer Green comments that the piece deserved wide dissemination. 'It clearly defines, illustrates, and urges real catholicity.'

Note the abundance of rhetorical questions in this sermon. Wesley fires them at his hearers in remorseless succession. 'Is thy heart right with God . . .?' 'Dost thou believe . . .?' 'Dost thou know . . .?' 'Dost thou seek . . .?' 'And dost thou find . . .?' These questions are not asked at random, nor do they repeat a single point in different guises. Most of them have their origin in the New Testament or the creeds. Wesley is urging, directing, *catechizing*, his audience in the dogmatics of salvation.

1. IT IS allowed even by those who do not pay this great debt, that love is due to all mankind; the royal law, 'Thou shalt love thy neighbour as thyself,' carrying its own evidence to all that hear it: And that, not according to the miserable construction put upon it by the zealots of old times, 'Thou shalt love thy neighbour,' thy relation, acquaintance, friend, 'and hate thine enemy:' Not so; 'I say unto you,' saith our Lord, 'Love your enemies, bless them that curse you, do good to them that hate you, and pray for them that despitefully use you, and persecute you; that ye may be the children,' may appear so to all mankind, 'of your Father which is in heaven; who maketh his sun to rise on the evil and on the good, and sendeth rain on the just and on the unjust.'

2. But it is sure, there is a peculiar love which we owe to those that love God. So David: 'All my delight is upon the saints that are in the earth, and upon such as excel in virtue.' And so a greater than he: 'A new commandment I give unto you, that ye love one another: As I have loved you, that ye also love another. By this shall all men know that ye are my disciples, if ye have love one to another.' (John xiii. 34, 35.) This is that love on which the Apostle John so frequently and strongly insists: 'This,' saith he, 'is the message that ye heard from the beginning, that we should love one another.' (1 John iii. 11.) 'Hereby perceive we the love of God, because he laid down his life for us: And we ought,' if love should call us thereto, 'to lay down our lives for the brethren.' (Verse 16.) And again: 'Beloved, let us love one another: For love is of God. He that loveth not, knoweth not God; for God is love.' (iv. 7, 8.) 'Not that we loved God, but that he loved us, and sent his Son to be the propitiation for our sins. Beloved, if God so loved us, we ought also to love one another.' (Verses 10,11.)

3. All men approve of this; but do all men practise it? Daily experience shows the contrary. Where are even the Christians who 'love one another as He hath given us commandment?' How many hinderances lie in the way! The two grand, general hinderances are, First, that they cannot all think alike; and, in consequence of this, Secondly, they cannot all walk alike; but in several smaller points their practice must differ in proportion to the difference of their sentiments.

4. But although a difference in opinions or modes of worship may prevent an entire external union; yet need it prevent our union in affection? Though we cannot think alike, may we not

love alike? May we not be of one heart, though we are not of one opinion? Without all doubt we may. Herein all the children of God may unite, notwithstanding these smaller differences. These remaining as they are, they may forward one another in love and in good works.

5. Surely in this respect the example of Jehu himself, as mixed a character as he was of, is well worthy both the attention and imitation of every serious Christian. 'And when he was departed thence, he lighted on Jehonadab the son of Rechab coming to meet him. And he saluted him, and said to him, Is thine heart right, as my heart is with thy heart? And Jehonadab answered, It is. If it be so, give me thine hand.'

The text naturally divides itself into two parts:—First, a question proposed by Jehu to Jehonadab:—'Is thine heart right, as my heart is with thy heart?' Secondly, an offer made on Jehonadab's answering, 'It is:'—'If it be, give me thine hand.'

I. 1. And, First, let us consider the question proposed by Jehu to Jehonadab,—'Is thine heart right, as my heart is with thy heart?'

The very first thing we may observe in these words, is, that here is no inquiry concerning Jehonadab's opinions. And yet it is certain, he held some which were very uncommon, indeed quite peculiar to himself; and some which had a close influence upon his practice; on which, likewise, he laid so great a stress, as to entail them upon his children's children, to their latest posterity. This is evident from the account given by Jeremiah, many years after his death: 'I took Jaazaniah and his brethren, and all his sons, and the whole house of the Rechabites,—And set before them pots full of wine, and cups, and said unto them, Drink ye wine. But they said, We will drink no wine; for Jonadab,' or Jehonadab, 'the son of Rechab, our father,' (it would be less ambiguous if the words were placed thus: 'Jehonadab *our father, the son of* Rechab;' out of love and reverence to whom, he probably desired his descendants might be called by his name,) 'commanded us, saying, Ye shall drink no wine, neither ye nor your sons for ever. Neither shall ye build house, nor sow seed, nor plant vineyard, nor have any; but all your days ye shall dwell in tents.—And we have obeyed, and done according to all that Jonadab our father commanded us.' (Jer. xxxv.3-10.)

2. And yet Jehu (although it seems to have been his manner, both in things secular and religious, to *drive furiously*) does not concern himself at all with any of these things, but lets Jehonadab abound in his own sense. And neither of them appears to

have given the other the least disturbance touching the opinions which he maintained.

3. It is very possible, that many good men now also may entertain peculiar opinions; and some of them may be as singular herein as even Jehonadab was. And it is certain, so long as we know but *in part*, that all men will not see all things alike. It is an unavoidable consequence of the present weakness and shortness of human understanding, that several men will be of several minds in religion as well as in common life. So it has been from the beginning of the world, and so it will be 'till the restitution of all things.'

4. Nay, farther: Although every man necessarily believes that every particular opinion which he holds is true; (for to believe any opinion is not true, is the same thing as not to hold it;) yet can no man be assured that all his own opinions, taken together, are true. Nay, every thinking man is assured they are not; seeing *humanum est errare et nescire*: 'To be ignorant of many things, and to mistake in some, is the necessary condition of humanity.' This, therefore, he is sensible, is his own case. He knows, in the general, that he himself is mistaken; although in what particulars he mistakes, he does not, perhaps he cannot, know.

5. I say, perhaps he cannot know; for who can tell how far invincible ignorance may extend? or (that comes to the same thing) invincible prejudice?—which is often so fixed in tender minds, that it is afterwards impossible to tear up what has taken so deep a root. And who can say, unless he knew every circumstance attending it, how far any mistake is culpable? seeing all guilt must suppose some concurrence of the will; of which He only can judge who searcheth the heart.

6. Every wise man, therefore, will allow others the same liberty of thinking which he desires they should allow him; and will no more insist on their embracing his opinions, than he would have them to insist on his embracing theirs. He bears with those who differ from him, and only asks him with whom he desires to unite in love that single question, 'Is thy heart right, as my heart is with thy heart?'

7. We may, Secondly, observe, that here is no inquiry made concerning Jehonadab's mode of worship; although it is highly probable there was, in this respect also, a very wide difference between them. For we may well believe Jehonadab, as well as all his posterity, worshipped God at Jerusalem: Whereas Jehu did not; he had more regard to state-policy than religion. And,

therefore, although he slew the worshippers of Baal, and destroyed Baal out of Israel; yet from the convenient sin of Jeroboam, the worship of the golden calves, he departed not. (2 Kings x. 29.)

8. But even among men of an upright heart, men who desire to 'have a conscience void of offence,' it must needs be, that, as long as there are various opinions, there will be various ways of worshipping God; seeing a variety of opinion necessarily implies a variety of practice. And as, in all ages, men have differed in nothing more than in their opinions concerning the Supreme Being, so in nothing have they more differed from each other, than in the manner of worshipping him. Had this been only in the heathen world, it would not have been at all surprising: For we know, these 'by' their 'wisdom knew not God;' nor, therefore, could they know how to worship him. But is it not strange, that even in the Christian world, although they all agree in the general, 'God is a Spirit; and they that worship him must worship him in spirit and in truth;' yet the particular modes of worshipping God are almost as various as among the Heathens?

9. And how shall we choose among so much variety? No man can choose for, or prescribe to, another. But every one must follow the dictates of his own conscience, in simplicity and godly sincerity. He must be fully persuaded in his own mind; and then act according to the best light he has. Nor has any creature power to constrain another to walk by his own rule. God has given no right to any of the children of men thus to lord it over the conscience of his brethren; but every man must judge for himself, as every man must give an account of himself to God.

10. Although, therefore, every follower of Christ is obliged, by the very nature of the Christian Institution, to be a member of some particular congregation or other, some Church, as it is usually termed; (which implies a particular manner of worshipping God; for 'two cannot walk together unless they be agreed;') yet none can be obliged by any power on earth but that of his own conscience, to prefer this or that congregation to another, this or that particular manner of worship. I know it is commonly supposed, that the place of our birth fixes the Church to which we ought to belong; that one, for instance, who is born in England, ought to be a member of that which is styled the Church of England; and, consequently, to worship God in the particular manner which is prescribed by that Church. I was once a zealous maintainer of this; but I find many reasons to abate of this zeal. I fear it is attended with such difficulties as no reasonable man

can get over: Not the least of which is, that if this rule had took place, there could have been no Reformation from Popery; seeing it entirely destroys the right of private judgement, on which that whole Reformation stands.

11. I dare not, therefore, presume to impose my mode of worship on any other. I believe it is truly primitive and apostolical: But my belief is no rule for another. I ask not, therefore, of him with whom I would unite in love, Are you of my Church? of my congregation? Do you receive the same form of Church government, and allow the same Church officers, with me? Do you join in the same form of prayer wherein I worship God? I inquire not, Do you receive the supper of the Lord in the same posture and manner that I do? nor whether, in the administration of baptism, you agree with me in admitting sureties for the baptized; in the manner of administering it; or the age of those to whom it should be administered. Nay, I ask not of you, (as clear as I am in my own mind,) whether you allow baptism and the Lord's supper at all. Let all these things stand by; we will talk of them, if need be, at a more convenient season; my only question at present is this,—'Is thine heart right, as my heart is with thy heart?'

12. But what is properly implied in the question? I do not mean, what did Jehu imply therein? But,what should a follower of Christ understand thereby, when he proposes it to any of his brethren?

The First thing implied is this: Is thy heart right with God? Dost thou believe his being, and his perfections? his eternity, immensity, wisdom, power; his justice, mercy, and truth? Dost thou believe that he now 'upholdeth all things by the word of his power?' and that he governs even the most minute, even the most noxious, to his own glory, and the good of them that love him? Hast thou a divine evidence, a supernatural conviction, of the things of God? Dost thou 'walk by faith, not by sight?' looking not at temporal things, but things eternal?

13. Dost thou believe in the Lord Jesus Christ, 'God over all, blessed for ever?' Is he revealed in thy soul? Dost thou know Jesus Christ and him crucified? Does he dwell in thee, and thou in him? Is he formed in thy heart by faith? Having absolutely disclaimed all thy own works, thy own righteousness, hast thou 'submitted thyself unto the righteousness of God,' which is by faith in Christ Jesus? Art thou 'found in him, not having thy own righteousness, but the righteousness which is by faith?' And art thou, through him, 'fighting the good fight of faith, and laying hold of eternal life?'

14. Is thy faith ἐνεργουμένη δι᾽ ἀγάπης, — *filled with the energy of love*? Dost thou love God (I do not say 'above all things,' for it is both an unscriptural and an ambiguous expression, but) 'with all thy heart, and with all thy mind, and with all thy soul, and with all thy strength?' Dost thou seek all thy happiness in Him alone? And dost thou find what thou seekest? Does thy soul continually 'magnify the Lord, and thy spirit rejoice in God thy Saviour?' Having learned 'in everything to give thanks,' dost thou find 'it is a joyful and pleasant thing to be thankful?' Is God the centre of thy soul? the sum of all thy desires? Art thou accordingly laying up thy treasure in heaven, and counting all things else dung and dross? Hath the love of God cast the love of the world out of thy soul? Then thou art 'crucified to the world;' thou art dead to all below; and thy 'life is hid with Christ in God.'

15. Art thou employed in doing, 'not thy own will, but the will of Him that sent thee?'—of Him that sent thee down to sojourn here awhile, to spend a few days in a strange land, till, having finished the work he hath given thee to do, thou return to thy Father's house? Is it thy meat and drink 'to do the will of thy Father which is in heaven?' Is thine eye single in all things? always fixed on him? always looking unto Jesus? Dost thou point at him in whatsoever thou doest? in all thy labour, thy business, thy conversation? aiming only at the glory of God in all;—'whatsoever thou doest, either in word or deed, doing it all in the name of the Lord Jesus; giving thanks unto God, even the Father, through him?'

16. Does the love of God constrain thee to serve him with fear?—to 'rejoice unto him with reverence?' Art thou more afraid of displeasing God, than either of death or hell? Is nothing so terrible to thee as the thought of offending the eyes of his glory? Upon this ground dost thou 'hate all evil ways,' every transgression of his holy and perfect law; and herein 'exercise thyself, to have a conscience void of offence toward God, and toward man?'

17. Is thy heart right toward thy neighbour? Dost thou love, as thyself, all mankind without exception? 'If you love those only that love you, what thank have ye?' Do you 'love your enemies?' Is your soul full of good-will, of tender affection, toward them? Do you love even the enemies of God, the unthankful and unholy? Do your bowels yearn over them? Could you 'wish yourself' temporally 'accursed' for their sake? And do you show this by 'blessing them that curse you, and praying for those that

despitefully use you and persecute you?'

18. Do you show your love by your works? While you have time, as you have opportunity, do you in fact 'do good to all men,' neighbours or strangers, friends or enemies, good or bad? Do you do them all the good you can; endeavouring to supply all their wants; assisting them both in body and soul, to the uttermost of your power?—If thou art thus minded, may every Christian say, yea, if thou art but sincerely desirous of it, and following on till thou attain, then 'thy heart is right, as my heart is with thy heart.'

II. 1. 'If it be, give me thy hand.' I do not mean, 'Be of my opinion.' You need not: I do not expect or desire it. Neither do I mean, 'I will be of your opinion.' I cannot: It does not depend on my choice: I can no more think, than I can see or hear, as I will. Keep you your opinion; I mine; and that as steadily as ever. You need not even endeavour to come over to me, or bring me over to you. I do not desire you to dispute those points, or to hear or speak one word concerning them. Let all opinions alone on one side and the other: Only 'give me thine hand.'

2. I do not mean, 'Embrace my modes of worship; or I will embrace yours.' This also is a thing which does not depend either on your choice or mine. We must both act as each is fully persuaded in his own mind. Hold you fast that which you believe is most acceptable to God, and I will do the same. I believe the Episcopal form of Church government to be scriptural and apostolical. If you think the Presbyterian or Independent is better, think so still, and act accordingly. I believe infants ought to be baptized; and that this may be done either by dipping or sprinkling. If you are otherwise persuaded, be so still, and follow your own persuasion. It appears to me, that forms of prayer are of excellent use, particularly in the 'great congregation. If you judge extemporary prayer to be of more use, act suitable to your own judgement. My sentiment is, that I ought not to forbid water, wherein persons may be baptized; and that I ought to eat bread and drink wine, as a memorial of my dying Master: However, if you are not convinced of this, act according to the light you have. I have no desire to dispute with you one moment upon any of the preceding heads. Let all these smaller points stand aside. Let them never come into sight. 'If thine heart is as my heart,' if thou lovest God and all mankind, I ask no more: 'Give me thine hand.'

3. I mean, First, love me: And that not only as thou lovest all

mankind; not only as thou lovest thine enemies, or the enemies of God, those that hate thee, that 'despitefully use thee and persecute thee;' not only as a stranger, as one of whom thou knowest neither good nor evil;—I am not satisfied with this;—no; 'if thine heart be right, as mine with thy heart,' then love me with a very tender affection, as a friend that is closer than a brother; as a brother in Christ, a fellow-citizen of the New Jerusalem, a fellow-soldier engaged in the same warfare, under the same Captain of our salvation. Love me as a companion in the kingdom and patience of Jesus, and a joint-heir of his glory.

4. Love me (but in a higher degree than thou dost the bulk of mankind) with the love that is *longsuffering and kind*; that is patient; if I am ignorant or out of the way, bearing and not increasing my burden; and is tender, soft, and compassionate still; —that *envieth not*, if at any time it please God to prosper me in his work even more than thee. Love me with the love that *is not provoked*, either at my follies or infirmities; or even at my acting (if it should sometimes so appear to thee) not according to the will of God. Love me so as to *think no evil* of me; to put away all jealousy and evil-surmising. Love me with the love that *covereth all things*; that never reveals either my faults or infirmities;— that *believeth all things*; is always willing to think the best, to put the fairest construction on all my words and actions; —that *hopeth all things*; either that the thing related was never done; or not done with such circumstances as are related; or, at least, that it was done with a good intention, or in a sudden stress of temptation. And hope to the end, that whatever is amiss, will, by the grace of God, be corrected; and whatever is wanting, supplied, through the riches of his mercy in Christ Jesus.

5. I mean, Secondly, commend me to God in all thy prayers; wrestle with him in my behalf, that he would speedily correct what he sees amiss, and supply what is wanting in me. In thy nearest access to the throne of grace, beg of him, who is then very present with thee, that my heart may be more as thy heart, more right both toward God and toward man; that I may have a fuller conviction of things not seen, and a stronger view of the love of God in Christ Jesus; may more steadily walk by faith, not by sight; and more earnestly grasp eternal life. Pray that the love of God and of all mankind may be more largely poured into my heart; that I may be more fervent and active in doing the will of my Father which is in heaven; more zealous of good works, and more careful to abstain from all appearance of evil.

6. I mean, Thirdly, provoke me to love and to good works. Second thy prayer, as thou hast opportunity, by speaking to me, in love, whatsoever thou believest to be for my soul's health. Quicken me in the work which God has given me to do, and instruct me how to do it more perfectly. Yea, 'smite me friendly, and reprove me,' whereinsoever I appear to thee to be doing rather my own will, than the will of Him that sent me. O speak and spare not, whatever thou believest may conduce, either to the amending of my faults, the strengthening my weakness, the building me up in love, or the making me more fit, in any kind, for the Master's use!

7. I mean, Lastly, love me not in word only, but in deed and in truth. So far as in conscience thou canst, (retaining still thy own opinions, and thy own manner of worshipping God,) join with me in the work of God; and let us go on hand in hand. And thus far, it is certain, thou mayest go. Speak honourably, wherever thou art, of the work of God, by whomsoever he works, and kindly of his messengers. And, if it be in thy power, not only sympathize with them when they are in any difficulty or distress, but give them a cheerful and effectual assistance, that they may glorify God on thy behalf.

8. Two things should be observed with regard to what has been spoken under this last head: The one, that whatsoever love, whatsoever offices of love, whatsoever spiritual or temporal assistance, I claim from him whose heart is right, as my heart is with his, the same I am ready, by the grace of God, according to my measure, to give him: The other, that I have not made this claim in behalf of myself only, but of all whose heart is right toward God and man, that we may all love one another as Christ hath loved us.

III. 1. One inference we may make from what has been said. We may learn from hence, what is a catholic spirit.

There is scarce any expression which has been more grossly misunderstood, and more dangerously misapplied, than this: But it will be easy for any who calmly consider the preceding observations, to correct any such misapprehensions of it, and to prevent any such misapplication.

For, from hence we may learn, First, that a catholic spirit is not *speculative* latitudinarianism. It is not an indifference to all opinions: This is the spawn of hell, not the offspring of heaven. This unsettledness of thought, this being 'driven to and fro, and tossed about with every wind of doctrine,' is a great curse, not a blessing; an irreconcilable enemy, not a friend, to true catholicism. A man of a truly catholic spirit, has not now his religion to seek. He is fixed as the sun in his judgement concerning the main branches of Christian doctrine. It is true, he is always ready to hear and weigh whatsoever can be offered against his principles; but as this does not show any wavering in his own mind, so neither does it occasion any. He does not halt between two opinions, nor vainly endeavour to blend them into one. Observe this, you who know not what spirit ye are of; who call yourselves men of a catholic spirit, only because you are of a muddy understanding; because your mind is all in a mist; because you have no settled, consistent principles, but are for jumbling all opinions together. Be convinced, that you have quite missed your way; you know not where you are. You think you are got into the very Spirit of Christ; when, in truth, you are nearer the spirit of Antichrist. Go, first, and learn the first elements of the gospel of Christ, and then shall you learn to be of a truly catholic spirit.

2. From what has been said, we may learn, Secondly, that a catholic spirit is not any kind of *practical* latitudinarianism. It is not indifference as to public worship, or as to the outward manner of performing it. This, likewise, would not be blessing, but a curse. Far from being an help thereto, it would, so long as it remained, be an unspeakable hindrance to the worshipping of God in spirit and in truth. But the man of a truly catholic spirit, having weighed all things in the balance of the sanctuary, has no doubt, no scruple at all, concerning that particular mode of worship wherein he joins. He is clearly convinced, that *this* manner of worshipping God is both scriptural and rational. He knows none in the world which is more scriptural, none which is more rational. Therefore, without rambling hither and thither, he cleaves close thereto, and praises God for the opportunity of so doing.

3. Hence we may, Thirdly, learn, that a catholic spirit is not indifference to all congregations. This is another sort of latitudinarianism, no less absurd and unscriptural than the former. But it is far from a man of a truly catholic spirit. He is fixed in his congregation as well as his principles. He is united to one, not only in spirit, but by all the outward ties of Christian fellowship. There he partakes of all the ordinances of God. There he receives the supper of the Lord. There he pours out his soul in public prayer, and joins in public praise and thanksgiving. There

54

he rejoices to hear the word of reconciliation, the gospel of the grace of God. With these his nearest, his best-beloved brethren, on solemn occasions, he seeks God by fasting. These particularly he watches over in love, as they do over his soul; admonishing, exhorting, comforting, reproving, and every way building up each other in the faith. These he regards as his own household; and therefore, according to the ability God has given him, naturally cares for them, and provides that they may have all the things that are needful for life and godliness.

4. But while he is steadily fixed in his religious principles, in what he believes to be the truth as it is in Jesus; while he firmly adheres to that worship of God which he judges to be most acceptable in his sight; and while he is united by the tenderest and closest ties to one particular congregation,—his heart is enlarged toward all mankind, those he knows and those he does not; he embraces with strong and cordial affection, neighbours and strangers, friends and enemies. This is catholic or universal love. And he that has this is of a catholic spirit. For love alone gives the title to this character: Catholic love is a catholic spirit.

5. If, then, we take this word in the strictest sense, a man of a catholic spirit is one who, in the manner above-mentioned, gives his hand to all whose hearts are right with his heart: One who knows how to value, and praise God, for all the advantages he enjoys, with regard to the knowledge of the things of God, the true scriptural manner of worshipping him, and, above all, his union with a congregation fearing God and working righteousness: One who, retaining these blessings with the strictest care, keeping them as the apple of his eye, at the same time loves,—as friends, as brethren in the Lord, as members of Christ and children of God, as joint-partakers now of the present kingdom of God, and fellow-heirs of his eternal kingdom,— all, of whatever opinion, or worship, or congregation, who believe in the Lord Jesus Christ; who love God and man; who, rejoicing to please and fearing to offend God, are careful to abstain from evil, and zealous of good works. He is the man of a truly catholic spirit, who bears all these continually upon his heart; who, having an unspeakable tenderness for their persons, and longing for their welfare, does not cease to commend them to God in prayer, as well as to plead their cause before men; who speaks comfortably to them, and labours, by all his words, to strengthen their hands in God. He assists them to the uttermost of his power in all things, spiritual and temporal. He is ready 'to spend

and be spent for them;' yea, to lay down his life for their sake.

6. Thou, O man of God, think on these things! If thou art already in this way, go on. If thou hast heretofore mistook the path, bless God who hath brought thee back! And now run the race which is set before thee, in the royal way of universal love. Take heed, lest thou be either wavering in thy judgement, or straitened in thy bowels: But keep an even pace, rooted in the faith once delivered to the saints, and grounded in love, in true catholic love, till thou art swallowed up in love for ever and ever!

THE GREAT ASSIZE
Romans 14:10.
We shall all stand before the judgment seat of Christ.

THIS SERMON was preached in St Paul's Church, Bedford, at
the time of the Assizes, on Friday, 10 March 1758, and is printed as sermon xv in volume V of Jackson's edition of the *Collected Works*.

Wesley notes in his *Journal* (27 February 1758): 'Having a
sermon to write against the Assizes at Bedford, I retired for a
few days to Lewisham.' There this model sermon was prepared
upon classical precepts. It begins with the traditional exordium,
followed by the division into subjects, development of those
subjects under three heads, viz.
1. The chief circumstances which will precede our standing
    before the judgement seat of Christ;
2. The judgement itself, and
3. A few of the circumstances which will follow it;
and then the application of 'the preceding considerations to all
who are here before God', followed by the visionary conclusion:
'See, see! He cometh!' (These categories of the formal sermon,
deriving from medieval times, were well known to Wesley, who
was more donnish and less rabid than the vulgar opinion would
have him.)

The Great Assize, preached when Wesley was in his strength,
and to a congregation which was as he says himself 'very large
and very attentive', is not as straightforward as it may at first
sight appear to be. Within the forcefulness of his forms, Wesley
finds it possible to develop his argument with much variety of
vocabulary. George Lawton, whose study *John Wesley's English*
(1962) shows that far from being 'plain and simple' Wesley's
word-usage was 'on the Shakespearean scale', and his prose 'a
stout three-fold cord having scriptural, classical and colloquial
strands interwoven, and flecked with other colourful threads',
provides a list isolating the Latinisms in this particular sermon:

concur	comprise	annihilate
concourse	explicit	minute philosophers
representative	eminent	superficial
solemnity	planetary	magazines
insignificant	import	commissioned
subservient	phantom	ethereal

terraqueous	inclination	experiments
concussions	complex	culinary
resounding	dispositions	quiescent
commotion	contexture	inflexibility
proceeding	dispensations	inexorably
inference	caprice	intercourse
transactions	conception	

Lawton comments:

No doubt there is an easy, or at least an easier synonym for
some of these words, but not for all. Yet it does not necessarily follow that the easy term is better, although it might
make the meaning clearer for an uneducated public. For instance, in place of 'concourse' we could read 'crowd', and the
word 'phantom' might give place to the word 'unreality'. Unquestionably Wesley's words are the richer. In this sermon it
is not simply a 'crowd' that he is concerned with, it is the
flowing together of many streams of society at the Assizes.
If he had written 'the unreality (or the illusion) of human
greatness' he would have lost the spectral associations of the
word 'phantom'.

Lawton goes on to demonstrate that if Wesley had simplified
his style he would have *lost* the power which makes *The Great
Assize* such a superb piece of prose:

In connection with several words in the list given, there is a
conciseness which would be lost by simplification, in as much
as this would necessitate the substitution of periphrasis. For
example, Wesley is saying that the 'ethereal fire' (this was
thought of as an elemental substance in the physics of his
day) is kept in bounds in the natural order, but if it were re-
leased it would do on a frightful, universal scale what the kitchen fire does to fuel, rubbish and food. His phrase for this,
i.e. 'culinary fire' is compact and colourful, and it is appropriate. Neither 'kitchen fire' not 'domestic fire' would be as
good in apposition to 'ethereal fire.'
Again, take the word 'contexture' which occurs in the
phrase 'the whole amazing contexture of divine providence'.
It is difficult to find a better word. 'Pattern' is too simple,
'texture' is ambiguous, 'intermixture' is too purposeless.

Once more, the difficult word is sometimes the appropriate word because of established usage. Two words from the above list occur in a description of the final cataclysm of history, in a sentence which runs: 'Meanwhile all the waters of the terraqueous globe will feel the violence of these concussions.' The adjective 'terraqueous' has long been associated with the noun 'globe'. Even if there is a synonym, which is doubtful, to break the association would cause the knowledgeable reader surprise. As for the word 'concussions', is there a more compendious term by which to denote the shakings, reelings, shocks and quakings pictured in the apocalyptic visions of Scripture concerning the end of the world? (Lawton, pp. 91-2.)

The circumstances in which this sermon was preached were as follows. Wesley came down to Bedford early on the Thursday, but found to his surprise that he did not have to preach until the next day, while he had engaged to be in Epworth on the Saturday. This meant that when the judge immediately after the sermon sent for him to dine, Wesley was obliged to excuse himself. Setting out between one and two o'clock, he rode thirty miles through snow, sleet and hail, slept, renewed his journey between four and five the next morning and accomplished the remaining ninety miles. On the Saturday he preached twice in the church of Epworth, where it was sometimes his custom to preach in the churchyard from his father's tomb, and afterwards again in the market-place, in heavy rain, which as he noted himself 'neither lessened nor disturbed the congregation.'

Rain is one thing, but it is hard to believe that the congregation at Bedford was not disturbed by *The Great Assize*. It contains Wesley's most eloquent passage on that vision of the final conflagration which haunted him all his life.

1. HOW MANY circumstances concur to raise the awfulness of the present solemnity!—The general *concourse* of people of every age, sex, rank, and condition of life, willingly or unwillingly gathered together, not only from the neighbouring, but from distant, parts; *criminals*, speedily to be brought forth, and having no way to escape; *officers*, waiting in their various posts, to execute the orders which shall be given; and the *representative* of our gracious *Sovereign*, whom we so highly reverence and honour. The *occasion* likewise of this assembly adds not a little to the solemnity of it: To hear and determine causes of every kind, some of which are of the most important nature; on which depends no less than life or death, death that uncovers the face of eternity! It was, doubtless, in order to increase the serious sense of these things, and not in the minds of the vulgar only, that the wisdom of our forefathers did not disdain to appoint even several minute circumstances of this solemnity. For these also, by means of the eye or ear, may more deeply affect the heart: And when viewed in this light, trumpets, staves, apparel, are no longer trifling or insignificant, but subservient, in their kind and degree, to the most valuable ends of society.

2. But, as awful as this solemnity is, one far more awful is at hand. For yet a little while, and 'we shall all stand before the judgment seat of Christ.' 'For, as I live, saith the Lord, every knee shall bow to me, and every tongue shall confess to God.' And in that day, 'every one of us shall give account of himself to God.'

3. Had all men a deep sense of this, how effectually would it secure the interests of society! For what more forcible motive can be conceived to the practice of genuine morality? to a steady pursuit of solid virtue? an uniform walking in justice, mercy, and truth? What could strengthen our hands in all that is good, and deter us from all evil, like a strong conviction of this, 'The Judge standeth at the door;' and we are shortly to stand before him?

4. It may not therefore be improper, or unsuitable to the design of the present assembly, to consider,

I. The chief circumstances which will precede our standing before the judgment seat of Christ;

II. The judgment itself; and,

III. A few of the circumstances which will follow it.

I. Let us, in the First place, consider the chief circumstances which will precede our standing before the judgment seat of Christ.

And, First, God will show 'signs in the earth beneath;' (Acts ii. 19;) particularly he will 'arise to shake terribly the earth.' 'The earth shall reel to and fro like a drunkard, and shall be removed like a cottage.' (Isa. xxiv. 20.) 'There shall be earthquakes,' κατα τοπως (not in divers only, but) 'in *all* places;' not in one only, or a few, but in every part of the habitable world; (Luke xxi.11;) even 'such as were not since men were upon the earth, so mighty earthquakes and so great.' In one of these 'every island shall flee away, and the mountains will not be found.' (Rev. xvi. 20.) Meantime all the waters of the terraqueous globe will feel the violence of those concussions; 'the sea and waves roaring,' (Luke xxi. 25,) with such an agitation as had never been known before, since the hour that 'the fountains of the great deep were broken up,' to destroy the earth, which then 'stood out of the water and in the water.' The air will be all storm and tempest, full of dark vapours and pillars of smoke; (Joel ii. 30;) resounding with thunder from pole to pole, and torn with ten thousand lightnings. But the commotion will not stop in the region of the air; 'the powers of heaven also shall be shaken. There shall be signs in the sun, and in the moon, and in the stars;' (Luke xxi. 25, 26;) those fixed, as well as those that move round them. 'The sun shall be turned into darkness, and the moon into blood, before the great and terrible day of the Lord come.' (Joel ii. 31.) 'The stars shall withdraw their shining,' (Joel iii. 15,) yea, and 'fall from heaven,' (Rev. vi. 13,) being thrown out of their orbits. And then shall be heard the universal *shout*, from all the companies of heaven, followed by the 'voice of the archangel,' proclaiming the approach of the Son of God and Man, 'and the trumpet of God,' sounding an alarm to all that sleep in the dust of the earth. (1 Thess. iv. 16.) In consequence of this, all the graves shall open, and the bodies of men arise. The sea also shall give up the dead which are therein, (Rev. xx. 13,) and every one shall rise with 'his own body;' his own substance, although so changed in its properties as we cannot now conceive. 'For this corruptible will' then 'put on incorruption, and this mortal put on immortality.' (1 Cor. xv. 53.) Yea, 'death and hades,' the invisible world, shall 'deliver up the dead that are in them.' (Rev. xx. 13.) So that all who ever lived and died, since God created man, shall be raised incorruptible and immortal.

2. At the same time, 'the Son of man shall send forth his angels' over all the earth; and they shall 'gather his elect from the four winds, from one end of heaven to the other'(Matt. xxiv. 31.)

61

And the Lord himself shall come with clouds, in his own glory, and the glory of his Father, with ten thousand of his saints, even myriads of angels, and shall sit upon the throne of his glory. 'And before him shall be gathered all nations, and he shall separate them one from another, and shall set the sheep,' the good, 'on his right hand, and the goats,' the wicked, 'upon the left.' (Matt. xxv. 31, &c.) Concerning this general assembly it is, that the beloved disciple speaks thus: 'I saw the dead,' all that had been dead, 'small and great, stand before God. And the books were opened,' (a figurative expression, plainly referring to the manner of proceeding among men,) 'and the dead were judged out of those things which were written in the books, according to their works.' (Rev. xx. 12.)

II. These are the chief circumstances which are recorded in the oracles of God, as preceding the general judgment. We are, Secondly, to consider the judgment itself, so far as it hath pleased God to reveal it.

1. The person by whom God will judge the world, is his only begotten Son, whose 'goings forth are from everlasting;' 'who is God over all, blessed for ever.' Unto Him, being 'the out-beaming of his Father's glory, the express image of his person,' (Heb. i. 3) the Father 'hath committed all judgment, because he is the Son of Man;' (John v. 22, 27;) because, though he was 'in the form of God, and thought it not robbery to be equal with God, yet he emptied himself, taking upon him the form of a servant, being made in the likeness of men;' (Phil. ii. 6, 7;) yea, because, being found in fashion as a man, he humbled himself yet farther, 'becoming obedient unto death, even the death of the cross. Wherefore God hath highly exalted him,' even in his human nature, and 'ordained him,' as man, to try the children of men, 'to be the Judge both of the quick and dead;' both of those who shall be found alive at his coming, and of those who were before gathered to their fathers.

2. The time, termed by the Prophet, 'The great and the terrible day,' is usually, in Scripture, styled, *the day of the Lord*. The space from the creation of man upon the earth, to the end of all things, is *the day of the sons of men*; the time that is now passing over us is properly *our day*; when this is ended, *the day of the Lord* will begin. But who can say how long it will continue? 'With the Lord one day is as a thousand years, and a thousand years as one day.' (2 Pet. iii. 8.) And from this very expression, some of the ancient Fathers drew that inference, that, what is commonly called the day of judgment would be indeed a

thousand years: And it seems they did not go beyond the truth; nay, probably they did not come up to it. For, if we consider the number of persons who are to be judged, and of actions which are to be inquired into, it does not appear, that a thousand years will suffice for the transactions of that day; so that it may not improbably comprise several thousand years. But God shall reveal this also in its season.

3. With regard to the place where mankind will be judged, we have no explicit account in Scripture. An eminent writer (but not he alone; many have been of the same opinion) supposes it will be on earth, where the works were done, according to which they shall be judged; and that God will, in order thereto, employ the angels of his strength—

> To smooth and lengthen out the boundless space,
> And spread an area for all human race.

But perhaps it is more agreeable to our Lord's own account of his coming in the clouds, to suppose it will be above the earth, if not 'twice a planetary height.' And this supposition is not a little favoured by what St. Paul writes to the Thessalonians: 'The dead in Christ shall rise first. Then we who remain alive, shall be caught up together with them, in the clouds, to meet the Lord in the air.' (1 Thess. iv. 16, 17.) So that it seems most probable, the great white throne will be high exalted above the earth.

4. The persons to be judged, who can count, any more than the drops of rain, or the sands of the sea? 'I beheld,' saith St. John, 'a great multitude which no man can number, clothed with white robes, and palms in their hands.' How immense then must be the total multitude of all nations, and kindreds, and people, and tongues; of all that have sprung from the loins of Adam, since the world began, till time shall be no more! If we admit the common supposition, which seems no ways absurd, that the earth bears, at any one time, no less than four hundred millions of living souls, men, women, and children; what a congregation must all those generations make, who have succeeded each other for several thousand years!

> Great Xerxes' world in arms, proud Cannae's host,
> They all are here; and here they all are lost.
> Their numbers swell to be discern'd in vain;
> Lost as a drop in the unbounded main.

63

Every man, every woman, every infant of days, that ever breathed the vital air, will then hear the voice of the Son of God, and start into life, and appear before him. And this seems to be the natural import of that expression, 'the dead, small and great:' All universally, all without exception, all of every age, sex, or degree; all that ever lived and died, or underwent such a change as will be equivalent with death. For long before that day, the phantom of human greatness disappears, and sinks into nothing. Even in the moment of death, that vanishes away. Who is rich or great in the grave?

5. And every man shall there 'give an account of his own works;' yea, a full and true account of all that he ever did while in the body, whether it was good or evil. O what a scene will then be disclosed, in the sight of angels and men!—while not the fabled Rhadamanthus, but the Lord God Almighty, who knoweth all things in heaven and in earth,—

> *Castigatque, auditque dolos; subigitque fateri*
> *Quae quis apud superos, furto laetatus inani,*
> *Distulit in seram commissa piacula mortem.* *

Nor will the actions alone of every child of man be then brought to open view, but all their words; seeing 'every idle word which men shall speak, they shall give account thereof in the day of judgment;' (Matt. xii. 36, 37;) so that 'by thy words,' as well as works, 'thou shalt be justified; or by thy words thou shalt be condemned.' Will not God then bring to light every circumstance also, that accompanied every word or action, and if not altered the nature, yet lessened or increased the goodness or badness of them? And how easy is this to Him who is 'about our bed, and about our path, and spieth out all our ways?' We know 'the darkness is no darkness to Him, but the night shineth as the day.'

6. Yea, he will bring to light, not the hidden works of darkness only, but the very thoughts and intents of the hearts. And what marvel? For he 'searcheth the reins and understandeth all our thoughts.' 'All things are naked and open to the eyes of Him with whom we have to do.' 'Hell and destruction are before him without a covering. How much more the hearts of the children of men!'

---

* O'er these drear realms stern Rhadamanthus reigns,
   Detects each artful villain, and constrains
   To own the crimes, long veil'd from human sight:
   In vain! Now all stand forth in hated light.

7. And in that day shall be discovered every inward working of every human soul; every appetite, passion, inclination, affection, with the various combinations of them, with every temper and disposition that constitute the whole complex character of each individual. So shall it be clearly and infallibly seen, who was righteous, and who unrighteous; and in what degree every action, or person, or character was either good or evil.

8. 'Then the King will say to them upon his right hand, Come, ye blessed of my Father. For I was hungry, and ye gave me meat; thirsty, and ye gave me drink: I was a stranger, and ye took me in; naked, and ye clothed me.' In like manner, all the good they did upon earth will be recited before men and angels; whatsoever they had done, either in word or deed, in the name, or for the sake, of the Lord Jesus. All their good desires, intentions, thoughts, all their holy dispositions, will also be then remembered; and it will appear, that though they were unknown or forgotten among men, yet God noted them in his book. All their sufferings likewise for the name of Jesus, and for the testimony of a good conscience, will be displayed unto their praise from the righteous Judge, their honour before saints and angels, and the increase of that 'far more exceeding and eternal weight of glory.'

9. But will their evil deeds too, (since, if we take in his whole life, there is not a man on earth that liveth and sinneth not,) will these be remembered in that day, and mentioned in the great congregation? Many believe they will not; and ask, 'Would not this imply, that their sufferings were not at an end, even when life ended?—seeing they would still have sorrow, and shame, and confusion of face to endure.' They ask farther, 'How can this be reconciled with God's declaration by the Prophet,—"If the wicked will turn from all his sins that he hath committed, and keep all my statutes, and do that which is lawful and right; all his transgressions that he hath committed, they shall not be once mentioned unto him?" ' (Ezek. xviii. 21, 22.) How is it consistent with the promise which God has made to all who accept of the gospel covenant,—'I will forgive their iniquities, and remember their sin no more?' (Jer. xxxi.34.) Or, as the Apostle expresses it, 'I will be merciful to their unrighteousness, and their sins and iniquities will I remember no more?' (Heb. viii. 12.)

10. It may be answered, It is apparently and absolutely necessary, for the full display of the glory of God; for the clear and perfect manifestation of his wisdom, justice, power, and mercy,

toward the heirs of salvation; that all the circumstances of their life should be placed in open view, together with all their tempers, and all the desires, thoughts, and intents of their hearts: Otherwise, how would it appear out of what a depth of sin and misery the grace of God had delivered them? And, indeed, if the whole lives of all the children of men were not manifestly discovered, the whole amazing contexture of divine providence could not be manifested; nor should we yet be able, in a thousand instances, 'to justify the ways of God to man.' Unless our Lord's words were fulfilled in their utmost sense, without any restriction or limitation,—'There is nothing covered that shall not be revealed, or hid that shall not be known;' (Matt. x. 26;) abundance of God's dispensations under the sun would still appear without their reasons. And then only when God hath brought to light all the hidden things of darkness, whosoever were the actors therein, will it be seen that wise and good were all his ways; that he saw through the thick cloud, and governed all things by the wise counsel of his own will; that nothing was left to chance or the caprice of men, but God disposed all strongly and sweetly, and wrought all into one connected chain of justice, mercy, and truth.

11. And in the discovery of the divine perfections, the righteous will rejoice with joy unspeakable; far from feeling any painful sorrow or shame, for any of those past transgressions which were long since blotted out as a cloud, washed away by the blood of the Lamb. It will be abundantly sufficient for them, that all the transgressions which they had committed shall not be once mentioned unto them to their disadvantage; that their sins, and transgressions, and iniquities shall be remembered no more to their condemnation. This is the plain meaning of the promise; and this all the children of God shall find true, to their everlasting comfort.

12. After the righteous are judged, the King will turn to them upon his left hand; and they shall also be judged, every man according to his works. But not only their outward works will be brought into the account, but all the evil words which they have ever spoken; yea, all the evil desires, affections, tempers, which have, or have had, a place in their souls; and all the evil thoughts or designs which were ever cherished in their hearts. The joyful sentence of acquittal will then be pronounced upon those upon the right hand; the dreadful sentence of condemnation upon those on the left; both of which must remain fixed

and unmovable as the throne of God.

III. 1. We may, in the Third place, consider a few of the circumstances which will follow the general judgment. And the First is the execution of the sentence pronounced on the evil and on the good: 'These shall go away into eternal punishment, and the righteous into life eternal.' It should be observed, it is the very same word which is used, both in the former and the latter clause: It follows, that either the punishment lasts for ever, or the reward too will come to an end:—No, never, unless God could come to an end, or his mercy and truth could fail. 'Then shall the righteous shine forth as the sun in the kingdom of their Father,' 'and shall drink of those rivers of pleasure which are at God's right hand for evermore.' But here all description falls short: All human language fails! Only one who is caught up into the third heaven can have a just conception of it. But even such a one cannot express what he hath seen: These things it is not possible for man to utter.

The wicked, meantime, shall be turned into hell, even all the people that forget God. They will be 'punished with everlasting destruction from the presence of the Lord, and from the glory of his power.' They shall be 'cast into the lake of fire burning with brimstone,' originally 'prepared for the devil and his angels;' where they will gnaw their tongues for anguish and pain, they will curse God and look upward. There the dogs of hell—pride, malice, revenge, rage, horror, despair—continually devour them. There 'they have no rest, day or night, but the smoke of their torment ascendeth for ever and ever!' For, 'their worm dieth not, and the fire is not quenched.'

2. Then the heavens will be shrivelled up as a parchment scroll, and pass away with a great noise: They will 'flee from the face of him that sitteth on the throne, and there will be found no place for them.' (Rev. xx. 11.) The very manner of their passing away is disclosed to us by the Apostle Peter: 'In the day of God, the heavens, being on fire, shall be dissolved.' (2 Pet. iii. 12.) The whole beautiful fabric will be overthrown by that raging element, the connexion of all its parts destroyed, and every atom torn asunder from the others. By the same, 'the earth also, and the works that are therein, shall be burned up.' (Verse 10.) The enormous works of nature, the everlasting hills, mountains that have defied the rage of time, and stood unmoved so many thousand years, will sink down in fiery ruin. How much less will the works of art, though of the most durable kind, the utmost

efforts of human industry,—tombs, pillars, triumphal arches, castles, pyramids,—be able to withstand the flaming conqueror! All, all will die, perish, vanish away, like a dream when one awaketh!

3. It has indeed been imagined by some great and good men, that as it requires that same almighty power to annihilate things as to create; to speak into nothing or out of nothing; so no part of, no atom in, the universe, will be totally or finally destroyed. Rather, they suppose, that, as the last operation of fire, which we have yet been able to observe, is to reduce into glass what, by a smaller force, it had reduced to ashes; so, in the day God hath ordained, the whole earth, if not the material heavens also, will undergo this change, after which the fire can have no farther power over them. And they believe this is intimated by that expression in the Revelation made to St. John, 'Before the throne there was a sea of glass, like unto crystal.' (Rev. iv. 6.) We cannot now either affirm or deny this; but we shall know hereafter.

4. If it be inquired by the scoffers, the minute philosophers, 'How can these things be? Whence should come such an immense quantity of fire as would consume the heavens and the whole terraqueous globe?' We would beg leave, First, to remind them, that this difficulty is not peculiar to the Christian system. The same opinion almost universally obtained among the *unbigoted* Heathens. So one of those celebrated *free-thinkers* speaks, according to the generally received sentiment:—

> *Esse quoque in fatis reminiscitur, affore tempus,*
> *Quo mare, quo tellus, correptaque regia coeli*
> *Ardeat, et mundi moles operosa laboret.* *

But, Secondly, it is easy to answer, even from our slight and superficial acquaintance with natural things, that there are abundant magazines of fire ready prepared, and treasured up against the day of the Lord. How soon may a comet, commissioned by him, travel down from the most distant parts of the universe! And were it to fix upon the earth, in its return from the sun, when it is some thousand times hotter than a red-hot cannon-ball, who does not see what must be the immediate consequence?

---

* The following is Dryden's translation of this quotation from Ovid:
  Rememb'ring, in the fates, a time when fire
  Should to the battlements of heaven aspire;
  And all the blazing world above should burn,
  And all the inferior globe to cinders turn.

But, not to ascend so high as the ethereal heavens, might not the same lightnings which 'give shine to the world,' if commanded by the Lord of nature, give ruin and utter destruction? Or, to go no farther than the globe itself; who knows what huge reservoirs of liquid fire are from age to age contained in the bowels of the earth? Aetna, Hecla, Vesuvius, and all the other volcanoes that belch out flames and coals of fire, what are they, but so many proofs and mouths of those fiery furnaces; and at the same time so many evidences that God hath in readiness wherewith to fulfill his word? Yea, were we to observe no more than the surface of the earth, and the things that surround us on every side, it is most certain (as a thousand experiments prove, beyond all possibility of denial) that we ourselves, our whole bodies, are full of fire, as well as every thing round about us. Is it not easy to make this ethereal fire visible even to the naked eye, and to produce thereby the very same effects on combustible matter, which are produced by culinary fire? Needs there then any more than for God to unloose that secret chain, whereby this irresistible agent is now bound down, and lies quiescent in every particle of matter? And how soon would it tear the universal frame in pieces, and involve all in one common ruin!

5. There is one circumstance more which will follow the judgment, that deserves our serious consideration: 'We look,' says the Apostle, 'according to his promise, for new heavens and a new earth, wherein dwelleth righteousness.' (2 Pet. iii. 13.) The promise stands in the prophecy of Isaiah, 'Behold, I create new heavens and a new earth: And the former shall not be remembered;' (Isaiah lxv. 17;)—so great shall the glory of the latter be! These St. John did behold in the visions of God. 'I saw,' saith he, 'a new heaven and a new earth; for the first heaven and the first earth were passed away.' (Rev. xxi.1.) And only righteousness dwelt therein: Accordingly, he adds, 'And I heard a great voice from' the third 'heaven, saying, Behold, the tabernacle of God is with men, and he will dwell with them, and they shall be his people; and God himself shall be with them, and be their God!' (xxi. 3.) Of necessity, therefore, they will be happy: 'God shall wipe away all tears from their eyes, and there shall be no more death, neither sorrow, nor crying; neither shall there be any more pain.' (xxi. 4.) 'There shall be no more curse; but they shall see his face;' (xxii. 3, 4;)—shall have the nearest access to, and thence the highest resemblance of, him. This is the strongest expression in the language of Scripture, to denote the most perfect happiness.

'And his name shall be on their foreheads;' they shall be openly acknowledged as God's own property, and his glorious nature shall most visibly shine forth in them. 'And there shall be no night there; and they need no candle, neither light of the sun; for the Lord God giveth them light: And they shall reign for ever and ever.'

IV. It remains only to apply the preceding considerations to all who are here before God. And are we not directly led so to do, by the present solemnity, which so naturally points us to that day, when the Lord will judge the world in righteousness? This, therefore, by reminding us of that more awful season, may furnish many lessons of instruction. A few of these I may be permitted just to touch on. May God write them on all our hearts!

1. And, First, how beautiful are the feet of those who are sent by the wise and gracious providence of God, to execute justice on earth, to defend the injured, and punish the wrong-doer! Are they not the ministers of God to us for good; the grand supporters of the public tranquillity; the patrons of innocence and virtue; the great security of all our temporal blessings? And does not every one of these represent, not only an earthly prince, but the Judge of the earth? Him, whose 'name is written upon his thigh, King of kings, and Lord of lords?' O that all these sons of the right hand of the Most High, may be holy as He is holy! wise with the wisdom that sitteth by his throne, like Him who is the eternal Wisdom of the Father! no respecters of persons, as He is none; but rendering to every man according to his works; like Him inflexibly, inexorably just, though pitiful and of tender mercy! So shall they be terrible indeed to them that do evil, as not bearing the sword in vain. So shall the laws of our land have their full use and due honour, and the throne of our King be still established in righteousness.

2. Ye truly honourable men, whom God and the King have commissioned, in a lower degree, to administer justice; may not ye be compared to those ministering spirits who will attend the Judge coming in the clouds? May you, like them, burn with love to God and man! May you love righteousness and hate iniquity! May ye all minister, in your several spheres, (such honour hath God given you also!) to them that shall be heirs of salvation, and to the glory of your great Sovereign! May ye remain the establishers of peace, the blessing and ornaments of your country, the protectors of a guilty land, the guardian-angels of all that are round about you!

70

3. You, whose office it is to execute what is given you in charge by him before whom you stand; how nearly are you concerned to resemble those that stand before the face of the Son of Man, those servants of his that do his pleasure, and hearken to the voice of his words! Does it not highly import you, to be as uncorrupt as them? to approve yourselves the servants of God? to do justly, and love mercy? to do to all as ye would they should do to you? So shall that great Judge, under whose eye you continually stand, say to you also, 'Well done, good and faithful servants: Enter ye into the joy of your Lord!'

4. Suffer me to add a few words to all of you who are at this day present before the Lord. Should not you bear it in your minds all the day long, that a more awful day is coming? A large assembly this! But what is it to that which every eye will then behold, the general assembly of all the children of men that ever lived on the face of the whole earth? A few will stand at the judgment-seat this day, to be judged touching what shall be laid to their charge; and they are now reserved in prison, perhaps in chains, till they are brought forth to be tried and sentenced. But we shall all, I that speak, and you that hear, 'stand at the judgment seat of Christ.' And we are now reserved on this earth, which is not our home, in this prison of flesh and blood, perhaps many of us in chains of darkness too, till we are ordered to be brought forth. Here a man is questioned concerning one or two facts, which he is supposed to have committed: There we are to give an account of all our works, from the cradle to the grave; of all our words; of all our desires and tempers, all the thoughts and intents of our hearts; of all the use we have made of our various talents, whether of mind, body, or fortune, till God said, 'Give an account of thy stewardship, for thou mayest be no longer steward.' In this court, it is possible, some who are guilty may escape for want of evidence; but there is no want of evidence in that court. All men, with whom you had the most secret intercourse, who were privy to all your designs and actions, are ready before your face. So are all the spirits of darkness, who inspired evil designs, and assisted in the execution of them. So are all the angels of God; those eyes of the Lord, that run to and fro over all the earth, who watched over your soul, and laboured for your good, so far as you would permit. So is your own conscience, a thousand witnesses in one, now no more capable of being either blinded or silenced, but constrained to know and to speak the naked truth, touching all your thoughts, and words, and

71

actions. And is conscience as a thousand witnesses?—yea, but God is as a thousand consciences! O, who can stand before the face of the great God, even our Saviour Jesus Christ!

See! See! He cometh! He maketh the clouds his chariots! He rideth upon the wings of the wind! A devouring fire goeth before him, and after him a flame burneth! See! He sitteth upon his throne, clothed with light as with a garment, arrayed with majesty and honour! Behold, his eyes are as a flame of fire, his voice as the sound of many waters!

How will ye escape? Will ye call to the mountains to fall on you, the rocks to cover you? Alas, the mountains themselves, the rocks, the earth, the heavens, are just ready to flee away! Can ye prevent the sentence? Wherewith? With all the substance of thy house, with thousands of gold and silver? Blind wretch! Thou camest naked from thy mother's womb, and more naked into eternity. Hear the Lord, the Judge! 'Come, ye blessed of my Father! inherit the kingdom prepared for you from the foundation of the world.' Joyful sound! How widely different from that voice which echoes through the expanse of heaven, 'Depart, ye cursed, into everlasting fire, prepared for the devil and his angels!' And who is he that can prevent or retard the full execution of either sentence? Vain hope! Lo, hell is moved from beneath to receive those who are ripe for destruction! And the everlasting doors lift up their heads, that the heirs of glory may come in!

5. 'What manner of persons then ought we to be, in all holy conversation and godliness!' We know it cannot be long before the Lord will descend with the voice of the Archangel, and the trumpet of God; when every one of us shall appear before him, and give account of his own works. 'Wherefore, beloved, seeing ye look for these things,' seeing ye know He will come and will not tarry, 'be diligent, that ye may be found of him in peace, without spot and blameless.' Why should ye not? Why should one of you be found on the left hand, at his appearing? He willeth not that any should perish, but that all should come to repentance; by repentance, to faith in a bleeding Lord; by faith, to spotless love, to the full image of God renewed in the heart, and producing all holiness of conversation. Can you doubt of this, when you remember, the Judge of all is likewise the Saviour of all? Hath he not bought you with his own blood, that ye might not perish, but have everlasting life? O make proof of his mercy, rather than his justice; of his love, rather than the thunder of his power! He is not far from every one of us; and he is now

72

come, not to condemn, but to save the world. He standeth in the midst! Sinner, doth he not now, even now, knock at the door of thy heart? O that thou mayest know, at least in this thy day, the things that belong unto thy peace! O that ye may now give yourselves to Him who gave himself for you, in humble faith, in holy, active, patient love! So shall ye rejoice with exceeding joy in his day, when he cometh in the clouds of heaven.

LAURENCE STERNE, great-grandson of an Archbishop of York who had been a High Church loyalist during the Civil War, was born at Clonmel, in Tipperary, in 1713. His father was a soldier, his mother an Irishwoman of lowly birth. Sterne's childhood was spent in Ireland, travelling with his father's regiment—a chapter of escapades which gave him matter for the adventures of Uncle Toby, Corporal Trim and Lieutenant Le Fever in *Tristram Shandy*.

At the age of ten he was sent to school at Halifax, and then went up to Jesus College, Cambridge, in 1733. Sterne was ordained deacon in 1736, priest in 1738. Thanks to his uncle Jacques, who was a canon of York Cathedral, he procured the living of Sutton-in-the-Forest, Yorkshire. His uncle's influence ensured further emoluments and sinecures, and Sterne's marriage to Eliza Lumley, in 1741, obtained for him another living, that of the parish of Stillington.

From 1738 to 1759, then, Laurence Sterne lived the life of a country parson. He was no worse than some and better than many. Nineteenth-century agnostic moralists liked to delight that Sterne must have been indifferently suited to the priesthood, but more recent research has indicated that while eccentric he was not without conscience in carrying out his parochial duties, allowance being made for the fact that his health was never good.

His first publication was in 1747, a sermon entitled *The Case of Elijah and the Widow Zerephath Consider'd*; this was followed by another sermon on *The Abuses of Conscience* in 1750. A quarrel among cathedral officials at York set Sterne off on the writing of a satirical skit, eventually developed into his masterpiece, *Tristram Shandy*, the first two volumes of which appeared in 1760. This novel was partly composed in a fit of energy which came upon him after his wife's removal to be placed in 'confinement under a lunatic doctor in a private house at York.' Some say that her insanity had been brought on by discovery of Sterne in compromising circumstances with a servant-girl. If this is true, it may be a little mitigated by the fact that he loved Eliza enough to humour her mad imaginings. 'She fancied herself the queen of Bohemia. He treated her as such, with all the supposed respect due to a crowned head.'

Tristram Shandy was an immediate success, and Sterne was

soon so famous that a wager was struck in London that a letter addressed 'Tristram Shandy, in Europe' would get to him in Sutton. It did. Third and fourth volumes appeared in 1761, fifth and sixth in 1762, seventh and eighth in 1765 and the last in 1767. On the strength of the fame of his fiction he also found a market for the *Sermons of Mr. Yorick* (1760). Ill health, amatory entanglements and depression dogged Sterne for the rest of his life. Despite this he found time to celebrate the Eucharist and to preach now and again—at the English Ambassador's chapel in Paris, for instance, in 1764.

Amongst other sins, Sterne introduced the word *sentimental* into the English language in its modern connotation. It can be taken as referring in his personal affairs to something more than self-indulgent sensual dallyings and wallowings. His tenderness to his only child, his daughter Lydia, might be remembered when his feverish romances with a number of ladies are forgotten.

The manner of Sterne's death is memorable. In March 1768 he wrote to his daughter that he was bowed down with a vile influenza—'I wish I had thee to nurse me, but I am denied that. Write to me twice a week at least. God bless thee, my child, and believe me ever, ever, thy affectionate father.' The influenza worsened into pleurisy. The last thing we have from his pen is a letter begging a friend to take care of Lydia when he is gone. 'My spirits are fled.' We have an account of his end from an unusual source, the *Memoirs* of John Macdonald, a servant employed by a company dining together in London on 18 March— the party including the Duke of Roxburghe, the Earl of March, the Duke of Grafton, David Garrick and David Hume. The talk turning on laughter, these gentlemen dispatched Macdonald to see how Mr Sterne, their mutual friend, was faring. Macdonald did so. This is his report: 'I went to Mr. Sterne's lodgings; the mistress opened the door. I inquired how he did; she told me to go up to the nurse. I went into the room, and he was just a-dying. I waited ten minutes; but in five he said, "Now it is come." He put up his hand as if to stop a blow, and died in a minute.'

Sterne's body was buried in 'the new burying-ground near Tyburn', of the parish of St George's, Hanover Square. It is said, however, that the corpse was stolen by body-snatchers two days after the burial and sold to a professor of anatomy at Cambridge, where one of Sterne's friends, attending the demonstration of dissection that followed, fainted when he recognized the face on the table.

BIBLIOGRAPHY

The Life and Opinions of Tristram Shandy, vols I and II, York, 1759; 2nd ed., London, 1760, with plate by Hogarth.

The Life and Opinions of Tristram Shandy, vols III and IV, 1761, with a second plate by Hogarth.

The Life and Opinions of Tristram Shandy, vols V and VI, 1762.

The Life and Opinions of Tristram Shandy, vols VII and VIII, 1765.

The Life and Opinions of Tristram Shandy, vol IX, 1767.

Sermons of Mr. Yorick, vols I and II, 1760.

Sermons of Mr. Yorick, vols III and IV, 1766.

Sermons of Mr. Yorick, vols V, VI and VII, 1769.

The Sentimental Journey, 2 vols, 1768.

THE PRODIGAL SON

Luke 15:13.

And not many days after, the younger son gathered all he had together, and took his journey into a far country.

THIS IS sermon v in the third volume of *Sermons of Mr. Yorick*, published in 1766. It could have been preached at Sutton-in-the-Forest, where Sterne was vicar from 1738 to 1759, or in the cathedral at York, of which he was prebendary from 1740. If it was in the cathedral it probably caused some stir, for they say that when Sterne climbed into the pulpit 'half the congregation usually left.' When not at York he preached each Sunday morning at Sutton and each Sunday afternoon at the adjoining parish of Stillington, walking from one church to the other across the fields. Once his dog sprang a covey of partridges on the way. Sterne went home for his gun. His Stillington congregation waited in vain.

Sterne's originality of sermon-technique has not been given its due. Because his sermons are often as witty, laconic and brilliantly digressive as chapters of *Tristram Shandy* he has even been accused of insincerity. Yet as a country parson he celebrated the Eucharist five times a year—more often than was common among English clergy of his day; and his record of giving instruction to his people is decent. 'I Catechise every Sunday in my Church during Lent,' he informed Archbishop Herring in 1743, 'But explain our Religion to the Children and Servants of my Parishioners in my own House every Sunday Night during Lent, from six o'clock till nine. I mention the Length of Time as my reason for not doing it in Church.'[1] This shows no indolence.

Sterne was a complicated man, and perhaps it is because he did not take off his complications before getting into the pulpit that he has been attacked. When he cries out, at the climax of retelling the story of the prodigal son, that 'Joy is another name for Religion' you can almost hear William Blake saying 'Amen' in the pew behind.

I think we may assume that *The Prodigal Son* was preached late in Sterne's clerical career—judging from its sureness of style and its syntactical similarity to *Tristram Shandy*. It has been said that the parable of the prodigal prompts Sterne only to remarks on the advantages of foreign travel and the desirability of confiding one's son when on the Grand Tour to a tutor of gentlemanly habits. He *does* have fun with his text along these lines, but at the same time he seems wiser than some in *not* treating this parable as an allegory. Allegorically, indeed, it has many defects, containing for a start no illustration of the central fact of the Gospel—that our forgiveness is earned for us by Christ's sufferings and death. A lesser point, but still worrying if we are to read the story as an allegory, is that Jewish wisdom counsels fathers against premature disposition of their property (Ecclesiasticus 33:19), so that the prodigal's father could be criticized for being himself prodigal in giving the younger son his third (Deuteronomy 21:16-17).

In other words, interpretations which leave us with the father in this parable standing for the First Person of the Holy Trinity do less than justice to its realism. From the start of the story we are hearing about human fallibility, a favourite subject of Sterne's and as he knew not a prerogative of sons. Criticism moves on firmer ground if it confines itself to the question: Does Sterne see the point that it is *conscience* which forms the pivot upon which the prodigal's *metanoia* is accomplished? The words in Luke, *when he came to himself*, denote that moment in human life when the heart, sickened by dissipation, becomes self-collected, and is no longer 'beside itself'. Sterne surely sees this well? 'Strange!—that we should only begin to think of God with comfort, when with joy and comfort we can think of nothing else.'

Later, the elder brother's sullen envy testifies again to the *human* reality of this parable. Yet the father entreats him to forget his own feelings and rejoice in his brother's return. There is no legalism here, nor in the father's attitude to either son, expiation having no place in the relations between man and man, save through penitential acts effected in union with the perfect expiation of the Cross. Sterne himself reminds us that Christ was speaking to Pharisees who discountenanced his mission to the lost, and refers half-heartedly to those who would identify the prodigal son with the Gentiles and the elder brother with the Jews. But his mind is so instinctively unconvinced by 'these uses' that he begs his congregation's leave not to pursue them, and sets off instead on that piece of inspired serendipity which gives the sermon its charm—I mean, the peroration concerning the Grand Tour, which his hearers must have *enjoyed*, and why not, for the Church has never taught that homilies are of necessity unenjoyable, and might not the words of Christ himself be sometimes found extremely strange and witty, as in that

78

surrealistic figure of the rich man's difficulties in entering heaven being like a camel trying to get through a needle's eye[2] — an image which probably upset the Pharisees as much as Sterne's verbal exuberance upset their eighteenth-century descendants.

To read the sermon thus is not to claim that Sterne is enthusiastic about doctrinal exposition, or even theology itself. But he is profoundly interested in persons, and in their feelings, and doings, and that is what this story of Christ's is 'about'. Sterne once deprecated his own sermonizing as no more than a 'theological flap upon the heart'. This particular 'flap' retells an intimate and plausible human story, of much depth, and elaborates upon it in a spirit of Shandyism by no means contradictory to the Christian faith.

NOTES

1. *Archbishop Herring's Visitation Returns*, 1929, III, section 93.
2. Matthew 19: 24; Mark 10: 25; Luke 18: 25.

I KNOW not whether the remark is to our honour or otherwise, that lessons of wisdom have never such power over us, as when they are wrought into the heart, through the groundwork of a story which engages the passions: Is it that we are like iron, and must first be heated before we can be wrought upon? or, Is the heart so in love with deceit, that where a true report will not reach it, we must cheat it with a fable, in order to come at truth?

Whether this parable of the prodigal (for so it is usually called) is really such, or built upon some story known at that time in Jerusalem, is not much to the purpose; it is given us to enlarge upon, and turn to the best moral account we can.

'A certain man, says our SAVIOUR, had two sons, and the younger of them said to his father, Give me the portion of goods which falls to me: and he divided unto them his substance. And not many days after, the younger son gathered all together and took his journey into a far country, and there wasted his substance with riotous living.'

The account is short: the interesting and pathetic passages with which such a transaction would be necessarily connected, are left to be supplied by the heart: the story is silent—but nature is not: much kind advice, and many a tender expostulation would fall from the father's lips, no doubt, upon this occasion.

He would dissuade his son from the folly of so rash an enterprize, by shewing him the dangers of the journey, the inexperience of his age, the hazards of his life, his fortune, his virtue would run, without a guide, without a friend: he would tell him of the many snares and temptations which he had to avoid, or encounter at every step, the pleasures which would solicit him in every luxurious court, the little knowledge he could gain—except that of evil; he would speak of the seductions of women, their charms, their poisons: what helpless indulgences he might give way to, when far from restraint, and the check of the giving his father pain.

The dissuasive would but inflame his desire.

He gathers all together.—

—I see the picture of his departure—the camels and asses loaden with his substance, detached on one side of the piece, and already on their way: the prodigal son standing on the foreground with a forced sedateness, struggling against the fluttering movement of joy, upon his deliverance from restraint: the elder brother holding his hand, as if unwilling to let it go:—the father,—

80

sad moment ! with a firm look, covering a prophetic sentiment, 'that all would not go well with his child,'—approaching to embrace him, and bid him adieu. Poor inconsiderate youth! From whose arms art thou flying? From what a shelter art thou going forth into the storm? Art thou weary of a father's affection, of a father's care? or, Hopest thou to find a warmer interest, a truer counsellor, or a kinder friend in a land of strangers, where youth is made a prey, and so many thousands are confederated to deceive them, and live by their spoils.

We will seek no further than this idea, for the extravagancies by which the prodigal son added one unhappy example to the number: his fortune wasted, the followers of it fled in course, the wants of nature remain,—the hand of GOD gone forth against him,—'*For when he had spent all, a mighty famine arose in that country.*'—Heaven! have pity upon the youth, for he is in hunger and distress, strayed out of the reach of a parent, who counts every hour of his absence with anguish, cut off from all his tender offices, by his folly, and from relief and charity from others, by the calamity of the times.

Nothing so powerfully calls home the mind as distress: the tense fibre then relaxes, the soul retires to itself, sits pensive and susceptible of right impressions: if we have a friend, 'tis then we think of him; if a benefactor, at that moment all his kindnesses press upon our mind. Gracious and bountiful GOD! Is it not for this, that they who in their prosperity forget thee, do yet remember and return to thee in the hour of this sorrow? When our heart is in heaviness, upon whom can we think but thee, who knowest our necessities afar off, puttest all our tears in thy bottle, seest every careful thought, hearest every sigh and melancholy groan we utter.

Strange!—that we should only begin to think of GOD with comfort, when with joy and comfort we can think of nothing else.

Man surely is a compound of riddles and contradictions: by the law of his nature he avoids pain, and yet *unless he suffers in the flesh, he will not cease from sin*, tho' it is sure to bring pain and misery upon his head for ever.

Whilst all went pleasurably on with the prodigal, no pang of remorse for the sufferings in which he had left him, or resolution of returning, to make up the account of his folly: his first hour of distress, seemed to be his first hour of wisdom:—*When he came to himself, he said, How many hired servants of my father have bread enough and to spare, whilst I perish!—*

Of all the terrors of nature, that of one day or another dying by hunger, is the greatest, and it is wisely wove into our frame to awaken man to industry, and call forth his talents; and tho' we seem to go on carelessly, sporting with it as we do with other terrors—yet, he that sees this enemy fairly, and in his most frightful shape, will need no long remonstrance, to make him turn out of the way to avoid him.

It was the case of the prodigal—he arose to go unto his father.—

—Alas! How shall he tell his story? Ye who have trod this round, tell me in what words he shall give in to his father, the sad *Items* of his extravagancy and folly;

—The feasts and banquets which he gave to whole cities in the east, the costs of Asiatic rarities, and of Asiatic cooks to dress them, the expenses of singing men and singing women, the flute, the harp, the sack-but, and of all kinds of music the dress of the Persian courts, how magnificent! their slaves, how numerous! their chariots, their horses, their palaces, their furniture, what immense sums they had devoured! what expectations from strangers of condition! what exactions!

How shall the youth make his father comprehend, that he was cheated at Damascus by one of the best men in the world; that he had lent a part of his substance to a friend at Nineveh, who had fled off with it to the Ganges; that a whore of Babylon swallowed his best pearl, and anointed the whole city with his balm of Gilead: that he had been sold by a man of honour for twenty shekels of silver, to a worker in graven images; that the images he had purchased had profited him nothing; that they could not be transported across the wilderness, and had been burnt with fire at Shusan; that the apes (*Vide Chronicles ix. 21.*) and peacocks, which he had sent for from Tharsis, lay dead upon his hands; and that the mummies had not been dead long enough which had been brought him out of Egypt: that all had gone wrong since the day he forsook his father's house.

—Leave the story—it will be told more concisely.—*When he was yet afar off, his father saw him,*—Compassion told it in three words—*he fell upon his neck and kissed him.*

Great is the power of eloquence: but never is it so great as when it pleads along with nature, and the culprit is a child strayed from his duty, and returned to it again with tears: Casuists may settle the point as they will: But what could a parent see more in the account, than the natural one, of an ingenuous heart too open for the world, smitten with strong sensations of pleasures, and suffered to sally forth unarm'd in the midst of enemies stronger than himself?

Generosity sorrows as much for the overmatched, as pity herself does.

The idea of a son so ruined, would double the father's caresses: every effusion of his tenderness would add bitterness to his son's remorse.—'Gracious heaven! what a father have I rendered miserable!'

And he said, I have sinned against heaven, and in thy sight, and am no more worthy to be called thy son.

But the father said, Bring forth the best robe.

O ye affections! How fondly do you play at cross-purposes with each other?— Tis the natural dialogue of true transport: joy is not methodical, and where an offender, beloved, over-charges itself in the offense,—words are too cold; and a concili-ated heart replies by tokens of esteem.

And he said unto his servants, Bring forth the best robe and put it on him; and put a ring on his hand, and shoes on his feet, and bring hither the fatted calf, and let us eat and drink and be merry.

When the affections so kindly break loose, Joy is another name for Religion.

We look up as we taste it: the cold Stoic without, when he hears the dancing and the music, may ask sullenly, (with the elder brother) What it means? and refuse to enter: but the hu-mane and compassionate all fly impetuously to the banquet, given *for a son who was dead and is alive again,—who was lost and is found.* Gentle spirits, light up the pavilion with a sacred fire; and parental love, and filial piety lead in the mask with riot and wild festivity! Was it not for this that GOD gave man music to strike upon the kindly passions; that nature taught the feet to dance to its movements, and as chief governess of the feast poured forth wine into the goblet, to crown it with gladness?

The intention of this parable is so clear from the occasion of it, that it will not be necessary to perplex it with any tedious explanation: it was designed by way of indirect remonstrance to the Scribes and Pharisees, who animadverted upon our SAVIOUR's conduct, for entering so freely into conferences with sinners, in order to reclaim them. To that end, he proposes the parable of the shepherd, who left his ninety and nine sheep that were safe in the fold, to go and seek for one sheep that was gone astray, telling them in other places, that they who were whole wanted not a physician,—but they that were sick: and here, to carry on the same lesson, and to prove how acceptable such a recovery was to GOD, he relates this account of the prodigal son and his welcome reception.

I know not whether it would be a subject of much edification to convince you here, that our SAVIOUR, by the prodigal son, particularly pointed at those who were *sinners of the Gentiles*, and were recovered by divine Grace to repentance;—and by the elder brother, he intended as manifestly the more froward of the Jews, who envied their conversion; and thought it a kind of wrong to their primogeniture, in being made fellow-heirs with them of the promises of GOD.

These uses have been so ably set forth, in so many good sermons upon the prodigal son, that I shall turn aside from them at present, and content myself with some reflections upon that fatal passion which led him, and so many thousands after the example, *to gather all he had together, and take his journey into a far country*.

The love of variety, or curiosity of seeing new things, which is the same, or at least a sister passion to it, seems wove into the frame of every son and daughter of Adam; we usually speak of it as one of nature's levities, tho' planted within us for the solid purposes of carrying forwards the mind to fresh inquiry and knowledge: strip us of it, the mind (I fear) would doze for ever over the present page: and we should all of us rest at ease with such objects as presented themselves in the parish or province where we first drew our breath.

It is to this spur which is ever on our sides, that we owe the impatience of this desire for travelling: the passion is no way bad but as others are, in its mismanagement or excess; order it rightly, the advantages are worth the pursuit; the chief of which are—to learn the languages, the laws and customs, and understand the government and interest of other nations, to acquire an urbanity and confidence of behaviour, and fit the mind more easily for conversation and discourse; to take us out of the company of our aunts and grandmothers, and from the track of nursery mistakes; and by shewing us new objects, or old ones in new lights; to reform our judgment—by tasting perpetually the varieties of nature; to know what *is good*—by observing the address and arts of men, to conceive what is *sincere*—and by seeing the difference of so many various humours and manners —to look into ourselves and form our own.

This is some part of the cargo we might return with; but the impulse of seeing new sights, augmented with that of getting clear from all lessons both of wisdom and reproof at home— carries our youth too early out, to turn this venture to much account; on the contrary, if the scene painted of the prodigal in his travels, looks more like a copy than an original,—will it not be well if such an adventurer, with so unpromising a setting out, —without *carte*,—without compass,—be not cast away for ever,— and may he not be said to escape well—if he returns to his country, only as naked, as he first left it?

But you will send an able pilot with your son—a scholar.—

If wisdom can speak in no other language but Greek or Latin, —you do well—or if mathematics will make a man a gentleman, —or natural philosophy but teach him to make a bow,—he may be of some service in introducing your son into good societies, and supporting him in them when he has done— but the upshot will be generally this, that in the most pressing occasions of address,—if he is a mere man of reading, the unhappy youth will have the tutor to carry—and not the tutor to carry him.

But you will avoid this extreme; he shall be escorted by one who knows the world, not merely from books—but from his own experience:—a man who has been employed on such services, and thrice made the *tour of Europe, with success.*

—that is, without breaking his own, or his pupil's neck;—for if he is such as my eyes have seen! some broken *Swiss valet de chambre,*—some general undertaker, who will perform the journey in so many months 'IF GOD PERMIT,'—much knowledge will not accrue;—some profit at least, he will learn the amount to a halfpenny, of every stage from Calais to Rome; he will be carried to the best inns, instructed where there is the best wine, and sup a livre cheaper, than if the youth had been left to make the tour and the bargain himself. Look at our governor! I beseech you:—see, he is an inch taller as he relates the advantages.—

—And here endeth his pride, his knowledge and his use.

But when your son gets abroad, he will be taken out of his hand, by his society with men of rank and letters, with whom he will pass the greatest part of his time.

Let me observe in the first place, that company which is really good, is very rare—and very shy: but you have surmounted this difficulty; and procured him the best letters of recommen-

85

dation to the most eminent and respectable in every capital.

And I answer, that he will obtain all by them, which courtesy strictly stands obliged to pay on such occasions,—but no more.

There is nothing in which we are so much deceived, as in the advantages proposed from our connections and discourse with the literati, &c. in foreign parts; especially if the experiment is made before we are matured by years or study.

Conversation is a traffic; and if you enter into it, without some stock of knowledge, to balance the account perpetually betwixt you, the trade drops at once: and this is the reason,— however it may be boasted to the contrary, why travellers have so little (especially good) conversation with natives, owing to their suspicion, or perhaps conviction, that there is nothing to be extracted from the conversation of young itinerants, worth the trouble of their bad language or the interruption of their visits.

The pain on these occasions is usually reciprocal; the consequence of which is, that the disappointed youth seeks an easier society; and as bad company is always ready, and ever lying in wait, the career is soon finished; and the poor prodigal returns the same object of pity, with the prodigal in the gospel.

'A LARGE, black, scowling figure, a ponderous body with a lowering visage, embrowned by the horrors of a sable periwig. His voice was growling and morose, and his sentences desultory, tart, and snappish.'[1] Samuel Ogden left a mark on the world. Another contemporary could not forget 'a real or apparent rusticity attending his address, which disgusted those who were strangers to his character.'[2] All agree that it was his *voice* which commanded attention—Ogden spoke in 'a most solemn, drawling, whining tone; he seemed to think he was always in the pulpit.'[3]

Ogden was George III's favourite preacher. Boswell admired him too—extolling his 'subtilty of reasoning' and consequent merits so enthusiastically during the tour of the Hebrides with Johnson, that if you look closely at Rowlandson's cartoons you will notice in several of them a book of Ogden's sermons in Boswell's hand or pocket. Johnson, at last prevailed upon to consider the rival hero, read aloud the sixth sermon from *Ten Sermons on the Efficacy of Prayer and Intercession* (1770), and conceding that it contained 'elegant language and remarkable acuteness' noted cogently that its author 'fought infidels with their own weapons'.

A dyer's son, Ogden was born in Manchester in 1716. He was educated at Manchester Free School and at Cambridge, ordained deacon in 1740, priested a year later. For nine years from 1744 he had a school at Halifax, serving at the same time as a local curate. In 1753 he returned to Cambridge. His pugnacious preaching soon drew crowds, mostly of undergraduates, to the round church of the Holy Sepulchre. It was noticed that he would have advanced further in the world had he not been 'singularly uncouth' in his manner. His uncouthness manifested itself most offensively in a habit of speaking his mind freely upon all occasions. We may be grateful that he had a habit of writing it with equal freedom. As well as his sermons, some letters have survived. These are of a piece with the bluntness already indicated. Thus we catch him writing to a fellow clergyman concerning an aspirant curate: 'I have promised him no civilities from you, on purpose, not that you may lessen them, but that he may think himself the more obliged.'

Ogden was a typical churchman of his day, robust and downright, famous apart from his sermons for the observation that the goose was a silly bird—too much for one, yet not enough for two. Proficient in languages, he produced verses in Latin, English and Arabic. In 1764 he was appointed Woodwardian Professor of Geology at Cambridge, retaining this post until his death in 1778. He went on preaching until his sixty-first year, when he was 'seized with a paralytic fit as he was stepping into his chariot'. He died of a second fit, a year later, and lies buried in the round church.

NOTES

1. From the account of Ogden's life which is prefixed to the fourth edition of his *Sermons* (1805).
2. ibid.
3. ibid.

BIBLIOGRAPHY

Two Sermons Preached before the University of Cambridge, 1758.
Ten Sermons on the Efficacy of Prayer and Intercession, 1770.
Twenty-three Sermons on the Ten Commandments, 1776.
Fourteen Sermons on the Articles of the Christian Faith, 1777.
Sermons, on the Efficacy of Prayer and Intercession: on the Articles of the Christian Faith: on the Ten Commandments: and on the Lord's Supper. 'To which is prefixed an account of the author's life, together with a vindication of his writings against some late objections.' 2 vols, 1780. 4th ed. in one volume, 1805.

ON THE RESURRECTION OF CHRIST

Acts 2:31.

His soul was not left in hell, neither his flesh did see corruption.

THIS IS the fifth sermon in Ogden's series instructing his congregation in the articles of the Christian faith. As it was first published in 1777, we can presume that it was preached in the church of the Holy Sepulchre earlier in the seventies. In taking up his text from the Acts of the Apostles, Ogden first overwhelms us with a shocking image of the crucifixion, then cries out as Christ in the first person singular (a favourite device), then calms down and examines the evidence for the first resurrection. 'The witnesses of this important event are competent, clear, and full.' That Christ rose again on the third day after his death and burial is a fundamental tenet of the Christian faith—indeed, the resurrection caused the faith, not the faith the resurrection, for if the apostles had not believed that they had seen the risen Christ then they would have performed no acts, since on his arrest 'all forsook him and fled' (Mark 14: 50).

Playing along with the scepticism of his age, Ogden casts a section of his sermon in the form of a rough Socratic dialogue, whereby he can use a second voice to impute an impure motive for the apostles' witness. 'Perhaps *Ambition* . . .' Yes, he says, 'you have detected their latent passion: they were indeed ambitious'—the sentence is sprung with irony—'they were indeed ambitious; aspiring to the great, but yet unenvied honour, of suffering in the cause of God.' Irony thickens into sarcasm as he goes further with the theme: 'Or it was *pleasure* perhaps those foolish persons had in view, and the plan of Christianity was projected as a scheme of sensual enjoyment.'

From the moment when he lets fall the word 'sceptic' Ogden has it in mind to confute Hume's essay on miracles. Note the remarks concerning the resurrection of the body in the third paragraph from the end, where Ogden is also reminding us of the difference between Christian teaching and the popular notion of the soul's immortality. Graeco-Roman and modern pagans prefer to think about resurrection only in a metaphorical sense. Yet here, as in sermon xii of the same series, *On the Resurrection of the Body*, Ogden's orthodoxy represents man as matter and spirit knit in a unique relationship, and reminds us that at the end of time it is promised that 'the exquisite knot, so rudely broken, shall be tied again, never to be dissolved more'—which is to say that our spirits will once again be knit to matter, although in what way we have not to enquire, and it might be as well to recall that the risen Christ was not at once recognized by his friends, which would perhaps suggest an *altered* relationship between spirit and matter.

We are wholly thine, both body and soul; in the hands of thy mercy, Father, in every stage of our existence: while we dwell first in the house of clay; next when we shall enter, as we shall quickly, unclothed into the world of spirits; and lastly when the two parts of us, after a long, perhaps, and unknown state of separation, shall be finally reunited never to be divided more.   (*Sermons*, pages 202-3.)

As to the resurrection of Christ, this mystery, seen by many, implies his dominion over the living and the dead, and the judgement to come, when he will name those who are to live eternally through him with God in the unity of the Holy Spirit.

WHEN THE Saviour of the world had now been suspended, with his arms stretched out, and his hands and feet nailed to the ignominious tree, from the third to the ninth hour; he perceived at length the approach of that welcome messenger, Death; and having *received the vinegar, He said, It is finished: and he bowed his head, and gave up the ghost.* (John xix. 30.)

It is finished. The important work, for which my Father sent me, and I came willingly into the world, is at last accomplished. I have done, and have now suffered, the whole will of God. The bitter *cup which might not pass away from me*, (Matth. xxvi. 42.) is emptied to the dregs. It remains that I repose a moment after this painful conflict. I will appear on the third day with the palm of victory, and again in the pomp of triumph at the day of judgment.

The Redeemer had no further sufferings, that we know of, to endure after his death. It is writted that *his soul was not left in hell, neither his flesh did see corruption.* But nothing is more common in Scripture than a repetition of the same sentiment in different words. The word Soul often denotes the *Person*, without regard to the distinction between Soul and Body, and that which is here rendered *hell*, may mean the *grave*, or the state and place of the dead, without implying either reward or torment.

The human Soul of our Lord was by death separated from the Body; and remained, till his resurrection, in the place or state of unclothed Spirits.

But its abode there was not long. The departed Soul, and the crucified Body of the Redeemer were soon reunited; and, according to his own express promise, on the third day he rose again from the dead. The witnesses of this important event are competent, clear, and full.

They who of all men had the best knowledge of the person of Christ, did themselves *see*, and *hear*, and *handle* him, after his resurrection. *Of these men which have companied with us all the time that the Lord Jesus went in and out among us, beginning from the baptism of John, unto that same day that he was taken up from us, must one be ordained to be a witness with us of the resurrection.* (Acts i. 21, 22.) They had been his attendants for some years before his passion; and conversed with him forty days after it. They do not amuse us with imaginations or conjecture: it is not a matter of tradition or probability which they deliver. But, *That which we have seen with our*

91

eyes, and our hands have handled of the word of life, that which we have seen and heard declare we unto you. (1 John i. 1, 3.) The Apostles had the repeated evidence of every sense, for the truth of the fact which they published to the world: and if they assure us that their *Lord is risen indeed*; it is because *he shewed himself alive after his passion, by many* infallible *proofs.* (Luke xxiv. 34; Acts i. 3.)

The witnesses of our Lord's resurrection were also *numerous. He was seen of Cephas, then of the twelve: after that, he was seen of five hundred brethren at once*: (1 Cor. xv. 5, 6.) what an air of truth in the words that follow! *Of whom the greater part remain unto this present.* It is obstinacy then, or vice, or folly, or any thing but reason that supports us, if we refuse to yield our assent, when *we are compassed about with so great a cloud of witnesses.* (Hebr. xi. 1.)

Nor are we yet possessed of the entire amount of their testimony, unless we reflect that they were most undoubtedly *uncorrupt.* To what end, for what purpose should they attempt to impose upon mankind? What interests or views of their own were these poor men pursuing? At what scope could they possibly aim? Or by what human principle be influenced?

Perhaps *Ambition.* Yes; you have detected their latent passion: they were indeed ambitious; aspiring to the great, but yet unenvied honour, of suffering in the cause of God; the dignity of bearing contempt and insult, for the sake of religion, truth, and virtue. *When they had called the Apostles, and beaten them, they commanded that they should not speak in the name of Jesus: and they departed from the presence of the council, rejoicing that they were counted worthy to suffer shame for his name; Unto you it is given,* as a peculiar favour and honour, *Unto you it is given in the behalf of Christ, not only to believe on him, but also to suffer for his sake.* (Acts v. 40, 41; Phil. i. 29.)

Or it was *pleasure* perhaps those foolish persons had in view, and the plan of Christianity was projected as a scheme of sensual enjoyment. Foolish indeed! if this was the object of their pursuits. Their pleasures were as little desirable as their honours. The only pleasures they expected, or experienced, beside the satisfaction of a good conscience, and the hopes of another life, were the pleasures of being scourged and beaten, of being imprisoned, and tortured, and killed. *If in this life only we have hope in Christ, we are of all men most miserable.* (1 Cor. xv. 19.)

92

Not only miserable, but impious, and mad, to abandon their friends, and family, and country; for the pleasure of spreading a known falsehood, and the reward of dying, both in body and soul, for the support of it.

But what Sceptic was ever satisfied? What caviller confuted? The adversaries of our faith finding no further resources on the plain ground of common sense, make their last retreat into the thorns of subtilty.

The resurrection, it seems, was an event so strange, that no testimony whatever is enough to prove it: the story, we may be sure, is not true; whoever he be that tells it.

On what foundation pray, do you build an assurance so very absolute?

On the foundation of Experience.

As how?

I am to tell you, then, that we know nothing of the essence of *causality*; but found all our assent upon *similitude*.

I am not sure that I comprehend you.

You cannot be possessed of so fine an argument in its perfection, without having recourse to the original Inventor: it may suffice to let you know in brief, that we believe always what is most *likely*, and call that most likely, which most *resembles* what we have before met with.

But things often fall out that were not likely.

Yes; so often, that we find it, in general, likely that they should; and in each particular case reflect which of the two is less likely, that the thing should be as it is represented, or the reporter represent it falsely.

Have you ever found in the course of your experience that any thing was not true, which had been as well attested as the resurrection?

It was a miracle: experience therefore, universal experience declares against it.

That of the *five hundred brethren* who saw it, was, sure, on the other side. (1. Cor. xv. 6.)

You must appeal to present experience. Nature we find unchangeable.

Nature! When I dispute with you about Christianity, I suppose that you believe a God.

You suppose perhaps too fast.

Then I have no further dispute with you: I leave you to other hands. Christianity desires no greater honour than to be received

93

by every one that is not an Atheist.

Suppose there be a God: what then?

Why, then he made the world.

Well.

And a multitude of things must have been done at that time of the Creation, which are not comprehended within the present course of nature. Every animal, every vegetable, must have been brought into Being at first in some manner of which the world now affords no examples. Of this we have no experience, yet we allow it to be true; and we need no testimony, for we know it must have happened.

And if the Son of God were to assume our nature a second time, and be once more *crucified and buried*; according to the unalterable laws of the Universe, he must rise again from the grave, and *the pains of death be loosed* as before, *because it was not* POSSIBLE *that he should be holden of it*.

The opinion that this present life is the whole of man, that death puts an entire end to his Being, and there can be nothing for any one to hope or fear after it, is of all the most contrary to religion, and destructive of virtue. This great error is in a special manner confuted by our Lord's resurrection; and the doctrine of a future state established beyond the reach of controversy.

He had indeed taken care, during his life, to inculcate a truth of so much consequence, and confirm it both by his authority and by arguments. *Be not afraid of them that kill the body, and after that have no more that they can do. He is not a God of the dead, but of the living: for all live unto him.* (Luke xii. 4; Luke xx. 38.) But our Lord has now demonstrated this article of faith to the senses of mankind; and by raising himself to life he gave at the same time a proof and a specimen of the great doctrine he had before delivered. Do we disregard his testimony? are his arguments not convincing? yet what can we object to so plain a fact? shall we dispute also against experience?

We are taught further to expect the resurrection of the *body*. The light of reason has been able to induce many good men to look for another life after death. But they did not extend their hopes to the resurrection of the body. They only trusted that they should not perish wholly, but their souls might survive the dissolution of this earthly frame. We now see that the body also shall be partaker of the life to come. The hand of death, though it lays hold on us, can keep nothing which belongs to us. The exquisite knot, so rudely broken, shall be tied again, never to be dissolved more. *Behold my hands and my feet; that it is I myself: handle me, and see; for a spirit hath not flesh and bones, as ye see me have.* (Luke xxiv. 39.)

The *dominion* of our Lord is also connected with his resurrection; which was his entrance, as it were, upon his universal government. *All power is given unto me in heaven, and in earth. To this end Christ both died, and rose, and revived, that he might be Lord both of the dead and living.* (Matth. xxviii. 18; Rom. xiv. 9.)

Lastly, that most important article of faith, a *future judgment*, is confirmed by the resurrection of our Lord; who is the appointed judge, to whom this high office is committed in reward of his great humiliation; and whose own return to life, and exaltation to power and glory, is the greatest instance, and the surest pledge of the just judgement of God. *As the Father raiseth up the dead and quickeneth them; even so the Son quickeneth whom he will. For the Father judgeth no man; but hath committed all judgement unto the Son. The hour is coming when the dead shall hear the voice of the Son of God: and they that hear shall live. For as the Father hath life in himself, so hath he given to the Son to have life in himself; and hath given him authority to execute judgement also, because he is the Son of man.* (John v. 21, 22, 25, 26, 27.)

JAMES ARCHER, one-time pot-boy in a public house called The Ship, in Turnstile, Lincoln's Inn Fields, grew up to attend Douay College and to return to London in 1780 as a Roman priest. This was the year of the Gordon Riots, when a mob marched on Parliament with 'No Popery' banners, demanding the repeal of the Roman Catholic Relief Act of 1778. The military had to be called in to disperse them. Houses of known Roman Catholics were burned to the ground and 285 people lost their lives through this disturbance, instigated by Lord George Gordon, afterwards acquitted on a charge of high treason before dying insane in Newgate prison. Even in the quieter weeks in the second half of the eighteenth century, the hearing of Mass according to the Latin rite was difficult unless you had access to one of the chapels attached to foreign embassies in London. It will be understood, therefore, that Archer set about his missionary work with circumspection—he returned to his starting place, The Ship Tavern, and had his congregation assemble there unobtrusively. Pots of beer would be set out half-filled on the tables as an excuse for the assembly, if their devotions happened to be interrupted.

Archer, born in London in 1751, and now to spend all his life there until 1834, when he died at the age of eighty-two, is a shadowy figure. He lived as he celebrated Mass—quietly, secretly, behind locked doors. He sought no preferments, though his services were recognized by Pius VII in the conferring upon him of the degree of Doctor of Divinity in 1821. Of the man, we know only that he stood just over five feet in height and favoured a long brown coat which reached almost to the ground. Of his soul, we know four little paper-covered volumes of sermons. They are full of extraordinary things—some of them too extraordinary for the liking of his Vicar Apostolic, who took occasion in 1813 to print a pastoral letter condemning 'the mixture of erroneous and dangerous morality' in them, specifically those preached on *Humility*, on *The Passions* and on *The Means of Subduing the Passions*. The Vicar Apostolic's anger was most directly derived from Archer having remarked that 'in certain moments of peculiar interest or exultation' and when 'men meet together to exhilarate their humanity' some deviation from the virtue of temperance might be permissible.

Archer must be typical of the many pious and decent Roman

96

Catholic priests who ministered in these islands during the period between 1570, when Pius V excommunicated Elizabeth I, and the Restoration of the Roman Catholic hierarchy in 1850. In his preaching, he is better than most. 'To almost every Protestant library, and to many a Protestant toilet, Mr. Archer's sermons have found their way,' a contemporary noted. He said himself that he had 'no natural relish' for controversy, while being desirous, at the same time, to unfold to the world 'coolly and ingenuously' the real tenets of Catholicism.

He haunts the imagination, this ordinary mysterious little man, with his confidence that 'those who sincerely desire and seek to know the Divine will, and are careful to regulate their actions, and the affections of their hearts, by the wisdom which they have already received, cannot fail to be approved of by Heaven.'[1] He is, I suppose, like an eighteenth-century version of Chesterton's Father Brown—the unobtrusive unobserved figure who observes everything, God's spy. I have been able to track down only one direct description of him, from Edward Price's *Sick Calls* (1850):

> Shortly after my conversion, in the year 1822, I saw the venerable little man for the first time out of the pulpit. He was busily employed in looking over some books in front of an old shop in Holborn. I stood behind him for more than five minutes gazing with reverence upon him whose eloquent sermons had been so mainly instrumental in promoting my conversion. His dress was certainly rather slovenly. A long brown great-coat, much the worse for wear, nearly down to his heels; an old broad-brimmed hat, and thick-soled shoes a world too wide for his feet, and which had evidently been soled a score of times. Though I took in these discrepancies at a glance, I thought not of them but of the mind and heart they concealed.

NOTE
1. From Archer's own preface to the first edition of his *Sermons*, dated 26 November 1785, Duke Street.

BIBLIOGRAPHY
Sermons on Various Moral and Religious Subjects for All the Sundays in the Year, and some of the Principal Festivals of the Year, 1787. 2nd ed., 4 vols, 1794.
A Letter to J. Milner, Vicar Apostolic of the Midland District (Being a Reply to a Letter in which he Accuses the Author of Immorality), 1810.

On the Effects Produced by a Worthy Participation of the Sacred Mysteries

Luke 14:16.

A certain man made a great supper, and invited many; and he sent his servants at supper-time, to say to them that were invited, that they should come, for now all things are ready.

'IT HAS been his aim to satisfy reason, whilst he pleased, charmed, and instructed her; to impress upon the mind just notions of the mysteries and truths of the Gospel; and to show that the ways of virtue are the ways of pleasantness, and her paths the paths of peace.' Butler's characterization of Archer's sermon-style, quoted here from his *Historical Memoirs of the English Catholics* (third edition, 'corrected, revised, and considerably augmented', four volumes, 1822), suits very well the sermon by which I have chosen to represent him in this book. We may suppose that it was preached to his flock in The Ship Tavern, sometime between 1780 when he returned from France and 1789, when it first appeared in print. The occasion was the second Sunday after Pentecost. The sermon is xxxiii in volume III of the four-volume edition of 1794, in which, as Archer notes, 'some errors are corrected, and some alterations are made, tending, as I hope, to some small improvement.'

The quotation with which the sermon opens is from St Thomas Aquinas, in one of the antiphons, *O Sacrum Convivium*, which he wrote for the Feast of Corpus Christi. Now the second Sunday after Pentecost falls three days after Corpus Christi, and the feast itself is referred to in Archer's third paragraph, so it seems reasonable to assume that, his congregation having been unable to attend Mass on the Thursday, Archer is now taking the opportunity of speaking to them on the subject, explaining indeed why 'the Church at this time, by the institution of a solemn festival in honour of the divine banquet, awakens our feelings to this love, and calls our attention to these blessings'—that is, the love and blessings expressed in the Body and Blood of Christ.

Archer begins with Aquinas since the Corpus Christi offices are themselves believed to have been drawn up by that saint, and those offices may be taken as the expression of the Church's mind on the nature and effect of the sacrament of the altar. Archer is at once celebrating and instructing, even as the Mass re-presents sacramentally that which it commemorates intellectually. This act, he reminds us, is the eternal fulfilment of those 'types and figures' (the sacrifice offered by Melchisedec, manna, the Paschal Lamb) which look forward to it in the Old Testament, and it is at the same time the very present drama of our redemption in Christ's death and resurrection. 'He whom they announced to us, is come.' The Mass is thus 'the divine banquet' which brings Christ and the Christian face to face, with Christ's glory made bearable to our humanity by the veils of bread and wine.

Archer is at one with the Fathers of the Church in giving his attention to the *effects* produced by the sacred species rather than to any controversy on the subject of the Real Presence. He puts emphasis upon the Mass as the initial transfiguration of worldly matter by pointing up its character as a *banquet*. In this family meal of God's children, Christ makes here and now present for us that self-sacrifice of his own life by which we are saved. Archer is mostly concerned to inspire in his hearers a hunger for the divine. Why else should we be offered Christ's Body and Blood but as nourishment in preparation for our own life as eternal beings? The character of the Mass as sacred meal was uppermost in the minds of early Christians meeting to celebrate it in private, and easily grasped no doubt by that congregation behind locked doors in The Ship Tavern. Yet the word 'Eucharist' also means thanksgiving, and Archer does not neglect this aspect. In his second paragraph, he has demonstrated the continuity of the mystery—Christ took the Passover and filled it with himself. Through the passages that follow Archer's concern is 'to make you conceive a hunger and thirst, a longing after this life-giving food'—and his eloquence is such that who could withstand it who understood? Finally he enumerates two effects produced by what he calls 'a worthy participation' in the Mass: first, the support and nourishment of the soul to eternal life; second, the re-awakening of the mind to those wonders which Christ worked in our favour. We are not even to envy the disciples who conversed with him, or the woman who touched his garment, or the pilgrims who over the centuries have journeyed to the Holy Land in order to stand where Christ stood. 'Oh! Christians, it is not necessary you should pass the seas . . .' Christ is here, visible to the eye, tangible to the tongue, in The Ship Tavern, Turnstile.

'O SACRED banquet! in which Christ is received, the memory of his passion is renewed, the mind is replenished with grace, and a pledge is given us of future glory!' This pious ejaculation is frequently repeated by the Catholic Church in these days of spiritual joy. The banquet here spoken of, my brethren, is the most excellent, the most salutary, the most sweet and delicious of all banquets. It contains truth, life, and grace itself: it contains Jesus in person, the author of sanctity, the source of happiness. Well indeed is it called a *great supper*. The food here set before us is the bread of Angels: the invited to eat of it are the whole Christian world: the master of the feast is the eternal word of God, *the brightness of* the Father's *glory, and the figure of his substance.* (Heb. i.) He has commanded the gates of his temples, where this divine feast is served up, to be thrown open to all the world; and with tender solicitude he invites and presses all to come, to sit down at his table, and be filled with blessings.

Now types and figures have passed away; the shadows of future good things have disappeared before the light of the Sun of truth and justice, who hath shed his enlivening rays on the earth in these our happier days. You are not now to partake of the sacrifice offered by the High Priest Melchisedec; you are not to be supported by the manna which was rained down from the clouds, in the desert, before the people of God; no longer are we commanded to eat the Paschal Lamb, as the sign of our deliverance and redemption. These illustrious figures, these mysterious rites and ceremonies, were great and venerable, only because they pointed out the banquet to which we are called. He whom they announced to us, is come. *Take ye and eat*, says our divine Redeemer; *this is my body.* (Mat. xxvi.) Yes, my beloved friends, this is the true victim of redemption; this the body which was immolated for you on the cross; this the blood which flowed so plentifully for you on Mount Calvary, and now pleads your cause before the throne of God. *Take ye and eat*; be nourished to immortal life; for, *if any man eat of this bread, he shall live for ever.* (John vi.)

That we might not be unhappily insensible to the love which Jesus hath shown us in this mystery; that we might not deprive our souls of the blessings it contains; the Church at this time, by the institution of a solemn festival in honour of the divine banquet, awakens our feelings to this love, and calls our attention to these blessings. At all times, your Saviour sends his servants to invite men to his great supper; and he hath given it in charge to me also, to exhort and excite his people, and particularly you, my brethren, to whom I have an opportunity of addressing myself, to approach frequently to his holy table. Ah! my friends, would to God I may succeed in this! That I may at least endeavour to do it, it is my intention to lay before you this day some of the admirable and truly desirable effects which this sacrament will produce in your souls, if worthily and frequently received. In the first place, I mean to point it out to you as the grand support of a virtuous life, and the nourishment of the soul to immortality: secondly, as a continual remembrancer of all the virtues which Jesus, the divine model of perfection, exhibited in his mortal life for your example. To me it will give heart-felt pleasure, and it will indeed be a happiness for you, if I can treat this important subject in such a manner as to make you conceive a hunger and thirst, a longing after this life-giving food, and make the frequent participation of it the highest enjoyment of your lives.

I. We must observe that, besides the general graces annexed to all the sacraments, each of them in particular produces effects in the soul, which are peculiar to itself. Thus, by the waters of Baptism, we are regenerated, and made adopted children of God: in Confirmation we are enlisted under the banners of Christ, and invigorated by the Holy Ghost: at the tribunal of Penance we are cleansed from our iniquities, and purified by the blood of the Lamb. *There are diversities of graces*, says St. Paul, *but the same Spirit . . . And there are diversities of operations, but the same God, who worketh all in all.* (1 Cor. xii.) Now the peculiar effect of the blessed Eucharist, is to support and nourish the soul to eternal life. It was for this reason, that our Divine Saviour, who could communicate his graces to us by any method he should choose, was pleased to impart himself to us under the form of bread; giving us to understand, that, as the corporal food which we take maintains the health and vigour of the body, repairs the defects which are variously occasioned in the natural system, and supplies the springs of life and strength; in the same manner this bread of Angels invigorates the soul, repairs the defects caused by our concupiscence, and nourishes our spiritual life with constant supplies of Divine Grace, till we grow up to that measure of perfection, which is attainable only in a future state.

This distinctive and admirable property of the blessed Eucharist is painted out to us under a beautiful image in the Old Testament. We read in the first book of Kings, that the prophet Elias, flying from the fury of the impious Queen Jezebel, who had determined on his destruction, went a day's journey into the wilderness, and came and sat down under a juniper-tree: there, fatigued with his wearisome journey, dejected by the ill success of his ministry, and almost broken hearted by distress and anguish, without a friend to relieve him, or even commiserate his hard lot, *he desired that he might die; and said, it is now enough, O Lord, take my soul; for I am no better than my fathers.* While he sat in this pensive and melancholy state, *behold, now an Angel touched him, and said unto him, Arise and eat: and when he looked about, behold, there was a cake . . . and . . . water at his head . . . And the Angel of the Lord came again the second time, and touched him, and said, Arise and eat, for thou hast a great journey to go through. Then he arose, and did eat and drink, and walked in the strength of that food, forty days and forty nights, unto Horeb, the mountain of God;* where he was favoured with a vision of the Lord.

You have, my friends, in this history, an accurate and fine representation of your condition and mine in this mortal life. We also are travelling through a wilderness, through a vale of sorrows, in which we are strangers and pilgrims, pursuing our way towards the holy mountain where God dwells, towards our true country, the abode of peace and joy, where we shall be favoured and blessed with the vision of the Lord, with the clear sight and possession of our sovereign good. Our great care and solicitude must be to escape the violence and fury of the enemies who seek our ruin, and lie in wait for us in our passage through life. We have many such enemies, my beloved; the delusive maxims of worldly wisdom prepare many snares before us to entrap our unwary feet. The flesh, with its flattering allurements, invites us to the embraces of guilt and misery, decked out in all the various counterfeit forms of pleasure and happiness. The fiery darts of the princes of darkness are likewise pointed against us. Ah! too frequently, like the prophet in the wilderness, we are almost wearied out with the contest, are ready to succumb under the weight of our difficulties, and give up the cause of virtue: too often overpowered by the raging heat of concupiscence, we faint, we lie lifeless on the ground, an easy conquest to every temptation; or lulled by the fascinating charms of sloth and indolence, we sleep supinely in the very arms of our enemies.

But, oh! my friends, we may yet be comforted. Arise: Jesus hath mercifully provided for our support: he hath placed a table before us, and commands us, not by the ministry of an Angel, but with his own sacred mouth, to arise and eat; and promises, that, if we nourish our souls with the divine food he hath prepared for us, we shall be strengthened; we shall be enabled to pursue our journey, amidst surrounding dangers, with security, ease, and alacrity; and come at length to the term of our desires. Give an attentive ear to his own divine words: *I am the living bread which came down from Heaven. If any man eat of this bread he shall live for ever: and the bread that I will give, is my flesh for the life of the world . . . As the living father hath sent me, and I live by the Father, so he that eateth me, the same also shall live by me. This is the bread that came down from Heaven: —not as your fathers did eat manna, and are dead: he that eateth this bread shall live for ever.* (John vi.) Again, my brethren, in how tender and engaging a manner does he invite us to approach to him! *Come to me*, says he, *come to me, all you that labour and are heavy laden, and I will refresh you*; come, *and you shall find rest to your souls.* (Mat. xi.) Let not your infirmities and your weaknesses dishearten you, and deter you from coming to partake of this life-giving food. It is to the weak, it is to the infirm, that I address this invitation: *come, all you that labour, and are heavy laden.* Here you will be inflamed by that charity which makes every burthen light, that charity which sweetens every labour; this is the bread of consolation; the bread of power and strength.

Come then, you among my present hearers who labour under great temptations; you who find a source of corruption within your breasts, which presses you down to the earth with an almost irresistible force, and makes all your affections bend towards the enjoyment of sensual gratifications; approach frequently to this sacred table: the bread you here receive will counteract all the efforts of a vitiated self-love, and raise your immortal souls to higher pursuits, to the pursuits of those noble objects for which they were originally formed. Come, you that are deluded and blinded by the false maxims of the world, to the ruin of your innocence and your peace; come to Jesus in this mystery: here a ray of divine light will dart upon your mind, and dissipate every cloud of error and falsehood. Come, you that are puffed up by the pride of prosperity; whose hearts are enchanted by the gaudy trappings of vanity, or eagerly intent on procuring every refinement of luxury: here you may learn to set a due value on all that passes with time, and make the first and warmest wishes of your hearts be fixed on the attainment of more permanent and substantial blessings, the nobler ornaments of virtue and holiness, and the good things which the Lord hath prepared for his elect in the future life. You likewise, whom poverty deprives of many of the enjoyments of this life; you, to whom the world presents a darker aspect, come, and be no longer disheartened by the disadvantages of your lowly condition; come, and make Jesus your friend, be united to him. With him you have all things; you may taste a pleasure which the world, in its brightest days, could never impart to its most-favoured votaries: you may enjoy a sunshine of content, and a peace which surpasseth all understanding. *Come to me: come, all you that labour and are heavy laden, and I will refresh you.*

Holy David, whose prophetic spirit carried him forward into the regions of futurity, and placed before him a distinct view of all the blessings which our Redeemer would bring with him to the earth, thus describes, as in his own person, the fortunate condition of those who are united to Jesus in this mystery of love. *The Lord,* says he, *is my shepherd, and nothing shall be wanting to me:* (Ps. xxii.) he hath conducted me into green pastures abounding with flowers and fruits, and placed me on the banks of refreshing streams. Then, expressing his lively confidence in that divine goodness which he had already so often experienced, he declares, that even death, that formidable spectre which damps all the joys of men, brings with it no terror to him: *Though I should walk in the midst of the shadow of death, I will fear no evil, for thou art with me.* Oh! my friends, the hour will come, when your heart may rejoice in this confidence. In those trying moments which announce your approaching dissolution; when standing on the confines of two worlds, on the brink of an awful eternity, you shall turn pale, and shudder at the prospect before you; when the bitter remembrance of former crimes shall crowd on your mind and be a torture to your soul; oh! Jesus will visit you himself in person, and smooth your bed of sorrows; he will enter into your breast, calm your tumultuous soul, support you in that agonizing state; and then, you will cheerfully resign your soul into his hands, with secure and triumphant hope: then you will sing with the Royal Prophet, *Thy rod and thy staff, they have comforted me: thou hast prepared for me a table*, to give me power to struggle *against those who afflict me: thou hast anointed my head with oil; and my overflowing chalice*, how delicious, *how exquisite it is!* These are the admirable effects of this heavenly food; it supports us under the pressure of affliction, conducts us securely through the perils of life, arms us against the terrors of death, and is a sure pledge of our future and immortal felicity.

But, methinks I hear you say: 'Frequently I have partaken of this bread of Angels; yet I discover not, that into my soul, those blessings have flowed from it, which you describe. Indeed, in the moment when I receive my Saviour into my breast, I feel myself tenderly affected; divine love then seems to hold dominion in my heart: but those emotions are short and transitory, and the impressions then made are quickly effaced. When I return from it, I find that my desires are still earthly, my inclinations still grovelling among sensual satisfactions, my resolutions feeble and fluctuating, easily carried away by every wind of temptation.' Ah! Christian brother, how came it that you reaped so little fruit from it? To what cause must we attribute this failure? Is the fountain of grace dried up? Is the power of Jesus diminished? Or does he bear less love to you, than to the most favoured of his servants? Certainly not. The blood, which he so freely spilt for the salvation of every individual among mankind, is a clear, a convincing proof of it. No: the dispositions you brought with you must have been the sole cause of your misfortune. Did you prove yourselves? Were you sincere in your endeavours to purify your hearts from the defilements of sin, before you eat of this bread? Examine into this matter.—If not, no wonder you were not benefited by it. An unworthy Communion converts the bread of life into a deadly poison, which preys on the very vitals of the soul for eternity: the severest vengeance of Heaven is not too great to punish so execrable a crime.

But God forbid you should have been thus wretched and impious! I will not suppose it. But, after using every means to cleanse your soul from the infection of sin, still, you say, 'I taste not that sweetness, I do not experience those comforts.' My brethren, the favours of Heaven are always dispensed to us in proportion to the desire and fervour of soul with which we seek after them. If you had not a lively faith, a firm hope, and a longing after this divine food; if your appetite still craved after the dainties of Egypt; if you dealt ungenerously with your God; if you approached him with distaste and reluctance; if you were disposed to do no more for his service, than you thought you must do to secure your own interests—that is, to avoid only mortal sin, and deliberately indulge yourself in habits of venial offences: if that be the case, is it to be wondered at, that the Lord should impart his graces to you with a sparing hand, and punish your coldness and indifference towards him, by depriving you of the sweets of his presence? Indeed, this is not any way surprising, my brethren. Besides, if one Communion produced less abundant fruits, that might have been a preparation for another, which would have brought you a still more copious supply of the graces of Heaven. But, perhaps you only approach once a year to this table; and would not then present yourselves, did not the Church fulminate its censures against those who, at the solemnity of Easter, refuse to partake of this heavenly food. Or, if you communicate at stated times of the year, when it is the practice of those with whom you live or associate to approach to the Altar, perhaps you do it rather as a thing of custom, a matter of ceremony, a disagreeable business, a painful servitude from which you wish to be disengaged; and then return with new avidity to the accustomed round of vanity and folly which fills up your days; to those dangerous, and perhaps even criminal, pleasures, which you were grieved to abstain from, even for the moment.

Ah! Christian hearts, formed for goodness, and for an union with the God of love, deal honourably, liberally, and generously with your God; show him that grateful mind which you pretend to admire and esteem on every other occasion; and then you will taste how sweet he is. Enlarge the vessel of your heart, by discharging from it every profane affection, and he will not leave it empty. No: he will fill it, he will make it overflow with his graces and consolations. Then you will truly put on Jesus Christ: his precious blood, flowing through your veins, will give you his inclinations, his sentiments, his features; will form you to an entire resemblance with him: like princes descended from a royal race, there will appear in your countenances, and whole deportment, an air of majesty which speaks the nobleness of your origin: your words, your desires, your actions, all will be heavenly, and worthy the blood which you inherit; and you will be able to say with St. Paul, *I live now, not I, but Christ liveth in me*.

II. A second fruit of this adorable Sacrament is, that, by receiving it, we make a memorial of all the wonders which Jesus hath worked in our favour. By his presence upon our altars, he awakens in our minds the dear remembrance of those sacred actions, those consoling words, that instructive conversation of his mortal life, which is capable of making so strong and salutary an impression on a loving heart: *Do this*, said our Redeemer, when he instituted this mystery, *do this in remembrance of me*. So inconstant is the human heart, that absence frequently loosens the bands of the most intimate friendship. Our Lord foresaw, that when he should have ascended into Heaven, his disciples would insensibly forget his benefits and his instructions. Alas! Moses had been but forty days on the mountain, and the Israelites remembered no more the prodigies he had performed for their deliverance from the slavery of Egypt. 'What is become of him?' they cried out: 'Let us make Gods for ourselves.' That we might not be thus unhappily lost to every grateful recollection, forgetful of all which the memory of man should hold most dear; Jesus, before he ascended to the heavenly Sion, to the right hand of his eternal father, left us a pledge of his presence, that we may console ourselves in our banishment, till we are admitted to behold him face to face, and that we may never erase from our minds the image of his divine and adorable person.

You envy the fortunate condition of his Disciples, who, on earth, conversed familiarly with him: you could have wished to have been in the place of the woman that touched the hem of his garment, of the sinner that bedewed his feet with her tears, of the multitude who caught the words of grace which flowed from his lips. The Patriarchs and Prophets longed to see his day. Come then to our altars: there you shall see him; you shall touch him; you shall embrace him; you shall give him a kiss of peace; you may bedew his feet with your tears; you may carry him in your breast, and be incorporated with him.

In former ages, the piety of your forefathers carried them to Palestine, to visit the places consecrated by his presence, and adore his footsteps. Walking and conversing together over that hallowed ground: 'In this spot,' said they, 'he came into the world: here he expired on the cross for our redemption: sitting near this well he conversed with the Samaritan woman.' The view of the scenes in which he had spent his mortal life; of the mountains on which he delivered his heavenly doctrines, or retired to converse with his eternal Father in the silence of the night, caused a new joy to spring up in their minds. They shed tears flowing from a tenderness which religion inspired. Then a fresh ardour was enkindled in their souls. Their faith became more active: their hopes were heightened; they were all on fire with divine love. Oh! Christians, it is not necessary you should pass the seas, in order to be inspired with these devout and virtuous sentiments. Your salvation is near at hand. Look with the eye of faith. What do you behold upon our altars, when we offer up the tremendous sacrifice? Not only places consecrated by his presence; but himself, on whom the Angels delight to fix their enraptured sight.

Come then, and renew your remembrance of him. Let his presence on our altars awaken in your minds all those pious emotions which the circumstances of his life and death have ever excited in your hearts. Let the memory of that meekness and gentleness which he displayed in his conversation among men, calm all your anger and impatience, quell the risings of passion, and diffuse tranquillity through your souls. Let the memory of his labour and toil for your salvation, make you ashamed of your own indolence in prosecuting that important business in which all your interests are centered. Come, and remember his humility, and repress the swellings of pride; blush at your vanity, and put a stop to your ambitious projects. Let the remembrance of that zeal with which he cast out those who profaned the temple of God, teach you with that reverential awe you should come to adore him in his Sanctuary. Let the amiable simplicity of his manners convince you how truly ridiculous are the vain affectations of ours. Remembering the solitary hours which he spent in communing with his heavenly Father, let us learn to court retirement; to shun, as much as we can be allowed to do it, the bustle and tumult of life; to make ourselves a solitude in our own chambers, where we may pour forth our hearts before the God that made us and all things.

In a word, let the dear memory of all the virtues which he exhibited in his divine person, renewed and impressed deeply on our minds by his presence in this mystery, correct all our defects, and carry us on from one degree of perfection to another, till we become like unto him. Thus we shall indeed communicate in remembrance of him: and this remembrance will give us that purity and dignity of conduct, which is suited to our divine hopes. Undefiled by the pleasures of the world, and unshaken by its terror, we shall preserve one constant tenor of goodness; ever looking forward, and consoling ourselves with the expectation of that brighter day, which will shortly begin to dawn; when Jesus will throw off these mean appearances which now conceal his glories, and disclose himself to our souls in all his splendour and beauty; when the Sun of righteousness shall rise before us, and all that is imperfect shall be done away for ever.

Augustus William Hare was born in Rome in 1792 and died there in 1834. This Roman beginning and ending is the only exotic item in a quiet life.

Educated at Winchester, Hare was prevented by ill health and indifference from fulfilling indications of academic prowess, and when he went up to New College his interest lay chiefly in the establishing of one of the first Oxford debating clubs, the Attic Society. His aunt wanted him to take orders to qualify for the rich family living of Hurstmonceaux. Hare had other ideas about the propriety of this, and refused. His health compelled him once more to Italy, but in 1818 he came back to New College as a tutor. 'He was *very* eccentric,' his nephew recalled being told by friends of his uncle's from this time. 'If excited in conversation he would spring up in the midst of his talk, twirl himself rapidly round three times, and sit down again without pausing in what he was saying, as if some external action was necessary to let off the force of his excitement.'

In 1824 Hare published his first work, a terse defence of the Gospel narratives of the Resurrection, directed against rationalist apologists. He was ordained a year later in Winchester College Chapel. In 1827 he published *Guesses at Truth*, written with his brother Julius. This collection of prose bits, modelled upon the *Pensées* of Pascal, contains epigrams which still have a sting of sense in them—for example, 'The ancients dreaded death: the Christian can only fear dying.' It is in effect a book, rather like Auden's *A Certain World* (1971), for those who prefer to think in small sips. Published anonymously, it brought Hare no reputation.

In 1829 he was appointed to the living of Alton Barnes, and in the same year married. His parish was small—there were never more than a hundred and fifty people in it. Alton itself was described by his nephew as 'perhaps the most primitive village in Wiltshire.' It consisted of a few white-washed mud cottages, their roofs thatched with straw, clustered about a tiny towerless church. Hare set to work diligently. Inspired by the ignorance of his people, he hammered out a style to meet it. The result was a set of sermons which went straight to the hearts and minds of his hearers. 'Mr. Hare does *long* to save our souls,' one of them remarked. (This was in contrast to his brother Julius, of whom it was said, 'Mr. Hare, he be not a good winter parson'

—meaning that his sermons, usually over the heads of his congregation, kept people too long in church so that they could not get home before dark.)

Hare's religion overflowed in affection for his people, whom he also helped in a practical way, setting up with his wife a shop in which they sold clothing at two thirds of the cost price. He also established a second service on a Sunday—something never known before in Alton—and gave instruction in a barn for those approaching confirmation. A fellow clergyman remembered a habit which speaks volumes—whenever he heard good of anyone Hare would instinctively rub his hands together with pleasure. In 1831 his uncle died, and the family living of Hurstmonceaux was again offered to this least ambitious of priests—again to be refused.

Failing health was the only thing that could remove Hare from what his wife called 'the dear Alton'. All through 1833 his lungs got worse and in the autumn his doctors commanded a winter in Italy. Hare left the village in October, after giving a farewell supper for his people in the barn. 'After he had parted from them with prayer and a short exhortation,' wrote his nephew, 'he was sitting quietly in the drawing-room, when the singers, underneath his window, unexpectedly began the Evening Hymn. Quickly unfastening the shutter, his face working with emotion, he threw up the sash, exclaiming, "Dear people, how can I leave you!" and then sank back on a chair quite exhausted by the mental conflict, and then a terrible fit of coughing came on.'

On his deathbed Hare said, 'But for Christ I could not have borne to have had the great moral eye of God's justice fixed on me.' He died on 18 February 1834 and is buried at the foot of the pyramid of Caius Cestus in the English cemetery in Rome.

BIBLIOGRAPHY

Sermons to a Country Congregation, 2 vols, 1836.
The Alton Sermons, 1837.
Memorials of a Quiet Life, A. J. C. Hare, 1872.

HOLY BRANCHES; OR, WHY WAS THE TRINITY
REVEALED?
Romans 11:16.
If the root be holy, so are the branches.

THIS WAS preached on a Trinity Sunday during one of the
four years of Hare's ministry in Alton. Notice not only the
Saxon simplicity of language but the way in which Hare uses
analogies drawn from the life of the countryside in making his
meaning as plain as he can to his congregation. Hare's sermons
set out to *teach*, and to do this through the offices of the Church,
showing the relevance of fast days and feast days, explaining
the significance of the Christian calendar, drawing out some of
the meaning of doctrine—as here—by means of such words and
images as can immediately be understood by persons unschooled
in theology. In another sermon, *Who are Invited? or Christ's
Disciples*, he says:

> A disciple means a learner and a follower. We read in St.
> Matthew of the disciples of John; they were persons who went
> to be taught by John. We read in St. Mark of the disciples of
> the Pharisees: they were persons who went to be taught by
> the Pharisees. In the same way a disciple of Jesus Christ is a
> person that seeks to be taught by Jesus Christ. Every one
> then who wishes to learn from Christ, every one who is trying
> to follow Christ, every such person is his disciple. He is a pupil
> of Christ's; he is a scholar of Christ's; he is, in plain English,
> going to school to Christ . . . .

Hare writes nearly always as well as this, taking his hearers, in
plain English, to school to Christ. The posthumous volumes first
published in 1836 remind us of Christian activity going on around
Oxford amongst people who heard little of the Movement and
its tracts. These sermons contain no trace of haste or slovenliness,
despite the fact that they were written for one of the smallest
parishes in England. Their stance is not that of a scholar lowering himself to the level of the meanest capacity, but of one who
has found common ground of thought and feeling, on which he
and his congregation can take their stand, and talk. Doubtless
Hare was not alone in this achievement. We may well wish that the
sermons of the poet William Barnes, preached in Dorset some thirty years later, did not exist now only in the form of phonetic notes

112

held in ten cardboard boxes in the Dorchester Public Library.

Holy Branches deals with difficult matter in simple terms. Talk of trees and roots moves in the second paragraph into talk of 'the doctrine which contains all the others, the doctrine of the ever-blessed Trinity'. Hare asserts that this docrine is a mystery which would never have occurred to the human mind without revelation. But if the thought of a Trinity of persons existing in the one divine nature is *above* reason, Hare insists that it is not *contrary* to it. We could not have deduced the Trinity from observation of the created universe, but given the Christian revelation that God exists in Three Persons and One Substance then we can find, as Hare now proceeds to do, 'comparisons' which comfort reason with thoughts that if this is the nature of God then it is 'not altogether unlike what we find in the natural world'. He directs the attention of his congregation to the sun (which is also light and heat, 'three separate and distinguishable things: yet distinct as they are, what can be more united?') and to water, the ways of which, in his ninth paragraph, are likened to the triune God. Now even if we know that Aquinas was of the opinion that nothing in the sensory world affords any real analogy for an understanding of the Trinity we might do well to allow that those Alton parishioners remembered what Mr Hare had said when they emerged from their little church into rain or sunlight. In fact, what Hare goes on to say is shrewd as well as sound—he reminds his hearers that there might have been a Trinity, and the Son of God might have died to save us, all without our knowing of the matter. 'Even this would doubtless have been a great mercy, and a great blessing.' But the deliberate *revelation* of these things is the Christian point—a greater mercy and a greater blessing. 'The sum of the whole is this: though the nature of God must needs be mysterious to our understandings, there is no mystery in the benefits we receive from him nor any darkness in the duty we owe him.'

The reference to the recitation of the Athanasian creed—the Quicunque Vult—strengthens the probability that this sermon was preached on a Trinity Sunday, that profession of faith being commonly recited in the Church of England on thirteen holy days, of which Trinity Sunday is one. Newman writes of this creed, in the *Grammar of Assent*:

> It is not a mere collection of notions, however momentous. It is a psalm or hymn of praise, of confession, and of profound,

self-prostrating homage, parallel to the canticles of the elect in the Apocalypse . . . . For myself, I have ever felt it as the most simple and sublime, the most devotional formulary to which Christianity has given birth, more so even than the *Veni Creator* and the *Te Deum*.

THE PURPOSE of our Saviour's coming was to redeem and deliver us from all iniquity, and to purify us as a peculiar people, zealous of good works. This is the great end of his teaching; and this end all the doctrines of his religion further. For instance, the doctrine of the everlasting pains of hell,—why has that been made known to us, except to frighten us from sin? Why again has the doctrine of the unspeakable joys of heaven been made known to us, except to comfort and encourage us in well-doing? In like manner all the other doctrines of our faith are designed either to warn us against going astray, or to quicken our steps along the right path, or at least in some way or other to keep us firm and steadfast in our duty. So that our religion may not unfitly be compared to a great tree; of which the doctrines are the roots, and uprightness is the trunk, and godly deeds and all the ministries of love are the outspreading branches, and piety is the heavenward pointing head. As a tree grows up from its roots, and they nourish and support it; so do the duties of religion grow out of its doctrines, and rest on its doctrines, and draw their life from them. If the trunk of a tree be separated from the roots, it falls: nor will a man's morality be able to stand, unless it be rooted and anchored deep in the great truths of religion. Any hour of trial, a gust of passion, a sharp blast of temptation from an exposed quarter, would lay such unsupported virtue low. It would fall, like the house built on the sand; and great and sad would its fall be. But as a tree is nothing without its roots, so the roots on the other hand are nothing without the tree. It is for the sake of supporting the branching, wide-spreading tree, that there are any roots at all. No one ever saw a root growing by itself and for itself. A root without a tree would be the same sort of thing among God's works, as a foundation without a house among man's works. Nor is this less true of the spiritual roots of faith. God, who does nothing in vain, has not revealed any doctrine to us for the mere sake of feeding our curiosity, or of making us stare and wonder. Doctrines from which nothing springs would be as much out of place in the book of God's word, as roots from which nothing grows would be in the book of nature. Such roots are not living, but dead. Whenever therefore you come to any doctrine in the Bible, bear in mind that the Scriptures were not written to make us wise merely, in that which the world deems wisdom,—but wise unto salvation. Instead of stumbling over the doctrine, as a blind or heedless man might stumble over a root that lay in his path, and stood a little way out of the ground,—instead, I say, of stumbling over it, and being offended at it, say to yourselves, 'Here is another root of godly living, a root which, if I can only plant it in my heart, is sure to bring forth a goodly tree of some christian grace or other.'

Thus it is with all the great truths, with all the great doctrines of our faith: nor is it otherwise with the greatest and most mysterious of all its doctrines, with the doctrine which embraces all the others, the doctrine of the ever-blessed Trinity. But what is the doctrine of the ever-blessed Trinity? Some of you may perhaps be glad to hear a short and simple explanation of it. And much does it behove you to understand what the Scriptures have revealed to us on this matter: seeing that it is the very doctrine into which you were all baptized, when you were baptized in the name of the Father, and of the Son, and of the Holy Ghost. On this great and wonderful mystery it becomes the ministers of Christ to speak, humbly indeed, but plainly and boldly, so far as Scripture bears them out,—no further. Where the Bible stops, we must stop too. Were you walking over a mountainous country, beset with steep and dangerous precipices, so long as the sun lit up your path, and showed you a safe footing, you would go on cheerfully and fearlessly. Still safer and more confident would you feel, if an angel were leading you by the hand. But if the sun went down, if a thick mist arose, if the angel let go your hand, if you found yourself in this dangerous country without light and without a guide, would you go on then? Surely the true wisdom would be to stop the moment the light faded away, lest, by walking rashly on, you might stumble or slip into the jaws of death. Thus, when we are talking of the Trinity, so long as we keep within the bounds of Scripture, we may walk safely: for the light of God is upon us, and his angel is leading us by the hand. But when the Bible stops, we must stop also. Every step beyond the written word is dangerous, and rash and foolish.

Still, though it would be most unwise to follow the dancing lights of our own fancies, where the risk of a false step is so great, yet, as long as the light of the Bible is on our path, we may, we ought, to go on, under the assurance that God has revealed nothing in his word, except what it behoves us to know. We may not be able to reach the very top: but let us mount as high as we can, keeping in mind that we are not walking by our own light, but by God's light, and therefore walking humbly, as

116

befits those who can do nothing of themselves. For as an excellent writer has said, 'What would it profit us to speak never so wisely of the Trinity, if by speaking proudly we offended the Trinity?' In this humble spirit would I speak, in this spirit would I have you listen to what I shall say, concerning the Holy Trinity.

'The Catholic faith (as you have just heard in the Athanasian Creed) is this: that we worship one God in Trinity, and Trinity in Unity.' This is the Catholic faith; that is to say, the universal faith, the faith held by every faithful part and member of Christ's Church. By whatever name the various branches of that Church may be called,—Roman Catholics, Greeks, Lutherans, we of the Church of England, our brethren of the Church of Scotland,—however they may disagree and differ on other points,—and alas! these differences are so many and so violent, that Christ's coat, which was woven without seam from top to bottom, setting forth the perfect union which ought to subsist among true believers, has been shamefully rent and almost torn to tatters amongst them,—still, these many violent differences notwithstanding, the several churches of Christendom all agree in this, that they worship one God in Trinity, and Trinity in Unity. Therefore this faith is called catholic, or universal; because it is held by all the churches. For this is the meaning of the word catholic: the Catholic faith is that which is held by all true believers: the Catholic Church is that which embraces and is made up of all true believers; and everybody is a member of that Church, who holds all the great doctrines of the christian faith. This is the Holy Catholic Church which we profess in the Creed to believe in. This is the Catholic Church for which we pray in the prayer for all sorts and conditions of men, and in the Litany, where we call it the holy Church universal.

Now, the great doctrine of that Church, the doctrine which is held by every branch of that Church,—the doctrine by which whoever holds it becomes a member of that Church, while whoever rejects it ceases to belong to that Church, and becomes a heretic,—is the doctrine of the Trinity: that is to say, the doctrine that in the Godhead there are three Persons, the Father, the Son, and the Holy Ghost; and the Father is God, the Son is God, and the Holy Ghost is God: and that yet there are not three Gods, but one God. To the carnal understanding this doctrine sounds strange and hard to believe: it is strange and hard to believe, that three should be one, and that one should be three. Why then does the whole body of the Catholic Church

117

hold this doctrine? Because it is plainly set down in Scripture. Because the Scripture tells us on the one hand that God is one, and on the other hand that the Father is God, that our blessed Lord Jesus Christ, the Word that was with God from the beginning, is God, and that the Holy Ghost is God. Because moreover we are convinced that it is not in man, by seeking, to find out God, and that we cannot know anything of God, except what God himself is graciously pleased to make known to us.

This then is the Catholic faith, that we acknowledge the Father, the Son, and the Holy Ghost, to be each of them God, and yet that they are not three Gods, but one God. How these three Persons are so united as to make up only one God, we are nowhere told in Scripture: therefore on this, as with regard to so many lesser matters, we must be content to remain ignorant. Does this seem a great hardship to the pride of the would-be wise? Let them come forward then, and prove their right to be admitted into the innermost mysteries of heaven, by shewing that they have fully mastered all the lesser mysteries of earth. Let them tell me why the needle of the compass always turns toward the north. Perhaps they will say, because it is its nature to do so. But that is no answer. My question is, why does the needle so turn? What secret and invisible hand twists it round, and teaches it to point always the same way? Or, if this be too puzzling a question, perhaps these wise men, who think it so great a hardship that they are not permitted to understand God, may tell us a little about themselves. They can perhaps teach us how it comes to pass that the blood keeps on flowing unceasingly through our veins without our being aware of it, except when we are in a high fever. We grow tired with labour, or with exercise; we tire even with doing nothing; we need sleep at certain seasons to refresh us for the taskwork of the morrow: but the blood never wearies. On it flows, from the hour of our birth, day and night, summer and winter; year after year it keeps on its silent round, never felt when we are in health, yet never stopping, and never sleeping, until it stops once for all, and sleeps the sleep of death. How, I ask, can these things be? What, again no answer! Tell me then at least, how it is that I dream; or if you cannot,—and no one can,—let those who know nothing about the how and the why in so many of the commonest earthly matters, not be so very much surprised that they cannot understand the essence of that invisible, that eternal, that infinite Spirit, whom we call God.

But though the Scripture has only told us that these things are, without teaching us how they are, yet for the sake of shewing that the mystery of the Trinity is not so utterly at variance with what we find in earthly things, as unbelievers would fain persuade us,—for the sake of proving how possible it is, even according to our limited notions, for that which is three in one sense, to be one in another sense,—learned and pious men have busied themselves in seeking out likenesses for the Trinity among the things of this world. It is most true indeed, and should be borne in mind, that these likenesses must be very imperfect, and that they cannot give us anything approaching to a full and just idea of the glorious Trinity. For so the prophet teaches us when he exclaims, 'To whom will ye liken God? or what likeness will ye compare to him? Have ye not known? have ye not heard? It is he that sitteth upon the circle of the earth, and the inhabitants thereof are like grasshoppers: that stretcheth out the heavens as a curtain, and spreadeth them out as a tent to dwell in.' (Isaiah xl. 18, 22.) To whom then, or to what created thing can we liken God, and not fall immeasurably below the glory of his infinite perfections? Still, although no likeness to which we can liken God, can be of any avail toward shewing him to us as he is, yet since so many find a stumbling-block in the mystery of the Trinity, and so many cast it as a stumbling-block in their brother's path, there can be no harm, and there may be some good, in comparisons, which shew that it is not altogether unlike what we find in the natural world. Moreover such comparisons may help you in attaching some sort of notion, though a very dim and imperfect one, to the words of your Creed, which declare that God is one, and yet that there are three Persons in the Godhead. They may keep these words from lying dead in your minds, or rather on your tongues.

One of the comparisons or likenesses I am speaking of is taken from the most glorious object which our eyes see, the sun. That ball of light and heat, which we call most properly the Sun, may be compared to the Father, from whom both the Word and the Spirit come. From this sun the light issues, and is as it were a part of it, and yet comes down to our earth and gives light to us. This we may compare to the Word, who came forth from the Father, and came down on earth, and was made man, and who, as St. John tells us, is 'the true light, which lighteth every man that cometh into the world.' But beside this there is the heat, which is a different thing from the light: for we all know, there may be heat without light: and so may there be light,—moonlight for example, and starlight,—without any perceivable heat. Yet the two are blended and united in the sun; so that the same rays, which bring us light to enlighten us, bring us heat also to warm us, and to ripen the fruits and herbs of all kinds which the earth bears. This heat of the sun may not unfitly be compared to the Holy Spirit, the Lord and Giver of life, as the Creed calls him, for heat is the great fosterer of life: as we see for example in an egg. As that is hatched by the warmth of the parent bird, sitting on it lovingly, and brooding over it, until it is quickened into life; just so does the Holy Spirit of God brood with more than dove-like patience over the heart of the believer, giving it life and warmth; and though he be driven away again and again by our backslidings, he still hovers round our hearts, desiring to return to them, and to dwell in them, and cherish them for ever. Moreover, if any seed of the Word has begun to spring up in any heart, the Spirit descends like a sunbeam upon it, and ripens the ear, and brings the fruit to perfection. Thus have we first the sun in the sky, secondly, the light, which issues from the sun, and thirdly, the heat, which accompanies the light,—three separate and distinguishable things; yet distinct as they are, what can be more united than the sun and its rays, or than the light and heat which those rays shed abroad?

The comparison which I have just set before you, is taken from the most glorious of the heavenly bodies known to us, the sun. Another is sometimes taken from the purest of earthly bodies, water. Here too we have first the fountain, high up among the rocks, far out of man's reach, answering to the Father; secondly, the stream, which issues from the fountain, and flows down into the valley for the use of man, and which may be likened to Jesus Christ, the Son; thirdly, the mist, which rises from the water, and falls in rain or dew upon the thirsty ground: this, I need hardly say, answers to the Holy Spirit, who in the days of the apostles came down visibly, like the rain, with a sound as of a rushing mighty wind, but who now descends gently and silently, like the dew in the silence of the night, on the heart of the humble believer, to refresh it, to soften it, and to make it fruitful.

Do not mistake me, my brethren. I do not mean that these comparisons will enable us to understand the mystery of the Trinity; any more than a farthing rushlight will enable us to understand the sun. But supposing a man, who had never seen the sun, were to say, 'it is impossible for the light to abide in the sun, and yet to be shed abroad over the earth,' a farthing rush-light would suffice to show him that the light, though it fills the room, may yet abide with the candle. In like manner the comparison I have been setting before you may suffice to convince you that the difficulty, by which so many have been offended, in the mystery of the Trinity, is not so irreconcilable with what we find in God's created works, as we are apt to fancy it. And this is all that we need. What God is in himself,—how the eternal Word is the only-begotten of the Father,—how the Holy Ghost proceeds from the Father and the Son,—how the Father, Son, and Holy Ghost abide for ever in indissoluble union and unity,—these are questions of no importance to the practical government of our lives. Therefore God has not thought fit to reveal them to us more clearly. That which it concerns us to know, that which is to act upon our hearts and souls, and through them on our conduct, has been declared to us. The holy root lies hid underground: the holy branches spread abroad before our sight, and offer us a safe shelter from all the evils of this world. Knowledge, a wise man has said, is power; but it is power only when we use it. Knowledge not applied, or misapplied, profits nothing. What good would knowing all the herbs and simples in the world do a sick man, if he did not use them to cure his sickness? Neither would it profit us to know the most secret mysteries of the divine nature, unless that knowledge helped us on in the paths of holiness and godliness.

But what, you may ask, are the practical uses and purposes, for which the doctrine of the Trinity was revealed to us? What good can it do us to know that the Son is God, and that the Holy Ghost is God, as well as the Father, and yet that there are not three Gods, but one God? What are the holy branches which spring from this most holy root?

Now, if the purpose and end of Christianity be, as it doubtless is, to bring us near to God in heart and life, it is easy to see, how much the revealing the doctrine of the Trinity to us is fitted to further that end. I say the revealing it to us: because there might have been a Trinity; the Son of God might have died to save us; the Holy Ghost might come and sanctify us; and yet we might know nothing of the matter. Even this would doubtless have been a great mercy, and a great blessing. But the having that mercy revealed to us so plainly,—the knowledge that these things are so,—the being made acquainted with the great works

121

which have been done, and are doing by the Son of God and the Spirit of God for our sakes,—this multiplies our debt, and makes the blessing and the mercy much greater.

For consider what would be the state of a sinner, on waking from his sin, if he did not know himself to be pardoned. What dread! what horror! what despair! what distracting thoughts of God's righteous indignation! What an ever-present vision of hell yawning to devour him! What a doleful voice ever ringing in his ears, Judgment! Judgment! Who could remain long in such a state? What mind could go on dwelling on such terrible and dismal thoughts, and not be driven mad? Yet this would be the state, the natural and reasonable state, of a sinner awaking from the sleep of sin, if he did not know of the propitiatory sacrifice which Christ has offered up for sin. But now that the good news of pardon and acceptance with God through the blood of Christ has been proclaimed to all who repent, the light of hope is let into the prison-house of sin: so that they who sat in darkness and the shadow of death, fast bound in misery and iron,—they who naturally could have nothing to look for but judgment and fiery indignation, for the misdeeds they have been wilfully guilty of,—for their drunkenness, for their lust, for their foul and evil-speaking, for the pains they have taken to learn mischief, for the opportunities of instruction and improvement which they have thrown away,—even these, on awaking from their slumber, and coming to a right mind, have only to lift up their eyes to heaven, to see the beams of mercy and forgiveness shining and ready to descend. They have only to take up their Bibles; and they will read there—what? That sin is a light matter? Far from it. That it does not signify whether a man goes on sinning or not? By no means. That God is easy, and will let sinners go unpunished? Quite the contrary. They will find that sin is hateful to God, that punishment must follow it, that God 'will by no means clear the guilty,' but, according to their deeds, will repay 'tribulation and anguish upon every soul of man that doeth evil.' (Rom. ii. 9.) Yet in the midst of all these terrible passages, which so awfully represent God's justice, they will find the freest and fullest and most merciful promises of pardon for Christ's sake, to every one without exception who repents and truly turns to God in time. They will read that 'the blood of Christ cleanseth us from all sin' (1 John i. 7); that God gave his only-begotten Son in order that all true believers in him should have everlasting life (John iii. 16); and many other passages to the same effect. These will be sufficient, not to banish the sinner's shame and sorrow for his past life,—God forbid that they should! —but they will make that shame and sorrow bearable. They will prevent his soul from sinking to the earth under an insupportable fear of God's wrath. They will save him from that recklessness and despair, which harden the heart and make it devilish. Instead of looking on himself as an outcast doomed to eternal torment, he will get to feel that he is pardonable, yea, and already pardoned, if he will only return home to God. He will learn that, during all his wanderings, he has been followed with a watchful eye by his merciful and heavenly Father: and then the thought of having wilfully offended such a father, of having run away from him to go and eat the husks of sin,—that thought, coming with a prospect of forgiveness, will soften his stubborn heart, and will make him sorrow with the godly sorrow which worketh repentance not to be repented of. Such are some of the blessed effects likely to be produced in the sinner's mind, by knowing that Christ came down from heaven to suffer death for sinners. Here then you see the benefit of knowing at least so much about the Trinity, as to be aware of all that the second Person of it, the eternal and only-begotten Son of God, has been pleased to do and suffer for our redemption.

The good of knowing what is done for us by the third Person of the Trinity is also very great and plain. It is a great benefit for us to have been taught that the Holy Ghost is ever ready to help us in our endeavours after holiness. I have set before you the case of a sinner, whose eyes have been opened to see the danger and the wickedness of offending God, and who is anxious to lead a better life. Let us follow this penitent a few steps on his road, and see what he will do next. Doubtless he will begin his reformation by studying the law of God; for to keep it, he must know it. The first steps will perhaps be easy enough. Not to murder, not to commit adultery, not to steal, not to bear false witness, crimes like these he may never have had any mind to: at any rate now he would rather die than be guilty of anything so wicked. But on reading a little further, he meets with other commandments as difficult as the first were easy; commandments far surpassing the utmost reach of human virtue, such as 'be ye holy as God is holy,' and 'perfect as God is perfect;' commandments the most contradictory to flesh and blood, such as, that we must love them that hate us, that we must deny ourselves, that we must take up our cross and follow Jesus;

commandments reaching to the very smallest actions, and even thoughts, such as, that we must cleanse and purify our hearts, that we must bridle our very tongues. Now who is sufficient for such things? Who can hope, try he never so much, to become perfect like God? The more a man thinks what God is, and what great goodness he requires from us, the more he learns of the divine law, how exceeding broad and high and deep it is, the further he sees into the spiritual nature of the service which we owe him,—the more he must needs feel his utter inability to serve and obey God as he ought to do. Here then a new despair threatens to overwhelm the penitent, a despair of being able to pay God a sufficient and acceptable service. He sees, and is forced to confess, to use St. Paul's words, 'that the law is holy, and the commandment holy and just and good.' But what does this profit him when the holiness of the commandment only shews him his own crookedness, but gives him no means of becoming upright? What does it avail him that he delights in the law of God and feels its excellence and purity so long as he sees another law in his members bringing him into captivity to sin, or at least crippling him from attaining to the purity he admires and longs for? Truly it avails and profits him just as much, and no more, than it profited the impotent man at the pool of Bethesda to be desirous of being made whole, and to lie on the edge of the healing waters, which he had not strength to step into. But thanks be to God! a remedy has been provided for this our natural weakness by the gracious kindness of the Holy Ghost; just as a remedy has been provided for our natural sinfulness by the blood-shedding of Jesus Christ. The Spirit of God takes the sinner out of the hands of the blessed Jesus: he nurses him; he cherishes him; he feeds him; he supports and strengthens him; and finally he takes up his abode within him and purifies him, and gradually changes his whole nature, filling him with love, joy, peace, long-suffering, gentleness, goodness, faith, meekness, and temperance. Surely the knowledge that the Spirit does all this is an inestimable benefit to the young Christian. It gives him courage: it excites him to persevere and struggle on: it sets before him the certainty of conquering, if he be not wanting to himself. Instead of crying out, as otherwise he might have done, 'O wretched man that I am, who shall deliver me from the body of this death!' he now exclaims, with humble confidence, 'I can do all things, through Christ that strengtheneth me: in spite of tribulation and temptation, through Christ I shall be more than conqueror.'

Nor is it merely to the sinner, or to the penitent, that the knowledge of the Son and of the Spirit of God is a root yielding blessed fruit. To the true followers of Jesus Christ, to those who have already made advances in holiness, to those who have tasted and learnt how gracious the Lord is,—to such persons the knowledge of these great truths is still more precious than to any others. Think of knowing that you have a Friend, a Saviour, a prevailing Advocate in heaven. Think of knowing that you have the Spirit of all peace and joy and purity dwelling in you. Think of knowing that, come what will, you have an almighty Shepherd, who once died to save you, and who now ever liveth to protect you. 'Who will harm you,' says St. Peter, 'if ye be followers of that which is good?' Let me wax bolder, and ask, what can harm you? What can harm you, if ye be followers of Christ? Can Satan, whom he has trampled on? can the world, which he made, and will destroy? can sin, which he expiated on the cross? can death, whose chains he burst at his resurrection? Fears then there can be none, except from human weakness, to the faithful followers of Jesus. Nor can there be doubts or lasting sorrow. What doubts can there be to that man, who hath God's word pledged for his salvation, and who has the promise of the Holy Spirit to teach him every necessary truth? As to sorrow, are we not expressly told that all things work together for good to them that love God? What room then to such blessed persons can there be for any lasting sorrow? Even that most incurable of earthly griefs, the grief for the loss of those who are gone before us,—even of that St. Paul speaks in these words: 'I would not have you to be ignorant, brethren, concerning them which are asleep, that ye sorrow not, even as others which have no hope; for if we believe that Jesus died and rose again, even so them also which sleep in Jesus will God bring with him. Wherefore comfort one another with these words.' (1 Thess. iv. 13-18.)

The sum of the whole is this: though the nature of God must needs be mysterious to our understandings, there is no mystery in the benefits we receive from him nor any darkness in the duty we owe him. Without comprehending how the three Persons of the Godhead are united in one eternal God, we may glorify each for his excellent greatness and goodness to man. We may glorify the Father, the original fountain of all things, who sent his only Son to work out our salvation. We may glorify the Son, who undertook and has accomplished that salvation. We may glorify the Holy Ghost, who is graciously present with the faithful in Christ to write his words in their hearts, to comfort and succour them, and to lead them in the steps of their Redeemer to the gates of heaven which he has opened. The Father, the Son, and the Holy Ghost, were not revealed to us that we might be more knowing than the heathens. We were told of the Father, that we might obey the Father: we were told of the Son, that we might be delivered from our sins by the Son: we were told of the Holy Ghost, that we might welcome him into our hearts, and throw them open to receive him. What will it avail us to have heard of the Father, if we choose to be cast out for ever from his presence? what, to have heard of the Son, if we reject the atonement of his blood? what, to have been brought up in the knowledge of the Holy Ghost, if we despise his warnings, drive him from our hearts by our impurities, and remain, like Gideon's fleece, dry in the midst of so much moisture, unregenerate and unsanctified amid the largest offers of the freest and most overflowing sanctification? Do not deceive yourselves so fatally, my brethren: do not repeat the error of the Jews. Do not fancy that knowing is doing, that right notions make a saving faith. True faith and true love, the trust in God and the love of God,—a trust shown by resignation to his will, a love proved by keeping his commandments,—these are the only things to rely on. Cling to them, and they will bear you through the world to heaven, where all mysteries will be cleared up, and all difficulties will be done away: for we shall be let into the presence of God, and shall see him as he is. And what is better, if possible, even than seeing and knowing God, we shall be ever growing more and more like him.

RICHARD HURRELL Froude has been well described as one
in whom angel and devil fought for mastery and it was not always the angel who won. The *enfant terrible* of the Oxford
Movement, he was also its Keats—dying young of tuberculosis,
lamented by his friends, but leaving a mass of papers which,
when edited by Newman and Keble and published posthumous-
ly in 1838-9, caused a critical furore, largely on account of their
truthfulness in recording Froude's struggles with his own divided nature, and because of the epigrammatic way in which his
mind worked. Such remarks as 'The Reformation was a limb
badly set—it must be broken again in order to be righted' could
scarcely be expected to endear him to the average Church of
England priest.

The *Remains* read differently now. The candour and completeness of their confession, as well as its absence of cant and
self-pretence (he observes, for example, how private prayer becomes stranger the longer one lives), make the pages sound as
though they were written yesterday, not a hundred and fifty
years ago. Froude's contemporaries saw for the most part only
something morbid and un-English in his introspection, his practice of certain forms of mild self-mortification, his praise of
clerical celibacy, and his devotion to the Blessed Virgin Mary.
Modern readers may be grateful for the record, loyally preserved
by his friends and bravely set forth upon public view, of a Catholic spirit managing to exist within the Church of England
during the first three decades of the nineteenth century.

Apart from the papers later published, Newman inherited
from Froude a copy of the Breviary. He chose it himself, when
invited to take one of his friend's books. The choice is interesting when it is remembered that at the time of their first meeting
Newman struck Froude as a kind of heretical Evangelical who
regarded the Pope as Anti-Christ and the Church of Rome as
not even the ugly sister, let alone the mother, of the Church of
England.

On his deathbed, Froude said that if he had done nothing else
he had made Newman and Keble understand each other. I think
he meant that he had effected a personal ecumenical act in bringing Anglican Evangelicalism and Anglican High Churchmanship
together. It is observable that Froude himself has been most
intelligently appreciated by Roman Catholic writers—notably,

Christopher Dawson in *The Spirit of the Oxford Movement*, and by his biographer Louise Imogen Guiney, also of the Roman communion.

Froude was an elegant, self-torturing, over-emphatic person, with a streak of sado-masochism in his temperament as well as a mischievous wit. But he was also a man of Keatsian intensity, whose sermons should be studied as exercises in self-restraint. The contrast between their deliberate severity, their dryness of tone, and the bright enigma of his personality as revealed in the personal journals could not be more marked. We fall back upon Newman's observation that his friend's mind afforded 'a remarkable instance of the temptation to rationalism, self-speculation, etc., subdued.' Newman adds, in the *Apologia*:

I speak of Hurrell Froude, in his intellectual aspect: as a man of high genius, brimful and overflowing with ideas and views, in him original, which were too many and strong even for his bodily strength, and which crowded and jostled against each other, in their effort after distinct shape and expression. And he had an intellect as critical and logical as it was speculative and bold. Dying prematurely, as he did, and in the conflict and transition-state of opinion, his religious views never reached their ultimate conclusion, by the very reason of their multitude and their depth. His opinions arrested and influenced me even when they did not gain my assent. He professed openly his admiration of the Church of Rome, and his hatred of the Reformers. He delighted in the notion of an hierarchical system, of sacerdotal power, and of full ecclesiastical liberty. He felt scorn of the maxim, 'The Bible and the Bible only is the religion of Protestants', and he gloried in accepting Tradition as a main instrument of religious teaching. He had a high severe idea of the intrinsic excellence of Virginity, and he considered the Blessed Virgin its great Pattern.

Froude's *Englishness* has not been better expressed than by Newman in the paragraph which follows this one. I quote again:

He had a keen insight into abstract truth; but he was an Englishman to the backbone in his severe adherence to the real and the concrete. He had a most classical taste, and a genius for philosophy and art; and he was fond of historical inquiry, and the politics of religion. He had no turn for

128

theology as such . . . . I should say that his power of entering into the minds of others did not equal his other gifts: he could not believe, for instance, that I really held the Roman Church to be anti-Christian. On many points, he would not believe but that I agreed with him, when I did not: he seemed not to understand my difficulties. His were of a different kind: the contrariety between theory and fact. He was a High Tory of the Cavalier stamp . . . .[1]

This is the point at which it would be as well to draw attention to the way Froude—fond as he was of Oxford—sprang from quite another environment. He was a Devon man. There is more than a touch of another Devonian, Sir Walter Ralegh, about the mixture of the ascetic and the cavalier in his character. 'Stab at thee he that will, / No stab thy soule can kill.' The Ralegh who 'gave the lie' to the rottenness of his own age would have found a friend in the Froude who proclaimed his faith in 'the ancient Church of England', adding as an explanation of what he meant: 'Charles the First and the Non-jurors.'

More than any other one figure, Hurrell Froude inspired the Oxford Movement. 'Keble is the fire,' he said, 'but I am the poker.' There is consolation here for those of us who mistrust the Oxfordiness of the enterprise. Christopher Dawson writes:

The roots of the Oxford Movement are to be found not so much in Oxford itself as in the country parsonages of Gloucestershire and Devon, by the banks of the Windrush and the Dart. It was there that the first links were forged of the chain that was to draw the Anglican tradition out of the rut of conventionality and Erastianism in which it had stuck so long. Dartington today hums with activity; the old church has been destroyed and the Froudes' home has become a parochial centre. But on the other bank of the Dart, in the woods of Little Hempston, there still stands the little 14th-century manor house, which Hurrell regarded as the most beautiful place in the world, with its effaced fresco of the mystery of the Resurrection, a memorial at once of Froude himself and of the old Catholic England to which he had pledged his faith.[2]

He was born at Dartington in 1803, on the Feast of the Annunciation, the son of a High Church west country clergyman.

After being educated at Eton and Oriel College, Oxford, he was ordained a priest in 1829. He died in his father's house on 28 February 1836, and his body lies buried in Dartington old churchyard.

NOTES

1. J. H. Newman, *Apologia pro Vita Sua*, 1864, pp. 85-6.
2. Christopher Dawson, *The Spirit of the Oxford Movement*,1933, p. 24.

BIBLIOGRAPHY

J. H. Newman and John Keble (eds.), *Remains of the Late Reverend Richard Hurrell Froude*, 2 vols., 1838; 2 vols., 1839.
Louise Imogen Guiney, *Hurrell Froude: Memoranda and Comments*, 1904.

RELIGIOUS INDIFFERENCE
Luke 17:26, 27.
And as it was in the days of Noe, so shall it be in the days of the Son of Man. They did eat, they drank, they married wives, they were given in marriage, until the day that Noe entered into the ark; and the flood came, and destroyed them all.

THIS IS sermon xv in the second volume of Froude's *Remains*. All his sermons were written and preached between 1829 and 1833, after his twenty-fifth but before his thirtieth year. His biographer observes that their style is quiet and sober, yet also 'searching, pitiless, unforgettable'.[1]

Religious Indifference deserves attention for at least two reasons. 'We indulge a notion,' Froude says, speaking of our attitude to the Old Testament, 'that a Dispensation so obviously miraculous as this appears *to us* to have been, while we are reading the sacred records, must have appeared so, no less obviously, to those who were actors in the scenes described.' Indicating the dangers of such condescension, he requires us to look hard at the psychological reality—in particular at the 'self-deceit and security in wickedness' of the inhabitants of Sodom, whose 'indifference and worldly-mindedness' brought about their downfall. He speaks levelly but critically of the opinion that statements in the Bible are 'somehow or other exaggerated', and that 'it was written for different times, or for persons differently circumstanced' from ourselves, or—most attractive of heresies— that 'it intentionally overstates the rule of conduct, on the assumption that men will aim at something short of the mark prescribed to them.' Froude cuts through these comfortable delusions by showing that they are not new. On the contrary, they were the sins of Sodom. The question which he raises at the end, *What then is the Ark which we are to prepare, or where is the Zoar we must fly to?* can be taken as the question which he did not live to answer. We may suppose that Newman did not forget it.

I have selected this sermon because it shows a different Froude from the maker of scornful aphorisms. I have selected it also because in its choice of text and treatment of that text, it can be used to discuss Sir Geoffrey Faber's fancy that Froude and Newman were homosexual.[2] No doubt when *Oxford Apostles* first appeared it seemed to say something fresh about the Tractarians. It now reads as a period piece—'the nemesis of a psychology which regards every spiritual or self-transcending tendency as a disguised form of the sexual impulse', as Christopher Dawson says. Worse, it confuses medical and moral values. It is Charles Kingsley updated. Dawson goes on:

> The Freudian concept of homosexuality involves no moral judgement, but as applied by Mr. Faber to the case of Newman it becomes charged with ethical significance and finally becomes equivalent to a lack of 'manliness' in the moral sense. This is, however, nothing else but the old prejudices of Kingsley and Abbott in a new Freudian dress. No doubt there is much to be said for the traditional English ideal of manliness which finds expression in Mr. Kipling's *If*. But it was not Newman's ideal, and we have no right to ignore his own ethical standards and to judge his character by a conflation of the Freudian psychology with the ethical ideals of Mr. Rudyard Kipling. The fact is that Newman offends the moral sense of his critics not because he was weak but because he was strong. His genius challenges the accepted standards of the ordinary Englishman who is accustomed to dismiss the great ethical paradoxes of Christianity as pious platitudes.[3]

Now it is clear that Froude had more than his share of the usual divisions and complications of human nature. We could speak of masochism from the evidence which he gives us himself; we could speak of sadism in what has been reported to have been his treatment of his younger brother Anthony, later well known as the historian J. A. Froude. But neither of these charges seems of much account when set beside the seriousness of his own self-accusations in the first volume of the *Remains*. Faber's disgust was excited by a homo-erotic element which he thought he noticed in the Oxford Movement. Froude sees the sin of Sodom as *religious indifference*. The contrast between the two views could not be sharper. Froude's might be recommended to all who believe that they have convincingly explained or discredited a man's faith if they can discover his erotic likes and dislikes. I doubt whether Faber knew more of Froude's or Newman's temptations than they did themselves.

NOTES

1. Louise Imogen Guiney, *Hurrell Froude*, 1904, p. 62.
2. Geoffrey Faber, *Oxford Apostles*, 1933, pp. 218-23.
3. Christopher Dawson, *The Spirit of the Oxford Movement*, 1933, p. ix.

IN THESE verses and the few following ones that relate to the destruction of Sodom, our Lord describes the state of persons who have been selected as the most signal examples of God's vengeance. Next to the universal destruction of the human race by water, the overthrow of Sodom and Gomorrah occupies the most prominent place in the records of His judgments. And to both of them there is given an additional and fearful interest by the manner in which our Lord here associates them with that last judgment of all: like as it was in the days of Noe, so shall it be in the Son of Man's days.

It cannot, then, but concern us intimately, to examine what was the *peculiarity* in the temper prevalent among these persons, which rendered them so *peculiarly* offensive in the sight of God; in what respect *their* guilt differed from that *of other men*, so as to merit such a pre-eminence of punishment. And it may perhaps at first appear a matter of some surprise to us, that in our Lord's account of the occupations in the midst of which their fate overtook them, we should find nothing mentioned which shocks our feelings, either by its uncommonness or enormity. He does not say they murdered, they stole, they worshipped idols, they dealt abominably, nor, which is very remarkable, does He characterise their condition by those crimes which the sacred historian lays to their charge.

The features of their behaviour, which He in both instances selects, are these: 'They did eat, they drank, they married, and were given in marriage; they bought, they sold, they planted, they builded.'

It is true, indeed, that the condition which these words describe is not insisted on as the *crime* of these most guilty persons, yet surely they are meant to convey some idea beyond that of the mere surprise which attended the lighting down of God's vengeance. If this had been the only thing intended to be impressed on us, the description would have lost nothing of its force by mentioning the crimes which the book of Genesis relates, instead of these seemingly innocent occupations; nor is it at all likely that such fearless abominations would have been passed in silence, unless our Lord had had a farther end in view, beyond giving force to the picture of unprepared destruction.

We are left, then, to infer that the words of the text convey a deeper meaning; that they are intended to divert our thoughts from what we suppose the crying sins of that guilty generation, to some other feature in their moral condition, some temper

in itself especially displeasing to God, however apparently innocent may be the actions which result from it.

Nor, indeed, need we feel much at a loss to discover what
this temper was; this additional feature of finished wickedness
which fills up the measure of their guilt. Our Lord is evidently
describing a state of *religious indifference*, an utter alienation of
mind from all serious thoughts, a forgetfulness of every motive
but pleasure and interest, a complete surrender of themselves to
this world. And as far as we can judge, from the short narrative
of the book of Genesis, we may infer this to have been their
spiritual condition.

We are told of the generation before the flood, that 'The sons
of God saw the daughters of men that they were fair, and they
took them wives of all *that they chose*;' a peculiar emphasis
seems to belong to the words 'of all that they chose;' they were
withheld by no consideration from executing their will, and in
consequence we hear that 'God saw the wickedness of man, that
it was great in the earth; and that every imagination of the
thoughts of his heart was only evil continually.' Jesus Christ describes these imaginations in the words of the text, 'they did eat,
they drank, they married, and were given in marriage:' that is,
these were the only objects which they kept in view; they pursued these as the sole ends of life, and disregarded all restraints
which the love of their neighbour or the fear of God could impose on them. Their sin does not seem so much to have consisted in an avowed opposition to God, as in an utter disregard of
Him; it was not so much that they defied His power to punish
them, as that the very notion of His exerting it against them
seemed absurd and impossible. Of this the history of the destruction of Sodom furnishes a striking example. 'Two Angels were
sent to summon Lot and his family out of Sodom. And the men
said unto Lot, Hast thou here any besides? son-in-law, and thy
sons, and thy daughters, and whatsoever thou hast in this city,
bring them out of this place. For we will destroy this place, because the cry of them is waxen great before the face of the Lord:
and the Lord has sent us to destroy it. And Lot went out and
spake unto his sons-in-law which married his daughters, and said,
Up, get you out of this place, for the Lord will destroy this city.
But he seemed as one that mocked unto his sons-in-law.' The
thing seemed to them utterly impossible, such as was not worth
even the thought of any but a fool.

Such was the temper of the men before the flood, and of the

inhabitants of those devoted cities; and how deeply it is displeasing to God the manner in which He has in these instances dealt with it is sufficient to show. It may not have been of itself enough to draw down the wrath of God so signally; it may not perhaps have held the first place in the catalogue of crimes, which together constituted their guilt. Yet it holds a place among them sufficiently marked and prominent, to have its proof embodied in the sacred narrative, and to have been alone selected in the comment of our Saviour.

Against such a temper, then, it becomes us to be most seriously on our guard, and we shall do well not merely to watch and examine our own condition with a view to trace its progress in ourselves, but also, as much as we can, to realise to ourselves the situation of those unhappy persons, and see how far we have room to hope that under the same circumstances we might have escaped the same destruction.

The second of these considerations is not less necessary to us than the first. For one of the commonest obstacles to our deriving benefit from the experience of others, especially if they have lived in an age or state of society very different from our own, is the vague and indistinct way in which we are in the habit of regarding all that we hear of them; we look on them almost as a different order of beings, and do not associate their feelings, their conduct, or their sufferings, with any thing which we feel, or do, or suffer.

This is the case very generally with regard to all history, but more especially is it so with the history of the Old Testament. We indulge a notion, that a Dispensation so obviously miraculous as this appears *to us* to have been, while we are reading the sacred records, must have appeared so, no less obviously, to those who were actors in the scenes described; and fancy that such familiarity with divine interpositions must have produced an involuntary effect on the views and feelings of persons even the least disposed to serious thought. Hence instances of virtue appear in such circumstances less praiseworthy, and faithlessness or disobedience seem to deserve less consideration. And the result is, that instead of profiting, as we ought, by applying to our own case, the warnings and the judgments with which their sins were visited, we delude ourselves with the hope that we may be tried by a different standard, and be summoned to a less rigorous account.

Let us see, then, whether in the two cases before us, we have

135

any reason to suppose exaggerating circumstances of this kind, such as would call for more than usual severity.

At the time when the Flood came upon the Earth, a space of 600 years had elapsed since the last recorded miracle,—the assumption of Enoch; and even this we have no reason to believe had been made public to the world in general, still less that any certain evidence had been given, such as could convince those who were unwilling to believe.

The conversations between God and the family of Noah were evidently not intended to be generally known; and the only way in which attention was likely to be called to them, was by the long preparation of the Ark. A work so extraordinary and apparently so useless as this, must indeed have excited very general wonder; yet it could not be used as a proof of any thing more, than that Noah and his family *believed* they had received an intimation from God. There was nothing as yet to show that their faith had better ground than superstition and enthusiasm. The evidence their conduct gave of the judgment God was bringing upon the earth was neither stronger nor more striking than that which is afforded us concerning our destiny in the world to come, by the existence of the Church visible among ourselves. Whatever excuses we are in the habit of making when we neglect the advice of good men now, we may be sure were equally availing then. They saw, as we do, that it made but little difference to their *outward* comfort and prosperity, whether they tied themselves down by strict and painful rules of duty, or gave free scope to the bent of their inclinations. 'They saw the daughters of men, that they were fair, and they took them wives *of all which they chose*.' And their children became 'mighty men, which were of old, men of reknown.' The offspring of these unholy unions bore no outward marks of God's displeasure against sin;—they were mighty men, the favoured of their race. Surely it might be said, God cannot in truth be so severe a master as He is represented; it cannot be that those whom He blesses with such prosperity, and to whom He gives such favour in the eyes of their brethren, can really be regarded by Him with so stern an eye, can indeed be objects of the vengeance of the Almighty.

This is no fictitious or exaggerated way of talking; it is a way of viewing things which is but too frequent among ourselves. It is the way we excuse our selfish worldly-minded pleasures and pursuits, our *partial* and *inconsistent* attempts to conform ourselves to the pattern which the Bible holds up to us, our *voluntary* submission to a different rule of right and wrong, from that which our Heavenly Father has prescribed:—and such are the very reasonings and excuses which the condition of mankind before the flood was certain to suggest.

Nor again does it appear that the men of Sodom were without like grounds for self-deceit and security in wickedness: 500 years had intervened between the time when the two Angels came into Sodom and the last great judgment which God had brought; all was ease and wealth around them; they seemed especially favoured among the inhabitants of the earth. 'Lot lifted up his eyes, and beheld all the plain of Jordan, that it was watered everywhere' before the Lord destroyed Sodom and Gomorrah 'even as the garden of the Lord.' Could it be that the Lord would all at once alter the course of His Providence; that while their conduct continued only the same as formerly, He would suddenly adopt a new manner of dealing with them; that His anger would be excited at one particular moment, by those very actions and agents whom He had hitherto allowed to pass unnoticed? 'Lot seemed as one that mocked unto his sons-in-law.'

These few remarks have been made upon the situation of those persons who have afforded the most marked examples of God's vengeance, to show that as far as appears from the sacred history, they were tempted by the same difficulties, and might shelter themselves behind the same excuses, which in these days afford a covering to practical infidelity; and that, therefore, if we would avoid their fate, we must avoid the indifference and worldly-mindedness which brought it on them; we must 'take heed to ourselves, lest at any time our hearts be overcharged with surfeiting and drunkenness, and the cares of this life, and so that day come upon us unawares. For as a snare shall it come upon all them that dwell upon the face of the earth.'

Is it *true*, then, that there exists among us at the present day, a temper such as that which our Lord attributes to the Sodomites? ARE WE such persons as He intended to describe under the terms, 'they ate, they drank, they married, and were given in marriage?' The question may be put in a rather different and more definite form: Is our conduct like that of persons who believe the Bible to be in earnest, and who are willing to take God at His word?

I fear it is impossible for any one to look around him at what is going on in the world, or even to question his own conscience with impartiality, without arriving at a most unsatisfactory conclusion on this important point. The aspect of Society is sadly unlike what we should expect from a Christian brotherhood, who own one Lord, one Faith, one Baptism, one God and Father of us all; and as little are the pursuits, the hopes, the pleasures of each individual Christian like those of a stranger and pilgrim upon earth.

But not to dwell on these surprising inconsistencies between the faith we own and the tempers we indulge, let us confine our attention to the open professions which men generally make, the principles which they avow and justify, and we shall find even here how little weight is given to the Bible among those who accept it as the word of God. Men, not only in their actions, show a preference of every other motive before that which their reason tells them to be of paramount importance; but even in their very opinions and modes of judging, deliberately put by the consideration of it. 'Knowing the judgment of God, that they who commit such things are worthy of death, they not only do the same, but have pleasure in those that do them.'

For instance, all men know in what strong language our Lord and His Apostles have spoken of the sins of sensuality; yet we know too that many of these sins are systematically indulged by numbers of Christians; persons who profess (when they turn their thoughts that way) to believe the Scripture *records*, and to respect the authority of the Scripture *precepts*. Now, how do these persons explain their conduct to themselves? Is it not their habitual practice to laugh down seriousness, and to look on any argument which is brought against them from the words of Scripture, as on that very account unworthy of attention? It seems as if the mere fact, that the objection turned on religious grounds was with some men a sufficient reason for putting it by, as part of a question into which they do not feel called on to enter.

How plainly do such persons resemble the profligate sons-in-law of Lot! The Bible seems to them as a book that mocketh.

And what has just been said of sensuality, is equally applicable to every other course which men knowingly persevere in against God's command, and yet without a feeling of uneasiness.

No persons, who intentionally put by religious considerations in the regulation of any part of their conduct, can possibly take the Bible to mean what it plainly says. They must suppose that its statements are somehow or other exaggerated, that it was written for different times, or for persons differently circumstanced from themselves, or that it intentionally overstates the rule of conduct, on the assumption that men will aim at something short of the mark prescribed to them.

These, and other devices of self-deceit, must be systematically cherished by a large portion of mankind. But there is yet a further step of indifference to be traced: we have to observe men not only putting the Bible intentionally out of their thoughts, wherever it is brought to bear upon their own conduct; but, at the same time that they do this, taking God's word into their mouth, praising religious sentiments, expressing the utmost respect for [religion]. 'They come unto thee,' says the Prophet Ezekiel of the faithless Israelites, 'as the people cometh, and they sit before thee as My people, and they hear thy words, but they will not do them; for with their mouth they show much love, but their heart goeth after their covetousness. And lo thou art unto them as a very lovely song of one that hath a pleasant voice, and can play well on an instrument; for they hear thy words, but they do them not.'

This is the last and most hopeless form of religious indifference; to this, more than to any other temper, the Bible seems as a book that mocketh; and those who cherish it would have been the least of all men likely either to follow Noah into the Ark, or to fly with Lot from the fate of Sodom. Yet it is to be feared that a way of viewing things not very unlike this, is sadly characteristic of our times; at any rate, we cannot doubt that it is very prevalent among us, and that it takes especial hold on refined and educated minds. The two first forms of practical infidelity which have been mentioned, are common to all times and all stages of society. In all the variety of circumstances in which history exhibits man to us, we see abundant instances of wilful sin against a knowledge of the truth, and a deliberate preference for the servants of mammon before the servants of God. But to combine the real contempt of sacred things with a hollow artificial respect which hears the word of the Most High 'as a very lovely song,' this is a kind of neglect reserved only for days of intellectual cultivation.

In these times we must be most zealously on our guard against such fatal delusions, if we would hope that it may not sometime be with us as in the days of Lot and in the days of Noe. If we would hope that God's third great judgment, the coming of the Son of Man, may not overtake us unawares.

Nor let us suppose it so very certain, that this fearful day is as yet far distant from us. The course of Nature may indeed seem firm and settled; the thought may suggest itself to us, which St.

Peter says shall arise among those who walk after their own lusts, 'which say, Where is the promise of His coming; for since the fathers fell asleep, all things continue as they were from the beginning of the creation.' But let us remember that this is to be the scoff of *the last days*; and that the Apostle states it in connexion with this solemn warning, 'The heavens and earth which are now, by the same word are kept in store, reserved unto fire against the day of judgment . . . . The Lord is not slack concerning His promise, as some men count slackness; but is long-suffering to us-ward . . . . But the day of the Lord *will* come, as a thief in the night.'

Let us be careful that this warning is not treated by us as was the warning of the Angels by Lot's sons-in-law.

What then is the Ark which we are to prepare, or where is the Zoar we must fly to?

'Sell that ye have and give alms; provide for yourselves bags which wax not old; a treasure in the heavens that faileth not . . . Let your loins be girded about, and your lights burning; and ye yourselves like unto men that wait for their Lord; . . . that when He cometh and knocketh, they may open unto Him immediately. Blessed are those servants whom the Lord, when He cometh, shall find watching.'

THE DUTY OF FOLLOWING THE GUIDANCE OF THE CHURCH
2 Tim. 3:14.
But continue thou in the things which thou hast learned, and been assured of, knowing of whom thou hast learned them.

THIS IS sermon xviii in the second volume of the *Remains*. It was preached, a footnote informs us, in 1831.

When Froude addressed himself to the subject of this sermon he did not have moral precepts in mind, so much as a half-formed vision of the *ecclesia*. He was soon to define rationalism as the tendency to attach undue weight to human experience, especially in the interpretation of Scripture. More generally, he was to contrast what he called 'Sight', or reliance on the evidence of our individual senses, and 'Faith', or reliance on the evidence of revelation as a something *shared* beyond individualism. The essence of rationalism he defined as 'a downright refusal to walk by faith, in opposition to sight'. Against such refusals he writes on *The Duty of Following the Guidance of the Church*.

Froude's sermon can be compared with an early sermon of Newman, *On the Duty of Public Worship*,[1] in which he speaks of the Church as not only the visible channel of invisible grace, but the means by which religious individualism is eliminated. Newman writes that:

> It has been the great design of Christ to connect all His followers into one, and to secure this, He has lodged His blessings in the body collectively to oblige them to meet *together* if they would gain grace each for himself. The body is the first thing and each member in particular the second. The body is not made up of individual Christians, but each Christian has been made such in his turn by being *taken into the body*.

Froude's teaching is much the same. It is to be noted that both of them were therefore writing and preaching orthodox Catholic sermons some years before the official beginnings of the Oxford Movement.

Froude's *Essay on Rationalism* having been mentioned, I refer attention to it for its argument against sermons. While the effect of preaching is subjective, depending as it does on the merit of the sermon in question, the sacraments have an objective efficacy *because* they are sacraments. 'To set up Sermons as

141

a means of grace, to the disparagement of Sacraments,' says Froude, is to judge by experience and not by faith, and thus 'a lower modification of Rationalism'. Those who regard preaching as the essence of the service are not making a mere theological mistake; they are putting man in the centre of the worship. 'In a Protestant church the parson seems either to be preaching the prayers or worshipping the congregation.'[2]

NOTES

1. Unpublished, at the Birmingham Oratory, MS. Sermon 213. Preached 25 October 1829.
2. J. H. Newman and John Keble (eds.), *Remains of the Late Reverend Richard Hurrell Froude*, vol. I, 1838, p. 365.

THE ADVICE which is here given by St. Paul to Timothy, may at first appear to countenance a notion which is very prevalent among ourselves, *i.e.* that the respect we owe to teachers of religion depends on the opinion we have of their personal qualities; that we may make up our minds as to the degree of attention they deserve, and that unless their doctrine, and their manner of inculcating it, agrees with the notions we have formed of what is becoming in a Minister of the gospel, we are justified in withholding from them that deference which we should pay to one whose views accorded with our own. This notion is now very prevalent, and in many cases leads people to desert those who had been appointed as their teachers, and to choose others for themselves, who can have no possible authority except that which they derive from the assent of their hearers. On this ground many leave their parish Churches, and join congregations with which they have no regular connexion, in order to place themselves under the instruction of Clergymen of whom they approve more than their own, and happy would it be if this were all;—many even desert Church altogether, and prefer being instructed by men who were never commissioned to teach God's word, only because these persons teach the kind of things which they like to hear, or happen to have some personal qualification, such as reputation for talent or power of speaking fluently, or a striking manner, which inclines others to assent to what they say. This practice of choosing religious teachers, each person for himself, as their own fancies direct them, is what many now allow themselves in; and they do so on principle, they think it right; they not only allow themselves in the practice, but they approve of it.

Now it may, perhaps, appear at first that the advice which St. Paul gives to Timothy in the text affords indirectly, at least, some sanction to this prevailing notion. He tells Timothy to feel confident in the truth of what he had been taught, 'as knowing those who had taught him,' 'Continue thou in the things which thou hast learned, and been assured of, knowing of whom thou hast learned them.' It may, perhaps, seem from this, that St. Paul is appealing to Timothy's good opinion of his instruction, in proof of the things which he had learned of them; and that thus by approving of this practice in his own disciple, he authorises us also to make up our minds as to the degree of confidence we should place in any particular minister, and to rely only on those whom we approve of.

143

Such a notion may at first seem to be countenanced in the text. But if we examine it attentively, we shall not find this to be the case; indeed, the conclusion to which closer observation leads is directly opposite to this. By a reference to the general tenour of St. Paul's writings, we might easily show that he is as far as possible from encouraging people in placing themselves under favourite teachers, and ranking themselves as their followers. But in this case it is not necessary to refer to the general tenour of his writings. An examination of the passage itself will be sufficient for the purpose.

First, we have to inquire who the teachers were to whom St. Paul alludes; and, secondly, what that knowledge of them was to which he refers as a ground for confidence.

On the first point there may, perhaps, exist a doubt whether it is of himself St. Paul is speaking, or of those instructors who had taught Timothy from his youth; we may not be able to ascertain with certainty whether the things here mentioned, which Timothy had learned and been assured of, were the doctrines of the Gospel which had been taught him by St. Paul, or those more elementary principles of religion which are inculcated in the Old Testament. Yet, let us suppose either to be the case, and it will be very clear what kind of knowledge of his teachers it was to which St. Paul refers, as a pledge for the truth of the things which had been taught.

Suppose that the things spoken of are the truths of the Gospel, and consequently that the teacher from whom Timothy had learned them was St. Paul himself, we then have to inquire what was the warrant to which St. Paul used to refer his converts as a proof that he himself was worthy of credit. Was it then to his great reputation, or to his learning or eloquence, or to the excellence of his doctrine that he referred; doubtless he possessed these advantages in a remarkable degree; but was it on these that he founded his claims to the confidence of his disciples? He says to the Corinthians, 'And I, brethren, when I came unto you, came not with excellency of speech and of wisdom; . . . and my speech and my preaching was not with enticing words of man's wisdom, but in demonstration of the Spirit and of power. That your faith should not stand in the wisdom of men, but in the power of God.' This is the warrant which he shows; he proves that he is a divinely commissioned teacher, by working miracles among them he is sent to teach. He refers them as a proof of his doctrines, not the character of these doctrines, nor to the

144

arguments with which he had enforced them, but to the authority with which he was invested as a teacher. And he calls on
them to believe, not because they were pleased or because they
were convinced, but because he was set over them as God's
minister to show them His will. Such was the ground he took
with his Corinthian converts, as we see by his own words; and
such, doubtless, was the knowledge to which he referred Timothy, when he called on him to continue in those things which
he had learned, as knowing of whom he had learned them.

Or suppose, which is perhaps the most probable, that the
things spoken of are those plain truths of religion which pious
Jews had known before the coming of our Saviour, the things
which St. Paul reminds Timothy he had known from his youth;
still the case is in material points the same.

If we consider who his teachers must in this case have been, it
will be evident that St. Paul, in reminding Timothy of his knowledge of them, is appealing not to their personal qualification,
but to their commission; that he still grounds their claim to confidence, not on their character, nor their ability, nor their arguments, but on their authority.

Timothy, as we know from the Acts of the Apostles, was a
native either of Derbe or Lystra, ignorant and obscure cities, so
much given to superstition and idolatry that they were disposed
to sacrifice to Paul and Barnabas, thinking them gods; and so
unsteady in their opinions, that within a few days, at the insti-
gation of the Jews, they drove from their coasts the very men
who just before had been the objects of their mistaken worship.
Of one or other of these cities Timothy was a native, and it is
not probable that in either of them he could have fallen in with
any of the celebrated Jewish teachers, who were not in the habit
of seeking disciples in distant countries. But he had the advantage, as we know from the Acts, of having a Jewish mother; and
the same thing we may collect from the chapter of the Epistle
from which the text is taken, where St. Paul reminds him of the
faith which dwelt in his grandmother Lois, and his mother
Eunice. To this circumstance he owed the knowledge of the
Holy Scriptures, which he had been taught from his youth; and
it is probable that he had heard them explained by the ruler of
some neighbouring synagogue, for we know from the Acts that
Jews dwelt in those parts, who knew Timothy and his mother.
Such, then, was the instruction from which Timothy had learned, and been assured of those things in which St. Paul exhorts

145

him to continue, as knowing from whom he had learned them. He had learned them as a child from his pious parent; and had been farther instructed in them by the ruler of some obscure synagogue. He had learned them as a child before he could judge of the arguments by which they were supported, yet this is considered by God's inspired Apostle as a reason why he should have the more confidence in their truth. 'Continue thou in the things which thou hast learned and been assured of, knowing of whom thou hast learned them; and that from a child thou hast known the Holy Scriptures, which are able to make thee wise unto salvation.'

Here, then, we have an authority, which cannot be doubted for stating, that in making up our minds on religious subjects, we are not to trust our own impressions alone; that on points of such importance our private judgments are not sufficient to direct us, but that we are to look in another direction for advice and security.

Of course, what we have ultimately to keep in view, is the *truth* of the opinion we embrace; and if we are once positively certain what is the truth, no deference to the judgments of others, or to their authority, can have any influence over us. But what St. Paul tells us is, that in making up our minds as to what *is* true, we are to take into consideration two things independent of our private judgment, viz. what is the doctrine that we have been taught from our youth, and what is taught by those who are authorized to be our religious instructors. And it will be observed, that both of these considerations are as applicable to our case as to the case of Timothy, or any of those whom St. Paul is speaking to. We, as well as they, have authority to appeal to in matters of religion. Instruction has been *appointed* for us just as much as for the Jews and first Christians, by God's own ordinance. The question, who are God's appointed ministers, is not one of any vagueness or uncertainty; it is one in which there is no room for difference of opinion, even among those who differ most widely, as to what God intended us to be taught. Every one admits the truth of the history which records the appointment of Christian teachers, and it is well known that to some among these teachers was committed the authority of ordaining successors to themselves. Nor is there any dispute that there exists in the world a set of men, and only one set of men, who derive their commission to teach religious truth, through an uninterrupted succession of persons themselves similarly commissioned, and deriving their first appointment from the Apostles themselves. Such a set of persons there are in the world, and every body knows and admits that this set of persons consists of those who have been ordained by Christian Bishops as ministers of the Catholic Church. This point is clearly established by history; and its truth is in no way affected by the supposed truth or falsehood of the doctrines which these ordained persons teach.

Here, then, are a set of persons who rest their claims to attention on their *authority*, not on their own personal *qualifications*, nor on the nature of their doctrines. Our speech and our preaching is not with enticing words of man's wisdom, but, as St. Paul's was, in demonstration of the Spirit and of power. People may doubt our wisdom or our sincerity, but they cannot doubt that we are persons, and the only persons, who derive our commission to preach from the Holy Apostles, and through them from our Lord Himself.

On these grounds, then, the ministers of the Church claim some degree of confidence and attention from those whom they are appointed to teach; and they claim it on an authority which cannot be disputed, on the authority of St. Paul's own words.

But though the Ministers of the Church are doubtless God's appointed servants, yet it must be admitted that they are not on this account secure from error; and it is also plain, that they may so far err as to forfeit the claims of their commission: in such a case, then, neither the words of St. Paul nor the general tenour of Scripture can be supposed to demand [for them] continued confidence. Now, the *possibility* of this case is what men take hold of when they justify secession from the Holy Catholic Church, and as it is one which certainly may occur; yet as it is equally plain that men are much too ready to suppose, on light grounds, that it has occurred, it may be profitable to suggest a few considerations which may teach caution on a point of so much importance.

It will be observed, then, that in a case in any way doubtful, when persons feel misgivings about the truth of what they hear at Church, but are not quite certain of the grounds on which they are proceeding, as long as there seems to them a chance that the error may be on their side, and not on that of God's commissioned Ministers, so long the authorized side is clearly the safe side; for, first, there is at least some degree of probability that the truth, if to be found any where, is to be found where God intended it to be sought. God's ministers, though liable to error because they are men, are surely, in some degree, less likely to fall into it, because they *are* God's ministers. It is not to be supposed that He instituted an Order of men for the preservation of the truth, and yet that He so instituted it that it should have no tendency to effect its purpose, but should be just as likely to fall into mistaken notions, as any self-constituted set of teachers who owned no guide but their own judgment.

To suppose this, is not to deem rightly or reverently concerning God and His ordinances; a truer wisdom would be to teach us to believe that whatever could be done to perpetuate a knowledge of the truth, has been done to perpetuate it among God's appointed messengers; and a pious person of any seriousness, or who had any regard for his best interests, would require very strong evidence indeed before he would believe that the truth was to be heard not at Church, but elsewhere.

In a case then where the arguments seem in any way balanced; where there seems nearly as good a chance that one opinion should be right as another; this additional presumption, in favour of what the Church teaches, should be sufficient to decide a prudent man 'to continue in those things which he had been taught and assured of; knowing of whom he had learned them.' Secondly, we may assist ourselves in conceiving the danger of neglecting God's ministers, in matters of religion, by reflecting how we are ourselves affected by similar conduct in our earthly concerns. Suppose then that a master has given certain instructions to his servants previously to his going a journey, and that he has appointed some, whom he trusted, to overlook the rest, and see that the others adhered to his orders: further; suppose that these servants cannot agree among themselves as to what their master intended them to do, but that the upper servants think one thing, and the under servants another, now how will these men act, if they have any regard for their master's approbation? will not the under servants see at once, that in case their superiors happen to be right, themselves will incur far severer censure by disobeying them, than they could possibly do by obeying them if they were wrong? will they not acknowledge at once, that the reason their master set other servants over them was that they should be obedient, and that it will be a far greater offence in them to neglect right orders than to follow mistaken ones.

Indeed in all common concerns, we must have observed that

nothing so much shuts a man out from the sympathy of his neighbours, as the fact that he has got into difficulties by neglecting advice, and determining to act on his own opinion, while ready allowance is always made for those who have been misled by acknowledged principles of prudence.

Now these feelings, which we entertain one towards another in our ordinary concerns, and which common sense sanctions as reasonable, are constantly appealed to by our Lord in His parables, as illustrating the way in which Almighty God regards the actions of His creatures; and hence we may readily conceive how much more leniently He will view the errors which we may fall into by obedience to His Church, than by secesssion from it.

The considerations which have just been presented to you through a parallel case, may be illustrated and enforced by a striking example from the thirteenth chapter of the first of Kings. We there hear of a prophet, who, by a singular and dreadful death, is marked as a monument of God's disapprobation; yet let us reflect what it is that he did to draw down on himself such an awful judgment. Few, perhaps, have read the chapter in which his story is contained, without feeling the thought cross them, as if he had been severely dealt with. His obedience throughout that part of his mission which seemed most beset with temptation, his fearlessness in the presence of Jeroboam when that wicked king would gladly have destroyed him, and after he had executed his commission, his resolute refusal to profit by the terrors which he had awakened, seem to mark him out as a sincere and faithful messenger. 'The man of God said to the king, If thou wilt give me half thine house, I will not go in with thee; neither will I eat bread, nor drink water in this place: for so it was charged me by the Lord.' It seems he was proof against both fear and enticement, and his disobedience at last hardly looks like more than an artless reliance on one who was unworthy of his confidence: The old prophet 'said unto him, I am a prophet also, as thou art, and an Angel spake unto me by the word of the Lord, saying, Bring him back to thy house, that he may eat bread and drink water; but he lied unto him: so he went back with him, and did eat bread in his house, and drank water.'

Such was the crime of the disobedient prophet, and for this a lion met him by the way and slew him. Now if we attend to this narrative, we shall see that his offence consisted in giving credit to one who pretended to be God's messenger, and yet gave no proof of his commission: he believed in what was declared to him, though he did not know of whom he heard it. And this offence was aggravated by the fact, that he did himself know the truth of his own commission, both by the manner in which it was conveyed to him, and the miracle he had wrought in attestation of it.

Thus then he allowed himself to disobey a command which he knew to have proceeded from God, because it was revoked by one claiming a divine commission which he did not prove. He did not 'continue in those things which he knew and had been assured of,' although he did 'know of whom he had learned them.' He chose his teacher for himself, and God has left his fate as a warning how conduct like his will be dealt with among us: excusable as his conduct may appear in our eyes, God, who cannot err, has pronounced his sentence; and 'whether it be right in the sight of God, to hearken unto men more than unto God, judge ye.'

NICHOLAS WISEMAN—who in adult life provided the original for Browning's Bishop Blougram—was born in Seville in 1802, of Anglo-Irish parents, and brought as a child to the cathedral in that city, where he was consecrated to the service of the Church. He was educated at Ushaw College, near Durham, and at the English College in Rome, where his talents obtained him a doctorate at the age of twenty-two. He was ordained deacon in January 1825, and priest two months later.

In 1827 Wiseman published his first book, *Horae Syriacae*, an exposition of a Syrian version of the Old Testament. This won him reputation among oriental scholars, and an appointment as curator of Arabic manuscripts in the Vatican. From 1828 to 1840 he was rector of the English College, and held Leo XII's brief to preach to the English in Rome. Newman and Froude were among the visitors in 1832. Wiseman commented, years after, 'From that hour I watched with intense interest and love the movement of which I then caught the first glimpse.'

He came to England in 1840 as coadjutor to the Vicar Apostolic of the Midland District, and was later himself translated to be Vicar Apostolic of the London District. His essay on the Donatists, published in the *Dublin Review*, drawing a parallel between the Church of England and an early schismatic body separated from the Church in Africa, worried Newman, who referred to it as 'the first real hit from Romanism', and added that it had given him a stomach-ache.

In 1841 Newman published Tract 90, advocating an interpretation of the Thirty-Nine Articles in a sense congruous with the Council of Trent. Wiseman reviewed this sympathetically, but took the opportunity to comment upon what he perceived to be a lack of logic. Wiseman's agility as a controversialist is best examined in the second volume of *Essays on Various Subjects* (1853), which reprints amongst other papers his reviews of Froude's *Remains* and Keble's sermon *Primitive Tradition*.

When Pius IX restored the Roman Catholic hierarchy in England in 1850, Wiseman was appointed cardinal and the first Archbishop of Westminster. His bombastic pastoral letter *From Out of the Flaminian Gate* (7 October) excited hostility in a public already roused by press denunciation of the restored hierarchy as 'papal aggression', and he was burned in effigy— together with the Pope—on Guy Fawkes's night. Wiseman's response was to issue a conciliatory *Appeal to the Reason and Good Feeling of the English People*. After 1855 he had more trouble from the old Catholics, who disliked his ultramontane sophistication, than he had from the Protestant mob. He died in 1865, in London, and was buried in Kensal Green cemetery. In 1907 his body was removed to the newly-built Roman Catholic Cathedral of Westminster, where it now lies beneath a Gothic altar.

BIBLIOGRAPHY

Sermons on our Lord Jesus Christ and on His Blessed Mother, Dublin, 1864.
Essays on Various Subjects, 3 vols., 1853.

THE TWO GREAT MYSTERIES OF LOVE
John 6:11.
And Jesus took the loaves, and when He had given thanks, He distributed to them that were sat down.

FROM INTERNAL evidence we may deduce that this sermon was preached in Rome to English visitors on 25 March, the day of the Annunciation of Our Lady. The place was probably the church of Gesù e Maria. The year would have been between 1828 and 1840, during which period Wiseman had the Pope's special appointment to preach on Sundays from Advent to Easter. He commented later on the character of his audience: 'It was not merely what is called a mixed one . . . . All was educated, learned, somewhat formal, and, perhaps, cold.' It is helpful to keep this in mind in reading *The Two Great Mysteries of Love*.

Wiseman draws his subject from the concurrence, on the day when he is preaching, of the festival of the Annunciation and the Gospel text which has fallen to be read on this occasion—the account of the feeding of five thousand persons with five loaves. The Annunciation calls the Incarnation to mind, and he extends the story of the loaves and fishes to remind his hearers of another miraculous meal: the Eucharist. The mystery of the Incarnation and the mystery of the Eucharist stand together, as the Fathers taught, and may be taken to clarify each other. 'In both,' says Wiseman, 'there is an outward veil, hiding from the eye of flesh a precious and divine deposit, visible only to that of faith.' Faith teaches us of the Eucharist that by the consecration of the priest the substance of the Body and Blood of Christ becomes present under the appearance of bread and wine. (This is to speak of the mystery which the Eucharist is, not of the mysteriousness by which it becomes what it is.) The mystery of the Incarnation is the mystery of God clothed in human nature, or of man enfleshed in the divine. (Those displeased here, as in Archer's sermon, by the word 'mystery', may be glad to know that scholars no longer favour the idea that early Christian apologists borrowed from pagan mystery religions to make Christianity understandable to the Greek world; the current view is that 'mystery' was an ancient Hebrew term of some theological respectability, current in Jewish circles at the time of Christ.) Mystery in Wiseman's sense implies a hidden reality or secret truth which man would not have discovered for himself without divine revelation and which, even after revelation, surpasses human understanding. He points out memorably that the Magi could have been *disappointed* to find at the end of their journeyings 'only a child in a manger'. Yet they managed to adore that child, by raising their belief 'above the range of their senses'. This, he suggests, is what is required of us in acknowledging the Real Presence of Christ in the sacrament of the altar. God on the other hand humbles himself by such a manifold extension of the Incarnation. 'Oh! it is too true that God seems to have made Himself too common .... Had He appointed but one place on earth wherein the adorable sacrifice could be offered, and but one priest who could administer it, what eager devotion would drive crowds of believing Christians to adore at so privileged a place!'

Referring back to the Incarnation, Wiseman reminds us that this also was an act of divine humility inspired as we suppose by love—love being the only constituent we can grasp when we try to consider the nature of the Godhead. Christ did not just 'put in an appearance' in human form. He put himself, as God, into our hands. This was the Incarnation: the supreme communication of divine life to created nature. It is also the Eucharist: the central act of Christian worship, which once more puts God into our hands, and raises our hearts to be heirs of heaven.

Wiseman's English sometimes has a foreign sound—witness the remark about Newman and Froude quoted in my biographical note above, it has an air as of someone translating his feelings from another language into a tongue which does not suit them quite. Yet in the last two paragraphs of this sermon he transcends such limitations and sounds a note of authentic ecumenical intensity in exhorting his audience to concentrate upon restoring 'the belief, the knowledge, the worship of the Blessed Eucharist', urging that other matters of Christian difference of opinion are unimportant by comparison. Since we may take it that few Christians of any complexion have preached the Real Absence of Christ in the Eucharist, and only formal heretics have entertained the thought that the Incarnation was a Real Absence also, then Wiseman on *The Two Great Mysteries of Love* can be found to be preaching as well upon that text in John 17:22: 'That they may be one, even as we are one.'

THERE WERE supposed conjunctions of the heavenly bodies, my brethren, which in ancient times were considered of favourable augury, as promising great blessings to all beneath their influence. And if such speculations were mere vanity, springing only from the foolish fancies of men, you will forgive me, if I own to myself to discover something similar in the peculiar concurrence of two most holy mysteries in the celebration of this day. For, on the one hand, the incident related in the Sunday's Gospel,—the feeding of five thousand persons with five loaves,—and the subsequent discourse thereon held by our Redeemer, forcibly turn my mind to the contemplation of that divine Sacrament, wherein He feeds us in this wilderness with bread truly descended from heaven,—His own adorable Body and Blood. But, at the same time, the festival which has fallen upon this same day, commemorative of the angel's annunciation to Mary, necessarily draws our thoughts to another still greater mystery on that occasion, wrought in favour of man; for no sooner had the spotless Virgin given her consent to the heavenly message, by those blessed words, 'Behold the handmaid of the Lord, be it done unto me according to thy word,' than the Incarnation of the Son of God took place in her womb, through the power of the Most High, and the Word made flesh entered on that course of blessing, which ended in our salvation.

Either of those two mysteries, my brethren, is a rich theme for discourse, but richer still for meditation. Each of them presents to us an act of self-devotion on the part of our dear Redeemer, whereby He gives Himself up unreservedly to us, and makes His own abasement a means of our sanctification. The more they are considered together, the stronger and more numerous the analogies they present, till one seems to be but the natural consequence and accomplishment of the other. Nor is it merely in the fancy of the moderns that this close resemblance between the mysteries of the Incarnation and the Eucharist is to be found. It has been remarked by the wise and venerable teachers of the ancient Church. For not only in matters of controversy regarding one of these mysteries, is the other employed to afford illustration or argument, but they are often compared together by the Fathers, as similar in grandeur, efficacy, and love.

St. Ambrose, after clearly stating that the words of consecration change the bread and wine into the Body and Blood of Christ, as much as Moses changed his rod into a serpent, proceeds to say: 'We will now establish this mystery by the truth itself of the Incarnation. Was the order of nature followed, when Jesus was born of a Virgin? Plainly not. Then why is that order to be looked for here?' (De Initiandis.)

'You believe,' says St. Ephraim, the glory of Edessa and the light of the Eastern Church—'you believe that Christ, the Son of God, was born for you in the flesh? . . . Believe then, and, with a firm faith, receive the Body and Blood of our Lord.' (De Nat. Dei.) In like manner, St. Augustine writes: 'Christ took upon Him earth from the earth, because flesh is from the earth, and this flesh He took from the flesh of Mary; and because He here walked in this flesh, even this same flesh He gave us to eat for our salvation.' (In Psalm.)

In like manner, not to multiply authorities, St. Peter Chrysologus says, that Christ is the bread which, first sown in the Virgin's womb, is finally brought to the altar, to be our daily food. (Serm. lxvii.) St. John Chrysostom compares the altar to the manger, in which Christ lies, not wrapped in swaddling-clothes, but surrounded on all sides by the Holy Spirit, and where we, like the wise men, adore Him. (Orat. de S. Philog.) And a later writer, the Patriarch Dionysius, though belonging to a separated Church, says, that the altar is the symbol of the Virgin's womb, on which the Holy Ghost descends, transmutes the bread and wine, and makes them become the Body and Blood of Christ. (Hor. Syr. p. 58.)

These examples, which might with little trouble have been multiplied, are sufficient to prove, that it is no result of scholastic ingenuity, no fanciful reasoning of modern theology, to discover a marked parallelism and resemblance between the two mysteries, which the circumstances of to-day have brought together before our consideration. Unwilling, therefore, to give up either, I will unite the two; and, after the venerable authorities I have quoted, will endeavour to unfold them, united to your pious contemplation; treating of them both, first as a twofold mystery of humiliation, and as a double mystery of grace. The whole struggle between faith and weak, yet haughty, reason, should, methinks, be directed to the conquest of a very narrow point, which, if faith has won, there remains no further room for contest. All the difficulty of belief should seem to rest upon the admission of only these two words: 'Ecce venio'—Behold I come. And well are they said to have been inscribed by the Eternal Word in the very head, or frontispiece, of the Book, wherein are registered the merciful counsels of God. For they are as a seed, from which fruits of incalculable abundance, as well as sweetness, must spring; they are as the theme from which the richest strains of harmonious music may be developed; they are a summary of deep incomprehensible wisdom, from which a successive series of heavenly truths may be evolved. Nay, if they are but on the first page of that blessed book, there must be much to come after them to fill the volume.

Admit these words, and where will your faith come to an end, or where shall you be able to say, 'I have believed enough'? When the Son of God, the consubstantial to the Father, hath once consented to take upon Him the nature of man, frail, disfigured, and disgraced by sin, it is not, surely, for man's reason to calculate what more He may be impelled to do. After the first step, from the glory of heaven, and the bosom of the Father, into the womb, however pure, of woman, the step from this to the cross, and from the cross to the altar, must seem but as comparatively short in His gigantic career of love. For, whatever may befall His humanity, insults, injuries, torments, death, is but as a mere nothing compared with what He Himself assumed to His divinity.

What is a cross upon the shoulders of the man, compared with the burden of the flesh united to the Godhead? What are blows upon His cheek, or thorns upon His head, compared to the humiliation of feeling, the cravings of human wants in the person of a God-Man? What were nails through His hands, or a spear in His side, compared with the ignominy of submitting to the temptations of the Evil One? What was death compared with the imputation of guilt to which His Incarnation brought Him—yea, of the guilt of the entire world? No; when once that first plunge into the abasement of human nature had been made—when the entire abyss of its misery had thus been absorbed into Himself, the rest must be as mere drops and sprinklings, concerning which a loving heart will not condescend to calculate.

Nay, there seems to be something ungenerous and unkind, in the attempt to establish anything like a proportion between our belief, and our powers of comprehension, or our powers of love, when once we have seen that the very first stride went so infinitely beyond our measurement. There should seem to have been laid in the first mystery of Christ's earthly existence, such a strong foundation of confidence, as would allow a super-structure of any extent and of any mass. There should appear, in His first words, a promise of so much, as should prevent all surprise at whatever might follow in fulfilment. Man should listen to its unfolding wonders, to its tale of love, with the simplicity of a very child, who upon each recital of a marvellous incident, only craves and expects another still more strange, and is only disappointed and grieved when the history is closed.

And, in like manner, when a man with a heart disposed to love, has learnt and believed, that out of affection to him, a God of infinite power and majesty has become a helpless infant, seeming completely as the children of men in a similar condition, yet possessing all the fulness of the Godhead; then that this infant, grown up to man's estate, has died an ignominious death, impelled by the same love, to save him lost, at the expense of His own life—will it any longer seem strange, or incredible to him, that even after these efforts of incomprehensible love, this untiring benefactor had discovered and adopted a new, unheard-of way to complete His scheme of benefits—has submitted to a new act of humiliation, so as to become our food?

It would be, indeed, too inestimable a benefit for him to admit without proof; but against this his heart, at least, would not allow him reason to start objections. For any of us might be called upon to give satisfactory evidence, that an affectionate Father has left him a magnificent legacy, but we shall think it nothing strange or wonderful if we were told that, being able, He had done so.

But the resemblance between the two mysteries of the Incarnation and Eucharist, will bear a closer investigation. In both there is an outward veil, hiding from the eye of flesh a precious and divine deposit, visible only to that of faith. When the wise men came from the East, under the conduct of a miraculous star, there can be no doubt that they were but little prepared for what they were to discover at Bethlehem. The very circumstance of their inquiry at Jerusalem for Him who was born King of the Jews, shows that they expected to find His birth treated as a public event, and His entrance into His kingdom hailed with festivals of joy. Yet they find Herod ignorant, not merely of the occurence, but of the place where it was likely to happen, and obliged to summon the priests to meet their inquiries. What a shock was here to their expectations! Still, encouraged by the re-appearance of the star, they prosecute their journey with undiminished ardour, and arrive at Bethlehem. Their miraculous guide points to a poor dilapidated shed, not likely to be tenanted by any but outcasts of human society; yet, strong in faith, they enter in.

What do they discover? A little babe, wrapped up as the poor-est infant would be, and laid upon a bundle of straw! And is this all that they could have crossed the deserts to see? Is this all that they abandoned their homes and palaces to discover? When they set off from their homes, their friends derided them, perchance, for undertaking so long a journey, and on the guidance of a way-ward meteor, that might abandon them in the midst of some frightful wilderness. Many, probably, thought it little better than madness to go so far in search of a foreign sovereign, only yet an infant. What an account will they have to give on their return of their success, and of the employment made of their precious gifts! Will not their very attendants ridicule them for their credulity, in coming so far to find only a child in a manger? Will they dare to report what they have discovered to Herod? In spite of all such obstacles, which pride must have raised to a simple faith, without any new assurances to encourage them; without any miraculous splendour, round the humble group they have found, to overawe them; without any evidences to convince them, they trust implicitly to the sure guidance of that star, which, having led them safe through all their journey, first to Jerusalem, and then to Bethlehem, they do not conceive like-ly now to turn traitor and mislead them; they prostrate them-selves before that Child, they adore Him, and by their gifts do Him supreme homage, acknowledging Him as their Lord and their God.

If we, then, have in like manner been led by the light of God, through all the obscure paths of faith, shall we hesitate to trust our guides to the utmost? If His word, which told us how His Son became man, and has been believed, tells us no less, that He has assumed another disguise of love, and shrouded His glories still further for our benefit, shall it not be equally believed? If His Church, which hath been our principal conductor through the mazes of early tradition, whereon alone the belief in the Di-vinity of the Incarnate Word can be solidly built, fixing its di-recting ray, in the end, upon that humble tabernacle, assures you, with the same voice that till now you have believed, that therein dwells the God of your souls, your dear Saviour, no longer under the form of flesh, but with that same flesh, in its turn, concealed under the appearance of bread, why will you hesitate to prostrate yourself and adore? If He Himself, of whom reverently we treat, whose words we unhesitatingly receive, when He tells us that He and His Father are one, taking up this

159

bread, solemnly declares it to be His Body, shall we make difference between word and word—reason away the glorious announcement of the one, and not fear that we are weakening the testimony of the other? No; like those eastern kings, we will hush and subdue every suggestion of pride; and if the humiliation of our blessed Saviour in either mystery shocks our sense, let it be honoured the more with a corresponding humility of our hearts.

But if a few, like the wise men and the shepherds, worshipped Him devoutly in the disguise of a child, there were many who, then and afterwards, refused to acknowledge Him for more than He outwardly appeared, a mere man, however privileged. And so should we not wonder, nor should our faith be shaken, if many now refuse to raise their belief above the range of their senses, and admit more to be contained in the Eucharistic species than they outwardly exhibit. For it is easier to abstract from the influence which our senses exercise upon our judgments, when they are not immediately called into use, than where the object of inquiry falls directly under them. Thus we find that the preaching of Christ's Divinity was more easily received from the apostles in distant countries, where His person had not been seen, than in Judea and Jerusalem, where men had been familiarized with His human form. And so may it be that many who, able to use the testimony of their senses in discussing the inquiry concerning the blessed Sacrament, prefer it to every other, would have acted similarly in regard of our Saviour's Godhead, had the same test been within their reach. Contrary to Thomas, they believe because they see not; peradventure, had they seen, they would not have believed.

But all this is only in the course of God's ordinary dispensation. It would seem that the love of our blessed Redeemer towards us, would never be sufficient for His heart, unless, in some way, it involved His suffering. The humiliation of the manger was but preparatory to the humiliation of the cross: and all the intermediate space was filled by privation, poverty and sorrow. He became man, to all appearance, that He might become the reproach of men. And so it is no small enhancement to His graciousness, in thus again abasing Himself in the adorable Sacrament, that thereby, even after returning to His glory, He has remained exposed to the insults and ingratitude of men.

I speak not of those ignorant blasphemies uttered against it by those who believe not, and know not what they do: still less of those frightful outrages which heresy and infidelity, in moments of impious frenzy, have committed. But I speak of our own conduct,—of the treatment which He receives from us who believe. Do you not sometimes think the world must have been stupidly blind to its own happiness and blessing, to have allowed Jesus for thirty years to live hidden in a poor carpenter's cottage, and not to have discovered the jewel it possessed, and begun, much earlier than it did, to enjoy His instructions, witness His example, be benefitted by His miracles, and be blessed by His presence? But there at least was a deep counsel of God that He should lie concealed.

What, then, shall we say of ourselves, who have Him ever in the midst of us, humble, indeed, and retired, yet ever accessible, day and night within the reach of our homage and petitions, and yet do so seldom visit Him, so seldom turn towards Him our eyes or thoughts? The churches, which should be crowded all day with adorers, are comparatively empty; if here, in Rome, what shall we say of our own country? And we seem to make over our duty to the lamps that burn day and night, as our hearts should do, before the altar. Oh! it is too true that God seems to have made Himself too common—that we act as though we thought He had demeaned Himself too low! For, as a devout author observes, had He appointed but one place on earth wherein the adorable sacrifice could be offered, and but one priest who could administer it, what eager devotion would drive crowds of believing Christians to adore at so privileged a place! And even so, it would be nothing more than He formerly did for the ark of His covenant, of settim wood and gold. But now that He has unreservedly made Himself over to us—that He dwells in every part of our cities and in every hamlet, as though but one of ourselves, we pass by the doors of His temples without a thought of Him, we enter them often without respect, we admire them and their riches, but their real treasure we heed not. And would to God, that only in this, our neglect, did Christ suffer from us in this blessed mystery, and not in a way which, in His Incarnation, was spared Him! When, on this day, He descended into the womb of Mary, He found His chosen place of confinement strait, indeed, but pure and holy; He dwelt with one whose heart was entirely His, whose soul was free from every stain, whose desires, whose thoughts were in every respect devoted unto God. But when, in this blessed Sacrament, He comes into our breasts, alas! what does He find? A chamber, perhaps, but lately tenanted by His hateful enemy, sin, ejected thence a few hours before by a hasty repentance. Its paltry furniture is yet in the disorder and confusion which this foe had caused there, bearing on every side traces of the riot and havoc committed within it so long and so late. A few shreds and tattered scraps of virtuous protestations collected together in half an hour, out of the stores of our prayer-books, have been hung around it, to cover its habitual bareness. The remains of many a once precious gift, presents from God's bounty, the torn fragments of contracts of love and promises of service, lie scattered about, patched up for the moment, by its passing fervour. And, perhaps, even in the corners of this den, yet lurk, skulking from His sight, irregular attachments and dangerous affections, which we have not had courage to expel when we turned out His full-grown enemies, but still to His eyes monsters of hateful shape and nature. Into this cell, this dungeon, we invite Him, the King of glory, and have the courage to introduce Him, the living God; and He remembers the first time He visited it, how clean and fair it was, how cheerful and pleasant a dwelling, and how He then decked it out for us with those gifts, and many others, long since broken or lost, or flung away. And we, oh! do not we feel our cheeks burning with shame, when we have thus received Him, to think what He has found within us; and to what a degradation we have dragged the Son of God! What was the hall of Herod, or the court of Pilate, or the house of Caiphas to this? And what, if when He is once there, you are so wretched as to strike and buffet Him by sin? If, as too often happens, on the very day that you have received Him into your bosom, you offend Him: and thus betray Him in your own house to your enemies, while dipping your hand with him into the same dish, and feasting at the same table? Oh, how has our dear Saviour drunk to the dregs the cup of humiliation and self-abasement, that He might enable us to drink of the chalice of His salvation!

If Jesus hath twice humbled Himself so low, it was love that constrained Him. For the moving cause, the active principle of both these mysteries, was affection for us. When John, in the sublime preface to his Gospel, describes to us the Divinity and Incarnation of the Word, he sums it up in these terms: 'And the Word was made flesh, and dwelt amongst us.' Here was a double blessing, in first assuming our human nature, and then retaining it. We frequently read in Scripture of angels appearing to the patriarchs in a human figure. But they merely put on this outward form as a garment, or disguise, which they threw off again as soon as their message had been delivered, and their commission discharged. One might also imagine that it would have been an intolerable hardship to those pure spirits, had any of them, who were sent on such errands to earth, been obliged to retain, for the rest of their existence, that body which they had joined to themselves for the occasion.

In like manner, might not our Saviour have appeared in the flesh to teach and instruct us, or, by some act of graciousness, save us, without assuming it so as for ever to retain it? But His object would not have been thus attained, of dwelling and conversing among men, and truly being as one of us. It was not merely for the one momentary act of redemption that He put on our nature; it was to procure thereby for us that abundance of grace which on every side flowed from His sacred humanity. The excellence of His example, the model of His prayer, His conduct under temptation, His suffering of hardship and distress, His resignation, His obedience and other virtues, would have been lost to us, had He not become truly man, dwelling upon earth. That pleading which His wounds, still open, keep up in our behalf; that light and joy which the presence of His humanity sheds over heaven; that glory which the exaltation of His flesh secures to man; that headship of His Church on earth which He retains; that mediatorship which He holds between His Father and us; these, and many other immense prerogatives, we should not have enjoyed, had He contented Himself with less than the absolute and permanent union of His manhood with His Godhead.

But then, how comparatively short of the object of His great design would the execution have fallen, had but one short visit to earth comprised the whole of His commerce with His new brethren here below? And, still more, what an undue advantage, so to speak, would they have enjoyed over us, whom accidental circumstances brought to live in the same time, and country, with Him. Were they to possess the privilege of touching His sacred body, and we not be allowed to touch even the hem of His garment? Was the woman of Chanaan to be admitted to partake of the fulness of His benefits, and we who are the children of the kingdom, be denied what she ventured to claim—the right of feeding on the crumbs from His table? Was He to place His hands upon the heads of children, some of whom, perhaps, joined in the outcries against Him, and be to us like Isaac, who had no blessing for Esau, when Jacob had anticipated him? Such is one motive assigned by the great Father of the Eastern Church, St. Maruthas, for the institution of the Blessed Eucharist.

No, my brethren, our dear Redeemer was too impartial in His love to treat us so. We who were to come eighteen hundred years too late to enjoy His company in the flesh, had as large and as warm a place in His heart, as they who entertained Him in their houses. It was but natural for us to expect from Him some ingenious contrivance, some institution of almighty love, whereby His sojourn upon earth should be prolonged until the end of time. Even in the Old Law, His presence by visible emblems, which gave assurance and promised mercy, was made permanent in His holy place. While Israel dwelt in the wilderness, His cloud overshadowed the tabernacle; and both there and in the Temple, the Holy of Holies contained a mercy-seat, whereon He sat between the cherubim, to receive the supplications of priests and people. And if this was a figure or symbol of Him, who alone has wrought propitiation for many, was it otherwise than reasonable to expect in that Law, when realities succeeded to shadows, truths to figures, there would be some provision for a corresponding token of God's presence, securing, however, its reality and truth? Such precisely was supplied us in the Blessed Eucharist, in which Christ is with us, our true Emmanuel, ever residing in our sanctuaries. There we may visit Him hourly, and pour our entreaties before His feet, assured of His listening to us with graciousness and sweetness. There we may grieve over our sins, sympathise with His sufferings, and protest to Him our love. And thus does the Sacrament of the altar hourly appear what it is—the full accomplishment of His manifestation in the flesh; the firmly securing to all ages and all places, of one of the greatest blessings of His Incarnation, His 'dwelling amongst us.' It is, indeed, the completing of this ineffable mystery.

Further, the Incarnation of Christ Jesus, was the preparation for redemption; the Eucharist was its application. He became man that, as man, He might suffer and die, and so procure for us all grace, inclusive of eternal salvation. He became our food, that so the remembrance of His passion might be ever kept before us; that His precious blood might be applied to our souls, and that we might be filled with all grace, by contact with its very source and author.

But, finally, the great and true analogy between those two mysteries, consists in the communication made in both of God to man. The love which inspired the Eternal Word to take upon Him our human nature, was in the form of an ardent desire to devote Himself to man—to sacrifice Himself for him. He became one of us, so to acquire an interest in all that concerns us. He gave to us, so far as He could, participation in that divine nature, which He associated to our humanity. He gave us heirship with Himself in heaven. And, after this, He gave up to man, and for man, all that He had acquired, if it could be considered an acquisition—His time, His mind, His strength, His happiness, His blood, His life.

But, then, all these communications and gifts were made to our race in general; and only through their connexion with it, to the individual man. Whatever He thus bestowed, was bestowed upon mankind. Not, however, there would His love rest; but it sought to communicate all this and more, individually and personally, to each of us; and this He accomplished in the Divine Eucharist. But strange as at first sight it may appear, there was a corresponding ardour of desire on the part of man for such a union, traceable among the ruined traditions of heathen superstitions. For, in many countries of the old and new world, did the idea prevail, that by partaking of victims offered to the Deity, man did become actually united and incorporated with Him; and many were the vain follies devised, whereby wiser and holier men were supposed to arrive at a close, and most intimate, union with God. Wherever nature, even in its degradation, has preserved a craving after anything good and holy, we need not be surprised if it be gratified.

And how, in this mystery of love, it is gratified, they who love their Saviour alone can tell. When, with a conscience cleansed by penance, of the lesser transgressions to which all are subject, and a heart at peace with itself, free from rancour, from anxiety, from disturbing fear, they approach their Saviour's feast, they feel their hearts so divided between eagerness and humility, love and a sense of unworthiness, as to tremble, they scarcely know if from hesitation or hope. But, when they have drawn nigh unto the altar, and received the pledge of their salvation, He seems to come into their souls as rain upon the fleece, in calm and sweet serenity. Their hearts are too full for analyzing their feelings; but there is a sense of silent, unalterable happiness —an absorbing overflow of tranquil joy, which disdains the feeble expression of the tongue. The presence of their God is felt with sufficient awe, to depress the soul into humble adoration; the presence of our loving Redeeemer is experienced with an intensity of affection, that burns in the heart, rather than breaks forth into a flame. But this deep paroxysm of heavenly feeling, this foretaste of future bliss, cannot last long, but that the outburst of contending affections must take place. It is as though so many different inmates of the heart, the children of the house, scarce restrained for a time from the presence of a brother they revere and love, at length broke open the door into his presence, and poured forth their tumultuous emotions upon him. There, hope seems to seize upon his strengthening hand, and faith to gaze upon his inspiring eye, and love to bury its face in his bosom, and gratitude to crown his head with garlands, and humble sorrow to sit down at his feet and weep. And amidst this universal homage and joy, of every affection and every power, the blessed Jesus sits enthroned, sole master of the heart and of the soul, commanding peace and imparting gladness, filling with sweetness, as with a heavenly fragrance, the entire being. True, the vision soon dies away, and leaves us to the drearier duties of the day, its burthen and its heat; but the dew of the morning will lie upon that Christian's soul, long after the bright cloud that dropt it hath faded away.

If, my brethren, there were any one point whereon I could concentrate the zeal of every order of men who have our dear country's true interest at heart; if by narrowing the sphere of our exertions, I could hope to increase their intensity, yet so as to neglect no claim, I own that I could turn the thoughts and hearts of all to the restoration of the belief, the knowledge, the worship of the Blessed Eucharist amongst us. I would beg that, comparatively, small stress should be laid upon other matters contested between us and our fellow-subjects; but that every energy of clergy and laity should be devoted to the vindication and adoration of this incomparable Sacrament. Three hundred years of public rejection of its true doctrine as idolatrous; three centuries of privation of the blessings which it alone can bestow upon man, so much written and spoken against the noblest institution of divine love,—these things are a fearful weight upon a nation's soul, not to be expiated but by many tears and much loving reparation by those that believe. Let the laity be ready to concur in every measure that may be proposed for man's public homage, a bolder worship, and a more frequent use of it in our country. Let us, who have dedicated ourselves to its ministry, whose standing-place is by God's altar, consider ourselves the apostles of this mystery of love. Let us be willing to suffer every extremity to promote its honour and glory, and diffuse its benefits among men. Happy they, who having collected thousands to hear them, shall take care not to let them depart contented with their words, but shall send them home nourished with this heavenly bread, divinely multiplied so as to suffice for all, possessing every savour of delight, medicine, food, sweetness, and strength, source of our hope, fuel of our love, security of our salvation, and pledge of a blessed eternity.

NEWMAN LIKED to compare Keble to St Philip Neri. 'This great saint,' he told his sister in 1847, 'reminds me in so many ways of Keble that I can fancy what Keble would have been if God's will had been that he should have been born in another place and age; he was formed in the same type of extreme hatred of humbug, playfulness, nay, oddity, tender love for others, and severity, which are lineaments of Keble.' It is an accurate tribute to a shy, awkward, remarkably unremarkable man, the patron saint of the Oxford Movement.

John Keble was one to whom the new is but the old understood more clearly. He was born at Fairford, Gloucestershire, in 1792, the son of a High Church priest, his family being one of those which has quietly maintained the Catholic faith within the Church of England down the centuries. This background is important. Of the triumvirate who effectively directed the Tractarians, Newman's earliest spiritual experiences were of an Evangelical character, Pusey had professed Whig sympathies, and only Keble *embodied* that Catholic continuity within the English Church which the Movement stressed—the catholicity which had survived the Reformation, passed on through Laud and the Caroline divines, and which, under the Georges, had identified itself mainly with the Non-Jurors. John Keble, in other words, did not need to *acquire* a view of the catholicity of the Christian Church. He inherited it. Newman *learnt* his early Catholicism, even reluctantly, from Froude and from Keble. Later, Keble was to feel as keenly as its author about the bishops' reaction to Tract 90—but he managed not to be driven out of the English Church by this, or by any other adversity.

'If the Church of England were to fail altogether yet it would be found in my parish,' he said once, according to Manning. His biographer Georgina Battiscombe comments:

It was a declaration of faith which might have been uttered by the North Country saint, Bernard Gilpin, or by any other of the many parish priests who, like Gilpin, stayed with their people through all the religious changes and chances of the reigns of Henry VIII, Mary, and Elizabeth I. These men were not turncoats, they were priests who saw the Church not in terms of theories but of souls. The Church was a living, breathing entity, a collection of people, the congregation of the faithful. Part of that congregation lived in their own parish, and it was to that local congregation that their loyalty was primarily due. So Keble knew the Church of England to be alive, knew it beyond doubt or question as a matter of experience.[1]

That the Catholic Church was *one* was second nature to Keble's thinking, and although he loved the man he probably saw Newman's secession as involving the risk of private judgement, and therefore even in some sense a return to Evangelical individualism. The Church in England had faults, and Keble grieved over them as sensitively as anyone, including Newman; at the same time, he felt it the more necessary for her sons to remain where they were, working to eradicate those faults. The introduction to his *Sermons Academical and Occasional* (1847) is an essay in defence of the Catholic faith, and of the duty of English Catholics to remain within the Church of England in a spirit of hope and penitence, while working for reunion with the Holy See, on the basis of full dogmatic agreement, and the healing of the schism of the sixteenth century, to be accomplished when that is the will of God.

Keble imbibed these ideas from his father, who educated him privately until his sixteenth year, when he went up to Oxford, where after a brilliant passage through Corpus Christi he was elected in 1811 to a fellowship at Oriel, being then only nineteen years of age. He was ordained deacon in 1815 and priest a year later. From 1817 to 1823 he was a tutor at Oxford (Hurrell Froude and Robert Wilberforce were among his pupils), but in the latter year he abandoned what had begun as one of the most successful academic careers of the century to retire to the Cotswolds and work as his father's curate. There seems to have been an element of deliberate *choice* of limitations in this decision, as there was in the verses which he wrote at the same time, eventually to be published anonymously in 1827 as *The Christian Year*. This modest collection celebrates the Church as the visible channel of invisible grace. Its aim, Keble declared, was to bring men's thoughts and feelings into line with their prayers, especially as these are given shape by the offices of the Church. Keble had no ambition to publish these verses in his own lifetime, and did so in deference to his father, who was dying. All profits from the book—which enjoyed an unusual success, running through ninety-five editions—were devoted to the restoration of Hursley Church.

In 1831 Keble was elected professor of poetry at Oxford, a chair he held for the next ten years. (His writings in this capacity, *De Poeticae Vi Medica*, 'on the healing power of poetry', are superior to his own poetic practice.) Meanwhile, in the company of Newman and Froude—as well as others such as Isaac Williams, Pusey, Robert Wilberforce and Hugh James Rose—he was growing increasingly aware of the dangers facing the *ecclesia anglicana* from liberal and 'reforming' movements. On 14 July 1833 he preached an assize sermon before the university, entitled *On National Apostasy*. Newman says in the *Apologia* that he always held this sermon—occasioned by the state's proposed suppression of ten Irish bishoprics—to mark the birth of the Oxford Movement. Its text was 1 Sam. 12:23, and it was delivered in the church of St Mary the Virgin, Keble giving voice boldly to indignation at the Church's enslavement by a secularized state.

From this point on, Keble played a leading—if elusive—part in the direction of the Oxford Movement. (The elusiveness derives from his conscious self-effacement.) He collaborated with Newman in the issue of the *Tracts for the Times*, and himself composed numbers 4, 13, 40, 52, 54, 57, 60, 78 and 89, all of them enforcing his awareness of the need for 'deep submission to authority, implicit reverence for Catholic tradition, firm belief in the divine prerogatives of the priesthood, the real nature of the sacraments, and the danger of independent speculation'. In 1836 he published a scholarly edition of Hooker's *Works*, having spent five years preparing it; this remains the standard edition. In 1838, with Pusey and Newman, he began editing the Library of the Fathers, in which he was himself the translator of St Irenaeus. His publication, with Newman, of Froude's *Remains* caused an outburst of Protestant anger in the same year. Tract 89 *On the Mysticism Attributed to the Early Fathers of the Church* (1840-1), also met with hostility, although it can now be seen as one of the most illuminating of all the Tracts. He remained a close friend of Newman's even after the Tracts stopped appearing, for when the storm broke over Tract 90 he confessed his share of the responsibility—pointing out that he had seen and approved the text before publication, and had not changed his mind now because others disliked it.

After 1845 Keble, with Pusey, remained to remind the English Church of its holy past, to continue its Catholic present, and to press for its Apostolic future. In 1857 he published a pamphlet

On Eucharistic Adoration, defending the doctrine of the Real Presence, and advocating the adoration of the sacred species; this has been described as 'one of the most beautiful of his contributions to the treasures of the Church of England'. It is to Keble's credit that he set greater store by such pamphlets than by his verses, the shortcomings of which were known to him. 'I wish,' he said, 'that people, instead of paying me compliments about what they call my poetry, would see if there were not some sense in my prose.' He also had much to do with the project of editing the Library of Anglo-Catholic Theology—and himself spent sixteen years working on a biography of Thomas Wilson, Bishop of Sodor and Man, published in two volumes as a preface to the complete collection of Wilson's works in six volumes as part of that library.

On the death of his father, in 1834, Keble had become vicar of Hursley, near Winchester. For the rest of his life he performed the usual offices of a country priest. He had no ecclesiastical ambitions. He died in 1866 and lies buried in Hursley churchyard.

NOTE

1. Georgina Battiscombe, *John Keble: A Study in Limitations*, 1963, p. 303.

BIBLIOGRAPHY

The Christian Year, 2 vols., 1827.
De Poeticae Vi Medica; Praelectiones Academicae Oxonii Habitae Annis MDCCCXXXII-XLI, 2 vols., Oxford, 1844.
Hooker, Oxford, 1836.
Sermons Academical and Occasional, 1847.
On Eucharistic Adoration, 1857.
Catholic Subscription to the XXXIX Articles, considered in Reference to Tract XC, 1865.
Sermons Occasional and Parochial, 1867.

Primitive Tradition Recognized in Holy Scripture

2 Tim. 1:14.

That good thing which was committed unto thee keep by the Holy Ghost which dwelleth in us.

THIS SERMON, which lasted one and a half hours, and which Keble described to Newman as having been 'thundered out', was preached in Winchester Cathedral on 27 September 1836, and afterwards published with notes in which its theme was illustrated with passages from the Fathers. I have chosen it, rather than the more famous *On National Apostasy*, since it is central to Keble as understood by Newman in the *Apologia*:

> A man who guided himself and formed his judgements, not by processes of reason, by inquiry or by argument, but, to use the word in a broad sense, by authority . . . . What he hated instinctively was heresy, insubordination, resistance to things established, claims of independence, disloyalty, innovation, a critical censorious spirit.

Primitive Tradition is designed to controvert the attitude of those who hold that, whatever may have been the value of tradition in the early Church, while the Canon of the New Testament was incomplete, its place has now been taken by Scripture. This is, of course, the Protestant argument against the authority of the Church. Opposing it, Keble suggests that tradition and scripture are complementary to one another, not antagonistic, that they are indeed so closely related that they may be compared to 'two streams flowing down from the mountain of God' whose 'waters presently became blended' so that 'it were but a vain and unpractical inquiry, to call upon every one who drinks of them to say, how much of the healing draught came from one source, and how much from the other.'[1]

On a deeper level, Keble's sermon deals with another difficulty—Why from the beginning has the Church regarded as essential certain articles of faith for which little or no Biblical authority exists? Newman's answer to this question may be studied in his *Development of Christian Doctrine*. Keble's answer, as set forth here, does not necessarily make a road to Rome. He lays it down that 'new truths, in the proper sense of the word, we neither can nor wish to arrive at', but in place of this 'the

172

monuments of antiquity may disclose to our devout perusal much that will be to this age new.' Newman was an evolutionist, Keble a conservative. That Newman's point of view strikes us as the more in keeping with twentieth-century thought-ways does not make it true. In the Fathers, it could be claimed in support of Keble's opinion as against Newman's, the word *traditio* does not mean something 'handed down' but something 'handed over'.

The question, however, occurs: Did Keble pay sufficient attention to the Church as the *living* Body of Christ on earth? Did he not tend rather to think of it as a divine society which petrified in purity round about the sixth century? It is perhaps significant that he chose to translate St Irenaeus who, writing in the year 180, taught that the law of tradition was most essential to the Church and would suffice for her *if it alone existed*. Compare Keble's own celebrated remark that if the Church of England were to deny herself everywhere else in the land, she would still be found in his parish.

After the Archidiaconal Visitation, when the text of the sermon was printed, someone wrote to Keble thus: 'What a stir you are making in the world! Who would suppose that so quiet and orderly a body was the author of such a combustion?'

NOTE

1. John Keble, Postscript, in *Primitive Tradition Recognized in Holy Scripture*, 3rd. ed., 1837, p. 73.

173

WHATEVER MEN may severally anticipate concerning the final issue of the many anxious discussions which at present occupy the Catholic Church in England, all, I suppose, must feel that for the time they occasion a great perplexity and doubtfulness of mind. We are beset on every side (the clergy more especially) with conflicting difficulties, and temptations to unworthy compromise. That man must be either very confident in the accuracy of his own views, or very highly favoured in respect of clearness of judgment, or very successful in keeping himself out of the way of all controversy, who has not repeatedly found himself at a loss, within the last seven years, on such points as the following:—What are the limits of the civil power in ecclesiastical matters, and how far we may venture in the way of submission without sacrifice of church principle: how the freedom of the Anglican church may be vindicated against the exorbitant claims of Rome, and yet no disparagement ensue of the authority inherent in the Catholic Apostolical Church: again, how the method of voluntary combination, so generally resorted to in our days for important ecclesiastical objects, may be reconciled with entire deference to episcopal prerogative; how CHRIST's ministers may 'study to be quiet,' and yet do their duty as watchmen, and not let their people slumber in the midst of danger; and how they may best unite unwearied meekness in judging, and active Christian love, with strict reserve and timely censure towards every one that walketh disorderly. The time was, not long since, when many of these points appeared to most of us as mere historical curiosities. We felt, perhaps, that they were, abstractedly, of grave importance, but we thanked GOD that our lot was cast in times which required not of us as pastors and stewards in CHRIST's service, any distinct consideration and settled views concerning them. Now things are different: the course of God's providence has permitted the enemies or prompted the defenders of the Church to lay bare her very foundations; and it has become imperative on us all, in discharge of our ordination vows, to make up our minds as well as we can, and endeavour to see our own way, on points which we should gladly, if we might, have taken on trust.

It cannot be safe to shrink from this duty, and say, as many seem inclined to do, that we could bear persecution itself better than the perplexity of considering such things, or the responsibility of deciding for ourselves, and agitating others, concerning them. We have put our hand to the plough, and we must not—

we dare not—look back. It is too late for sworn and ordained priests and ministers in the Church of GOD to dream of drawing back from responsibility. The nature of the case contradicts the very thought. For what responsibility can be more fearful than *his*, who indolently and unthinkingly gives his assent to changes, which, for aught he knows, may prove not only ruinous in the event, but in theory and principle also opposed to the truths and ordinances wherewith CHRIST has put him in trust? Dismissing, therefore, as a snare of our great enemy, the false comfort which many of us, perhaps, are too much inclined to take to ourselves, from a notion that by not interfering we keep ourselves irresponsible, let us see whether the unprejudiced study of those parts of Scripture, which are obviously best suited to our case, may not supply us with a better and more genuine comfort, by furnishing some one clear and unquestionable rule, which may go a good way in guiding us rightly, independent of all results: showing us where our chief responsibility lies, and to which, among interests and duties apparently conflicting, we are bound always to give the preference.

It is natural, in such an inquiry, to turn immediately to the two Epistles to Timothy, especially the last. For, undoubtedly, it must have been to that holy Bishop a time of very great perplexity, when his guide and father in the faith was on the eve of departing from him: the heretics also, as appears from many passages, already beginning to infest the Asiatic churches, according to St. Paul's own prophecy. It appears from the opening of the second Epistle, that when all doubt was taken away as to St. Paul's approaching martyrdom, his affectionate disciple was in danger of being overwhelmed by his sorrow for so great a loss, joined to his sense of the heavy burden which would be laid on himself, now left comparatively alone. To these two feelings in the breast of Timothy the Apostle in his farewell letter addresses himself: remembering, as he says, (iii. 4) the tears which Timothy had shed, perhaps when they had last parted from each other, and longing the more for the satisfaction of seeing him again. In the mean time, there are two words, which he seems studiously to repeat again and again, that he may leave them sounding, as it were, in his disciple's ears, for remembrancers of the two duties most pressing at the moment: 'endure hardness,' and 'keep that committed to thy charge.'

First, with reference to the dejection of mind, by which Timothy was then suffering: 'endure hardness,' says the Apostle, 'as a good soldier of JESUS CHRIST' (ii. 3); 'endure affliction, make full proof of thy ministry' (iv. 5); 'be thou partaker of of the affliction of the Gospel, according to the power of GOD' (i. 8). The drift of all which warnings is the same as where he reminds the Thessalonians, 'When we were with you, we told you that we should suffer tribulation; even as it came to pass, and ye know' (Thess. iii. 4). Affliction, hardness, trial, tribulation, is the very atmosphere of the Gospel ministry: we never had cause to expect any thing else. 'Do not, therefore,' (so the Apostle implies,) 'do not shrink thus over-tenderly from the thought of losing me, which, you now see, comes into your ordained portion of trouble.' 'Be not ashamed of the testimony of our LORD, nor of me his prisoner;' do not carry your affectionate regret so far as almost to cause an appearance of defective faith. Do not take it to heart so very bitterly, as if you in some sort regretted your Christian engagement, finding so much to be borne beyond your expectation; as if you were sorry that you had put so much confidence in me. But, instead of vain regret, take comfort in doing your duty; resort to that fountain of supernatural grace which was opened for you when you were consecrated to be an Apostle. 'Remember that thou stir up the gift of GOD which is in thee by the imposition of my hands. For the SPIRIT which we both of us then received was not a spirit of fear,' of unworthy sadness and cowardice; excessive, unreasonable dejection can be no fruit of it. Such were the tender expostulations and chidings of St. Paul, well beseeming the kindest and most thoughtful of parents recalling his own son in the faith to a manly firmness. Then, in the temper of a noble and true soldier, he propounds his own example, teaches his younger comrade the way of consolation which he found most effectual for himself. 'Because I am ordained a herald and apostle and teacher, I suffer these things: but I am not ashamed, for I know in whom I have believed, and am persuaded that he is able to keep that which I have committed unto him against that day.' And elsewhere, 'I suffer evil, as a malefactor, even unto bonds, but the word of GOD is not bound' (ii. 9). What can be more animating, what more affecting, than to witness a person like St. Paul, full of conscious energy, power, and usefulness, thus devoutly reconciling himself to that which, humanly speaking, would have seemed the most untimely interruption of his labours? It is clear, I think, that even St. Paul found this a severe struggle; but he cheers himself, as in his former imprisonment;

when he wrote to the Philippians, that the taunts of his enemies on his confinement had turned out rather to the furtherance of the Gospel, causing his bonds in CHRIST to be spoken of in the palace of the Caesars, and in all places: so that even those who in speaking of his sufferings meant nothing but envy and strife, did in a manner preach CHRIST, *i.e.* make His Gospel known, and draw popular attention to His Name. Such I take to be the true meaning of that often alleged text; far from conveying the encouragement, which some think they find in it, to irregular and schismatical efforts, but fraught with abundant consolation for those, who being anxious for the Church in evil times, feel themselves precluded from active exertions on her behalf. They can always say to themselves, 'The Word of GOD is not bound: He can make even envy and strife involuntary heralds of His cause.' Their fidelity in acting while they could is rewarded with the assurance of a strong faith, that when *their* work is over, GOD's eternal and glorious work is still in progress, although they cannot see how.

But we dare not take this comfort to ourselves,—we dare not, in those instances where we find the Church bound and fettered, mitigate our regret by exulting remembrance of the expansive inherent force of divine truth,—except we be really, in some tolerable measure, doing our best for her, so far as we are at liberty. The sense of our own responsibility, and of our faithfulness to it, must lie at the root of all true and solid consolation. To this, therefore, as the one thing needful, both for the cause and for himself, the Apostle most emphatically bespeaks his disciple's attention. He loses no opportunity of reminding him of the charge, trust, deposit, which had been left jointly in both their hands, and in the hands of all commissioned as they were. Observe how naturally, with what dexterity of affection, he passes from the mention of his own trust to that of the same trust as committed to Timothy: 'I am not ashamed, for I know in whom I have believed, and am persuaded that He is able to keep my deposit against that day. Hold fast the form,' or, 'abide by the pattern or standard, of wholesome words which thou hast heard from me, by faith and love which is in CHRIST JESUS. That good thing committed unto thee' (literally, the good and noble deposit) 'keep, by the HOLY GHOST which dwelleth in us.' Surely these are words in which we ourselves are concerned, as deeply as he was, to whom they were first written. We are so far in Timothy's case, that we are full of sorrow and perplexity

at the condition in which we find the Church and Body of
CHRIST JESUS: we would fain lay hold of Timothy's and St.
Paul's consolation: let us first see to it, that we neglect not the
warning given. To the companion of Apostles that warning was
plain and simple. The duty imposed on him, paramount to all
others, was simply to keep safe and entire a certain trust committed to his charge; to that one vital object all considerations
of present expediency, temporal comfort, visible, apparent edification, were to give way. What that treasure was, Timothy
could not be ignorant; nor yet could he be doubtful as to the
celestial aid, by which, if not wanting to himself, he would
surely be enabled to preserve it. But in both respects some consideration is requisite, before we of this day can fully apply the
case to ourselves. It is not obvious at first sight, what this trust
or treasure was: nor (of course) whether we are partakers of it:
and even supposing those points settled, there might still remain
a doubt, whether we have the same help for the faithful discharge of our trust, the HOLY GHOST dwelling in us. The consideration of these points in their order may not unfitly employ
us on the present occasion.

1. And, first, as to the exact notion which we are to attach to
the word παρακαταθήκη, 'trust or deposit,' in this place: I observe
that the very use of so general a word with the article implies
that it had been by that time received among Christians as a
term (if one may so speak) of their own, a part of the vocabulary of the holy Catholic Church. A diligent eye may detect, in
St. Paul's Epistles, many traces of the like use of language:
current sayings, or senses of words, or formulae, which the
Apostle only just alludes to, as well known to all his readers. For
instance, the expression, 'This is a faithful saying,' which occurs
repeatedly in these latter Epistles, indicates, in all probability,
so many Christian proverbs, familiar in the mouths of that generation of believers. Thus in the first Epistle to Timothy, we have,
'This is a faithful saying, and worthy of all men to be received,
that "Christ Jesus came into the world to save sinners" ' (i. 15):
'This is a faithful saying, "If a man desire the office of a Bishop,
he desireth a good work" ' (iii. 1); 'This is a faithful saying,
"That therefore we both labour, and suffer reproof, because we
trust in the living God, who is the Saviour of all men, especially
of them that believe" ' (iv. 9, 10). In the second Epistle, 'It is a
faithful saying, "If we be dead with Him, we shall also live with
Him; if we suffer, we shall also reign with Him; if we deny Him,

He also will deny us" ' (ii. 11). And to Titus, after a brief summary of the gospel way of salvation, which by the exact rhythm and order of its members might almost appear to be part of a primitive hymn, St. Paul adds the same clause, 'Faithful is the saying.' From all which I argue, that there was a certain set of 'sayings' current among the Christians of that time, to which any allusion or appeal, however brief, would be presently understood. Nor will it be hard to find examples of single words, which had evidently acquired by that time a Christian sense; so that, even when used absolutely, they could only be taken by Christians in a particular relation: such words, I mean, as τὸ μυστήριον, for 'the scheme of supernatural truth revealed in the Gospel, and more especially in the doctrine of our Lord's incarnation;' ὁ ἐχθρὸς, for 'the evil spirit;' ἡ ὁδὸς, for 'the profession of Christianity.' These, and other examples which might be mentioned, make it surely not incredible, that ἡ παρακαταθήκη, 'the deposit, trust, or charge,' conveyed to Christian ears in those days a peculiar and definite, I had almost said, a technical, meaning.

Now both this word and its kindred term, ἡ ἐντολὴ, 'the commandment,' are mentioned in connection with errors to be avoided in *doctrine*. Thus, Timothy is warned to 'keep the deposit, avoiding profane and vain babblings, and oppositions of science falsely so called' (vi. 20). Again, on mention made of the good confession, made by the same Timothy before many witnesses, at the time of his first calling to eternal life,—which 'good confession' can only mean the Apostles' Creed, or some corresponding formula, recited at baptism,—St. Paul proceeds thus: 'I exhort thee before God and the Lord Jesus Christ, who before Pontius Pilate witnessed a good confession, that thou keep *the commandment* without spot, unrebukable, until the appearing of our Lord Jesus Christ.' Does not this appear as if 'the confession' in the former verse had suggested the caution about 'the commandment' or 'commission' in the latter? and if so, what more probable than that 'the commission' means the same treasure of doctrine which we know to have been embodied in the Confession or Creed?

The interpretation of the noun παρακαταθήκη, 'deposit,' is confirmed by the repeated use of the kindred verb, παρατίθεσθαι, 'to entrust, or commit,' in reference to Christian doctrine. For example, 'This *commandment* I *commit* unto thee, son Timothy, that thou mightest charge some that they *preach no other doctrine*' (i. 18, 3). Elsewhere (a passage which seems to

179

be sufficient alone to warrant the proposed interpretation) Timothy is instructed concerning the things which he had heard from St. Paul, 'before many witnesses,' *i.e.* as it should seem, as a kind of public charge at his ordination:—these he is directed to commit or entrust 'to faithful men, who shall be able to teach others also' (2 Tim. ii. 2). Ability to *teach* is the thing required: it is plain, therefore, that the test related principally to *doctrine*.

Further, it will be observed that the phrase of the Apostle is absolute: *the* trust, not *your* trust; the great trust of all, in which whosoever participates has reason to consider himself especially responsible to the great Judge of heaven and earth. And it is implied that the charge of St. Paul and that of Timothy were one and the same. 'Keep the good deposit,' says the Apostle, 'by the Holy Ghost which dwelleth in us.' Now, what St. Paul's trust was, the trust uppermost in his heart, he himself teaches, exclaiming, 'I have fought a good fight, I have finished my course, *I have kept the faith*' (2 Tim. iv. 7). He does not say, 'I have kept the flock, I have kept those left in my charge;' but, 'I have kept the *faith*, the *truth* of Christ, the *doctrine* of the Gospel. I have watched it, and preserved it entire.' Great as was the holy Apostle's anxiety for the souls which GOD had put under his care, his anxiety for the system of CHRIST, the kingdom of heaven, did at that moment apparently engross him more entirely. And it is clearly probable, that what he felt himself to be the main care, the chief trust of all, that he would recommend to his disciple in such words as those of the text, 'That good thing which is committed unto thee, keep;' especially considering that those words immediately follow a caution which can only relate to doctrinal formulae: 'Hold fast,' as a model for thyself, 'the form of sound words,' the course of healthful, orthodox interpretations and doctrines, 'which thou hast heard of me.' That 'form of sound words,' is it not obviously the same with 'the good deposit' in the next verse.

Thus the context leads to the same exposition which, as we have seen, the parallel passages suggest—an exposition ratified also by the general consent of Christian antiquity. The good deposit is commonly understood by the Fathers to mean the *truths* committed by St. Paul to Timothy. Thus, in the paraphrase ascribed to St. Jerome: 'Watch over the deposit *of the faith*, entrusted to thy keeping by us. What thou hast not heard of me, though it were spoken by an angel, receive it not willingly.' And a venerable father of the third century, Hippolytus, having quoted the expressions, 'O Timothy, keep that which is committed to thy charge,' and, 'The things which thou hast heard of me before many witnesses, the same commit to faithful men,' remarks that 'the blessed Apostle used religious care in delivering these *truths*, which were easily accessible to all.' And Vincent of Lerins; 'Keep,' says the Apostle, 'that which is committed to thy charge: *the Catholic faith*, as a talent, preserve thou inviolate and unalloyed.'

Upon the whole we may assume with some confidence that the good thing left in Timothy's charge, thus absolutely to be kept at all events, was the treasure of apostolical doctrines and church rules:[1] the rules and doctrines which made up the charter of CHRIST's kingdom.

2. The next question to be settled is, whether the precept in the text apply literally to us: *i.e.* in other words, whether we have yet in our possession the identical deposit which St. Paul left with Timothy. For, *if* we have, mere natural piety would teach us to reverence and guard it as he was required to do.

Some will reply to this question at once, We have the Holy Scriptures, and we know for certain that they contain all that is important in Timothy's trust. These would resolve the custody of the good deposit into the simple duty of preserving the Scriptures incorrupt, and maintaining them in their due estimation among Christians. Undoubtedly this would be in some respects the least troublesome, if it could be proved the most correct and dutiful way. But can it be so proved?

We are naturally, if not reasonably, jealous of the word Tradition, associated as it is in our minds with the undue claims and pernicious errors of Rome. Yet must it not be owned, on fair consideration, that Timothy's deposit did comprise matter, independent of, and distinct from, the truths which are directly Scriptural? that it contained, besides the substance of Christian doctrine, a certain form, arrangement, selection, methodizing the whole, and distinguishing fundamentals; and also a certain system of church practice, both in government, discipline, and worship; of which, whatever portion we can prove to be still remaining, ought to be religiously guarded by us, even for the same reason that we reverence and retain that which is more properly scriptural, both being portions of the same divine treasure.

To these conclusions we are led by the consideration, first, that the truths and rules committed to Timothy's charge were at the time almost or wholly unwritten. This is clear from the very date of the Epistles which mention that charge: the latest of which must have been composed many years before St. John's gospel, and in the first of them the deposit in question is spoken of, not as an incomplete thing on its progress towards perfection, but as something so wholly sufficient, so unexceptionably accurate, as to require nothing but fidelity in its transmitters (1 Tim. i. 3; vi. 14. 20). The holy writings themselves intimate, that the persons to whom they were addressed were in possession of a body of truth and duty, totally distinct from themselves and independent of them. Timothy, for instance, a few verses after the text, is enjoined to take measures for the transmission, not of holy Scripture, but of things which he had heard of St. Paul among many witnesses (2 Tim. ii. 2). The Thessalonians had been exhorted to hold the traditions which they had received, whether by word or apostolic letter (2 Thess. ii. 15). They could not be exhorted to hold the Christian Scriptures, since at that time in all probability no Christian Scriptures yet existed, except perhaps St. Matthew's gospel. Much later we find St. Peter declaring to the whole body of Oriental Christians, that in neither of his Epistles did he profess to reveal to them any new truth or duty, but to 'stir up their minds by way of remembrance of the commandment of the Apostles of the Lord and Saviour' (2 S. Pet. iii. 1). St. John refers believers, for a standard of doctrine, to the word which they had heard from the beginning (1 S. John ii. 24), and intimates that it was sufficient for Christian communion if that word abode in them. If the Word, the Commandment, the Tradition, which the latest of these holy writers severally commend in these and similar passages, meant only or chiefly the Scriptures before written, would there not appear a more significant mention of those Scriptures; something nearer the tone of our own divines, when they are delivering precepts on the Rule of Faith? As it is, the phraseology of the Epistles exactly concurs with what we should be led to expect: that the Church would be already in possession of the substance of saving Truth, in a sufficiently systematic form, by the sole teaching of the Apostles. As long as that teaching itself, or the accurate recollection of it, remained in the world, it must have constituted a standard or measure of Christian knowledge, though it had never seemed good to the Almighty to confer on us the additional boon of the books of the New Testament.

It can hardly be necessary to remind this audience, that these scattered notices are abundantly confirmed by the direct and formal testimony of the ecclesiastical writers of the age immediately following the Apostles. As often as Tertullian and Irenaeus have false teachers to reprove, or unevangelical corruptions to expose, do they not refer to the tradition of the whole Church, as to something independent of the written word, and sufficient at that time to refute heresy, even alone? Do they not employ Church tradition as parallel to Scripture, not as derived from it? and consequently as fixing the interpretation of disputed texts, not simply by the judgment of the Church, but by authority of that HOLY SPIRIT which inspired the oral teaching itself, of which such tradition is the record. Their practice is throughout in accordance with the following sentence of Irenaeus:—'We ought not to be still seeking among others for the truth, which it is easy to receive from the Church; since therein, as in a rich depository, the Apostles did most abundantly lodge all things appertaining to the truth: so that whoever will, may receive from her the waters of life. For the Church is the entrance to life: all the rest are but thieves and robbers . . . . And what if the Apostles themselves had left us no Scriptures? Ought we not to follow the course of tradition, such as they delivered it to those whom they entrusted with the Churches? Which rule is followed by many nations of the barbarians, those I mean who believe in Christ, without paper or ink, having salvation written in their hearts by the Spirit, and diligently keeping the old tradition.' Then having recited the substance of the Apostles' Creed as a specimen of that tradition, he adds, 'this faith those who without letters have believed, in respect of our language are indeed barbarians, but in respect of their views, habits, and conversation, have attained by faith a very high measure of illumination, and please God, walking in all justice, chastity, and wisdom. And if any one should relate to them in their own language the new inventions of the heretics, they would presently shut their ears and escape as far as possible, not enduring so much as to hear the profane discourse.' This noble passage I the rather quote, because it shows that the case which was just now put, of persons left without the Scriptures to depend on tradition alone, is not a mere dream of imagination, but at that time actually existed in some parts of the Christian world. There were instances, it seems, known to Irenaeus, of true believers who did not as yet know any thing of the New Testament, yet were able to stop the mouths of heretics by merely avouching the ancient apostolical tradition. As was the condition, duty, and privileges, of those faithful and simple men, such would have been those of the whole Christian world, had the inspired Scriptures either remained unwritten, or perished with so many other monuments of antiquity. Faith in those divine truths with which the Church was originally entrusted would still have been required at the hands of Christian men; but the task of ascertaining those truths would have been far harder and more delicate. Now that it has pleased our gracious GOD to bestow on us, over and above, the use of His written word, can we be justified in slighting the original gift, on pretence of being able to do without it? Surely, in whatever respect any tradition is really apostolical, to think lightly of it must be the same *kind* of sin, as if those unlearned and remote Christians, of whom Irenaeus speaks, had thought lightly of the New Testament when it came to be propounded to them. We see at once in what manner sincere reverence for GOD's truth would lead them to treat the portions of His *written* word, as they were brought successively under their notice. If we will be impartial, we cannot hide it from ourselves, that His *unwritten* word, if it can be any how authenticated, must necessarily demand the same reverence from us; and for exactly the same reason: *because it is His word*.

But, further: the fact is clearly demonstrable from Scripture, that as long as the canon of the New Testament was incomplete, the unwritten system served as a test even for the Apostles' own writings. Nothing was to be read, as canonical, except it agreed with the faith delivered once for all to the first generation of the saints. The directions of St. Paul on this subject are perfectly clear, and without reserve. 'Though we or an angel from heaven preach any other Gospel unto you than that which we have preached unto you, let him be anathema.' And St. John, in his Epistles, strikes continually on the same chord. His language sounds like an emphatical protest against any suspicion of novelty or originality in his teaching. 'Brethren, I write no new commandment unto you, but the old commandment which ye had from the beginning. The old commandment is the word which ye heard from the beginning.' He writes to them as to persons knowing the truth; knowing all things; not needing that any man teach them. He forbids their acquiescing without trial in any pretensions to spiritual gifts: he would have the spirits tried, whether they be of GOD, whatever their claim to be confirmed even by miracle; and the test or touchstone which he recommends is, agreement with the orthodox doctrine of the Incarnation. 'Every spirit that confesseth that Jesus Christ is come in the flesh, is of God; and every spirit that confesseth not that Jesus Christ is come in the flesh, is not of God' (S. John ii. 7. 20, 21. 27; iv. 1. 3). And his second Epistle speaks just the same language: 'Whosoever transgresseth, and abideth not in the doctrine of Christ, hath not God; he that abideth in the doctrine of Christ, he hath both the Father and the Son' (2 S. John 9).

I do not see how we can be wrong in inferring, from these and similar passages, that the faith once for all delivered to the saints, in other words, Apostolical Tradition, was divinely appointed in the Church as the touchstone of canonical Scripture itself. No writing, however plausible the appearance of its having come from the Apostles, was to be accepted as theirs, if it taught any other doctrine than what they at first delivered: rather both it and its writers were to be anathema.

This use of apostolical tradition may well correct the presumptuous irreverence of disparaging the Fathers under a plea of magnifying Scripture. Here is a tradition so highly honoured by the Almighty Founder and Guide of the Church, as to be made the standard and rule of His own divine Scriptures. The very writings of the Apostles were to be first tried by it, before they could be incorporated into the canon. Thus the Scriptures themselves, as it were, do homage to the tradition of the Apostles; the despisers, therefore, of that tradition take part, inadvertently or profanely, with the despisers of the Scripture itself.[2]

On the other hand, it is no less evident that Scripture, being once ascertained, became in its turn a test for every thing claiming to be of Apostolical Tradition. But on this part of the subject there is the less occasion to dwell, it being, I suppose, allowed on all hands. Only it may be well to notice a distinction not always sufficiently kept in view by modern writers on the rule of faith; viz. that whereas Scripture was from the beginning appealed to, of course, as a test of *positive* truth, it could only then be appealed to *negatively*, i.e. its silence could then only be quoted as excluding any point from the list of truths necessary to salvation, when itself had attained a certain degree of completeness. And this perhaps may be one reason why the doctrine of the sufficiency of Scripture is nowhere expressly affirmed in Scripture itself. The character which our Article justly assigns to the Bible, of 'so containing all things necessary to salvation, that whatsoever is not read therein, nor may be proved thereby, is not to be required of any man that it should be believed as an

article of faith, or be thought requisite or necessary to salvation:'
—this character the Bible could not, from the very force of the
terms, acquire, until a sufficient portion of its contents had
appeared, to include in one place or another every one of such
fundamentals. Nor are we sure of this condition having been fulfilled until the appearance of St. John's Gospel and first Epistle,
the latest, probably, of those canonical Scriptures of whose
authority was never any doubt in the Church. This consideration
may serve to account for the comparative rareness of quotations
from the New Testament in the writings of the first century; in
the Epistle of St. Clement, for instance, who, while he produces
in almost every paragraph some testimony from the Jewish Scriptures, has only three or four references to the New Testament:
where such might be expected, he rather uses to remind men of
'the depths of divine knowledge, which they had looked into;'
of 'the immortal knowledge, whereof they had tasted;' and of
the apostolical examples which they had seen. Whereas the writers of the following age, Irenaeus, Tertullian, and the rest, add
to the argument from tradition, on which in itself they lay as
much stress as St. Clement, authorities and arguments from the
New Testament, much in the manner of controversialists of
our own time.

From all this I gather, that in the interval between Clement
and Ignatius on the one hand, Irenaeus and Tertullian on the
other, the canon of the New Testament had first become fixed
and notorious, and then the fact had been observed, which is
stated in our Article: That every fundamental point of doctrine
is contained in the unquestioned books of that canon, taken
along with the Hebrew Scriptures. And this observation, being
once made, would of course immediately suggest that golden
rule, not of the Anglican only, but of the Catholic Church; That
nothing is to be insisted on as a point of faith necessary to salvation, but what is contained in, or may be proved by, canonical
Scripture. At any rate it is unquestionable that by the time of
Irenaeus, *i.e.* towards the end of the second century, the fact
had been universally recognized, and the maxim thoroughly
grounded and incorporated into the system of the Catholic
Church.

Reserving thus the claim of Scripture to be sole and paramount as a rule of faith, we may now, I think, venture to assume,
from the nature of the case, the incidental testimony of Scripture, and the direct assertions of the Fathers, that it was an

unwritten system which the holy writers spoke of, when they so earnestly recommended the deposit, the commandment, the word heard from the beginning, to the reverential care both of pastors and of all Christian people.

Will it be said, 'This is no concern of ours; it may be true in fact, but it yields no practical result; the traditionary system, whatever it was, having long ago passed away, except so far as it has been preserved in inspired writings?' This may be stated, and often is so, but can hardly be proved.

For in the first place, as long as it is only doubtful whether any statement or precept is part of the Apostolic system or no, so long a mind imbued with true devotion will treat that statement or precept with reverence, will not rudely reject or scorn it, lest he refuse to entertain an angel unawares. So long, the mere fact of its not being contained in Scripture cannot be felt as a justification for casting it aside, any more than we should venture to disparage it on account of its not being revealed in any particular *book* of Scripture, which we might happen to value above the rest. Although not in Scripture, it may yet be a part of *their* rule, concerning whom the SON of GOD has declared, 'He that heareth you, heareth ME; and he that despiseth you, despiseth me.'

But in truth it may be proved to the satisfaction of any reasonable mind, that not a few fragments yet remain, very precious and sacred fragments, of the unwritten teaching of the first age of the Church. The paramount authority, for example, of the successors of the Apostles in Church government; the threefold order established from the beginning; the virtue of the blessed Eucharist as a commemorative sacrifice; infant Baptism; and above all, the Catholic doctrine of the Most Holy Trinity, as contained in the Nicene Creed. All these, however surely confirmed from Scripture, are yet ascertainable parts of the primitive, unwritten system, of which we yet enjoy the benefit. If any one ask, how we ascertain them; we answer, by application of the well-know rule, *Quod semper, quod ubique, quod ab omnibus*: Antiquity, Universality, Catholicity: tests similar to those which jurists are used to apply to the common or unwritten laws of any realm. If a maxim or custom can be traced back to a time whereof the memory of man runneth not to the contrary; if it pervade all the different courts, established in different provinces for the administration of justice; and, thirdly, if it be generally acknowledged in such sort, that contrary decisions have been disallowed and held invalid: then, whatever the exceptions to it may be, it is presumed to be part and parcel of our common law. On principles exactly analogous, the Church practices and rules above mentioned, and several others, ought, we contend, apart from all Scripture evidence, to be received as traditionary or common laws ecclesiastical. They who contend that the very notion of such tradition is a mere dream and extravagance; who plead against it the uncertainty of history, the loss or probable corruption of records, the exceptions, deviations, interruptions which have occurred through the temporary prevalence of tyranny, heresy, or schism; must, if they would be consistent, deny the validity of the most important portion of the laws of this, and of most other old countries.

It is not, therefore, antecedently impossible that a system of tradition, subsidiary to the Scriptures, might yet exist in the commonwealth or city of GOD. The rest is matter of investigation in each case, whether any given rule, interpretation, or custom, be traditionary in the required sense. But it will not be going too far into particulars, and may help to the understanding and application of the whole argument, if I point out three distinct fields of Christian knowledge, in neither of which can we advance satisfactorily or safely without constant appeal to tradition, such as has been described.

The first is, the *System and Arrangement of fundamental Articles*, so far as they have come down to us systematic and arranged. We, that is all of the Anglican Church who have had any regular training in theology, are so early taught to trace the Creed in the Scriptures, and to refer at once certain portions of both Testaments to certain high mysteries of the Catholic faith, that it commonly appears to ourselves as though we had learned those mysteries directly from the Scriptures. But there are few, surely, who on careful recollection would not be compelled to acknowledge that the Creed, or some corresponding catechetical instruction, had prepossessed them with these truths, before ever they thought of proving them from Holy Writ. I need hardly remind you of the unquestioned historical fact, that the very Nicene Creed itself, to which perhaps of all *formulae* we are most indebted for our sound belief in the proper divinity of the SON of GOD—even this Creed had its origin, not from Scripture, but from tradition. The three hundred Bishops who joined in its promulgation did not profess to have collected it out of the Bible, but simply to express the faith which each of them had found in the Church which he represented, received by tradition from the Apostles. Nor is this any disparagement to Scripture, nor need it excite any alarm for the great fundamental verity itself, which the Creed was meant to assert; any more than it would disparage the works of God, or shake the foundation of our faith in natural religion, were one to affirm that the power and Godhead of the Creator, although unquestionably provable from the things which are made, would yet have remained unknown to the mass of mankind, but for primitive tradition, or subsequent revelation of it.

The second great subject on which most of us are unconsciously indebted to the ancient Catholic tradition, is the *Interpretation of Scripture*, especially those parts of which less obviously relate to the mysteries of the Gospel. Catholic tradition bears upon Scripture interpretation, not only indirectly, by supplying, as just now stated, certain great landmarks of apostolical doctrine, conformably to which the written statements are all to be interpreted; but also, in numerous cases, directly; setting the Church's seal, as it were, upon one among many possible expositions of particular passages. For example: how else could we know, with tolerable certainty, that Melchisedek's feast is a type of the blessed eucharist?[3] or that the book of Canticles is an allegory, representing the mystical union betwixt CHRIST and his Church?[4] or that Wisdom, in the book of Proverbs, is a Name of the second Person in the Most Holy Trinity?[5] All which interpretations, the moment they are heard, approve themselves to an unprejudiced mind, and must in all likelihood have come spontaneously into many readers' thoughts. But it may be questioned whether we could ever have arrived at more than a plausible conjecture regarding them, but for the constant agreement of the early Church, taking notice every where, in these and the like instances, of the manner in which the Old Testament was divinely accommodated to the wonders of CHRIST's religion.

The third great field of apostolical tradition lies among *practical* matters, the *Discipline, Formularies*, and *Rites* of the Church of CHRIST: in regard of which, reason tells us that the Church Apostolical must here have had *some* method and system; yet it is evident to the very eye that the New Testament exhibits no such system in form, but only fragments and other indications of one in full operation at the time, and well known

189

to those for whom the Apostles were writing. These fragments being found to coincide with similar but more copious indications in later Church records; consideration also being had of the religious reverence wherewith in those ages every thing primitive was regarded, and of the charitable jealousy of the Churches, watching each other for the purpose of remonstrating against unwarrantable deviations; we need not fear to accept in its fulness, on all such matters, the well-known rule of St. Augustin, which I give in the words of Hooker: 'Whatsoever positive order the whole Church every where doth observe, the same it must needs have received from the very Apostles themselves; unless, perhaps, some general council were the authors of it.' In this kind no one at all versed in Church history can be at a loss for examples of the benefit which the present Church derives from the chain of primitive tradition. Without its aid, humanly speaking, I do not see how we could now retain either real inward communion with our LORD through his Apostles, or the very outward face of God's Church and kingdom among us. Not to dwell on disputable cases: how, but by the tradition and practice of the early Church, can we demonstrate the observance of Sunday as the holiest day, or the permanent separation of the clergy from the people as a distinct order? or where, except in the primitive Liturgies, a main branch of that tradition, can we find assurance that in the Holy Eucharist we consecrate as the Apostles did, and, consequently, that the cup of blessing which we bless is the communion of the blood of CHRIST, and the bread which we break the communion of the body of CHRIST?[6]

Whether, then, we look to Discipline, to Interpretation, or to Doctrine, every way we see reason to be thankful for many fragments of apostolical practice and teaching, most needful to guide us in the right use of Holy Scripture.

So it is, however, that either from impatience of authority, or dislike of trouble, or excessive dread of Romish error, tradition has become to most of us an unpalatable word, and we love not to allow that in any sense we rest our faith and practice upon it. And, as commonly happens when the mind is first made up, and reasons are to be found afterwards, objections the most contradictory are brought to justify this our determined disregard of antiquity. Sometimes it is urged that the matters involved are so many, so intricate and various, and demand such minute research, that it is out of the question bringing them within the reach of the great body of the clergy, however learned; sometimes, on

190

the contrary, it is maintained, that the points agreed on in the whole ancient Church are obviously so few, there have been such constant discussions and waverings of opinion, that after all there is no such thing as primitive Catholic tradition; what is called such being merely the register of the dictates of that which has proved, on the whole, the strongest and most fashionable party in the Church. The one statement makes the field so wide, that it is impossible not to lose one's way in it; the other so contracted, that occupying it is no advantage. It is obvious that both objections cannot stand together; and as might be expected, the truth lies between the two. On the one hand, we are not to imagine that every usage which has prevailed in any part of the Church, every opinion which has been upheld even among orthodox Fathers, claims to have been part of the system of the Apostles. On the other hand, we cannot surely deny such claim to those rules, in which *all* primitive Councils are uniform, those rites and formularies which are found in *all* primitive Liturgies, and those interpretations and principles of interpretation in which *all* orthodox Fathers agree; more especially when they produce them as undoubted and authoritative. Now the genuine canons of the primitive Councils, and the genuine fragments of the primitive Liturgies, are reducible into a small space; even although we go so low down in both as the division of the Eastern and Western Churches, including the six first Councils general, and excluding image-worship and similar corruptions by authority. As far, therefore, as the Councils and Liturgies are concerned, tracing the remnant of apostolical tradition need not prove such a very overwhelming task. To establish consent among the Fathers is, doubtless, a far more laborious process; easiest, however, where it is most desirable, *viz.* in the great points of faith and worship, as recurring continually, and implied in all other discussions. What remains is chiefly interpretation of Scripture; a precious, inexhaustible mine of primitive knowledge, to such as have the zeal to explore it, but not essential to the fixing of the main outlines. Leaving out, for the present, all such incidental discussions, and confining our view to that which touches the foundation, we shall find that the matters are neither few nor unimportant, which are settled by traditionary evidence within reach of common students. Were they much fewer than they are, and less important, still, as unquestionable relics of the Apostles, a devout and thoughtful mind would prize them for their authors' sake, and for the sake of the lost treasure, whereof they are portions. To forget and disparage them, would be a hard and unnatural thing, like coldly refusing due reverence to the dead. As it is, by the gracious Providence of Almighty GOD, the points of Catholic consent known by tradition constitute the knots and ties of the whole system; being such as these: the canon of Scripture, the full doctrines of the Trinity and Incarnation, the oblation and consecration of the Eucharist, the apostolical Succession; truths and orders soon enumerated, but such as to extend in vital efficacy through every part of the great scheme of the Church. What, then, if the Church in our time, for the sins of Christians, should have lost more or less of 'that good thing,' the perfect apostolical body of government, doctrine, and sacramental grace, committed to St. Paul first, and by him to Timothy? It is not the less our duty, and by GOD's grace we will regard it as our high privilege, to keep unwearied watch over what remains, and to preserve it, 'by the HOLY GHOST which dwelleth in us.'

3. These concluding words, while they supply an additional reason for extreme jealousy of our precious apostolical relics, open to us the appointed way of guarding what remains, and if one might be so happy, of recovering more: a way not our own, but strictly and properly supernatural. And thus we are conducted to the final point of our enquiry. Whether we, the existing Ministers of the Church, have the same grace dwelling in us, by which Timothy was exhorted to maintain his trust.

Now certainly the obvious meaning of the text is, that the treasure of sound doctrine was to be guarded by the grace of the apostolical succession. For St. Paul speaks of the HOLY GHOST dwelling *in us; i.e.* in himself and Timothy: and how it had passed from him to Timothy had been expressed a few verses before; 'I will that thou stir up the grace of God which is in thee by the imposition of my hands.' The Church of England, you will remember, supplies full warrant for this interpretation; by directing the same phrase to be solemnly repeated at the consecration of every Bishop: 'Remember that thou stir up the grace of God *which is given thee by this imposition of our hands;'* and also where, in ordaining a Bishop or Presbyter, the solemn words are spoken, 'Receive the Holy Ghost.' Our Church, therefore, does not teach us to consider the HOLY GHOST dwelling in St. Paul and Timothy as properly miraculous, a gift of extraordinary grace; but as their portion of that SPIRIT which was to be poured out on all Apostles and successors of the Apostles, for ever. It was not what is commonly called miraculous; yet it was altogether supernatural. For no natural or acquired virtue or talent, though it might be called the *gift* of the HOLY GHOST, would ever be designated as the HOLY GHOST himself abiding in a man. Neither was it the preventing or assisting grace, common to all Christian persons; for it was given to Timothy in particular by imposition of St. Paul's hands. It could only be, what the Church interprets it, apostolical or episcopal grace.

Apostolical, then, or episcopal grace is by GOD's ordinance the guardian of sound doctrine; the SPIRIT abiding in Timothy is to watch incessantly the deposit or trust of divine truth left in his charge: and where the one, the succession, fails, there, as this verse should lead us to expect, and as all Church history proves, the other, the truth of doctrine, is immediately in imminent jeopardy.

Here, then, we seem to have arrived at one cardinal point at least, whereby we may shape our course in times and emergencies more than usually perplexing. We are to look before all things to the integrity of the good deposit, the orthodox faith, the Creed of the Apostolical Church, guaranteed to us by Holy Scripture, and by consent of pure antiquity. Present opportunities of doing good; external quietness, peace, and order; a good understanding with the temporal and civil power; the love and co-operation of those committed to our charge;—these, and all other pastoral consolations, must be given up, though it be with a heavy heart, rather than we should yield one jot or one tittle of the faith once delivered to the Saints.

And whereas the dangers to that faith vary according to the differences of times, interests, and opinions; and sometimes the scriptural, sometimes the traditionary safe-guards of it appear to be more immediately threatened; both must be watched with jealous and impartial care, since comparative neglect of either is sure to be attended with ill consequences to both. Thus the reverence of the Latin Church for tradition, being applied unscrupulously, and without the necessary check from Scripture, to opinions and practices of a date comparatively recent, has led a large portion of Christendom to disuse and contempt, not of Scripture only, but of that real and sure tradition, which they might and ought to have religiously depended upon. On the other hand, is there not reason to fear that the Holy Scriptures

193

themselves are fast losing reverence, through the resolute defiance of tradition, which some affect, in conformity, as they suppose, with the maxim, that the Bible only is the religion of Protestants? Surely it is no rare nor unnatural result, if such as are trained to this principle, being left, as some one has said, alone with their Bibles, use their supposed liberty of interpretation, first in explaining away the mysterious meaning, and afterwards in lowering or evading the supernatural authority, of the very Scriptures which at first they deferred to exclusively. And no wonder; since among the traditionary truths which they are taught to undervalue is the canon of Scripture itself, and the principle also, that fundamental articles of belief must be sought for in Scripture. In short, the sacred building is so divinely, though invisibly cemented, that for aught we know it is impossible to remove any portion, either of scriptural or traditionary truth, without weakening the whole arch. We, to whom the whole is committed, under the most solemn of all pledges, and with the actual gift of the all-sufficient SPIRIT to aid us in redeeming that pledge; let us, above all things, beware of the presumption of selecting for ourselves among the truths and laws of the Most High, *which* we will retain, and *which* we may venture to dispense with.

In the next place, let us beware of Novelty: novelty, I mean, as compared with the apostolic age; not the mere appearance of novelty as compared with the current notions of our time. For it is self-evident that if in any age or country any portion of apostolical truth be lost, whenever it is revived it must for the time look new; and its maintainers will have to contend with the prejudice which constantly waits on the disturbers of things established. Not novelty, therefore, relative to us, but novelty relative to the primitive and original standard, is the thing above all to be deprecated in the whole of theology, by whatever plausible air of originality, ingenuity, completeness, it may seem to recommend itself.

Observe under what a fearful penalty, in a warning parallel to that of the text, St. Paul, writing to the Thessalonians, discourages every intrusion of speculative doctrine. The apostacy, he tells them, will come; the wicked one shall be revealed, actuated by Satan to deceive them that perish; 'on whom God will send strong delusion, that they may believe a lie.' And then he proceeds, 'Wherefore, brethren, stand fast, and hold the traditions which ye have been taught, whether by word or our epistle.' Is not this equivalent to saying, that whoever is studious of novelty

194

in religion is in a way to take part with Antichrist; that the only security against him, and the spirit which prepares the way for him, is to hold the apostolical doctrine, whether taught in word or in writing; and to exclude all additions, however tempting to human ingenuity and love of system, however acutely they may appear to be reasoned out, and to fall in with allowed principles?

Had this rule been faithfully kept, it would have preserved the Church just as effectually from transubstantiation on the one hand, as from the denial of CHRIST's real presence on the other hand. The two errors in the original are but rationalism in different forms; endeavours to explain away, and bring nearer to the human intellect, that which had been left thoroughly mysterious both by Scripture and tradition. They would both turn the attention of men from the real life-giving miracle to mere metaphysical and grammatical subtilties, such as our fathers never knew.

Observe, again, the phraseology of the Apostle, how it is formed throughout upon the supposition that in the substance of the faith there is no such thing as improvement, discovery, evolution of new truths; none of those processes, which are the pride of human reason and knowledge, find any place here. Here the one thing needful is to '*retain* the mystery of the faith;' to '*abide* in the good instruction whereto we have already attained;' to teach no *other* doctrine, to be on our guard against those who resist the truth under pretence of 'proceeding further,' assured that such, although they seem to be 'ever learning,' shall never be able to 'come to the knowledge of the truth;' they will '*proceed*' indeed, but it will be from bad to worse (1 Tim. iii. 9; iv. 6; i. 3. 2 Tim. iii. 7. 9. 13). All these cautions, and others no less fearful, the HOLY SPIRIT has left for our admonition, directed not against any positive wrong opinion, but in general against the fatal error of treating theology like any human science, as a subject in which every succeeding age might be expected to advance on the former.

Nor is the warning less important, nor the application to our times less certain, where Timothy is enjoined to 'keep that committed to his charge, turning away from profane, empty verbal discussions, and oppositions of knowledge falsely so called' (1 Tim. vi. 20, 21). The allusion was probably in the first instance to the low-minded empirical system of the Gnostics. But the words are not much less appropriate to that which may be called the *Nominalism* of our days; I mean the habit of resolving the high mysteries of the faith into mere circumstances of language, methods of speaking adapted to our weak understanding, but with no real counterpart in the nature of things. Whoever takes this line must needs hold the tradition of antiquity cheap, since it is based altogether on the supposition which he rejects as unphilosophical. Thus slighting tradition, and explaining away Scripture, there is no saying what pernicious heresy such a theorist may not fall into, if not happily guarded against himself by feelings and prejudices more reasonable than all his reasoning. Meantime, the warning of Scripture is express: that they who 'profess' such things may be expected to 'err concerning the faith.' And it is plain that if at any time either the high places of the Church, or the schools of theological knowledge, should be left in such keeping, the guardians of the good deposit would be bound to direct especial attention that way, and not permit things to pass away, as in a dream, before men are aware.

This leads directly to the recollection of a third danger, to which the Church seems especially exposed at this moment; I mean, that which is commonly entitled *Erastianism*; the Church betraying to the civil power more or less of the good deposit, which our LORD had put exclusively into her hands. This is a form of compromise with the world, for which no occasion was given by the circumstances of the Apostles: a trial peculiar to times like ours, when the governors of the world profess to have become the servants of our LORD and of HIS CHRIST. We cannot therefore look in the New Testament for literal instruction how to behave with regard to this delicate and dangerous part of our duty. The Gospel affording no express rules or precedents, we are thrown first upon the many analogous cases which the inspired records of the Jewish history supply; and then upon the conduct and determinations of the Catholic Church, in those centuries of her establishment during which the primitive system existed in something like integrity, to guide her demeanour in her altered condition. Yet, undoubtedly, the general rule, Keep the deposit, affects our relations to the civil authorities more immediately than persons unversed in Church matters might imagine. If we are to understand by 'the deposit,' the faith once for all committed to Christians; and if the apostolical succession be the appointed guard of that faith; and if the charter of the succession, 'As my Father hath sent me, even so send I you,' convey the power of Church government as well as that of administering sacraments; then every undue sacrifice of the power of Church government to any earthly power is an infringement of the charter, and renders the deposit of the faith less secure. For the sake therefore of the very foundation of sound doctrine, and not only for the sake of peace and order in the Church, ecclesiastical government, as well as the custody of the Sacraments, should be jealously reserved in those hands to which CHRIST originally entrusted it. Nor do I see how it can be less than a sacred duty, however painful, and to human eyes unavailing, to protest, if we can do no more, against unauthorized intrusions on Church government, as every one will readily allow we ought to protest against unauthorized administration of Sacraments.

Such being the object for which we are set in defence, and such the enemies with whom we have to contend; such also the heavenly Assistant, dwelling in us and fighting on our side; it cannot be hard to perceive with what dispositions we ought to address ourselves to that holy warfare. It will not do to shrink from responsibility, or to be over scrupulous in calculating immediate results. Once let us be reasonably assured that we are in the way of our duty, really keeping the good deposit; and then, to use the words of the Prophet, we may 'set our faces like a flint, and need not be ashamed.' Then, as often as misgivings and alarms come over us, we must 'stir up the grace of God which is in us by imposition of apostolic hands.' For 'God hath not given us a Spirit of cowardice, but of power, and of love, and of brotherly correction and reproof;' a SPIRIT that brings with Him an invisible but real *power*, to open and shut the kingdom of heaven in the name of our LORD JESUS CHRIST; a SPIRIT of never-failing *love* and *charity* to men's souls, to guide us in the exercise of that more than human power; and, lastly, a SPIRIT of kind and fatherly, yet, if need be, uncompromising and fearless *rebuke*.

Let us be only true to our sacred trust: let us put every thing else by for the sake of handing down the whole counsel of GOD, our good deposit, entire as we received it: and who knows but we may by GOD's mercy be made instrumental in saving the English Church from ruin not unlike that which has fallen on Ephesus, Smyrna, or Sardis? At any rate, the Church Catholic, in one country or another, we are sure, will survive and triumph. As of old she has stood before kings and governors, and it turned to her for a testimony, so now blessed are they whom divine Providence shall choose and enable worthily to support her cause against popular delusion and tyranny. We, indeed, as Priests of the second order, are but under-labourers in that most holy cause. Yet the least and lowest among us may look for his share of the blessing, as he has undoubtedly his share of the bur-then and of the peril. Is there not a hope, that by resolute self-denial and strict and calm fidelity to our ordination vows, we may not only aid in preserving that which remains, but also may help to revive in some measure, in this or some other portion of the Christian world, more of the system and spirit of the apo-stolical age? New truths, in the proper sense of the word, we neither can nor wish to arrive at. But the monuments of antiqui-ty may disclose to our devout perusal much that will be to this age new, because it has been mislaid or forgotten; and we may attain to a light and clearness, which we now dream not of, in our comprehension of the faith and discipline of CHRIST. We may succeed beyond what humanly appears possible in rekind-ling a primitive zeal among those who shall be committed to our charge. Even as Abraham, neglecting all earthly objects, 'taught his children and his household after him, to keep the way of the Lord, to do justice and judgment;' and one part of his re-ward was, that 'God would not hide from Abraham the thing which he did' (Gen. xviii. 17-19); another, that he was made the glorious and favoured instrument for transmitting divine truth through a fallen and corrupt age.

NOTES

1. The insertion of 'Church Rules' here has been objected to, as not being warranted by the preceding citations. But the Sacraments, at least, were from the beginning Church Rules; and were not they part of the trust committed to Timothy, in common with all 'Stewards of the Mysteries of God?'
2. It is assumed in this paragraph, that where Scripture is silent or ambiguous, consent of the Fathers is a probable index of Apostolical tradition.
3. For this, see S. Cyprian, S. Augustin, S. Jerome. These with the distinct acknow-ledgement in the ancient Roman Liturgy, may perhaps be considered sufficient to represent the sense of the Western Churches. Among the Greeks, S. Chrysostom (on Gen. xiv) clearly implies the same construction. But the reserve maintained by them on all liturgical subjects may account for their comparative silence on this point, even supposing them to have received the same interpretation.
4. In this I believe all the Fathers who quote that divine Book (and most of them do so often) are agreed.
5. The disputes on the text, Proverbs viii.22, at the Nicene Council, are sufficient to prove agreement on this point. It is well known that the Arians alleged it, as it stands in the Septuagint, as a proof of the Son's inferiority. The Catholics never disputed the application of the text to our Lord, but denied the deduction from it.
6. Of course, in points of this kind, persons are at liberty, if they will, to content themselves with the common remark, 'Some order must have been adopted, and the Church had a right to adopt which she pleased.' It is among the privileges reserved for serious inquiring piety, to discern an express will of God, as well in these ecclesiastical laws, as in others more immediately scriptural.

FREDERICK DENISON Maurice was born at Normanstone, near Lowestoft, in 1805, of dissenting stock, his father being a Unitarian minister. Bitter religious quarrels within the family left him with a hunger for orthodoxy and the conviction, later expressed, that 'a society founded upon opinions has no real cohesion'.

Refusing to satisfy his father's wish that he should follow him in the Unitarian part, Maurice read law at Cambridge, with a view to becoming a barrister. A further refusal to subscribe to the Thirty-Nine Articles excluded him from a degree, however, and he removed to London, where he picked a meagre living with his pen. Refusal rather than independence seems the key to Maurice's character when young. His intellectual energy was given over to attacking Bentham and his disciples in their pursuit of happiness, and to admiring Coleridge in his pursuit of truth. These activities did not hinder the weaning of his own mind from dissent. In 1831 he was baptized, and then went up to Exeter College, Oxford, where he was ordained a priest in 1834 and took up the curacy of Bubbenhall, near Leamington, in Warwickshire, in the same year.

It is noteworthy that Maurice does not seem to have had personal contact with any of the leaders of the Oxford Movement while at Oxford, just as he never actually met Coleridge while in London. His inquiring spirit was complicated by shyness, although in print he had the courage both to speak his mind and to change it.

Parish work was not his style; in 1836 he found a more congenial niche by becoming chaplain of Guy's Hospital, where in addition to other duties he lectured the students twice a week upon moral philosophy, yet found time to write what remains the least tautological of his multifarious books, *The Kingdom of Christ*. In 1840 he was appointed professor of English literature and history in King's College, London, and to this post in 1846 was added the chair of divinity. The revolutionary events in France in 1848 peculiarly inflamed his imagination, and with Charles Kingsley and others he was soon busy in attempts to baptize republican ideas.

Maurice's subtlety, or confusion, had meanwhile made him suspect with the various religious parties, and when he published an essay criticizing the common view of the eternity of hell, and maintaining that in the New Testament eternity has nothing to do with duration, his enemies made such a noise that he had to resign from King's College. Public feeling was on Maurice's side in this issue, although as has been pointed out perhaps the popular objections to everlasting punishment did not quite coincide with his own.

In 1854 Maurice furthered his socialistic ideals and solved his own unemployment problem by opening a Working Men's College in London and becoming its first principal. In 1860 he was appointed to the Chapel of St Peter's, Vere Street, and from 1866 until his death he taught moral philosophy at Cambridge. Ruskin, who found him 'by nature puzzle-headed and indeed wrong-headed', was one of those who wondered about Maurice's soundness as a teacher of anything, but Tennyson and Gladstone professed themselves pleased. He died in Cambridge on April Fools' Day, 1872. His body is buried at Highgate, within reach of Karl Marx.

BIBLIOGRAPHY

Christmas Day and Other Sermons, Cambridge, 1843.
The Kingdom of Christ; or Hints to a Quaker Concerning the Principle, Constitution and Ordinances of the Catholic Church, 1838.
Moral and Metaphysical Philosophy, 2 vols., 1871-2.
Life and Letters, ed. his son Frederick Maurice, 2 vols., 1884.

CHRISTMAS DAY
John 1:14.
The Word was made flesh and dwelt among us, and we beheld His glory, the glory as of the only begotten of the Father, full of grace and truth.

THIS WAS preached at Guy's Hospital on Christmas Day, 1839. Maurice ministered there 'to sick and dying people', publishing a collection of the sermons he preached in these circumstances under the title *Christmas Day and Other Sermons*, that name being chosen, he explains, 'not because I desire to impart to the reader a festal tone of feeling, which is in no wise characteristic of the preacher', but rather 'to signify that the highest gifts of God, like the days that testify of them, are common gifts which we must be content to enjoy as members of one body with the most ignorant and wretched, if we would enjoy them at all.'

The refusal to rejoice, which may seem grudging or over-scrupulous, could be judged typical of Maurice when he feels self-compelled to comment upon the posture of his own mind. When he is at his priestly task, and preaching, he appears more straightforwardly endowed with an ability to *speak* his mind instead of moralizing round and about its processes. The simplicity of this sermon might be recalled when his own phrase in description of some of his writings—that they were the work of a 'muddy mystic'—is thrown back at him by theological opponents. Early experience of the painful effects of dissent within a family had left him with an ideal of the national Church as embodying the vital principle of Christian unity—an ideal which he never abandoned, and which caused him to dislike all talk of 'high', 'low', and 'broad' parties within that Church.

The beginning of the sermon is clumsy with affection—in a way that many sermons, preached by priests uncertain of their congregations, are necessarily clumsy. If the reader forgives Maurice his clichés in the first two paragraphs he will be rewarded by what follows.

MY BRETHREN, You that are here to-day, have come together from various places. Many of you do not know each other now, scarcely any of you knew each other a few weeks ago. You have been brought up in different families, perhaps many miles, or hundreds of miles apart. You have had different joys, and different sorrows. Each of you has some ache or sickness of his own. Each of you knows a whole world of things about himself, and knows very little about his neighbours. And yet I can wish you all a happy Christmas to-day. And I know that the words belong to one of you as much as to another. To you that were born here in London, and to him that was born (if there be such a one) over the sea; to you who have a wife and children, and to you who have none; to healthy men, and sick men, be their sickness what it may. It is strange that it should be so; but you know that so it is. These same words 'A happy Christmas to you!' have been spoken this morning by people who never heard of us. The like of them have been spoken in other languages. They have been spoken now for nearly eighteen hundred years. The persons who heard them through all that time, and in all those places, understood that they were addressed to themselves.

It is a pleasant thought, this, that we are not shut up, each in his own narrow circle; that people have some common thing to be glad about, if it were but for a little while; for one day in the whole year. And yet, I think, there would be a sadness in that thought too. It would be sad to feel 'We have been brethren in joy for a few hours, but it could not last. In a little time the flood of our private feelings, and sorrows, and sins, broke in upon us, and we were divided and solitary again.' It would be better, would it not, if this joy, in which we are all sharers, was one which had something to do with each of us, one which each of us, in his private chamber, had been crying after; something that would give another meaning to our own pleasures, and that would take the sting out of our pains. Then that common day of happiness would be one which we might remember, it would not be a day of twenty-four hours, but a day to last for ever.

Let us see whether Christmas day be such a day as this. You are told what it means in the verse I have just read, 'And the Word was made flesh, and dwelt among us; and we beheld his glory, the glory as of the only begotten of the Father, full of grace and truth.' These words explain Christmas to us; the Church uses them for that end. But the words themselves are most wonderful—who shall interpret *them*? Perhaps you may say, 'The

202

chapter which you read to us from the desk interprets them. That tells us when and how the Word was made flesh.' You would say rightly; but still that answer would not be enough. It is true that the event which that chapter speaks of, is the event which the text speaks of. But what did that event mean? What does St. John mean when he says THE WORD was made flesh? We turn back a few verses, and we find him saying, 'In the beginning was the WORD, and the Word was with God, and the Word was God. The same was in the beginning with God. All things were made by Him, and without Him was not anything made that was made. In Him was life, and the life was the light of men. And the light shineth in the darkness, and the darkness comprehended it not.' 'What,' you will exclaim, 'and do such words as these make Christmas day clearer to us? Surely they speak of things almost too deep for an angel to think of. Can you suppose that they will help us poor and ignorant men to understand anything? Christmas day we have kept for many years; old men and children, young men and maidens, have kept it. Must we go back to the beginning of the world before we can learn how to keep it rightly?'

Yes! brethren, I believe that you must give heed to these words if you would know what Christmas day is, or what any day of your lives is, or what you yourselves are, or why you have come into this world, and what you have to do in it. But I believe, also, that they are not hard words; not words which poor and ignorant need turn away from. I am sure they are meant especially for those who find that the things which are told them in books puzzle them very much, and that they cannot make out the sense of what is told them from pulpits; for men who have a livelihood to get by the sweat of their brows; for men whose bodies and minds are wasted by disease. I say this confidently, and I think when you have considered what it is that perplexes you in books and in sermons, you will agree with me. Is it not the *words* you read and hear in them? They float about you; they tell you of something that you are sure you want to know, but you cannot see them or handle them, and the things you can see and handle, do not tell you what they signify. Whence do they come? Who has given them to you? Who has taught you to utter them? St. John reveals the secret. He speaks to us of THE WORD. Of One from whom all words have come; of One in whom the very life and sense of them dwells. 'In him,' he says, 'was life,' and not only this, but 'the life was the light of men.' All the light or intelligence that has ever been in any man's mind, has come from him, has been communicated by him. All those thoughts and questionings with us which words try to explain, are awakened by him. It is he who leads each man to ask, 'What am I? Whither am I going? What is it to be a man?' It is he who gives the answer. But this is not enough. We are living in the midst of a strange world; we have eyes and ears to take in the sights and sounds of it; but we do not know what all these sights and sounds have to do with us; what use we are to make of them; whether they are our masters or our servants. 'All things,' says St. John, 'were made by him, and without him was not anything made that was made.' What clear bright sunbeams are these! It seems as if they caught light from the very source of light. This world, that is so beautiful when we look at it, and yet seems so confused when we think about it, was made by him who is the Lord of men; by that Word who inspires their thoughts, who gives them language. Out of him came the light that makes each thing distinct from the other, and the life that brings all things into one. He is the maker of the world, and the interpreter of it.

This is strange and amazing; but it is not all. You are confused about yourselves, and your own lives, and you are confused about the world that surrounds you. But is there no other thought more confusing and overwhelming still? Is there not a whisper in your hearts about One who is higher than yourselves; and higher than the world; about One who is all Powerful and all Right; One who cannot look upon any evil thing, or be satisfied with anything that is less good and holy than himself? Is there no whisper about God? Hear once again: 'In the beginning was the Word, and the Word was with God, and the Word was God. The same was in the beginning with God.' He then who made the worlds, he who is the light of men, was with God before all things were. He knew the absolute and awful Being whom our lips tremble to speak of; He held converse with Him; He delighted in Him. Yea, he *was* God. This unseen Teacher of men, this source of our light and our life, was perfectly one with Him whom no man hath seen or can see; the brightness of his glory, the express image of his person.

Brethren, am I speaking of things too deep and fearful for men to utter? I should think so indeed, if St. John had not uttered them, and if the Church had not bidden me set them before you to-day. The more deep and awful they seem to you and to me, the better it is for us. Let us pray God that every day we may grow into the feeling which Moses had when he drew nigh to the bush, and was commanded to put his shoes from off his feet, because the place whereon he stood was holy ground. But we shall not have this feeling unless we do approach when God speaks to us and bids us approach him. The coward has no reverence; only a vague dread of something that he thinks will do him harm. If we would tremble with a real holy fear, we must come into the light, and see every thing as it stands out beautifully and gloriously, not stay in the darkness, where there are nothing but dim shadows and spectres which frighten us, and which we wish to fly from. St. John warns us of this. After he has spoken of him who is the light of man, he says, 'And the light shineth in the darkness, and the darkness comprehended it not.' This light is with us, about us, at every hour and moment. It comes to us, and brings a thousand things back to us that we thought were gone for ever—words that were spoken to people who have left the world; acts that no human eye saw; thoughts that passed in the depths of our own souls. You know—you that have been on sick beds—that what I say is true; you know that all these have visited you as you lay at night, longing for sleep and not finding it. And have you not also felt this? 'Now, even now there is an evil near me, clinging to me, that I cannot get rid of: it is part of my own self; if it dies, I must die.' And then how dark the future has looked to you. You have said to yourselves, 'It *may* be better, the light may break in upon it:' you could not wholly lose that hope. But it has grown dimmer and dimmer, and you have feared that the time to come would be darker and more miserable than the time gone by, and you could see no end of it. Here, brethren, is the Light shining in the darkness. Some one there is who has power to recall those things that you thought had perished, to set them clearly and fully before you. Some one there is who is admonishing you of your state now. Some one there is who can enable you to look onward. And, oh! brethren, have you not oftentimes felt, 'He who has *this* power, has another too. He might deliver me out of this evil, even of that past evil which seems to possess me. He might give me a new life in the midst of this death. If I could see and know him, and converse with him, I believe that he would; for he must be good, else why does the evil in me so struggle with him, why does he condemn it?' 'The light shineth in the darkness, and the darkness has not comprehended it.' It tries to inclose it, and

205

quench it; but in vain. The light is there still, and by it we know what the darkness is.

I have spoken to you in this way, because I know that you have all hearts and consciences, which testify of the presence of Him whom these verses declare unto us. I hope that some of you have more than this; but my message is to all, and what I am saying now is true, not only about you who are here, but about all men who have ever been in the world.

'He hath ordered the times before appointed (saith St. Paul), and the bounds of men's habitation, that they should seek the Lord, if haply they might feel after him, and find him.' That is to say, God hath placed one man in this period, one man in that; one man in this country, one man in that; but in every age and in every country, He has been, by some means or other, stirring men up to feel his presence, and to inquire after him. And therefore men have said, 'Where is he, and how can we know him? Where does that Word dwell who is speaking to me inwardly, and making me feel that he is my Lord, and that I ought to serve him? Where is he? Is he in the air, or in the clouds; is he in the ocean when it rages against me, or in the woods through which the wind is roaring at night? Who can declare him to me?' This was the question which men were asking of each other; and now they seemed to find him here, now there; now in animals more mean than themselves, which did them good or harm; now in the beautiful lights of heaven, now in the creatures of their own race, who had lived on the earth and left it. Still they sought him, and dreamed of him; but could not discover him. He must be like themselves, they said, and yet he must be most different. He must hate their evil, and yet they wanted one who could sympathize in it. He must bring them together, and keep them as one, and yet each man seemed to need a separate God for himself, to enter into his miseries. Yet all this while 'He was not far from every one of them, for in Him,' says St. Paul again, 'we live, and move, and have our being.' Though it seemed as if the thought of his presence confounded them, and made them wretched; yet from that presence came all their light, and their freedom, and their hope. In spite of all disappointments, they could not but believe that he would make himself known, and that their blindness should not hinder them from beholding Him.

'The Word was made flesh and dwelt among us.' This is St. John's declaration. He does not invent a great many arguments to prove it; he simply says, 'So it was.' This poor fisherman, who was once upon a time sitting in his father's ship on the lake of Galilee, mending his nets,—this man who was infinitely humbler and less self-conceited now than he was then, says out boldly and without hesitation, 'This everlasting Word, in whom was life, and whose life was the light of men, this Word who was with God and was God, was made flesh and dwelt among us; He whom all nations and kindreds and people have been longing to see, He whom they have been worshipping in the sun and the moon and the stars; He whom their consciences have been confessing and witnessing of, He has actually shewn himself to us; He has been born into the world in a little village in our country; He has grown up among us, we have seen Him, heard Him, handled Him; He has walked about with us, we have had the most intimate converse with Him; we are sure that He was a real man, that He was in all outward respects like us, speaking with a human voice, sensible of bodily fatigue, enduring bodily pain; we are certain that He had all the feelings and sympathies of a man; we are certain that He had friends, that He sorrowed with them and for them, that He cared for little children; in everything he was human.'

'And yet (he adds) we beheld his glory—the glory as of the only begotten of the Father.' We are sure that in this man—this poor man, thus entering into our feelings and circumstances,—we beheld the living God. Not *some* unseen power—some angel or divine creature who might have been sent down on a message of mercy to our little corner of the earth, or to us poor fishermen of Galilee—it is not such a being whom we saw hidden under this human form; we declare that we saw the glory of the Father, of Him who made heaven and earth and the sea, of Him who has been, and is, and is to be; of Him to whom all nations and kindreds belong, and who shall be at last acknowledged as the one living and true God of all. We say that the Father revealed himself fully and perfectly in this man, that he was with him before the worlds were, that he held unbroken converse with him while he was upon earth, that he is upon the right hand of his glory now. He told us that when we saw him we saw the Father: the lowliest of men told us so, and we believed him. We are certain that all the Love and Grace and Holiness of God came forth in Him; we are certain that he exercised the power of God; and we are appointed to declare this truth to all men, that they may believe it and rejoice in it. We say that God has made himself known to men, and that in the flesh of Jesus Christ there is a bond between all creatures and their Creator.

That a meek, humble man, who believed that nothing was so horrible as to trifle with God's name, should have spoken such words as these, so boldly, and yet so calmly, with such a certainty that they were true and that he could live and act upon them, this is wonderful. But yet, this might have been, and the world might have gone on as if no such sounds had ever been proclaimed in it. What is the case actually? These incredible words have been believed. In the east, in the west, in the north and the south, men there were, who said, 'They are and must be true.' Though all their interests went the other way, they said so; though they had to give up the most cherished notions and feelings, they said so; though they had to believe despised men of a despised nation, they said so; though the world was against them and would not leave them quiet in their faith, they said so. The world could not leave them quiet in their faith; for it was not a faith about themselves, but about the world. They did not say, 'The Son of God has been made flesh for *us*.' They said, 'By this act He has redeemed our race, He has declared that mankind is created in Him, that men have a new eternal life in Him. He has proclaimed himself the King and Lord of the universe. And we do not live and die to claim some glory for ourselves because we are good men or saints. If we are good men or saints, it is because we renounce all pretensions to goodness and saintship in ourselves, because we say that all we have is in Him who has been made flesh, and in that flesh has made us one with Him, that we might receive the Spirit of the Father and the Son. If we are saints and good men it is because we will have no honour but what we claim for the poorest beggar who will enter into God's covenant, and put on Christ by holy baptism.' You see, then, it was not a question whether this man or that should hold a certain opinion. The question was, 'Who is the Ruler of the world?' The apostles said, 'This Jesus of Nazareth is its Ruler.' Their words prevailed. The masters of the earth confessed that they were right. Here in England, at the other end of the world, the news was heard and received. Then the day which said the Word has been made flesh and dwelt among us, became the queen-day of the year. All the joy of the year was felt to be stored up in it. Every man, and woman, and child, had a right to be merry upon it.

And has this right ceased? There are some who will tell you that it has; and it seems the general opinion, that people are not as merry now on this day as they used to be. One says that this

208

is a grievous thing, that we should try if we can to bring back the old times. Another says, 'This cannot be, people are wiser now. They know that one day is no better than another; the thing is to be real Christians in our hearts.' Another tells us 'Christmas day is forgotten, because that of which Christmas day speaks of does not signify so much as it once did. It was good for the people who lived a thousand years ago to believe such tales; but we have better and more solid things to care for.' Brethren, I will tell you what I believe is the truth about these notions, which different people will puzzle you with. To those who say, 'Let us bring back the old times—let us be merry as we used to be,' I would say, 'Well! but we cannot be merry merely because we try to be so. We cannot be merry unless there is something to make us merry. If our hearts be glad we shall find ways to express our gladness, but we do not make our hearts glad by pretending that they are so, or by putting on the outward signs of jollity.' Now, this is what men have been endeavouring to do, and they find that it is a vain thing. They have heard from their forefathers that Christmas day was a good day; a day when children and parents, brothers and sisters, should meet together and rejoice; they have, accordingly, met and kept holiday. As long as they remembered that they were kinsfolk, and liked coming together for the sake of greeting old friends, and looking at the happy faces of children, they had the savour of Christmas day in them, even though they might not always recollect in whose name they were assembled, and what his coming into the world had to do with their good fellowship. But by degrees, the song, and the cup, and the dance, which were signs of the pleasure that friends and brothers had in seeing one another, were more thought of than their friendship and their brotherhood; then the joy wasted away, and went so much the faster because they were trying to invent ways of keeping it up. Good hearty English gladness must have some root; all the contrivances in the world will not make it grow when it is severed from its root. If we care about nothing but ourselves, we shall not be merry at Christmas time, or at any other time.

And therefore, brethren, I do not know what those mean who say, that we are to be good Christians in our hearts, but are not to think about Christmas day. That seems to me like saying that we are to be very good Christians for ourselves, but that we are not to care whether our neighbours have any share in the blessing or not. Now how a man can be a good Christian and only be concerned about himself, I do not know. These days are witnesses to all men, everywhere, young and old, rich and poor, of a blessing which God has bestowed upon them: if there be no such blessing we ought to say so plainly; but if there be, it is a base and miserable thing not to like the plain, simple testimonies of it which come down from generation to generation, and which all alike may own and rejoice in whether they have book-learning or no. And mark this, also, brethren; they who would cheat us of these days, and send us to a book, though it be the best book in the world, for all our teaching, soon forget that our faith is not in a book, but in Him of whom the book speaks. They forget that the Word is a living person, and that he was made flesh and dwelt among us. These days bear witness of that truth—bless God for them.

Yes, bless God for them! for he is a liar who says that the words which St. John speaks to us to-day, are not as fresh, as living, as necessary now as they were when he first wrote them down. It may be, brethren, that easy, comfortable people make less of Christmas day than they once did. Perhaps they will presently make less of it than they do now. If the Bible be true this was to be expected. If Christmas is a real and true thing it was to be expected. For hear what Isaiah says, and St. Peter repeats the words, 'The grass withereth, the flower thereof falleth away, but the Word of our God endureth for ever.' As if he had said, 'All that has grown out of this root shall drop off in order that it may be seen how deeply the root itself is fixed in the soil.' We do not keep Christmas in the bright, sunny time of the year, but now in the heart of winter, when everything is bare and dry. And our Lord himself is said to be 'a root out of a dry ground,' that, indeed, from which all the blossoms of hope and joy are to come, but which must first be owned in its own nakedness before they shall appear. If then, brethren, men have begun to fancy that their gladness has another root than this, it is meet that for a time they should be left to try whether they can keep it alive by any efforts and skill of theirs. If Christmas joy has been separated from Christ, it is no wonder and no dishonour to Christ that it should grow feeble and hollow. But Christmas is not dead, because the mirth of those who have forgotten its meaning is dead. It is not dead for you, it is not dead for people who lie upon beds tormented with fevers, and dropsies, and cancers. It is not dead for the children in factories, and for the men who are working in mines, and for prisoners who never see the light of the sun. To all these the news, 'The Word who was in the beginning with God and was God, in whom is life, and whose life is the light of men, by whom all things were made, and without whom was not anything made that was made, became flesh and dwelt among us, entered into our poverty, and suffering, and death,'—is just as mighty and cheering news now as it was when St. Peter first declared it to his countrymen on the day of Pentecost. You want this truth, brethren, you cannot live or die without it. You have a right to it, no men can have a greater. By your baptism God hath given you a portion in him who was made flesh; by your suffering he is inviting you to claim that portion, to understand that it is indeed for you Christ lived and died. You may live as if no such news as this had ever been proclaimed in the world, but it is not the less true that it has been proclaimed, and proclaimed for you. And blessed be God, this proclamation is not made merely through weak, mortal lips; that altar bears a more deep and amazing witness of it than it is possible for these words of mine to bear. There you may learn how real the union is which the living Word of God established with the flesh of man; how truly that flesh is given to be the life of the world. Christmas day declares that He dwelt among us. To those who there eat his flesh and drink his blood, he promises that he will dwell *in* them, and that they shall dwell in Him. This is the festival which makes us know, indeed, that we are members of one body; it binds together the life of Christ on earth with his life in heaven; it assures us that Christmas day belongs not to time but to eternity.

EDWARD BOUVERIE PUSEY

PUSEY WAS born at Pusey. This piece of Englishness fell out because his father, Philip Bouverie, son of the first Viscount Folkestone, chose to assume the name of a village in Berkshire on inheriting certain estates there in 1789. The background is rich, amiable and cultivated. Edward Bouverie Pusey, born in 1800, was not unconscious of it. His mother was also of noble birth. From the start Pusey fitted into the English fabric more securely than Newman or Manning, those sons of mere bankers. He was educated at Eton and Christ Church, and elected a fellow of Oriel College in 1823.

Not long afterwards Pusey went to Germany, attending the universities at Göttingen, Berlin and Bonn, where he studied under Schleiermacher and acquainted himself with what was then known as the 'higher criticism'. A wish to prevent similar developments in England prompted his first work of consequence, an essay entitled *An Historical Enquiry into the Probable Causes of the Rationalist Character Lately Predominant in the Theology of Germany*, published in 1828. This, like all Pusey's writings, is an extremely thorough treatment of its subject. His mind was receptive rather than reflective. He absorbed other people's ideas and then gave them out again in sentences sustained by quotations from the Fathers. The process won him a deserved reputation for scholarship, although the modern reader may notice that the ideas overflow the thought too often for Pusey to be considered a true intellectual. He was an eclectic who found a home for his reading in the service of the Church.

In June 1828, Pusey was ordained deacon and then in November priested. In the same year he was appointed Regius Professor of Hebrew and Canon of Christ Church, Oxford, offices he held until his death. As an academic, Pusey set himself a high standard of duty—he gave from the first three sets of lectures three times a week, where he was obliged only to give one lecture twice. He treated the study of Hebrew as a religious subject, and aimed at imparting a full idiomatic knowledge of the language, so that his students might 'enter more fully into the simple meaning of God's word'.

Pusey attached himself to the Oxford Movement in 1833 by the publication of a Tract (No. 18) entitled, *Thoughts on the Benefits of the System of Fasting, Enjoined by Our Church*. This was the first Tract to be issued with an indication as to its author's identity. Pusey's insistence on this point was sensible, since his style changed the character of the Tracts from pamphlets to doctrinal treatises. 'He was able', as Newman wrote later, 'to give a name, a form, and a personality to what was without him a sort of mob.' Pusey also supported the founding of the Library of the Fathers, supplying its first volume (St Augustine's *Confessions*, 1838) with a careful preface on the importance of patristic theology.

Bookish and reserved by temperament, Pusey's defence of Newman over Tract 90 does him honour. He identified himself with the interpretation which his friend had put upon the Thirty-Nine Articles, and published a letter in which he contended that Newman's interpretation was not 'only *an* admissable, but *the* most legitimate' interpretation of them.

After 1841, and Newman's withdrawal from the Movement, Pusey became its leader. By this time the Protestant faction in Oxford was spoiling for a fight. It found an occasion or excuse in Pusey's sermon on the Eucharist, included in the present book. He was suspended from the university pulpit for two years, although the authorities found it difficult to say why.

Unlike Newman, Pusey did not despair of the Church of England. In 1845 his efforts to revive the religious life within that Church were rewarded when a community of nuns was established in London—the first Anglican sisterhood for at least two hundred years. Other communities followed—in Oxford, Devonport, Wantage, Clewer and East Grinstead. In 1846 he preached another important sermon before the university, on *The Entire Absolution of the Penitent*, in which he insisted upon the power of the keys and the reality of priestly absolution after private confession—all within the context of the English Church. His treatises on the sacraments, *The Doctrine of the Real Presence, as Contained in the Fathers* (1855) and *The Real Presence of the Body and Blood of Our Lord Jesus Christ, the Doctrine of the English Church* (1857) may also be mentioned as useful documents.

Pusey made no declarations against the Church of Rome, but asserted that he would die as he lived—in the Church of England. He favoured the idea of working to find a basis for corporate reunion of the Sees of Canterbury and Rome, and maintained this ideal despite such setbacks as the secession of Manning and Robert Wilberforce, publishing in 1865 a letter to Keble on *The Church of England a Portion of Christ's One Holy Catholic*

Church, and a Means of Restoring Visible Unity: An Eirenicon.
At the same time, he reissued Newman's Tract 90. Several Roman
Catholic writers responded favourably—notably the Archbishop
of Paris, Monsignor Darboy. Newman, however, answered the
Eirenicon in 1866, holding out little hope for effective reunion
at that time.

In 1869 Pusey published a second *Eirenicon*, addressed to
Newman directly, and in 1870 a third. He sent this to Roman
Catholic bishops attending the Vatican Council, but his expectations were discouraged by what he took to be the insuperable
problem presented by the definition of Papal Infallibility. He
continued to work patiently, all the same, and one of the most
moving sentences in his many writings is to be found at the end
of a book on the subject of the reunion of the Church of England
and the Orthodox Church, where he speaks of it as his 'last con-
tribution to a future which I shall not see'.

Pusey's own position was that the Church of England was the
Church of Augustine and Bede and Anselm and Becket, as well
as Donne and Andrewes and Nicholas Ferrar and George Herbert;
his life's work aimed to prove that she still held the faith which
these men had held. He believed that the doctrines of the English
Church were enshrined in the writings of the Anglican divines
of the seventeenth century, but that the influences of Whig in-
differentism, deism, and ultra-Protestantism had obscured their
significance. 'My life', he said once, 'has been spent in a succession
of isolated efforts, bearing indeed upon one great end—the
growth of Catholic truth and piety among us.' He died at Ascot
Priory, Berkshire, in 1882, and his body now lies buried in the
nave of Christ Church Cathedral, Oxford.

BIBLIOGRAPHY

University Sermons, 3 vols., Oxford, 1872.
Sermons during the Seasons from Advent to Whitsuntide, 2 vols., Oxford,
1848.
Parochial Sermons, 3 vols., Oxford, 1873.
Parochial and Cathedral Sermons, 1883.
Nine Sermons, 1885.
The Doctrine of the Real Presence, 1855.
*The Real Presence of the Body and Blood of Our Lord Jesus Christ, the
Doctrine of the English Church*, 1857.
*The Church of England a Portion of Christ's One Holy Catholic Church,
and a Means of Restoring Visible Unity: An Eirenicon*, 1865.

The Holy Eucharist a Comfort to the Penitent
Matt. 26:28.
This is My Blood of the New Testament, which is shed for many for the remission of sins.

THIS WAS preached on the fourth Sunday after Easter 1843, at Christ Church Cathedral, Oxford, before the university. Things were brewing for a storm. Newman had preached his last sermon as an Anglican a month before, with Pusey celebrating on that occasion. The air was full of rumours as to what the Oxford Movement would do with itself if the community at Littlemore went over to Rome. In the circumstances, Pusey could have been forgiven for choosing a neutral theme, and treating it lightly. As it is, his sermon, a piece of aggressive orthodoxy, was immediately condemned by the vice-chancellor and six doctors of divinity as teaching error. Pusey asked to be heard in defence. No answer was returned to his request. When a copy of the sermon was demanded, he insisted on pointing out which passages in it derived from the Fathers, being anxious not to see communicant members of his own Church making fools of themselves by finding heresy in 'e.g. St. Cyril of Alexandria when they thought they were only condemning me'. Despite this, the vice-chancellor again condemned the sermon, and Pusey was suspended from preaching in the university for two years. There was a general outcry. Gladstone protested—the vice-chancellor returned his protest 'by the hands of his bedel', as if to stamp it further with his disapproval. The effect of the suspension was the sale of eighteen thousand copies of the condemned text. Pusey was never told the precise charge against his sermon, or the reasons for which it was condemned.

Pusey's main object is to show that the penitent finds comfort in the Eucharist such as is to be found nowhere else, because the Eucharist is both sacrifice wherein he pleads Christ's sacrifice for all his sins, and sacrament wherein he receives spiritual food and sustenance. The argument is strengthened by quotations from the Fathers, and the whole is closely modelled upon patristic precepts. A secondary object of Pusey's in preaching this sermon was perhaps to balance the severity of his Tract on Baptism. As Dean Church remarks, it is not easy for a reader even to put his finger on the probably incriminating passages in the piece—'except on the supposition of gross ignorance of English divinity on the part of the judges'. The sermon is intense and in places so clotted with references that it is hard to follow —yet seldom can the Greek Fathers in particular have been expounded so thoroughly from an English pulpit. Not that Pusey offers much in the way of *argument*; his concern is practical and material—simply to affirm that the Eucharist is nothing less than the offering of Christ, really present in the consecrated elements.

As a preacher, Pusey lacked the graces of oratory, but compelled attention by his seriousness. He is worth reading patiently, as one imagines he wrote. Sara Coleridge described his demeanour during a sermon which she heard him preach:

He is as still as a statue all the time he is uttering it, looks as white as a sheet, and is as monotonous in delivery as possible. While listening to him you do not seem to see and hear a preacher, but to have visible before you a most earnest and devout spirit, striving to carry out in this world a high religious theory.

IT IS part of the manifold wisdom of God, that His gifts, in nature and in grace, minister to distinct, and, as it often seems, unconnected ends; manifesting thereby the more His own Unity, as the secret cause and power of all things, putting Itself forward in varied forms and divers manners, yet Itself the one Cause of all that is. The element which is the image of our Baptism, cleanses alike and refreshes, enlighteneth the fainting eye, wakens to life, as it falls, a world in seeming exhaustion and death, changes the barren land into a garden of the Lord, gives health and nourishment and growth. And if in nature, much more in the Gifts of Grace. For therein God, not by Will or by Power only, but by Himself and the Effluence of His Spirit, is the Life of all which lives through Him. Our One Lord is to us, in varied forms, all, yea more than all, His disciples dare ask or think. All are His Life, flowing through all His members, and in all, as it is admitted, effacing death, enlarging life. As blind, He is our Wisdom; as sinful, our Righteousness; as hallowed, our Sanctification; as recovered from Satan, our Redemption; as sick, our Physician; as weak, our Strength; as unclean, our Fountain; as darkness, our Light; as daily fainting, our daily Bread; as dying, Life Eternal; as asleep in Him, our Resurrection.

It is, then, according to the analogy of His other gifts, that His two great Sacraments have in themselves manifold gifts. Baptism containeth not only remission of sin, actual or original, but maketh members of Christ, children of God, heirs of Heaven, hath the seal and earnest of the Spirit, the germ of spiritual life; the Holy Eucharist imparteth not life only, spiritual strength, and oneness with Christ, and His Indwelling, and participation of Him, but, in its degree, remission of sins also. As the manna is said to have 'contented every man's delight and agreed to every taste' (Wisd. xvi. 20), so He, the Heavenly Manna, becometh to every man what he needeth, and what he can receive; to the penitent perhaps chiefly remission of sins and continued life, to those who have 'loved Him and kept His word,' His own transporting, irradiating Presence, full of His own grace and life and love; yet to each full contentment, because to each His own overflowing, undeserved, goodness.

Having then, on former occasions, spoken of the Fountain of all comfort, our Redeeming Lord, His Life for us and Intercession with the Father, as the penitent's stay amid the overwhelming consciousness of his sins, it may well suit, in this our season of deepest joy, to speak of that, which, flowing from the throne of the Lamb which was slain, is to the penitent, the deepest river of his joy, the Holy Mysteries; from which, as from Paradise, he feels that he deserves to be shut out, from which perhaps, in the holier discipline of the Ancient Church, he would have been for a time removed, but which to his soul must be the more exceeding precious, because they are the Body and Blood of His Redeemer. While others joy with a more Angelic joy, as feeding on Him, Who is the Angels' food, and 'sit,' as St. Chrysostom says, 'with Angels and Archangels and heavenly powers, clad with the kingly robe of Christ itself, yea clad with the King Himself, and having spiritual armoury,' he may be the object of the joy of Angels; and while as a penitent he approaches as to the Redeemer's Side, he may hope that having so been brought, he, with the penitent, shall not be parted from It, but be with Him and near Him in Paradise. 'To the holier,' says another (S. Ambrose), 'He is more precious as God; to the sinner more precious is the Redeemer. Of higher value and avail is He to him, who hath more grace; yet to him also to whom much is forgiven, doth He the more avail, because 'to whom much is forgiven, he loveth much.'

Would that in the deep joy of this our Easter festival, the pledge of our sealed forgiveness, and the earnest of endless life in God, we could, for His sake by Whom we have been redeemed, lay aside our wearisome strifes, and that to speak of the mysteries of Divine love might not become the occasion of unloving and irreverent disputings. Would that, at least in this sacred place, we could dwell in thought, together, on His endless condescension and loving-kindness, without weighing in our own measures, words which must feebly convey Divine mysteries; rather intent (as so many in this day seem) on detecting that others have spoken too strongly on that which is unfathomable, than on ourselves adoring that Love, which is past finding out. 'When we speak of spiritual things,' is S. Chrysostom's warning, on approaching this same subject, 'be there nothing of this life, nothing earthly in our thoughts; let all such things depart and be cast out, and be we wholly given to the hearing of the Divine word. When the Spirit discourseth to us, we should listen with much stillness, yea, with much awe. For the things this day read are worthy of awe. "Except ye eat the Flesh of the Son of man and drink His Blood, ye have no life in you." '

The penitent's joy, then, in the Holy Eucharist is not the less deep, because the pardon of sins is not, as in Baptism, its direct provision. The two great Sacraments, as their very signs shew, have not the same end. Baptism gives, the Holy Eucharist preserves and enlarges life. Baptism engrafts into the true Vine; the Holy Eucharist derives the richness and fulness of His life into the branches thus engrafted. Baptism buries in Christ's tomb, and through it He quickens with His life; the Holy Eucharist is given not to the dead, but to the living. It augments life, or—death; gives immortality to the living; to the dead it gives not life, but death; it is a savour of life or death, is received to salvation or damnation. Whence the ancient Church so anxiously withheld from it such as sinned grievously, not as an example only to others, but in tenderness to themselves, lest they break through and perish; 'profane,' says S. Cyprian, 'the Holy Body of the Lord,' not themselves be sanctified; fall deeper, not be restored; be wounded more grievously, not be healed; since it is said, he adds, 'Whoso eateth the Bread and drinketh the Cup of the Lord unworthily, is guilty of the Body and Blood of the Lord.'

The chief object, then, of the Holy Eucharist, as conveyed by type or prophecy, by the very elements chosen, or by the words of our Lord, is the support and enlargement of life, and that in Him. In type[1], the tree of life was within the Paradise of God, given as a nourishment of immortality, withheld from Adam when he sinned; the bread and wine, wherewith Melchizedek met Abraham, were to refresh the father of the faithful, the weary warrior of God; the Paschal Lamb was a commemorative sacrifice; the saving blood had been shed; it was to be eaten with the unleavened bread of sincerity and truth, and with bitter herbs, the type of mortification, and by those only who were undefiled. The Manna was given to them after they had passed the Red Sea, the image of cleansing Baptism, and, as He Himself interprets it, represented Him as coming down from heaven, to give life unto the world, the food of Angels and the holy hosts of heaven; the Shew-bread was eaten only by those hallowed to the Priesthood, (as the whole Christian people has in this sense been made kings and priests,) and, when once given to David and those that were with him, still on the ground that the 'vessels of the young men were holy' (1 Sam. xxi. 5). The Angel brought the cake to Elijah, that in the strength of that food, he might go forty days and forty nights unto the Mount of God. In verbal prophecy, it is foretold under the images of the very elements, and so of strengthening and overflowing joy. 'Wisdom,' that is, He Who is the Wisdom of God, in a parable corresponding to that of the marriage feast, crieth, 'Come eat of My bread and drink of the wine I have mingled.' Or, in the very Psalm of His Passion and atoning Sacrifice, it is foretold, that 'the poor shall eat and be satisfied;' or that He, the good Shepherd, shall prepare a Table for those whom He leadeth by the still waters of the Church, and giveth them the Cup of overflowing joy; or as the source of gladness, 'Thou hast put gladness into my heart, since the time that their corn and wine and oil (the emblem of the Spirit of which the faithful drink) increased,' and 'the wine which gladdeneth man's heart, and the oil which maketh his face to shine, and bread which strengtheneth man's heart;' or of spiritual growth, 'corn and wine shall make the young men and maidens of Zion to grow;' or as that which alone is satisfying, 'buy wine without money and without price,' for that 'which is not bread;' or as the special Gift to the faithful, 'He hath given meat unto them that fear Him;' or that which, after His Passion, He drinketh anew with His disciples in His Father's kingdom, 'I have gathered my myrrh, I have drunk my wine with my milk; eat, O friends; drink, yea, drink abundantly, O beloved.'

In all these varied symbols, strength, renewed life, growth, refreshment, gladness, likeness to the Angels, immortality, are the gifts set forth; they are gifts as to the Redeemed of the Lord placed anew in the Paradise of His Church, admitted to His Sanctuary, joying in His Presence, growing before Him, filled with the river of His joy, feasting with Him, yea Himself feasting in them, as in them He hungereth[2]. Hitherto, there is no allusion to sin; it is what the Church should be, walking in the brightness of His light, and itself reflecting that brightness.

And when our Lord most largely and directly is setting forth the fruits of eating His Flesh and drinking His Blood, He speaks throughout of one Gift, life; freedom from death, life through Him, through His indwelling, and therefore resurrection from the dead, and life eternal. 'This is the Bread, which cometh down from heaven, that a man may eat thereof and not die. If any man eat of this Bread, he shall live for ever; and the Bread that I will give is My Flesh, which I will give for the life of the world.' 'Except ye eat the Flesh of the Son of man and drink His blood, ye have no life in you.' 'Whoso eateth My Flesh and drinketh My Blood hath eternal life, and I will raise him up at the last Day.' 'He that eateth My Flesh and drinketh My Blood dwelleth in Me and I in Him.' 'As the Living Father hath sent Me and I live by The Father, so he that eateth Me, he also shall live by Me.' 'He that eateth of this Bread shall live for ever.' No one can observe how this whole discourse circleth round this gift of life, and how our Lord, with unwearied patience, bringeth this one truth before us in so many different forms, without feeling that He means to inculcate, that life in Him is His chief gift in His Sacrament, and to make a reverent longing for it an incentive to our faith. Yet although life in Him is the substance of His whole teaching, the teaching itself is manifold. Our Lord inculcates not one truth only in varied forms, but in its different bearings. He answers not the strivings of the Jews, 'how can this man give us His Flesh to eat?' Such an 'how can these things be?' He never answereth; and we, if we are wise, shall never ask how[3] they can be elements of this world and yet His very Body and Blood. But how they give life to us, He does answer; and amid this apparent uniformity of His teaching, each separate sentence gives us a portion of that answer. And the teaching of the whole, as far as such as we may grasp it, is this. That He[4] is the Living Bread, because He came down from Heaven, and as being One God with the Father, hath life in Himself, even as the Father hath life in Himself; the life then which He is, He imparted to that Flesh which He took into Himself, yea, which He took so wholly, that Holy Scripture says, He became it, 'the Word became flesh,' and since it is thus a part of Himself, 'Whoso eateth My Flesh, and drinketh My Blood,' (He Himself says the amazing words,) 'eateth Me,' and so receiveth into Himself, in an ineffable manner, his Lord Himself, 'dwelleth' (our Lord says) 'in Me and I in Him,' and having Christ within him[5], not only *shall* he *have*, but he *'hath'* already 'eternal Life,' because he hath Him Who is 'the Only True God and Eternal Life;' and so Christ 'will raise him up at the last Day,' because he hath His life in him. Receiving Him into this very body[6], they who are His, receive life, which shall pass over to our very decaying flesh; they have within them Him Who is Life and Immortality and Incorruption, to cast out or absorb into itself our natural mortality and death and corruption, and 'shall live for ever,' because made one with Him Who Alone 'liveth for evermore.' It is not then life only as an outward gift, to be possessed by us, as His gift; it is no *mere* strengthening and refreshing of our souls, by the renewal[7] and confirming our wills, and invigorating of our moral nature, giving us more fixedness of purpose, or implanting in us Christian graces; it is no gift, such as we might imagine given to the most perfect of God's created beings in himself. Picture we the most perfect wisdom, knowledge, strength, harmony, proportion, brightness, beauty, fitness, completeness of created being; fair as was that angel 'in the garden of God' before he fell, 'the seal of comeliness, full of wisdom, and complete in beauty—perfect in his ways from the day he was created' (Ezek. xxviii. 12,15). Yet let this be a perfection, upheld indeed of God, yet external to Him, as a mere creation, and it would fall unutterably short of the depth of the mystery of the Sacraments of Christ, and the gift, the germ whereof is therein contained for us; although such as we actually are, we know that, for strength we have weakness, for knowledge ignorance, our nature jarring still, disharmonized, obscured, deformed, both by the remains of original corruption and our own superadded sins. For the life therein bestowed is greater than any gift, since it is life in Christ, life through His indwelling, Himself Who is Life. And Holy Scripture hints, that the blessed Angels, who never fell, shall in some way to us unknown, gain by the mystery of the Incarnation, being with us gathered together under One Head, our Incarnate Lord, into His One Body,[8] the fulness of Him Who filleth all in all. Certainly, Scripture seems to imply, that, although He 'took not the nature of angels' but 'of man,' yet all created beings, 'thrones and dominions and principalities and powers,' shall, if one may reverently say it, be more filled with God, when, this His body being perfected, there shall be no check or hindrance to the full effluence of His Divine Nature, circulating through the whole Body, into which He shall have 'knit things in heaven and things in earth,' 'the innumerable company of the Angels,' and 'the just made perfect;' and the whole glorified Church shall be clothed and radiant with Him, the Sun of Righteousness.

And of this we have the germs and first beginnings now. This is (if we may reverently so speak) the order of the mystery of the Incarnation[9], that the Eternal Word so took our flesh into Himself, as to impart to it His own inherent life; so then we, partaking of It, that life is transmitted on to us also, and not to our souls only, but our bodies[10] also, since we become flesh of His flesh, and bone of His bone[11], and He Who is wholly life is imparted to us wholly[12]. The life which He is, spreads around, first giving Its own vitality to that sinless Flesh which He united indissolubly with Himself and in It encircling and vivifying our whole nature, and then, through that bread which is His Flesh, finding an entrance to us individually, penetrating us, soul and body, and spirit, and irradiating and transforming into His own light and life. In the words of a father[13] who in warfare with the Nestorian heresy, lived in the mystery of the Incarnation, 'He is life by nature, inasmuch as He was Begotten of the Living Father; but no less vivifying also is His Holy Body, being in a matter brought together and ineffably united with the all-vivifying Word; wherefore It is accounted His, and is conceived as one with Him. For, since the Incarnation, it is inseparable; save that we know that the Word which came from God the Father, and the Temple from the Virgin, are not indeed the same in nature; for the Body is not consubstantial with the Word from God, yet is one by that ineffable coming-together and concurrence; and since the Flesh of the Saviour became life-giving, as being united to That which is by nature Life, the Word from God, then, when we taste It, we have life in ourselves, we too being united with It, as It to the indwelling Word.' 'I then, He saith, being in him will by Mine own Flesh raise up him who eateth thereof, in the last Day. For since Christ is in us by His own Flesh, we must altogether rise, for it were incredible, yea rather, impossible, that Life should not make alive those in whom It is.' To add the words of one father only of the Western Church, ever had in honour, as well for his sufferings for the faith, as for his well-weighed and reverent language. S. Hilary adduced the very actualness of this union in proof against the Arians, that the unity of the Father and the Son, was not of will but of nature, because our union with the Son is by unity of nature, not of harmony of will only. 'For if the Word was truly made Flesh, and we, in the Supper of the Lord, truly receive the Word, being Flesh, how must He not be thought to abide in us, by the way of nature, Who, being born man, took to Himself the Nature of our flesh, now inseparable from Him, and under the Sacrament of the Flesh which is to be communicated to us, hath mingled the Nature of His own Flesh with His eternal Nature. So then, we are all one, because both the Father is in Christ, and Christ in us. Whosoever then shall deny that the Father is in Christ by way of Nature, let him first deny that himself is by way of nature in Christ or Christ in Him; because the Father in Christ and Christ in us, make us to be one in them. If then Christ truly took the Nature of our Body, and that Man, Who was born of Mary, is truly Christ, and we truly, under a mystery, receive the Flesh of His Body, (and thereby shall become one, because the Father is in Him and He in us,) how is it asserted that the Unity is of will only, whereas the natural property (conveyed) through the Sacrament is the Sacrament of a perfect unity?' And a little after, alleging our Blessed

Lord's words, 'My Flesh is truly meat, My Blood is truly drink.' 'Of the truth of the Flesh and Blood, there is no room left for doubt. For now, according both to the declaration of the Lord and our faith, It is truly Flesh and truly Blood. And these, received into us, cause, that we are in Christ and Christ in us. Is not this truth? Be it not truth to those who deny that Christ Jesus is true God. He then is in us through the flesh, and we are in Him, since this, which we are, is with Him in God.'

Would that, instead of vain and profane disputings, we could but catch the echoes of these hallowed sounds, and forgetting the jarrings of our earthly discords, live in this harmony and unity of Heaven, where, through and in our Lord, we are all one in God. Would that, borne above ourselves, we could be caught up within the influence of the mystery of that ineffable love whereby the Father would draw us to that oneness with Him in His Son, which is the perfection of eternal bliss, where will, thought, affections shall be one, because we shall be, by communication of His Divine Nature, one. Yet such is undoubted Catholic teaching, and the most literal import of Holy Scripture, and the mystery of the Sacrament, that the Eternal Word, Who is God, having taken to Him our flesh and joined it indissolubly with Himself, and so, where His Flesh is, there He is[14], and we receiving it, receive Him, and receiving Him are joined on to Him through His flesh to the Father, and He dwelling in us, dwell in Him, and with Him in God. 'I,' He saith, 'in the Father, and ye in Me, and I in you.' This is the perfection after which all the rational creation groans, this for which the Church, which hath the first fruits of the Spirit, groaneth within herself, yea this for which our Lord Himself tarrieth, that His yet imperfect members advancing onwards in Him, and the whole multitude of the Redeemed being gathered into the One Body, His whole Body should, in Him, be perfected in the Unity of the Father. And so is He also, as Man, truly the Mediator between God and Man, in that being as God, One with the Father, as man, one with us, we truly are in Him who is truly in the Father. He, by the truth of the Sacrament, dwelleth in us, in Whom, by Nature, all the fulness of the Godhead dwelleth; and lowest is joined on with highest, earth with heaven, corruption with incorruption, man with God.

But where, one may feel, is there here any place for the sinner? Here all breathes of holy life, life in God, the life of God imparted to man, the indwelling of the All Holy and Incarnate Word, the Presence of God in the soul and body, incorruption and eternal life, through His Holy Presence and union with Him, Who, being God, is Life. Where seems there room for one, the mansion of whose soul has been broken down, and he to have no place where Christ may lay His head[15]; the vessel has been broken, if not defiled, and now seems unfit to contain God's Holy Presence; the tenement has been narrowed by self-love, and seems incapable of expanding to receive the love of God, or God Who is love; or choked and thronged with evil or foul imaginations; or luxury and self indulgence have dissolved it, or evil thoughts and desires have made room for evil spirits in that which was the dwelling-place of the Trinity?

Doubtless, God's highest and 'holy' gift, is as the Ancient Church proclaimed, chiefly 'for the holy.' 'Ye cannot be partakers of the Table of the Lord, and the table of the devils.' And as Holy Scripture, so also the Ancient Church, when alluding to the fruits of this ineffable gift, speak of them mostly as they would be to those, who, on earth, already live in Heaven, and on Him Who is its life and bliss. They speak of those 'clothed in flesh and blood, drawing nigh to the blessed and immortal nature;'[16] of 'spiritual fire;' 'grace exceeding human thought and a gift unutterable;' 'spiritual food, surpassing all creation visible and invisible,' 'kindling[17] the souls of all and making them brighter than silver purified by the fire;' 'removing us from earth, transferring us to heaven,' 'making angels for men, so that it were a wonder that man should think he were yet on earth,' yea, more than angels, 'becoming that which we receive, the Body of Christ.' For that so we are 'members[18] of Him, not by love only, but in very deed, mingled with that Flesh, mingled with Him, that we might become in a manner one substance with Him,' 'the one Body and one Flesh of Christ[19];' and He the Eternal Son and God the Word in us, 'commingled[20] and co-united with us,' with our bodies as with our souls, preserving both for incorruption; 're-creating the spirit in us, to newness of life, and making us "partakers of His Divine Nature;" ' 'the bond of our unity with the Father, binding us to Himself as Man,' Who is 'by nature, as God, in God His own Father;' 'descending to our nature subject to corruption and to change, and raising it to Its own excellencies,' and 'by commingling it with Itself, all but removing it from the conditions of created Nature,' and 're-forming it according to Itself.' 'We are,' adds S. Cyril, 'perfected into unity with God the Father, through Christ the Mediator. For having received into ourselves, bodily and spiritually, Him Who is by

225

Nature and truly the Son, Who hath an essential Oneness with Him, we, becoming partakers of the Nature Which is above all, are glorified.' 'We,' says another (S. Cyril), 'come to bear Christ in us, His Body and Blood being diffused through our members; whence, saith St. Peter, we become "partakers of the Divine Nature." '

Yet although most which is spoken belongs to Christians as belonging already to the household of saints and the family of Heaven and the Communion of Angels and unity with God, still, here as elsewhere in the New Testament, there is a subordinate and subdued notion of sin; and what wraps the Saint already in the third Heaven, may yet uphold us sinners, that the pit shut not her mouth upon us. The same reality of the Divine Gift makes It Angels' food to the Saint, the ransom to the sinner. And both because it is the Body and Blood of Christ. Were it *only* a thankful commemoration of His redeeming love, or *only* a shewing forth of His Death, or a strengthening *only* and refreshing of the soul, it were indeed a reasonable service, but it would have no direct healing for the sinner. To him its special joy is that it is His Redeemer's very[21] broken Body, It is His Blood, which was shed for the remission of his sins. In the words of the ancient Church, he 'drinks his ransom,' he eateth that, 'the very Body and Blood of the Lord, the only Sacrifice for sin,' God 'poureth out' for him yet 'the most precious Blood of His Only-Begotten[22];' they 'are fed from the Cross of the Lord, because they eat His Body and Blood;' and as of the Jews of old, even those who had been the betrayers and murderers of their Lord, it was said, 'the Blood[23], which in their phrenzy they shed, believing they drank,' so of the true penitent it may be said, whatever may have been his sins, so he could repent, awful as it is to say,—the Blood he in deed despised, and profaned, and trampled under foot, may he, when himself humbled in the dust, drink, and therein drink his salvation. 'He Who refused not to shed His Blood for us, and again gave us of His Flesh and His very Blood, what will He refuse for our salvation?' 'He,' says S. Ambrose, 'is the Bread of life. Whoso then eateth life cannot die. How should he die, whose food is life? How perish, who hath a living substance? Approach to Him and be filled, because He is Bread; approach to Him and drink, because He is a Fountain; approach to Him and be enlightened, because He is Light; approach to Him and be freed, because, where the Spirit of the Lord is, there is liberty; approach to Him and be absolved, because He is

Remission of sins.'

In each place in Holy Scripture, where the doctrine of the Holy Eucharist is taught, there is, at least, some indication of the remission of sins. Our Blessed Lord, while chiefly speaking of Himself, as the Bread of life, the true meat, the true drink, His Indwelling, Resurrection from the dead, and Life everlasting, still says also, 'the Bread that I will give is My Flesh, which I will give for the life of the world.' As amid the apparent identity of this teaching, each separate oracle enounces some fresh portion of the whole truth, so also does this; that His Flesh and Blood in the Sacrament shall give life, not only because they are the Flesh and Blood of the Incarnate Word, Who is Life, but also because they are the very Flesh and Blood which were given and shed for the life of the world, and are given *to* those, *for* whom[24] they had been given. This is said yet more distinctly in the awful words, whereby He consecrated for ever[25] elements of this world to be His Body and Blood. It has been remarked[26], as that which cannot be incidental, (as how should any words of the Eternal Word be incidental?) how amid lesser variations in the order or fulness of those solemn words, they still, wherever recorded, speak of the act as a present act. 'This is my Body which *is* given for you;' 'This is My Body which *is* broken for you;' 'This is My Blood of the New Testament which *is* shed for many for the remission of sins;' 'This Cup is the New Testament in My Blood, which *is* shed for you.' He saith not, 'which shall be given,' 'shall be broken,' 'shall be shed,' but 'is being given,' 'being broken,' 'being shed,' and this in remarkable contrast with His own words, when speaking of that same Gift, as yet future, 'The Bread which I will give is My Flesh, which I will give for the life of the world.' And of one of the words used, S. Chrysostome remarks how it could not be said of the Cross, but is true of the Holy Eucharist. 'For "a bone of Him," it saith, "shall not be broken." But that which He suffered not on the Cross, this He suffers in the oblation for thy sake, and submits to be broken that He may fill all men.' Hereby He seems as well to teach us that the great Act of His Passion then began; then, as a Priest, did He through the Eternal Spirit offer Himself without spot to God; then did He 'consecrate' Himself[27], before He was by wicked hands crucified and slain[28]; and all which followed, until He commended His Blessed Spirit to the Hands of His Heavenly Father, was One protracted, willing, Suffering. Then did He begin His lonely journey, where there was none to help or uphold, but He 'travelled in the greatness of His strength;' then did He begin to 'tread the wine-press alone,' and to 'stain all His raiment;' then to 'wash the garments' of His Humanity 'with' the 'Wine' of His Blood; and therefore does the Blood bedew us too; it cleanses us, because it is the Blood shed for the remission of our sins[29]. And this may have been another truth, which our Lord intended to convey to us, when He pronounced the words as the form which consecrates the sacramental elements into His Body and Blood, that that Precious Blood is still, in continuance[30] and application of His One Oblation once made upon the Cross, poured out for us now, conveying to our souls, as being His Blood, with the other benefits of His Passion, the remission of our sins also. And so, when St. Paul says, 'The cup of blessing which we bless, is it not the participation of the Blood of Christ?' remission of sins is implied by the very words. For, if we be indeed partakers of His atoning Blood, how should we not be partakers of its fruits? 'That which is in the Cup,' S. Chrysostome paraphrases, 'is that which flowed from His side, and of that do we partake.' How should we approach His Sacred Side, and remain leprous still? Touching with our very lips that cleansing Blood[31], how may we not, with the Ancient Church[32], confess, 'Lo, this hath touched my lips, and shall take away mine iniquities and cleanse my sins[33]?'

There is, accordingly, an entire agreement in the Eucharistic Liturgies of the universal Church, in prayer, in benediction, in declaration, confessing that in the Holy Eucharist there is forgiveness of sins also. Those of S. James and S. Mark so paraphrase the words of Consecration as to develop the sense that they relate not only to the past act of His Precious Bloodshedding on the Cross, but to the communication of that Blood to us now. 'This is My Body which for you is broken and given for the remission of sins.' 'This is My Blood of the New Testament, which for you and for many is poured out and given for the remission of sins.' Again, the Liturgies join together, manifoldly, remission of sins and life eternal, as the two great fruits of this Sacrament. Thus in the prayer for the descent of the Holy Ghost on the sacred elements, 'that they may be to all who partake of them to the remission of sins, and to life eternal;' or in intercession[34], 'that we may become meet to be partakers of Thy holy mysteries to the remission of sins and life eternal,' or in the words of communicating, 'I give thee the precious and holy and undefiled Body of our Lord and God and Saviour Jesus

Christ for the remission of sins and life eternal.' And the prayer in our own liturgy is almost in the very words of an Eastern[35] and in the character of a Western Liturgy[36], 'that our sinful bodies may be made clean by His Body and our souls washed by His most precious Blood.' Even the Roman Liturgy, though less full on this point, has prayers, 'that the Communion may cleanse us from sin,' 'may be the washing away of guilt, the remission of all offences[37].'

It will then seem probably too refined and narrowing a distinction, when some Divines of that Communion, countenanced by the language of the Council of Trent[38], maintain, in opposition to other error[39], that venial sins only are remitted by the Holy Eucharist, since to approach it in mortal sin were itself mortal sin. For although our own Church also requires at least confession to God, and pronounces His absolution over us before we dare approach those holy Mysteries, yet because we are so far freed from our sins, that we may approach, to our salvation not to condemnation, yet can we say that we are so freed, that nothing remains to be washed away? that the absolution, which admits to that cleansing Blood, is every thing, that cleansing Blood Itself, in this respect also, addeth nothing? Rather, the penitent's comfort is, that, as, in S. Basil's words on frequent communion, 'continual participation of life is nothing else than manifold life,' so, often communion of that Body which was broken and that Blood which was shed for the remission of sins, is manifold remission of those sins over which he mourns, that as the loving-kindness of God admits him again and again to that Body and that Blood, the stains which his soul had contracted are more and more effaced, the guilt more and more purged, the wounds more and more healed, that atoning Blood more and more interposed between him and his sins, himself more united with his Lord, Who Alone is Righteousness and Sanctification and Redemption.

Since then, this Divine Sacrament has, as its immediate and proper end, union with Him Who hath taken our manhood into God, and the infusion into us of His Spirit and life and immortality, making us one with His glorified Humanity, as He is One in the Godhead with the Father, and, besides this, it is ulteriorly, the cleansing of our sins, the refining our corruptions, the repairing of our decays, what must the loss of the Church of the latter days, in which Communions are so infrequent! How can we wonder that love should have waxed cold, corruptions so

229

abound, grievous falls have been, among our youth, almost the rule, to stand upright the exception, Heathen strictness reproach Christian laxity, the Divine life become so rare, all higher instances of it so few and faint, when 'the stay and the staff,' the strength of that life is willingly forfeited? How should there be the fulness of the Divine life, amid all but a month-long fast from our 'daily Bread?' While in the largest portion of the Church, the people mostly gaze at the threshold of the Heaven where they do not enter[40], what do we? We seem, alas! even to have forgotten, in our very thoughts, that daily Communion, which once was the common privilege of the whole Church, which, when the Eastern Church relaxed in her first love, the Western continued, and which they from whom we have our Communion Service in its present form, at first hoped to restore. It implies a life, so different from this our common-place ordinary tenor, a life so above this world as knit with Him Who hath overcome the world; so Angelic as living on Him Who is Angels' Food[41]; an union with God so close; that we cannot mostly, I suppose, imagine to ourselves, how we could daily thus be in Heaven, and in our daily business here below, how sanctify our daily duties, thoughts, refreshment, so that they should be tinged with the hues reflected by our daily Heaven, not that heavenly Gift be dimmed with our earthliness; how our souls should through the day shine with the glory of that ineffable Presence to which we had approached, not we approach to it with earth-dimmed souls. It must ever be so; we cannot know the Gift of God, if we forfeit it; we must cease mostly even to long for what we forego. We lose the very sense to understand it.

It is not in blame of others, my brethren, God forbid! it is as the confession of a common fault, to which others have contributed least who have been least unworthy, and which, if we confess, God may the rather teach us how to amend, that I dare not but notice, how, even in this privileged and protected place, we still mostly forego even what remains, and what our Liturgy still enjoins. We have learned even, as people needs must, to justify the omission. As those, who know not our privileges of daily service, think set daily prayers must become a lifeless form, so right-minded persons speak, (and perhaps until they know it, must needs speak,) as though not we needed more reverence to partake worthily of the Communion weekly, but as though weekly Communions must needs decrease, not increase, reverence. And thus in this abode, which God has encompassed and blessed with privileges above all others, where so many have been brought into an especial nearness to Him, and a sacredness of office, so many look to be so brought, and yet on that account need the more watchfulness and Divine strength that they fall not,—where, if we will, we may retire into ourselves, as much as we will, and have daily prayers to prepare our souls,—we have, in very many cases, not even the privileges which are becoming common in village-Churches; we all, to whom it is expressly, as by name, enjoined, to 'receive[42] the Holy Communion with the Priest every Sunday *at the least*,' have it perhaps scarcely monthly[43]; and the thanksgiving for the Ascension of our Lord stands in our Prayer Book year by year unuttered, because when He ascended up on high to receive gifts for men, there are none here below to receive the Gift He won for us, or Himself Who is the Giver and the Gift. Nor has this been ever thus; even a century and a half ago, this Cathedral was remarked as one of those, where, after the desolation of the Great Rebellion, weekly Communions were still celebrated[44].

But, however we may see that our present decay and negligence should not continue, restoration must not be rashly compassed. It is not a matter of obeying rubrics, but of life or death, of health or decay, of coming together for the better or for the worse, to salvation or to condemnation. Healthful restoration is a work of humility, not to be essayed as though we had the disposal of things, and could at our will replace, what by our forefathers' negligence was lost, and by our sins bound up with theirs is yet forfeited. Sound restoration must be the gift of God, to be sought of Him in humiliation, in prayer, in mutual forbearance and charity, with increased strictness of life and more diligent use of what we have. We must consult one for the other. There is, in our fallen state, a reverent abstaining from more frequent Communion, founded on real though undue fears; there is and ought to be a real consciousness that more frequent Communion should involve a change of life, more collectedness in God, more retirement, at times, from society, deeper consciousness of His Presence, more sacredness in our ordinary actions whom He so vouchsafeth to hallow, greater love for His Passion which we celebrate, and carrying it about, in strictness of self-rule and self-discipline, and self-denying love. And these graces, we know too well, come slowly. Better, then, for a time forego what any would long for, or obtain it, where by God's bounty and Providence that Gift may be had, than by premature urgency, 'walk not charitably,' or risk injury to a brother's soul. He Who alone can make more frequent Communion a blessing, and Who gave such strength to that one heavenly meal, whereby through forty days and forty nights of pilgrimage He carried Elijah to His Presence at the Mount of God, can, if we be faithful and keep His Gift which we receive, give such abundant strength to our rarer Communions, that they shall carry us through our forty years of trial unto His own Holy Hill, and the Vision of Himself in bliss. Rather should those who long for it, fear that if It were given them, they might not be fitted for it, or, if we have it, that we come short of the fulness of its blessing, than use inconsiderate eagerness in its restoration. Ask we it of God, so will He teach us, how to obtain it of those whom He has made its dispensers to us. They too have their responsibilities, not to bestow it prematurely, though they be involved in the common loss. Let us each suspect ourselves, not others; the backward their own backwardness, the forward their own eagerness; each habitually interpret well the other's actions and motives; they who seek to partake more often of the heavenly Food, honour the reverence and humility which abstains, and they who think it reverent to abstain, censure not as innovation, the return to ancient devotion and love; restore it, if we may, at such an hour of the day, when to be absent need not cause pain or perplexity, and may make least distinction; so, while we each think all good of the other, may we all together, strengthened by the Same Bread, washed by the Same Blood, be led, in the unity of the Spirit and the bond of peace and holiness of life, to that ineffable Feast, where not, as now, in Mysteries, but, face to face, we shall ever see God, and be ever filled with His Goodness and His Love.

Meantime such of us, as long to be penitents, may well feel that we are less than the least of God's mercies; that we have already far more than we deserve; (for whereas we deserved Hell, we have the antepast of Heaven;) that the children's bread is indeed taken and given unto dogs; that He, Who is undefiled, spotless, separate from sinners, cometh to be a guest with us sinners; and therein may we indeed find our comfort and our stay. For where He is, how should there not be forgiveness and life and peace and joy? What other hope need we, if we may indeed hope that we thereby dwell in Him and He in us, He in us, if not by the fulness of His graces, yet with such at least as are fitted to our state, cleansing our iniquities and healing our infirmities, Himself the forgiveness we long for; we in Him, in Whom if we be found in that Day, our pardon is for ever sealed, ourselves for ever cleansed, our iniquity forgiven, and our sin covered.

NOTES

1. All the following types, as also that of the 'burning coal' referred to hereafter, are received (with some others) even by the learned Lutheran J. Gerhard, as are some of the verbal prophesies; all are currently found among the Fathers.

2. S. Jerome, 'Moses gave us not the true Bread, but the Lord Jesus; Himself feasting, and the feast: Himself eating, and Who is eaten; we drink His Blood, and without Himself we cannot drink it.—Let us do His will—and Christ will drink with us His own Blood in the kingdom of the Church.'

3. S. Cyril, 'Marvel not hereat, nor inquire in Jewish manner "how," ' &c.

4. S. Cyril, 'When the Son saith that He was sent, He signifieth His Incarnation and nothing else; but by Incarnation we mean that He became wholly man. As then the Father, He saith, made Me man, and since I was begotten of That Which is, by nature, Life, I, being God the Word, "live," and, having become man, filled My Temple, that is, My Body, with Mine own nature, so then, in like manner, shall he also who eateth My Flesh, live by Me. For I took mortal flesh; but, having dwelt in it, being by nature Life because I am of The living Father, I have transmuted it wholly into My own life. The corruption of the flesh conquered not Me, but I conquered it, as God. As then (for I again say it, unwearied, since it is to profit) although I was made flesh, (for the "being sent" meaneth this,) again I live through the living Father, that is, retaining in Myself the natural excellence of Him Who begat Me, so also he, who, by the participation of My Flesh, receiveth Me, shall have life in himself, being wholly and altogether transferred into Me, Who am able to give life, because I am, as it were, of the lifegiving Root, that is, God the Father.'

5. S. Cyril, 'So receive the Holy Communion, believing that it hath power of expelling not death only, but the diseases in us, [i. e. in the soul.] For Christ *thus coming to be in us* lulleth in us the law which rageth in the members of the flesh, and kindleth carefulness to Godward, and deadeneth passions,' &c. S. Chrysostome, 'He saith, he that eateth My Flesh dwelleth in Me, shewing that He is mingled in him.' 'Thou hast, not the Cherubim, but the Lord Himself of the Cherubim indwelling, not the pot, nor the manna, the tables of stone and Aaron's rod, but the Body and Blood of the Lord.' 'Thou art about to receive the King within thee by communion. When the King entereth the soul, there ought to be a great calm.'

6. S. Cyril, 'Why do we receive it [the Holy Eucharist] within us? Is it not that it may make Christ to dwell in us corporeally also, by participation and communion of His Holy Flesh? For S. Paul says that the Gentiles are embodied with, and coheirs, and copartakers of Christ? How are they shewn to be "embodied?" Because being admitted to share the Holy Eucharist, they become one body with Him, just as each one of the holy Apostles. For why did he [S. Paul] call his own, yea, the members of all, as well as his own, the members of Christ? (1 Cor. vi. 15.) And the Saviour Himself saith, "Whoso eateth My Flesh, and drinketh My Blood, dwelleth in Me and I in Him.' For here it is especially to be observed, that Christ saith that He shall be in us, not by a certain relation only as entertained through the affections, but also by a natural participation. For as, if one entwineth wax with other wax, and melteth them by fire, there resulteth of both one, so through the participation of the Body of Christ and of His precious Blood, He in us, and we again in Him, are co-united. For in no other way could that which is by nature corruptible be made alive, unless it were bodily entwined with the Body of That Which is by nature Life, the Only-Begotten. And if any be not persuaded by my words, give credence to Christ Himself, crying aloud, "Verily, verily, I say unto you, Except ye eat," &c. (S. John. vi. 53, 54.) Thou hearest now Himself plainly declaring, that, unless we "eat His Flesh and drink His Blood," we "have not in ourselves," that is, in our flesh, "Eternal Life;" but Eternal Life may be conceived to be, and most justly, the Flesh of That Which is Life, that is, the Only-Begotten.' S. Irenaeus, 'How say they that the flesh goeth to corruption, and partaketh not of life, which is nourished by the Body of the Lord and by His Blood. Our doctrine agreeth with the Eucharist, and the Eucharist confirmeth our

233

doctrine. For as bread out of the earth, receiving the invocation of God, is no longer common bread but Eucharist, consisting of two things, an earthly and a heavenly, so also our bodies, receiving the Eucharist, are no longer corruptible, having the hope of the Resurrection for ever.'

7. But, in the words of our Catechism, 'by the Body and Blood of Christ,' i. e. by receiving them.

8. S. Nicetae, 'I say more, even angels and virtues and the higher powers are confederated in this one Church, as the Apostle teaches that in Christ all things are reconciled, not only things in earth, but things in heaven.'

9. Hooker, 'Doth any man doubt but that even from the flesh of Christ our very bodies do receive that life which shall make them glorious at the latter day, and for which they are already accounted parts of His blessed Body? Our corruptible bodies could never live the life they shall live, were it not that here they are joined with His Body which is incorruptible, and that His is in ours as a cause of immortality, a cause by removing through the death and merit of His own flesh that which hindered the life of ours. Christ is therefore both as God and as man that true vine whereof we both spiritually and corporally are branches. The mixture of His bodily substance with ours is a thing which the ancient fathers disclaim. Yet the mixture of His flesh with ours they speak of, to signify what our very bodies through mystical conjunction receive from that vital efficacy which we know to be in His; and from bodily mixtures they borrow diverse similitudes rather to declare the truth, than the manner of coherence between His sacred and the sanctified bodies of the saints.' —The thoughtful study of these chapters of Hooker on the connection of the Sacraments with the Incarnation of our Blessed Lord would do much, in pious minds, to remove existing difficulties in the reception of the truth.

10. S. Cyril, 'The Holy Body then of Christ giveth life to those in whom It is and keepeth them from incorruption, mingled with our bodies. For we know it to be the Body of no other than of Him Who is, by Nature, Life, having in Itself the whole Virtue of the united Word, and in-qualitied as it were, yea rather filled with His mighty working, whereby all things are made alive and kept in being.'

11. S. Chrysostome, 'Wherefore we needs ought to learn what is the miracle of the Mysteries, why they were given, and what their benefit. We become one body, members, he saith, of His Flesh and of His Bones.'

12. S. Chrysostome, 'If they who touched the hem of His garment drew such great virtue, how much more they who possess Him wholly.'

13. S. Cyril. The words just preceding are, 'For wholly destitute of all share and taste of that life which is in sanctification and bliss, are they who do not through the mystical Communion receive the Son.'

14. S. Ambrose, 'Where His Body is, there Christ is. When the adversary shall see thy dwelling-place filled with the brightness of the heavenly presence,' &c.

15. Bishop Andrewes' Devotions for Holy Communion, (from ancient Liturgies,) 'O Lord, I am not worthy, I am not fit, that Thou shouldest come under the roof of my soul; for it is all desolate and ruined; nor hast Thou in me fitting place to lay Thy head.'

16. S. Chrysostome, 'Consider that, being earth and ashes, thou receivest the Body and Blood of Christ—now when God inviteth thee to His own Table, and setteth before thee His own Son,—let us draw near as approaching to the King of Heaven.'

17. S. Chrysostome, 'This Blood is the salvation of our souls; by this the soul is washed; by this beautified; by this kindled; this maketh our mind gleam more than fire; this maketh the soul brighter than gold.'

18. S. Chrysostome, 'But that we may be thus [one body, members of His Flesh and of His Bones,] not through love only, but in very truth, be we mingled with that Flesh. For this taketh place through the Food He gave us, wishing to shew the longing He hath towards us, wherefore He hath mingled Himself with us, and blended His Body with us, that we might be in a manner one substance as the body joined to the head.' 'It sufficed not to Him to become man, nor to be buffeted and slain, but He

234

mingleth Himself also with us, and not by faith only, but in the very deed maketh us His Body.' S. Cyril, 'For as if one joineth wax with wax, he will see the one in the other, in like manner, I deem, he who receiveth the Flesh of our Saviour Christ, and drinketh His precious Blood, as He saith, is found as one substance with Him, commingled as it were and immingled with Him through the participation, so that he is found in Christ, and Christ again in Him.—As when Paul saith that a little leaven leaveneth the whole lump, so the least portion of the consecrated elements blendeth our whole body with itself, and filleth it with its own mighty working, and thus Christ cometh to be in us and we in Him.'

19. S. Chrysostome, 'That whereat the Angels gaze with awe, thereby are we nourished, therewith are we mingled, and we become the one body and the one flesh of Christ.'

20. The whole passage stands thus in S. Cyril, 'We are united [not only with each other but] with God also. And how, the Lord Himself hath explained. "I in them, and Thou in Me, that they may be perfected in one." For the Son is in us corporeally as Man, commingled and co-united with us by the Holy Eucharist. And again spiritually as God, by the power and grace of His own Spirit, re-creating the spirit in us to newness of life, and making us partakers of the Divine Nature. Christ then appeareth to be the bond of our unity with God the Father, binding us to Himself, as Man, but being, as God, in God His own Father. For in no other way could the nature, subject to corruption, rise aloft to incorruption, unless the Nature, superior to all corruption and change, had descended to it, lightening in a manner that which ever sunk downwards, and raising it to Its own excellencies, and by communion and commingling with Itself all but uplifting it from the conditions conformable to created nature, and re-forming according to Itself that which is not so of Itself. We are &c. [as in the text.] For Christ willeth that we be received into the oneness with God the Father.'

21. S. Chrysostome, 'I willed to become your Brother; I became partaker of Flesh and Blood for your sake; again, that same Flesh and Blood, whereby I became akin to you, I give forth to you.' S. Ignatius, 'They [the Docetae] abstain from the Eucharist and prayer, because they confess not that the Eucharist is that Flesh of our Saviour Jesus Christ which suffered for our sins, which by His loving-kindness the Father raised.'

22. S. Augustine, 'Whom He accounteth so dear, that for you He poureth out daily &c.'

23. S. Chrysostome, 'This is My Blood, which is shed for you for the remission of sins. And Judas was present when the Lord said this. This is the Blood, which thou didst sell for thirty pieces of silver.—Oh how great the lovingkindness of Christ! oh, what the ingratitude of Judas! The Lord nourished, the servant sold. For he sold Him, receiving the thirty pieces of silver; Christ shed His own Blood as a ransom for us, and gave It to him, who sold Him, had he willed. For Judas also was present before the betrayal, and partook of the Holy Table, and received the mystical Feast.'

24. S. Chrysostome, 'If of His Birth it is said, "all this," what shall we say of His being crucified, and shedding His Blood for us, and giving Himself to us for a spiritual feast and banquet?' S. Cyril, 'Christ then gave His own Body for the life of all, but again through It He maketh life to dwell in us; and how, I will say as I am able. For when the life-giving Word of God dwelt in the flesh, He transformed it into His own proper good, i. e. life, and by the unspeakable character of this union coming wholly together with it made It life-giving, as Himself is by Nature. Wherefore the Body of Christ giveth life to all who partake of It, for It expels death when It entereth those subject to death, and removeth corruption, producing by Itself perfectly that Word which abolisheth corruption.' S. Cyprian, 'His Blood whereby we were redeemed and brought to life cannot seem to be in the Cup, when wine is wanting to the Cup, whereby the Blood of Christ is set forth.' S. Clement, 'He blessed wine when He said, Take, drink, this is My Blood, the blood of the vine; for the Word, Which is poured forth for many for the remission of sins, he calls in image, the holy fountain of joy.'

25. S. Chrysostome, 'As that voice, "increase and be multiplied," was uttered

once, but throughout all time doth in act enable our race to produce children, so also that voice [This is My Body], once spoken, doth, on every Table in the Churches, from that time until this day, and until His Coming, make the Sacrifice perfect.'

26. Johnson's Unbloody Sacrifice. Of Roman Catholic Divines it is maintained by Jansenius and others quoted by Vazquez, rejected by Vazquez.

27. S. Chrysostome, 'What meaneth "I sanctify Myself?" I offer Thee a sacrifice; but all the sacrifices are called "holy;" and properly, "holy" are what are dedicated to God.' S. Cyril, "That, according to the usage of the law is said to be sanctified, which is by any one brought unto God, as a gift or offering, such as every first-born which openeth the womb among the children of Israel. For He saith unto Moses, "sanctify unto Me &c." i. e., dedicate, set apart, write down as holy.—Taking, then, according to usage, "sanctify" as meaning "to dedicate and set apart," we say that the Son "sanctified" Himself for us. For He offered Himself, as a Sacrifice and holy Offering to God The Father, reconciling the world unto Him, &c.'

28. S. Gregory, 'He Who disposeth all things according to His supreme Will awaiteth not the compulsion from the Betrayal, nor the violent assault of the Jews, and the lawless judgment of Pilate, so that their malice should be the beginning and cause of the common salvation of man; but by this dispensation He anticipateth their assault according to the mode of His Priestly Act, ineffable and invisible to man, and offered Himself as an Offering and Sacrifice for us, Priest at once and The Lamb of God, Who taketh away the sins of the world.'

29. S. Ambrose, 'That you may eat the Body of the Lord Jesus, wherein is remission of sins, the imploring of Divine reconciliation and everlasting protection.' 'He receiveth who examineth himself, but whoso receiveth shall not die the sinner's death, for this Bread is the remission of sins.'

30. Bishop Overall, 'This word ["sufficient Sacrifice"] refers to the Sacrifice mentioned before, for we still *continue* and commemorate that Sacrifice, which Christ once made upon the Cross.' S. Chrysostome, 'What then? Do not we [Christians] daily offer? We do offer, but making a Memorial of His Death. And this is one and not many. How one and not many? Because it was once offered, as was that which was brought into the Holy of Holies. This is a type of that, and this itself of That. For we always offer The Same; not now one animal, tomorrow another, but always the same thing. So then the sacrifice is one. Else since it is offered in many places, there were many Christs. But no. There is but One Christ every where, here fully and there fully, One Body. As then He, being offered in many places, is One Body, and not many bodies, so also there is One Sacrifice. Our High Priest is He, Who offered the Sacrifice which cleanseth us. That same Sacrifice which was then also offered, we offer now too, That, the inexhaustible. For this is for a Memorial of That Which took place then. For, He saith, "This do, as a Memorial of Me." We do not make a different, but always the same Sacrifice; or rather we make a memorial of that Sacrifice.'

31. S. Gregory, 'His Blood is there received, His Flesh distributed to the salvation of the people; His Blood poured out, not now on the hands of the unbelievers, but into the mouths of the faithful.' S. Chrysostome, 'While the Blood in the Cup is being poured out out of the undefiled Side.' Hooker, 'We are dyed red within and without.' Bishop Wilson, 'Seeing the Blood of the true Paschal Lamb upon your lips.'

32. The coal from the altar is regarded as a type of the Holy Eucharist by S. Chrysostome and others.

33. S. Chrysostome, 'The Lord bless us and make us worthy to take with the pure "tongs" of our hands the fiery coal and to place it on the mouths of the faithful, for the cleansing and purifying of their souls and bodies, now and ever.'

34. S. Mark, 'For the remission of sins, for the communication of the Holy Spirit.' Nestorian Lit., 'May Thy Living Body, O Lord, which we have eaten, and Thy pure Blood which we have drunk, not be to us, Lord, to hurt or weakness, but to the expiation of offences and blotting out of sins, Lord of all.' [See also the Gallic-Gothic, Armenian and Mozarabic Liturgies.]

35. Syriac Liturgy, 'Vouchsafe to us, O Lord God, that our bodies may be sancti-fied by Thy Holy Body, and our souls cleansed by Thy propitiating Blood, and that it may be to us forgiveness of our debts and pardon of our sins.' S. Ephraim, 'Leave me not in hell, most merciful Lord, Who hast given me Thy Body to eat, and made me to drink Thy Blood which is life; through Thy Body may I be cleansed, and through Thy Blood my trespasses be forgiven.'

36. Gallic Sacrament, '—by Whose Flesh, sanctified by Thyself, while fed, we are strengthened, and by His Blood, while given us to drink, we are washed.'

37. Breviary, 'Grant that this holy foretaste of Thy Body and Blood, which I, unworthy, look to receive, may be the perfect cleansing of sins, &c.'

38. 'An antidote, whereby we may be set free from sins of daily incursion, and preserved from mortal sins.'

39. 'That forgiveness of sins was the chief object of the Holy Eucharist.'

40. *Hearing* Mass' in the Roman Communion. This is, of course, said of the ge-neral declension of Communions; at early Masses, even on week-days, the writer is informed that there are Communicants, but not to what extent.

41. S. Augustine, 'That Eternal Word, wherewith the Angels are fed, Which is equal with the Father, men ate, because "being in the Form of God, &c." The Angels are satisfied with Him; but He "emptied Himself" that men might eat Angels' food.'

42. Rubric after Communion Service.

43. One College, it should be said, has, for some time past, restored weekly Communion.

44. Archdeacon Grenville, 'I am informed that his Grace my Lord of Canterbury hath determined on the setting up a weekly Celebration of the Holy Communion, according to the Rubric, in the Church of Canterbury, and that my Lord Archbishop of York is likewise doing the same in his Cathedral, and that they are both writing letters to the Bishops within their Provinces, to follow their example; a noble work of piety, which will prove to their everlasting honour, and very much facilitate conform-ity in the land, which hath been very much wounded by the bad example of Cathe-drals, which have (for the most part) authorized the breach of law, in omitting the weekly celebration of the Eucharist, which hath not been constantly celebrated on Sundays in any Cathedral but Christ Church, Ely, and Worcester.'

Henry Edward Manning

Henry Edward Manning was born at Copped Hall, Totter-idge, in Hertfordshire, in 1808, being descended from a family which made and lost its fortune in merchant banking from generation to generation. In a good patch the young Manning received his education at Harrow and Balliol College, Oxford, intending to follow his father in a parliamentary career. In a bad patch, the family bank failing, he was forced to accept a supernumerary clerkship in the Colonial Office as his first employment. At the age of twenty-four, however, he was rescued from this fate by having his thoughts turned towards an ecclesiastical career by a young lady of Evangelical opinions, and he returned to Oxford, where he was elected to a fellowship at Merton College and ordained first deacon and then priest. A year later he was presented to the living of Woollavington-cum-Graffam, in Sussex.

Manning was a good parish priest, and wrote long afterwards (in *England and Christendom*, page 124) of the affection he retained for 'the little church under a green hillside, where the morning and evening prayers and the music of the English Bible for seventeen years became a part of my soul'. He began his ministry as an Evangelical, and he kept to the end a crusading awareness of social ills and the abuses of wealth. The Tracts were in the air, however, and Manning ran through them as enthusiastically as any. By 1834 he had absorbed Hooker on the Eucharist, assimilated the doctrine of apostolical succession, and learned to attach value to tradition—see his first published work, the sermon in this volume.

Erastianism disgusted Manning, because it was contrary to any view of the Church as the divine society, founded by Christ, and owing its duty ultimately to no authority on earth. His eloquence on this and allied subjects was noted by his superiors, and he was appointed Archdeacon of Chichester before reaching the age of thirty-three. He contributed number 78 to the *Tracts for the Times* and after Newman's secession in 1845 he was looked on as one of the leaders of the High Church party, along with Keble and Pusey and Charles Marriott.

Manning's own disillusionment with the Church of England did not come until 1850, when the Privy Council appointed an elderly Calvinist theologian, George Gorham, to the living of Brampford Speke, despite the opposition of the Bishop of Exeter. (This event, notorious at the time, allowed Catholics who remained in the Church of England to draw attention to the limitations of the Privy Council as an ecclesiastical court of appeal.) Manning found the Gorham judgement a proof of what he took to be the supremacy of the temporal over the spiritual in the English Church. He was consequently received into the Church of Rome on Passion Sunday, 1851. A mere two months later Cardinal Wiseman ordained him priest, and after studying for three years in Rome, he returned to London first as diocesan inspector of schools and then as provost of the Westminster Metropolitan Chapter, from 1857.

In 1865 he succeeded Wiseman as Archbishop of Westminster, and held the see until his death. At the First Vatican Council (1869-70) he was an eager advocate of the promulgation of the definition of Papal Infallibility, pointing out that it was 'not a quality inherent in the person, but an assistance inseparable from the office.' His opposition to the idea of Roman Catholic families sending their sons to the universities, allied to his determination to Christianize the new scientific liberalism and his friendliness with the Irish Catholic element in the London working class, brought out differences with Newman. These cannot be explained merely by reference to their personalities. Manning's passion for social reform—his intervention in 1889 ended the Great Dock Strike—was mistrusted by the old Catholic families, who preferred Newman's conservatism. Manning also found himself in conflict with the Jesuits, whom he once described as 'a mysterious permission of God for the chastisement of England.'

Authoritarian and ascetic but always on what he took to be 'the people's side', a prince of the Church who admired the Salvation Army and signed the pledge, Manning was a more complex personality than there is room here to suggest. What is certain is that Lytton Strachey's caricature of him as a ruthless schemer deserves to be forgotten. Manning was made a Cardinal in 1875. He died in 1892, at the age of eighty-three, and his body, buried first in Kensal Green Cemetery, was later brought back to Westminster Cathedral, which he had founded.

BIBLIOGRAPHY

The English Church, 1835.
The Unity of the Church, 1842.
Sermons, Preached before the University of Oxford, Oxford, 1844.
England and Christendom, 1867.

THE ENGLISH CHURCH
Luke 24:48.
And ye are witnesses of these things.

THIS SERMON was preached in Chichester Cathedral on 7 July 1835, at the Visitation of the Archdeacon, and printed as a pamphlet by the Tractarian publisher Rivington in London in the same year.

It may seem mischievous to represent one of the leading Roman Catholics of his century by a sermon preached on the subject of *The English Church: Its Succession, and Witness for Christ*, but I have other motives than mischief in mind in bringing an almost forgotten aspect of Manning back to notice. (It would be impossible, in any case, to represent him in an anthology of English sermons, 1750-1850, by any of the sermons which he preached as a priest of the Church of Rome since he was not received into that Church until 1851.)

When he preached *The English Church*, Manning was a young man—only twenty-seven—and he had been an Anglican priest for barely two years. He had begun clerical life as an Evangelical, but he was now a convert to the Tractarian cause, and eager to add his voice to those already persuasive on its behalf. Picking up the theme of the first of the *Tracts for the Times*, published anonymously, but written by Newman, which had exhorted priests of the Church of England to 'magnify their office', Manning presents the historical evidence for believing that the apostolic succession has been maintained in the English Church and then speaks of the office of the priest as 'invested with a dignity of unequalled brightness', although far from making priests proud this should leave them humble.

We magnify our office, not to exalt ourselves, but to abase; for it is ever seen that those who lay the least stress on the commission, lay the most on the person; and they that esteem lightly of the derived authority of Christ's ministers, exalt personal qualifications, intellectual or spiritual, into credentials of their ministerial office. 'But we have this treasure in earthen vessels', fragile, and vile, formed of the dust, and to the dust returning, 'that the excellency of the power may be of God, and not of us'.

This sense of the significance of the priesthood is supported

240

in the sermon by an equal sense of the significance of the Church. At this stage, Manning of course believed that it was 'the providential design of God to his Church' that it had thrown out branches. The Church of England was one of those branches, together with the Church of Rome, and the Orthodox Church of the East, but—even at twenty-seven—Manning had grown beyond confusing the witness of the English Church with its established character. The Church in England might be disestablished —that would not matter, since its establishment is but one of those 'accidental adjuncts' or 'perishable dignities' which he insists are 'separable altogether from its indestructible essence'.

And in what does that indestructible essence consist? Manning at that time would have answered as he answers here: in 'the invisible spiritualities of our apostolic descent, and our ministerial power in the Word and the Sacraments', which 'no prince, no potentate, no apostate nation, can sully with a breath of harm'.

I have retained Manning's 'Appendix' to this sermon, printing it at the end of the text and incorporating references to it in the text.

IN OBEYING the call I have received to address you, my Reverend Brethren, to-day, it seemed right to select a topic of the simplest nature, and of the most extended interest, as being the fittest for me to handle, and, therefore, the worthiest for you to hear. Leaving then, for others, the more perfect wisdom, and the higher mysteries of our Holy Faith, I have chosen a subject, with which to be familiar is a pre-requisite to the right undertaking of our sacred ministry, and under the continual influence of which to live, is essential to its right discharge. While, as inferior ministers of Christ, we carefully refer the discussion of passing events, the state and prospects of the Church in this land, to those who, by the providence of God, stand charged with its administration and defence, we cannot deem it remote from the original scope and purpose of these solemn meetings before our Ecclesiastical Superior, if we should consider, in some measure, our ministerial duties and commission, as they are affected by the spirit and course of these latter days.

For the first fifteen hundred years of Christian antiquity, Christ's earthly Church was one, and His ministry one, till apostolical unity of faith and practice withered away in the hollow sameness of the Romish ceremonial. And now, for these three hundred years, men have seemed to sicken at the very name of unity; and to contemplate the unhealthy self-production of sects and divisions within the bosom of the Church with a spurious charity, a cold indifference, and even a misguided satisfaction. At length it has come to pass, that every one of the self-separated fragments of the body Catholic has successfully preferred a claim for itself, and its teachers, to be regarded as the Church and ministry of Christ:—all sects equal, all faiths alike, all ministrations, ordained or unordained, all ambassadors, sent or unsent, equally the institution of one God and Saviour.

We do not speak this in harshness, but in heaviness of soul. We grieve over the divisions and separations from the family of Christ, and our hearts' desire, and prayer to God for his Church is, that its scattered parts may be again fused, and recast into a perfect and indissoluble unity. (A)

It is a hard task, so to speak of our office, as neither to overbear with high pretensions, nor to understate its worth and dignity. In dependence, then, on the help and blessing of the Holy Spirit, whose presence and support was invoked upon us at our ordination, and for the establishment and comfort of our minds in the discharge of our ministerial commission, we will review the subject brought before us by these words of our Master; that is—*the witness He has appointed for Himself in the ministry of His Church*: and in following out this point, we will consider, firstly, *The character*; and secondly, *The influence of our Holy Office on our mind and conduct*.

I. *The character of our Holy Office*, how peculiar to itself; to which no other office of moral teacher or labourer in God's service can bear affinity. There are, indeed, those who imagine the difference of character to result only from the difference of the subject-matter, which, as it is infinitely pure, and infallibly certain, demands for its teachers and propagators a greater esteem and a higher dignity. But this is not all. We rest and rejoice in the peculiar character stamped upon our sacred ministry by its heavenly origin, and its exclusive privileges.

The Apostles of the Lord were not only the companions of Christ on earth, the propagators of God's revealed will after Christ's ascension into heaven, and the inspired writers of a book, on which, in after ages, the people of Christ should rest, as the unchangeable foundation of the faith; they bore a higher dignity, as *witnesses* for Christ, and *representatives* of their exalted and glorified Master. A high privilege it was to be the familiars of the Lord on earth; a glorious function to be the propagators of His kingdom; a sacred work to write the records of His hallowed life, and to fix an unchangeable rule of faith and holiness for His people; but a higher privilege, a more glorious function, and a more sacred work, to be the witnesses of His resurrection and the representatives of Himself. 'As my Father hath sent me,' the image of the invisible God, 'so send I you' (John xx. 21), the personal representatives of Myself. Thus He intimated the sameness of their mission, and His own. 'Verily, verily, I say unto you, he that receiveth you, receiveth me; and he that receiveth me, receiveth Him that sent me' (Matt. x. 40). 'He that despiseth you, despiseth me; and he that despiseth me, despiseth Him that sent me' (Luke x. 16). This strictly representative character of the apostleship, and the official identity of the Apostles with their Master, depended upon two essential constituents; that they had been with Him from the beginning; and that they were commissioned and sent by the Son, as the Son by the Father. This constituted the validity of their mission, and the value of their testimony. And these qualifications we find pointedly observed by the Apostles in adopting a successor into the vacant apostolate or bishopric of Judas. Evidently referring to the act and design of the Lord in ordaining twelve, that they should be with Him, whom also He might send forth to preach (Mark iii. 14), Peter stood up, and said, 'Wherefore of these men, which have companied with us, all the time that the Lord went in and out among us, beginning from the Baptism of John unto that same day that He was taken up from us, must one be ordained to be a witness with us of His resurrection' (Acts i. 21, 22).

And thus the Lord went forth in His representatives, and by His Spirit; beginning from Jerusalem unto the uttermost parts of the earth, preaching the Gospel of the Kingdom, for a witness unto all nations: and to us as many as received Him, to them gave He power to become sons of God, even to as many as believed on his name: and among them that believed, in every place, the Lord planted a Church, and erected a framework of spiritual ordinances, to be governed and applied by his appointed ministers, the *witnesses* of His resurrection, and the *representatives* of His personal presence. The fountain for sin and for uncleanliness, which was first opened to the House of David, and to the inhabitants of Jerusalem, sent forth its healing waters in diverging streams, which, bursting up in every land, multiplied their parent Source; a Bethesda with its many porches, standing open in every city and nation under heaven, to receive all comers, the halt and the maimed, the lame and the leprous; and to give them, not at casual and transitory seasons, but at all times, and for ever, a perfect soundness, by the spiritual presence and invisible energy of Christ.

And for ourselves, my Reverend Brethren, we may indeed be propagators of a doctrinal scheme, and upholders of a time-honoured fabric; and this we may be by man's delegation and authority; but witnesses for Christ crucified, risen, and ascended, and representatives of His person, we cannot be: we cannot offer forgiveness in our Master's name, seal it with baptism, and confirm it in the sacrament of the Lord's body and blood, unless we can show, that the testimony we bear is a direct personal testimony, and the authority we exercise a valid commission derived to us from Himself.

Now it is clear that how long soever the line of transmission be drawn out, the validity of all depends upon the soundness of the first, and the union between each successive link: so that if there be any where a break, the whole must fall; and what man dare, on his own authority, renew what the authority of Christ began? But if we can trace a sound and continuous junction, link by link, between ourselves and his Apostles, the last link of which mysterious chain is held in the hand of God the Son, as the representative of God the Father, we, while invested with a dignity of unequalled brightness, may well nigh sink under the weight of glory, that is put upon us.

We assume then, at once, that this personal testimony was designed to be transmissive; that what the first family of witnesses saw and heard, they were charged to commit to others after them, who believing without sight, should bear a testimony no less authentic than their own. That the order of Bishops are the lineal descendants of those first witnesses, the depositories of their testimony, and the links of this succession, was undisputed in the Church of Christ for fifteen hundred years (B): and how much soever it be gainsayed without, yet within the English Church there is still no other judgment. And ourselves, therefore, the inferior grade of the ministry, being lawfully ordained and sent, derive our representative character from him that laid hands on us. So that, as in every larger section of the Church, the Bishop is the chief official representative of Christ (C), we, in our several cures, are representatives of Christ's witness, and therefore directly, though subordinately, of Himself.

Our commission to witness for Christ, then, hangs upon this question:—*Are the Bishops of our Church the successors, in lineal descent, of the Lord's Apostles?*

As on the one hand it would be needless, if becoming, in this place to enter upon a laboured argument; so neither, on the other, would it be right to advance a bare assertion: for unsupported claims provoke a recoil in the hearer's mind; and pretensions unsustained by proof, savour rather of pride than soberness. You will not be unwilling, therefore, my Reverend Brethren, to review the line of evidence, upon which we rest our ministerial authority. We may distribute the episcopal succession of our Church, in order of time, into two periods: the first, from the present day upward, to the date of Augustin's mission from Rome, in the year 596: the second, from that event to the planting of the British Church.

As to the first period, excepting only the futile objection of the Papists (D), there can arise no controversy: the line of succession even through the transition from Popish corruption to our pure and reformed state, being unbroken throughout the English sees. And here we might close the question at once, by either of two assertions, both equally capable, to any patient,

245

candid mind, of direct and conclusive proof. The one already advanced, that for the first fifteen hundred years of Christian antiquity there was no Church rightly claiming to be Apostolical, which was not Episcopal: the other, that a direct succession may be traced to the origin of the Churches either of Rome or Ireland (E). But we are able to show that the Churches of Britain also were Episcopal, and of the very highest antiquity, even hardly younger in their birth than the apostate and usurping see of Rome.

The question, therefore, is narrowed to the second period, of six hundred years.

Surely, in proving these points, we suffer ourselves to be too much infected by the doubting spirit of these latter days. We consider not so much, what do we believe a valid and sufficient proof, but what will our hearers bear; and thus timidly shrink from exhibiting the evidences of remote history before the coarse incredulity of the world. It behoves the gainsayers of these things to arm themselves, how unused soever they may be to such a warfare, with other weapons of a keener proof, and temper, than impotent denials and a pointless ridicule. They must study, and weigh with patient and judicious discrimination, the rolls and annals of Christian, and especially of British antiquity, before they venture to throw off with a shallow cavil, what the learned and holy of other, why shall I not say, of wiser and better days, laboriously demonstrated, and implicitly believed; or, if they will not study, let them at least be silent.

And, 1st. We have sufficient proof that Augustin on his arrival found the British Churches, although compressed into narrow limits, and shut up in the fastnesses of the mountains by Saxon persecutors, governed by their own Bishops, and claiming absolute independence of all foreign sees (F).

The well known conference also, between the Romish Missionary and the seven British Bishops, of whose sees five or six remain to this day, in which Augustin attempted to bring over the British Churches to the Roman rule of observing Easter, the administration of baptism, and many other customs, which up to that time, and for some years after, the British Churches continued to celebrate after the Eastern model, affords a proof of their Asiatic descent, and therefore a high presumption that they were planted by the first missionary labours of the apostolic age.

This is the testimony of Bede, who wrote about 100 years after the event.

2dly. We find twenty-two counties of England, which had been overrun by the Saxon invasion, reconverted to the faith, and reduced to ecclesiastical discipline, by six or more Bishops from Ireland, who consecrated again an episcopal order in the sees that had been dishallowed by Pagan conquerors (G).

3dly. We have proof, in the year 420, of one Fastidius, Bishop in the see of London, who is designated by some writers Bishop of Britain; not as sole Bishop, but because that to London, as the capital of the civil empire, the metropolitical power, according to the rule of the Church, would also belong. Thus proving the existence of Episcopacy, not as an isolated point, but as a system (H).

4thly. That British Bishops sat in the Councils of Ariminum, Sardica, Nice, and Arles, the latest of which was convened in 359, the earliest in 314. The Council of Arles is a seal upon the Episcopacy of Britain at that date; proving that the lineal descent of our Bishops from the Apostles was then acknowledged. There were present at that Council three (I) Bishops from Britain. These were, it is most likely, the delegates of the whole body; the principle in convening such assemblies being to summon one or more from each province, according to its importance and extent. The question on which they were called to decide, involved the validity of a consecration to the see of Carthage (J),—a sufficient proof that none would have been admitted to pronounce upon the validity or invalidity of consecration, but those who could verify their own (K).

Now, it matters not whether we pursue the thread of the history higher, or leave it here; because, whether Britain received the Gospel from the Apostles, from apostolic, or post-apostolic men, at what time soever it was received, it came through a succession then acknowledged, and was preserved in a succession, which was then confirmed.

But we may add, lastly, on the evidence of Tertullian, who wrote about the year 200 A.D., that Christianity was then received even beyond the wall of Severus, and therefore throughout the south of Britain (L). Origen, at the same date, bears witness to the faith of Britain (M); and to this we may join the testimony of Theodoret and Eusebius, who expressly name the British islands as receiving the Gospel from the Apostles (N): so that, dismissing the variety of opinions, as to which (O) of the Lord's Apostles might have preached in these regions, in obedience to the express and reiterated charge of Christ, to teach all nations, the fact is made probable, even to moral proof, that the liv̄ waters, which were conducted into every other western province of the Roman empire, in Britain also, which, as a conquest comparatively recent, was an especial object of attention, and point of concourse, broke up into a springing well; and although choked and poisoned for awhile by Pagan and Popish invaders of the soil, has never ceased to run, and to this day pours forth the pure unsullied streams of everlasting life.

Wheresoever, then, we can trace its course, there also we find the apostolical order of Bishops; and if here and there, from defect of annals and histories, it bury itself out of sight, as it disappears, so again it emerges, having the marked and distinguishing qualities of its parent spring.

They who gainsay this proof must show that the stream which rises is not that which sunk, and that all these broken reaches owe themselves to so many several heads. And why then were they all Episcopal? But even though this should fail, we may trace our lineage distinctly upwards to apostolical institution, through the Churches of Ireland or Rome.

We have then to learn, when the English Church was not Episcopal. We can show not only that wheresoever its history is traceable, it was Episcopal; but that its Episcopacy is the basis of all its history. *'For we cannot trace the history of Churches further than we can do that of their Bishops,'* is the decision of one among our profoundest antiquarian authorities (P): the succession of Bishops, as of Kings in civil affairs, being in fact the links of history, and their sees the depositories of all ecclesiastical memorials.

Therefore, as a ministry lineally descended from the original witnesses; as a Church identical in faith and form with those they planted; of which also the foundations were laid by apostolic men, if not by the very Apostles of the Lord, there is impressed, both upon our commission a validity, and upon our witness a value, which none may rightfully assume, who cannot cite the Apostles as the forefathers of their Bishops, and the Catholic creeds and symbols as the standards of their faith.

But lest we be thought, out of the frailty of our swerving nature, to taunt in an unseemly way those Christian brethren, of whom we doubt not, that in the day of the Lord they will be found upon the corner-stone; though we believe they must render an account for overthrowing the perfect superstructure of his Church, we choose rather that one, who followed within one

248

hundred years of the last Apostle should speak for us. 'Let them,' he says to those who then divided the body of Christ, 'let them produce the originals of their churches, and unroll the line of their Bishops, running down in such wise by a succession from the beginning, that the first Bishop should have an Apostle, or an apostolic man, who continued faithfully with the Apostles unto the end, as his authority and predecessor; for thus the apostolical Churches trace their descent' (Q).

We especially desire to make clear in what spirit these claims are preferred; not with a desire of unduly exalting ourselves, or of fostering a corrupt pride, by a boastful challenging of spiritual pre-eminence, God knoweth; but to impress upon ourselves, my Reverend Brethren, that in virtue of our high privileges, a necessity of far more exceeding weight is laid upon us, as in an especial way the witnesses and representatives of Christ; and woe unto us if, in all its convincing, converting, humbling, sanctifying, and saving power, we preach not the Gospel. We magnify our office, not to exalt ourselves, but to abase; for it is ever seen that they who lay the least stress on the commission, lay the most on the person; and they that esteem lightly of the derived authority of Christ's ministers, exalt personal qualifications, intellectual or spiritual, into credentials of their ministerial office. 'But we have this treasure in earthen vessels,' fragile, and vile, formed of the dust, and to the dust returning, 'that the excellency of the power may be of God, and not of us' (2 Cor. iv. 7).

And once more, if any feel grieved that we thus unordain other men, and so act uncharitably and proudly against useful servants of our Common Master, we answer, that we unordain no man. We prove the validity of our orders, and leave to them a task we know not how to do for them, to prove the validity of their own (R); and bid them render an account, not to us, but, in an hour of calm self-examination, to their own instructed consciences, and to the Head of the Church in heaven, if they have entered uncalled upon this holy ministration. And what good is wrought by them we hinder not; nay, we rejoice, and bless God that bringeth rivers of water out of the dry ground. 'Some indeed preach Christ even of envy and strife; and some also of good-will . . . Notwithstanding, every way, whether in pretence or in truth, Christ is preached, and I therein do rejoice, yea, and will rejoice' (Phil. i. 15, 18). 'John answered and said, Master, we saw one casting out devils in thy name, and we forbade him, because he followeth not with us. And Jesus said unto him, Forbid him not, for he that is not against us is for us' (Luke ix. 49, 50).

II. And now, my Reverend Brethren, to show that this view of our holy office does not terminate in empty speculation, barren of results, nor fade away from the mind as a pageant, and shadow of the past, but, according to the design of Him who ordained this sacred ministry, exercises a most searching and constraining power over those that consider it aright, we proceed to show *what should be the influence of our holy office on our mind and conduct.* What are our duties as bearing this witness for our Master?

1. *As witnesses of Christ, we should continually revert to the origin of our commission.*

The providential design of God to his Church seems to be, that in every land, where it strikes a root, it should throw out its branches, and overshadow the whole population, becoming thereby *national*;—that it should be supported by the pious liberality of the rich and noble, becoming thereby *endowed*;—and that it should blend itself with every rank of society, and enter into the courts and councils of the state, and climb up even into the throne itself, thus winning over the aid of human laws to promote its extension and security, and becoming, in our common language, a Church *established*. But these are only accidental adjuncts, and perishable dignities, separable altogether from its indestructible essence, against which alone the gates of hell shall not prevail. Perpetuity is no where promised to its national, endowed, or established character; but to the essentials of the lineal ministry, and congregation of faithful men.

As ministers, then, of the national religion we dispense the advantages of an endowed system, and the privileges of legal security; but we deny that these things enter into the essence of the spiritual kingdom of which we are stewards, or of the commission under which we act. We will enjoy our blessings without doubting, and lay them out in God's service with thankfulness; but we will not rest upon them as our authority, or exhibit them as credentials of our office. The world gave, and the world may take away, is written broadly on them all; but the invisible spiritualities of our apostolical descent, and our ministerial power in the Word and Sacraments, no prince, no potentate, no apostate nation, can sully with a breath of harm. Though we should be brought down, and bid sit in the dust of humiliation;—though we should be repudiated by law, despoiled of rights, and, were these latter days zealous enough to persecute, driven up, a shortened remnant, as our British forefathers, into mountain-holds—yet, though minished and brought low by oppression, the witnesses would prophesy in sackcloth still, and, praying for their destroyers, hand on their holy privilege and unbroken testimony unto children's children.

It is well for us to distinguish for what we are contending, and to make clear to the eyes of all who will see, that while we stand for the earthly rights and privileges of the Church, we do not contend for existence, but only for the accidental blessings wherewith God in his Providence has furnished us for His work. And while this is of great importance in beating back the insinuations of avarice and worldly covetousness upon the uncandid minds that so allege against us, and in directing the attention of an attached and faithful laity, daily growing round us, to the real distinction between the spiritual pastors of the Church and other teachers of religion, it is also of the highest and chiefest importance in constraining our own minds to deeper, more exalting, more abasing, more encouraging views of the office we are charged to execute; and in calling us off from the earthly, separable, and transitory elements of our ecclesiastical system, to the heavenly, essential, and eternal character of the Church and Ministry of Christ. We remind ourselves that we are not ministers of men, nor by men, but witnesses called and commissioned by Jesus Christ, and God the Father, who raised him from the dead. And thus we are brought into closer communion with the invisible world, and the unseen Master, whose kingdom we are charged and empowered to administer. But though this our spiritual origin and mission be never so clear, it is no sufficient security, taken alone, that our message be according to the truth. An accredited ambassador may pervert his message, and betray his master's charge.

2. Therefore *as witnesses of Christ, we should be so much the more watchful over the message we deliver, by how much the more authority we have to treat in His name.* We may not borrow the wild and wandering light of cold philosophy; we may not adulterate our message with the corruptions of an evil world, or accomodate its holy severities to the fastidious taste of an unhealthy refinement; we may not explain away its mysteries to flatter a haughty intellect, nor lower the standard of its holiness to spare the unrenewed affections of the heart. In opposition to all this, and to all the inexhaustible varieties of error and deceit, we have to preach the truth as it is in Jesus, impressed with the

251

peculiar characteristics which bespeak it of unearthly origin, the eternal offspring of a higher state, the gracious visitant of this lower world, come down to bid them that believe ascend upward from the abodes of sin and death into the realms of life and glory.

Thus, we speak things above and beyond all human demonstration, things which the blind eye of man hath not seen, nor the dull ear heard, neither have entered into the corrupt and darkened heart to conceive: things of a celestial sound, which refuse to be comprehended, and demand implicit faith. As witnesses, our proof is, '*The Lord hath said*,' and in confirmation we point to the Scriptures, and say, '*It is written*.' And, taking our stand on this foundation, we testify of the world, which its worshippers revere with a prostrate adoration, that it lieth in wickedness, and is by nature guilty before God: of the heart, which philosophy would cleanse of its original stain, and imagination brighten with a guileless purity, that it is born enmity against God: of man, vaunting himself in the pride of life, that in his Maker's sight he is spiritually dead: of sin, which men will not recognise, except in vehement passion and external act, that every inward declension from absolute sinlessness is sin; that Christ takes cognizance of evil thoughts, and sits in judgment upon impure imaginations: of God's law, the breach whereof men deem a trivial thing, all but impeaching their Redeemer of undue severity, that the least offence, as surely as the greatest, brings us in guilty of all; and that the lightest as well as the heaviest sin can alone be cancelled in the blood of a crucified Redeemer; of man's return from death to life, from sin to holiness, we testify that the same Spirit, which raised up Jesus from the dead, alone can quicken our mortal bodies, alone regenerate and renew the soul: and in this we bear our Master's witness, as well against the schemes and calculations of political science, falsely so called, by which legislators would dispense with the aid and offices of the Eternal Spirit in raising and restoring mankind, as against the low, unspiritual, and hollow rectitude, which men esteem a substitute for the pure and heaven-born holiness of the redeemed and sanctified.

And what we testify we also seal; what we declare we also convey; being charged and empowered to conclude a peace with all that believe, and to seal it to their souls with the effectual graces of Christ's holy sacraments.

And when, my Reverend Brethren, if not now, shall there be need to witness this good confession faithfully, boldly, unflinchingly,—before kings and governors, before rulers and all the people,—when the standard and symbols of the Church seem fast departing from the course and order of society; when men recoil from the unsparing boldness of Christian truth, and take refuge in modified forms and vague generalities, buying a hollow peace with the world, at the cost of treason against the Majesty of Heaven. If they will not preserve inviolate, and honour with reverence the symbols and standard of the faith, we must give the greater heed that they may read in us the living witnesses for Christ, the form of sound words, written and engraven in tablets over which the world has no dominion. They must see in our persons, and hear in our words, what they will not endure in creeds and formularies.

3. And therefore, lastly, *as witnesses of Christ, we must continually seek a growing conformity to the mind and conduct of our Master.* We shall be ill representatives of Christ if our examples be at variance with His, and belie the letter of our message. The mind of Christ must be transfused into our own. There must be somewhat of the same intense love of perishing sinners, of the same patient endurance of moral evil, and unwearied striving to bring the impenitent to God: a portion of the same holy boldness and fearless inflexibility of purpose: a measure of that perpetual self-denial and self-sacrifice to the service and glory of His Father: of that acute, affectionate, and universal sympathy with the sick, the suffering, the tempted, and without partaking of their contamination, even with the sinful: and somewhat also of that intuitive penetration of heart and character, which His omniscience apprehended at a glance, but we can gather only by keen observation, strict analysis, and rigid search, under the guidance of the Holy Ghost, into all the depths and windings of our own. What a mission, Brethren, is ours! 'As my Father hath sent me, so send I you,' to arrest sinners in the career of death; to convert their souls to God; to open and shut the gates of his invisible kingdom; to feed with the bread of heaven; to conflict with every shade of corruption, and to wrestle with every shape of moral evil; to watch over and to ripen the varied and several developments of spiritual life, the bud, the blossom, and the fruit; to present every soul that is given to us perfect in Christ Jesus, an offering acceptable to God; and joyfully pour out, if need be, even ourselves also, as a crowning libation on our holy sacrifice!' (Phil. ii. 17.)

Woe to the covetous and greedy steward, woe to the careless and insensate minister, woe to the loitering and unprofitable servant, woe to him whom the gain, the honour, and the ease, of the world, whom a trifling temper, a selfish heart, and an unspiritual mind shall make a cumberer of Christ's ministry, a hinderer of the Lord's service, and a blight upon his Church. If there be in heaven no brighter crown than that which is studded with souls gathered by our hands, then surely in the gloomiest abode of hell there is no darker doom than awaits the hinderer of the Lord's glory, and the destroyer of a brother's soul—and, what if we destroy a flock! To witness for Christ on earth, and to dwell with everlasting burnings, is a linking together of most repugnant and intolerable things. The seal of our dignity here will then be a brand of the blackest infamy, eating into the soul with an unutterable anguish: and to this accumulated condemnation, we, if we be unfaithful, are hastening with a headlong speed. For we propagate not doctrines only but characters: whether we will or no, our example reproduces itself. A low tone of daily life chills, and depresses all around us; and so intimate is the correspondence, that such as the pastor is, such is the flock. And we have bound ourselves to implant and mature the mind of Christ in our people. In the most solemn hour of our mortal life we consented to this question, 'Will you be diligent to frame and fashion your own-selves and your families according to the doctrine of Christ, and to make both yourselves and them, as much as in you lieth, wholesome examples and patterns to the flock of Christ' (Service for ordering of Priests). By this vow we shall be tried in the day of doom, and who shall abide when God doeth this?

We should maintain, then, a continual remembrance, amounting to an habitual consciousness that, as witnesses and representatives of Christ, we are bound to walk as he walked: not so, indeed, as that this consciousness should produce an artificial carriage, or a forced insincere ostentation, but that it should be cultivated with diligence; and by daily and reiterated prayer, watchfulness, and exercise, so wrought into the mind, as to become an insensible habit, indistinguishable at last from its ordinary workings; unperceived indeed in its operation, but most evident in its effects. And to this end we have need to set Him continually before us. For the habitual contemplation of the Redeemer's life, made vivid by his mysterious grace and a sense of his nearness to us, has a transforming power, subduing the whole frame of the faithful mind, and assimilating it to Himself. And as in the discharge of His earthly ministry he was much in communion with His Father, so must we be with Himself, that we may catch somewhat of his Spirit, and that our faces may shine with the reflected outlines of His likeness, when we pass from our oratory and solitude into our family and flock. Like Him also we must be continual intercessors for our people, spreading day by day the account of their condition and of our ministry before Him, 'that holdeth the seven stars in His right hand, and walketh in the midst of the seven golden candlesticks' (Rev. ii. 1). And happy is the servant that, in this review of his ministry, has no need to say, 'Lo I have sinned, and I have done wickedly; but these sheep, what have they done?' (2 Sam. xxiv. 17.) Like Him also, who in the darkest hour of trial and desertion could say, 'I am not alone, because the Father is with me' (John xvi. 32), so we, pleading before Him his last promise, 'Lo, I am with you, even unto the end of the world' (Matth. xxviii. 20), may fully assure our hearts, that whithersoever we go in the lawful discharge of our ministry, He bears us company: howsoever we be tried, though men obstruct with ill-repressed hostility, or Satan urge with the last and hottest wrath, we have this confidence—He is ever with us, who can wither the might of spiritual evil, confound the malice of the world, pass the bars of the prison-house, mingle with our daily toils, wake with us in our nightly watchings, our companion in solitude, our defender in the throng of men, our sword and shield in the warfare of his kingdom. And this ever remembered and sensibly felt presence of Christ, reflecting upon our hearts the realities of the invisible world, is the secret of our power and peace, inexhaustible in the variety of its adaptation to all the imaginable contingencies of this stormy and tempestuous state; almighty in its sanctifying and sustaining energies, and as inseparable from the soul as consciousness from life.

For designs and purposes, which the exalted head of the Church hath put in his own power, He hath permitted the outward boundaries of His heritage and ministry to be broken down. Therefore while men, called and uncalled, commissioned and uncommissioned, alike approach and minister at the altar, while our apostolical descent is gainsayed, and the necessity of rightful ordination set at nought, it is bounden on us to show that we bear no visionary dignity, no barren privilege, but a most sacred office, full of a divinely appointed power, to strengthen and to sanctify those that in faith discharge it. We will show, my Reverend Brethren, by God's help, in our lives and labours, that in the apostolical ministry there resides a living influence, stamping it as the ordinance of Christ, and conforming His servants to Himself. If His word and witness be found in us, his Spirit will not be wanting. But if there should be found in us a less, or even an equal amount of self-devotion, deadness to the world, tender love of souls, fearlessness in rebuking high-born vice, and low corruption, forwardness in contending for the faith, and proclaiming the Gospel of the Redeemer's kingdom, of patient, unwearied daily intercourse, from house to house, with the people of our charge, in all their trials, afflictions, and offences; and, on the other hand, of their affections, reflected back upon ourselves, won by self-evidencing watchfulness, and care for their earthly and eternal welfare, than in those, whom we believe to have no part nor lot in our holy ministry, shall we be surprised if plain men, and unlearned in the mysteries of Christ's Church, should deem our commission no better, that I should not say less blessed and sealed of God than theirs? If they must account for assuming a commission never given to them, we must account for the abuse and neglect of that we have received; and ours will be the heavier reckoning. Let us then consider one another, within and without, to provoke unto love, and to good works. Here is a rivalry without collision, a contention without strife. And God grant that a more abundant measure of a holier spirit, and a closer conformity to our Master's pattern, impressed as a countersign upon our testimony, may henceforth and ever bear witness unto us, that if any are Christ's so are we Christ's.

And whom shall not these things constrain? To be the Lord's especial portion, a remnant quickened from the dead; forgiven and sanctified in the blood and spirit of the Lord; raised to a middle space between the throne of our exalted Master, and the spirits of a world redeemed: to be the visible representatives of an invisible Saviour, associated with him in the administration of his earthly kingdom; concluding eternal peace, or denouncing eternal war, a savour of life unto life, or of death unto death; doomed ourselves to an eternity of woe that cannot be deepened, or of glory that cannot be exalted:—who shall minister before Him, and not tremble? who shall draw nigh to Him, and not rejoice? who can forecast our condemnation without despair, or contemplate our blessedness without an ecstacy.

Which of us that be worldly, heedless, unprofitable, shall endure His withering scrutiny, when He shall be revealed from heaven with fire; or in the sunshine of his final acceptance remember our toil and labour? Who shall remember the contradiction and the cross, when the dead shall ascend up out of the depths of the sea, spread over the plains, and stand upon the mountains, when we and our people shall meet in the day of that mighty gathering, when the judgment shall be set, condemnation utter its thunders, and its voice die away in the peace of heaven; and the New Jerusalem, the foundation and corner-stones (Eph. ii. 20; Rev. xxi. 14) whereof, with Him, we are, shall be for ever filled with the unimaginable glories of Almighty God.

APPENDIX

A. 'From whence it appears that the first unity of the Church, considered in itself, besides that of the Head, which is one Christ, and the life communicated from that one Head, which is one Spirit, relieth upon the original of it. 1 Cor. iii. 11. Eph. ii. 19-21. 1. The unity of origination. 2. Of faith. 3. Of sacraments. 4. Of hope. 5. Of charity. 6. All the Churches of God are united into one, by the unity of discipline and government, by virtue whereof the same Christ ruleth in them all.'

B. – 'Catholic and Anti-Episcopal are contradictory terms.

'From Christ's time till this day, there was never any one Catholic, in the Eastern, Southern, or Northern Churches, who professed himself to be Anti-Episcopal, but only such as were cast out for heretics or schismatics. The same I say of the Western Church for the first fifteen hundred years. Let him [Baxter, against whom Bramhall writes] show me but one formed Church without a Bishop, or the name of any lay Presbyter, in all that time, who exercised or challenged Ecclesiastical jurisdiction, or the power of the keys in the Church before Calvin's return to Geneva in the year 1538, after he had subscribed the Augustan Confession and Apology for Bishops, and I will give him leave to be as Anti-Episcopal as he will. I will show him the proper and particular names of Apostles, Evangelists, Bishops, Presbyters, Deacons,in Scriptures, in Councils, in Fathers, in Histories: if he cannot name one particular lay Elder, it is because there never was any such thing in rerum natura for fifteen hundred years after Christ.' (Archbishop Bramhall)

For the same assertion, see Bishop Hall's 'Two undoubted propositions touching Church government.' Jeremy Taylor, Preface to a Sermon at the Consecration of the Archbishops and Bishops of Dublin. Hooker's Preface to Eccl. Pol.. Overall's Convocation Book. Jer. Taylor's Episcopacy asserted, &c. '. . . The Catholic practice of Christendom for fifteen hundred years is so insupportable a prejudice against the enemies of Episcopacy, that they must bring admirable evidence of Scripture, or a clear revelation proved by miracles, or a contrary undoubted tradition apostolical for themselves, or else hope for no belief against the prescribed possession of so many ages.'

C. Ignatius ad Ephes., Ad. Magnes.

D. The Nag's Head consecration.

E. Palmer's Origines Liturgicae, vol. ii. 249-251, and note f.

F. 'Things continued thus, when, anno 596, Pope Gregory the Great sent Austin the monk to convert these Saxons, who, after his first expedition, being at Arles, consecrated Archbishop of Canterbury, applied himself more closely to this his errand than he had done before. He found Paganism covering the greatest part of the Island, but withal a considerable Church among the Britains; seven Bishops they had, as Bede informs us . . . Their sees were Hereford, Tavensis or Llandaff, Lhan-Padern-Vaur, Bangor, Elviensis or St. Asaph, Worcester, and Morganensis, supposed by many to be Glamorgan, but that being the same with Llandaff, R. Hoveden reckons Chester in the room of it, or, as Bishop Usher thinks not improbable, it might be Caer-Guby, or Holy-head, in the Isle of Anglesea. These seven were under the superintendancy of a Metropolitan, whose Archi-episcopal See had been formerly at Caerleon upon Uske, (the famous river Isca,) in Monmouthshire, but some years before Austin's arrival, had been translated to Menevia, or St. David's, (so called from the Bishop that translated it,) in Pembrokeshire, though for some time after retaining the title of Archbishop of Caer-Leon. And to him were the Welsh Bishops subject; and by him ordained, as he by them, until the time of King Henry the First. . . . –This Church had rites and usages vastly different from them of Rome, both for the administration of baptism and many other customs—a most infallible argument that the Britannic Churches had no dependence upon, had held no communication with the Church of Rome. Their celebration of Easter after the manner of the Asiatic Churches, clearly showing that they had originally derived their religion from those Eastern parts.'-Cave on the Government of the Church, pp. 247-250; Stillingfleet's Origines Britannicae, 356-358;

Hooker, vii. c. 1; Bingham's antiquities, book 2, xviii. 2. and 9, 1, 11. and 9. vi. 20.

G. Palmer's Origines Liturgicae, vol. ii. 250.

H. Stillingfleet, 194, 195.

I. 'Three British Bishops subscribed the decrees of that Synod,' Eborius of York, Restitutus of London, and Adelfius de civitate Coloniae Londinensium, forsan Camalodunum, Colchester.—Cave's Government of the Church, 245.

J. The schism of Donatus, involving the conflicting claims of Majorinus and Caecilianus to the see of Carthage.

K. Taylor's Episcopacy asserted, &c. sect. xli.

L. Tertullian says—'The kingdom of Christ was advanced among them (the Britains), and that Christ was solemnly worshipped by them.' He was a man of too much understanding to expose himself to the contempt of the Jews, by mentioning this as a thing so well known at that time, if the Britains were then known to be no Christians.

He also says that 'the Gospel had access to those parts of Britain whither the Romans had none. Which doth prove, that Christianity was then received beyond the wall, but not by the Scots, who were not yet settled in those parts; but by old Britains, who were driven thither, as appears by the account given by Xiphilin, out of Dio, who saith that the Britains were divided into two sects, the Maeatae and the Caledonii. The former dwelt by the wall, and the latter beyond them. These were the extra-provincial Britains.'—Stillingfleet.

M. Stillingfleet, 57.

N. Stillingfleet, 36, 37.

O. Palmer's Origines Liturgicae, vol. ii. 250, note e; Stillingfleet, 38-48.

P. Stillingfleet, 77.

Q. Tertullian, de Praeser. Haeret. xxxii.

R. 'The second [scandal] is intended to raise envy against us, as the uncharitable censurers and condemners of those Reformed Churches abroad which differ from our government; wherein we do justly complain of a slanderous aspersion cast upon us. We love and honour those sister Churches as the dear spouse of Christ. We bless God for them, and we do heartily wish unto them that happiness, in the partnership of our administration, which, I doubt not, but they do no less heartily wish unto themselves. . . . When we speak of Divine Right, we mean not an express law of God, requiring it upon the absolute necessity of the being of a Church, what hindrances soever may interpose; but a Divine institution, warranting it where it is, and requiring it where it may be had.'—Bishop Hall's Divine Right of Episcopacy, vol. ix. 634, &c. &c. &c.

OF ALL the members of the Oxford Movement, Robert Wilberforce was the most scholarly—a systematic theologian. His trilogy on sacramental doctrine—*The Doctrine of the Incarnation of Our Lord Jesus Christ* (1848), *The Doctrine of Holy Baptism* (1849), and *The Doctrine of the Holy Eucharist* (1853)—shows Tractarian thinking on this subject at its most developed. As Dr A. Hardelin says in his *Tractarian Understanding of the Eucharist* (Uppsala, 1965):

> In 1830 Newman had started by insisting strongly on the sacrificial character of Christian worship and the ministerial functions, but the sacrifice offered was limited to the prayers and self-oblations of Christians in holy obedience. Later, Newman and the other Tractarians so concentrated on the preaching of the reality and importance of sacramentally mediated grace that the sacrificial aspect of worship was for a time almost forgotten. Since however belief in the real presence had become one of their central convictions, the problem of the eucharistic sacrifice inevitably recurred. In the eucharist, both as sacrament and sacrifice, Tractarian religion found an external object and a focus in which all its intentions were gathered up. For as faith and justification could not be divorced from love, obedience, and sanctification, so neither could sacramental grace be from sacrificial worship and self-dedication through it. The Church was not only a channel of grace to men, but the mystical body, humanity incorporated in Christ to be dedicated to God. What Newman in 1830 thought to be the only acceptable sacrifice to God, namely, the self-offering of obedient worshippers, Wilberforce, two decades later, *taught to be acceptable only as assumed in the body of Christ, sacramentally present, and offered up to the Father through His priests.* [p. 219, my italics.]

Robert Wilberforce was born at Clapham in 1802, the second son of William Wilberforce (1759-1833), philanthropist and chief advocate of the abolition of the slave trade. He was educated privately and at Oriel College, Oxford, where he graduated with a double first in 1823, and was elected a fellow in 1826. For three years thereafter he was a tutor at Oriel, his two fellow tutors being Newman and Froude. Wilberforce was ordained a deacon in 1826, and priested in 1828. In 1832 he was instituted to the benefice of East Farleigh, Kent, which he exchanged for that of Burton Agnes, near Beverley, some eight years later.

In 1841 Wilberforce was appointed Archdeacon of the East Riding. Soon after he became friendly with Manning, then rector of Lavington, and carried on with him a correspondence in which each man examined the claims of the Roman Catholic Church in England. Manning had made the first approach, turning to Wilberforce as a confessor since he was already beset with doubts as to the sufficiency of the English Church—he was received into the Church of Rome in 1851. A little later he wrote pointedly to his friend, following the publication of the third volume of Wilberforce's trilogy: 'Your private judgement has convinced you of the Incarnation, Baptism, and the Eucharist. Apply it now to the third and last clause of the Baptismal Creed, "I believe in the Holy Ghost, the Holy Catholic Church." Write a book on this next.'

Instead of writing such a book, at the end of August 1854 Wilberforce resigned his preferments, and on the eve of All Saints' Day of that year he was received into the Roman Catholic Church in Paris, not wishing to embarrass or annoy his friends and relations at home. After hesitating for a year, he proceeded to Rome and entered the Academia Ecclesiastica with a view to studying for the Latin priesthood, his expenses being defrayed by the Pope. He died, however, in minor orders, at Albano, near Rome, from an attack of gastric fever, in February 1857, at the age of fifty-four. Manning described that death in a letter to his brother Henry:

> On Monday morning he made his confession with full self-possession and received the Blessed Sacrament in Viaticum, with perfect recollection and calmness, and yesterday morning Extreme Unction, but his mind was less clear and present. He joined from time to time in words of prayer: and many times kissed the crucifix with very marked devotion. Through the whole of his illness he has been perfectly free from pain. We have never seen a moment of suffering: nor has he at any moment been distressed in mind. I never saw a death of more perfect peace.

The body of Robert Wilberforce is buried in the St Raymond Chapel of the church of S. Maria sopra Minerva, where there is also a tablet to his memory.

BIBLIOGRAPHY

Sermons on the New Birth of Man's Nature, 1850.
The Doctrine of the Incarnation of Our Lord Jesus Christ, 1848.
The Doctrine of Holy Baptism, 1849.
The Doctrine of the Holy Eucharist, 1853.
An Inquiry into the Principles of Church Authority, 1854.

THE SACRAMENTAL SYSTEM
1 John 4: 2, 3.
Hereby know ye the Spirit of God: Every spirit that confesseth that Jesus Christ is come in the flesh, is of God: And every spirit that confesseth not that Jesus Christ is come in the flesh, is not of God; and this is that spirit of Anti-Christ, whereof ye have heard that it should come.

THIS SERMON was preached before the University of Oxford on 10 March 1850, and first published as sermon xix in *Sermons on the New Birth of Man's Nature* in the same year. It is in itself a handy synthesis of Wilberforce's thinking as set forth in *The Doctrine of the Incarnation, The Doctrine of Holy Baptism* and *The Doctrine of the Holy Eucharist*; more importantly, it affirms Tractarian understanding of the relatedness of the Incarnation to the two sacraments of Baptism and the Eucharist.

Wilberforce argues for a whole sacramental system of religion not because this appeals to him aesthetically or intellectually, but because the Incarnation—the enfleshment of God—demands no less.

> For since the doctrine of our Lord's mediation is founded upon His taking our flesh; since its primary law is the re-creation in His person of our common nature, the entrance of divine grace into humanity in its Head and Chief:—therefore some medium is required, by which those things, which were stored up in Him, may be distributed to His brethren. To speak of the Head as the fountain of grace, is to assume the existence of streams, by which it may be transmitted to His members. Now this function is so plainly assigned to Sacraments, that nothing else can be alleged to supply their place.

The Incarnation of Christ implies the recovery of man's likeness to God, lost in Adam, or as Wilberforce puts it in another sermon, *The Mediation of Christ*, 'The manhood of our Lord . . . is the bridge whereby the gulf between heaven and earth has been spanned over.' The Incarnation is 'the great objective fact of Christianity'—as he writes in *The Doctrine of the Incarnation*. The Eucharist is the further incarnation of that fact, extending to individuals 'those gifts which were bestowed in the Incarnation upon humanity at large.'[1]

A vision of the glory of this fact is at the heart of the three theological volumes. But it is nowhere stated more concisely or precisely than in this sermon on those sacraments, or mysteries, which are sacred signs instituted by Christ to signify sanctifying grace and to communicate that grace to our souls. 'Not that communion with Christ is confined to the occasions of sacramental approach; but they supply the principle, on which all the other ordinances of grace are dependent.'

Wilberforce contrasts in this sermon what he calls 'the Sacramental and Anti-Sacramental systems of religion', criticizing the latter as a species of gnosticism because of its assertion that only by mental processes may the limited and the finite be brought into relation with the unlimited and the infinite. Wilberforce goes so far as to condemn the Anti-Sacramental system as blasphemy—since it implies that there is a means of intercourse between man and God apart from Christ's humanity.

NOTE

1. St Irenaeus observes a similar connection between the Incarnation and the Real Presence in the Eucharist, and Jeremy Taylor speaks of the sacraments as 'the extension of the Incarnation'.

HERE IS a statement brought before us of the utmost moment —how we are to discriminate between God's Spirit and that which is opposed to Him, between Christ and Anti-Christ, between truth and error. Its importance is enhanced by its place, amidst the latest portions of Scripture; and by the earnestness with which the warning is repeated by the holy Apostle. He returns to it in the seventh verse of his second Epistle: 'Many deceivers are entered into the world, who confess not that Jesus Christ is come in the flesh. This is a deceiver and an Anti-Christ.'

Now though this passage found its immediate fulfilment in the heresies of the early age, yet those who appreciate the depth of Holy Scripture will not suppose that its meaning was thereby exhausted. For the first heresies by which the Gospel was opposed, did but indicate what was the natural course of error; and thus show in what manner human passion must always come into collision with Divine truth. The same phenomena must perpetually recur, so long as man's nature is corrupt, and God's counsels are unalterable. So that the general principle which is here laid down will be found applicable in every age. For the Apostle enounces it as an universal truth, that the main opposition to the Gospel, the principle which deserves to be called Anti-Christian, that which is the Anti-Christ itself, is to be found here—in the denial that the work effected by the Son of God has been effected through His taking our flesh. Let us consider then, first, what is the exact nature of that truth, which the Apostle declares to be essential—'every spirit which confesseth that Jesus Christ is come in the flesh, is of God.' This will lead us to inquire, secondly, what that error is by which it is contradicted. And thus we shall be able, in conclusion, to appreciate the nature and extent of their opposition.

Now the doctrine insisted upon by the Apostle, may be said in one word, to be that of *Mediation*. He is not speaking to persons who were ignorant that such a being had existed as Our Lord Jesus Christ, or that through his instrumentality advantages had been bestowed upon men. But he dwells on the point that it was through the taking our flesh that these benefits were conferred by the Son of God. They resulted, that is, from the fact that He became truly a middle person between us and the Father. For on this rests not only the sacrifice offered upon the cross, but that whole work of Atonement, whereby man is reconciled to God. When mankind fell, in their first father Adam, no mean was left for their recovery save through their Second Head,

Jesus Christ. In the fulness of time there came forth a rod out of the stem of Jesse, wherein the ancient purity of man's being was again exhibited. Into this new heir and representative of manhood did the Godhead pour all the divine gifts, which can have been originally designed to be the portion of the human family. In Him were all graces concentrated, which would render the creature acceptable in the eyes of the Creator. Thus was Christ fitted not only to be the one sacrifice for sin—the only perfect offering which should ever be presented to the Father, but likewise to be the sole Mediator, the only channel, through whom divine gifts should be bestowed upon men. They came from God to Him by unity of nature, they come from Him to His brethren by sanctification and grace. Thus did Our Lord render His own humanity the true medium for communicating that renewed nature, which should leaven the whole mass of corrupted mortality, and declare Mediation to be the great law of the Gospel kingdom, the central fact in the economy of grace. The spiritual manna, whereby the new Israel is sustained in its weary journey through the wilderness of life—what is it but that very Body which He endued with life-giving energy by the taking of the manhood into God? This is that great truth of the actual Mediation of the God-man, which ancient heresy robbed of its reality, but which the Apostle declares to be characteristic of the Gospel. We may sum it up in St. Paul's words: 'as we have borne the image of the earthy, we shall also bear the image of the heavenly:' the process, namely, which has its end in the resurrection of saints, has its beginning in the regeneration of sinners.

II. And can this truth possibly be gainsayed? Is there any principle which can be arrayed against it? Is it not so suited to the wants of man, as to convey its evidence in itself? How comes it then to be in theory but partially admitted among ourselves; and to be almost universally disallowed in act? For whatever may be the language of our Public Offices, yet silent Churches, deserted altars, infrequent Eucharists, are but too plain a witness to the national unbelief. The counteracting system must appeal surely to some principle of our nature, and be built upon some law, which we are compelled to admit. And so it doubtless is: for if the principle of mediation be our revealed mode of intercourse with God, yet is there another channel, which the very constitution of our being forbids us to neglect. This compound being, compacted of soul and body, has in it two distinct principles, and while the one supplies our means of holding converse with

266

our brethren, our relation to God depends upon the other. For the external frame, which enables us to play our part in the delusive pageant of life, is not really ourselves. And the hidden principle, which witnesses by intuitive consciousness in each man's bosom, claims natural kindred with the Most High. For it is still the image of the parent Spirit, which has never been wholly expunged from the minds which it created.

Hence arises the feeling, of which men are naturally possessed, that the inward spirit can address itself by immediate resort to the Supreme Mind. Whether man walks abroad to meditate in the lonely valley, or whether conscience opposes itself to temptation amidst the throng of life—in either case his thoughts arise to the Being who created him, with a confidence that no medium of intercourse can increase the closeness of that relation, whereby the mind tends towards its parent source. And especially when he enters into some majestic temple, which the piety of early times has reared to the unseen God, and hears 'the pealing organ blow, to the full-voiced quire below:' then does his heart swell within him, 'all heaven' rises up before his eyes, and he feels a strong conviction that enthusiasm, mystery, divine communion, are not things which are forbidden to the mere worshipper of nature: seeing that they ally themselves with those modes of access with Himself, which the Highest has left open to every being, in whom remain traces of the Divine Mind.

III. Such, brethren, are the two systems of opinion which we have to contrast: that which the Apostle declares to be the truth of God, and that which he stigmatizes as the spirit of Anti-christ. And these two we may term respectively the Sacramental and Anti-sacramental systems of religion. For since the doctrine of Our Lord's Mediation is founded upon His taking our flesh: since its primary law is the re-creation in His person of our common nature, the entrance of divine graces into humanity in its Head and Chief;—therefore some medium is required, by which those things, which were stored up in Him, may be distributed to His brethren. To speak of the Head as the fountain of grace, is to assume the existence of streams, by which it may be transmitted to His members. Now this function is so plainly assigned to Sacraments, that nothing else can be alleged to supply their place. If union with Christ be union with His manhood, it is clearly through those means, whereby we become members of His Body that we are united to Himself. Now it is explicitly revealed that we are 'baptized into one body,' and that 'those who are baptized into Christ, have put on Christ.' And what perpetuates our union, save that participation in His flesh and blood, which is not less distinctively declared to be the means whereby we continue to be one body in Himself?

On these means of union are built all those affections and sympathies, which ripen into the fulness of the divine life. Prayer, praise, the converse of the thoughts; public worship or private meditation—all these are means of intercourse with Christ, which have their origin in the Christian's oneness with the Church's Head. Not that communion with Christ is confined to the occasions of Sacramental approach; but they supply the principle, on which all the other ordinances of grace are dependent. For that real union must underlie them all, whereby men are truly, and not only in name united to Christ. And this union has its being through that Sacramental relation, whereby we are members of His Body, of His flesh, and of His bones. And as this is the Sacramental, so that which is opposed to it may be called the Anti-sacramental system. For its characteristic is the assertion of such immediate union between the creature and the Creator, that no link is needed to unite them. The Unembodied Power, the Merciful One, regarded only according to His Divine nature, is supposed to be so near to each man's spirit, that man's thoughts need only to travel forth in order to find Him. To what purpose then were priest, or altar, or Sacrament—nay, to what purpose the mediating humanity of the Son of God Himself, since that which is desired is attained without them.

Neither let it be supposed that the contrariety between these two systems is a mere technical distinction; resulting from certain arbitrary rules, which have been observed in the dispensation of divine blessings. To suppose that artificial restraints had been imposed on the free course of that spiritual life, which is the principle of man's recovery, would be intolerable to earnest minds. Our short-sighted wisdom could not indeed have prescribed limits beforehand to the divine counsels; but it is not forbidden us to meditate on the actions of Supreme Goodness, and to observe the light which they throw on the great cause of all things—the nature of God Himself. Now this may be seen especially in the case before us. For what is all religion but a reaching forth of the finite after the infinite, the supplying of those wants, which our higher nature renders us competent to feel, but which our lower nature renders us incompetent to satisfy?

For there is a double nature in man. His finite being is bounded by the conditions of time, and place, and circumstance. These assign his individual position in the world of being. But then he is conscious of another mode of existence. The unlimited combination of his thoughts opens a vista into the infinite. They can find satisfaction in nothing, which is less unbounded than themselves. So that the thoughts which range at large through the unseen and eternal, lead us up to God Himself, as the only centre and end of the beings, whom He has created.

Now in what manner can the limited be brought into relation with the unlimited? How can the finite become one with the Infinite? Is this a process which is confined to man's intellect alone? Is a privilege allowed to the superior part of his being, which his inferior nature does not share? What were this but the error of the Gnostics; and how singular to recognize the ancient delusion among those who smile at the fanciful shape in which their own opinions were formerly dressed? For what was the alleged opposition between matter and God, but the idea that in the limitations of our finite being lay the origin of evil, and that to escape from them was to enter at once upon a higher mode of existence. And this is identical with the thought, that though our complex nature is bound down to earth by the law of its material being, yet that in the mind we have an open door, which enables us at once to enter into communion with God. If this were so, then would the alienation, which has separated man from God, be attributable, not to the perverseness of his will, but to the conditions of his nature. It would seem as though the pure spirit, which could range unchecked through the regions of the infinite, were contaminated by its imprisonment in those material frames, which gave to its several portions an individual life and separate consciousness. So that the material structure would be the true cause of debasement, and man would be separated from his Maker by the accident of isolation, and not by the malignity of sin.

Such is the necessary result of denying that Sacramental system which is built upon the notion of Our Lord's humanity. For it is to imply that a channel of intercourse exists already; and where can such a thing be looked for, save in that portion of our nature which retains the most lively traces of the Image of God? And this erroneous estimate of man's nature leads to an analogous misconception respecting the nature of God. A false Anthropology finds its complement in a false Theology. For if the limitation of his being is the secret of man's weakness, God's excellence must consist in His exemption from the like defect.

So that mere infinity would be supposed to be the characteristic of God. And thus would those Moral Attributes be lost sight of, which rest upon His Personal existence as the Only Good. And we should be precipitated into that abyss of Pantheism, in which the heresies of modern times will finally result.

Thus does the identity between ancient and recent error render the Apostle's warning against the one no less applicable to the other. And as the error is the same, so is the principle which is opposed to it the same also. Is it asked how can things which are wholly diverse be brought into relation with one another, how can the finite become one with the Infinite? the answer is given in one word, through the Incarnation of Christ. Let us confess only 'that Jesus Christ is come in the flesh,' and however far we may be from comprehending this mystery, we cannot choose but believe it. For was not this the very work which was effected by 'the taking of the manhood into God?' Were not the finite and the infinite bound together by that personal existence, whereby man and God were united in the instant of His taking our flesh? Thus did Deity become capable, in the human nature of the Word, of sympathizing with human sorrows; and manhood became capable of being the seed of grace, through its being taken into God. The one was able to participate through its inferior nature in the weakness of limited humanity; the other through its alliance with a superior nature was endued with heavenly efficacy. Thus did Our Lord's humanity become that very source of life, which is distributed through Sacraments as the life of His brethren: the Infinite Head communicates Himself through these channels to His finite brethren: God is in Christ reconciling to Himself the world: so that the efficacy of these ordinances depends wholly upon our estimate of Him, with whom they ally us: and to accept His Mediation as a truth is to receive that Sacramental system, whereby He is come in the flesh as the re-creator of mankind.

Here let us pause for a moment to observe the utter futility of that common notion, that the casual perusal of Holy Scripture will enable men to appreciate the mysteries of God's kingdom. True, the word of God, when studied with that aid which is supplied by His Church's teaching, is the very mirror which reflects the secrets of the divine will. But here we have a point of primary importance; in what manner, namely, man is brought into relation with God; and nothing is more common than to hear men decide it by appealing to some detached words of Holy

Writ. Whereas it has been shown that elementary as this question is, direct as is its relation to all the practical affairs of life, its settlement involves the deepest of all considerations; it implies an inquiry into the nature of man, and into the nature of God, which leads into the most mysterious secrets of Theology.

IV. To such an inquiry the present time is too brief to do justice; it will be sufficient to observe the practical conclusion which the text suggests—the absolute contrariety, namely, between those two systems which have been opposed to one another. The Sacramental and Anti-sacramental systems are two different religions, and to rest our hope of salvation on the one, is to say anathema to the other. Such is plainly the force of the Apostle's words. To affirm the doctrine of Mediation and to deny it—to assert the reality of those things, which the Son of God effected by coming in the flesh, and to call their reality into question—are as much opposed as light and darkness, as truth and error. The discrepancy may pass unobserved for a time, as at the commencement of the Arian struggle, that dispute was at times evaded by an ambiguous phraseology; but it is a fundamental question, on which rests the Church's life or death, and which, when once discerned, must of necessity be decided. Nothing is more hateful than to raise unnecessary contentions in the Church of Christ. But 'to every thing there is a season, and a time to every purpose under the heaven. There is a time to keep silence, and a time to speak—a time of war and a time of peace.' And it was the Apostle of love who taught us that every spirit that confesseth not that Jesus Christ is come in the flesh, is a deceiver and an Anti-christ.

For take the case of the Sacrament of Baptism. In this ordinance of the Gospel a natural emblem of purification was invested with supernatural force. The washing of the body must always have seemed typical of the inward ablution of the mind. But Baptism received a new meaning, when it was no longer 'the putting away of the filth of the flesh, but the answer of a good conscience toward God by the resurrection of Jesus Christ, who is gone into heaven, and is on the right hand of God.' Thus did it find an analogy in that new world on which Noah entered through the deluge waters: for 'we are buried with Him by Baptism into death, that like as Christ was raised again by the glory of the Father, even so we also should walk in newness of life.' In Baptism, that is, we partake of that hallowed nature, which entered into the line of humanity in the New Head of our race,

271

that from Him it might be communicated to all His brethren. Thus does the recreation, which began in Him, extend to His members. For Christ, according to His manhood, is 'the first-born of every creature, the beginning of the creation of God.' And into us also there is a new life infused by supernatural process, which is the spring of our new being. 'If any man be in Christ he is a new creature, old things are passed away, behold all things are become new.' The Apostle's words are too weighty, surely, to be resolved into a mere figure of speech: if we are really to be saved, we need a *real*, and not a metaphorical regeneration. Yet how shall it be obtained, save through the extension of that divine power, which became one with manhood, in the miraculous instant of Our Lord's conception? In this manner is the finite re-constructed by the Infinite. And thus is a true work effected in Holy Baptism, whereby heaven and earth are brought into union; Christ is truly born again in all His members; and the seed of the corrupt is superseded by that of the regenerate Adam.

Such is the Sacramental theory; now take the opposite one. And by the opposite one is not meant only the theory of those who reject Baptism; for the parties who employ it as it was employed by the Jews or Heathen, are not less really opposed to its Christian signification, as our means of union with the manhood of Christ. For the use of Baptism may be retained as a harmless concession to custom, or as an indulgence in the taste for acted services, or as a graceful adoption of ancient manners, or as a sign or seal of past acts and future expectations; but unless it be believed to be the real means of union with the manhood of Christ, it can only be a superfluous and unnecessary action. And on this supposition, the movement whereby a child who is born in the corrupt image of his parents, is refashioned after the perfect image of God, cannot have an external source in that re-creation of nature, which began in the Incarnation of Christ, but must have an internal one in that rectification of the child's nature, which has its beginning in his individual mind. Men may seek a further cause of this movement in God's immediate influence on the minds of His creatures (they may assume that in some cases there is an arbitrary gift of prevenient grace); but such a theory leads directly to Fatalism, because it implies that those renewing gifts, without which corrupt nature cannot be restored, are bestowed only on those whom the Almighty, by arbitrary selection, impels to use them. And yet to attribute capability of action to every child, but to suppose that it waxes effectual through that grace of God, which He bestows on those whom He discerns will use it, is not less distinctly allied to the Pelagian heresy. For to rest the efficacy of Baptism, in this manner, on foreseen obedience, is to suppose that God's grace can be purchased by human merit.

But whether men's denial of the doctrine of Baptismal grace be rested on Fatalism or on Pelagianism, it is equally incompatible with the Mediation of Christ. For in either case Baptism is of no real efficacy. It is not the mean through which a supernatural work is done, but the sign by which a natural work is represented. There is no engrafting into the nature of Christ; but the mere eliciting of those principles of the child's nature which belong to its original stock. That fundamental Article of the Creed, the doctrine of 'one Baptism for the remission of sins,' is contradicted. The office of Our Lord's manhood is superseded. So far as regards practice, there is a virtual denial that Jesus Christ is come in the flesh.

And is not this system absolutely incompatible with that which was before exhibited? Are they not two different religions? If we adopt one, must we not discard the other? Can we confess Christ's Mediation, and also deny it? Allow the one, and the Sacramental system is a groundless superstition: allow the other, and the Anti-Sacramental system is a presumptuous unbelief.

The same contrast might be exhibited in respect to the Holy Eucharist. If Our Lord's intercession as man be a real act, whereby we participate through that perpetual oblation, wherein we show the Lord's death till He come, then should this service be the very centre of our worship, and the basis of our prayers. We should look upon it as our continual means of participating in that divine nature, which mercifully submitted to the conditions of humanity, in order that the finite might be pervaded by the Infinite. Is such a thing impossible? Then has not God become man: then is Christianity a dream, and the Doctrine of the Cross a fable. For if nature can save us, then is it an idolatry to rest on grace; but if we can only be saved by grace, then to rest on nature is an infidel delusion.

Which of these systems, brethren, shall be adopted by ourselves? I ask not as if the question were doubtful, but because the Church looks to this place, and to this congregation, to show that they are ready to testify to the truth by their deeds. For why have you a faculty of theology, and a local government, and institutions which are independent of the popular voice, and associations which bind you to past times, save that in you the Church should have a rallying-point in moments of trial, and a safeguard against the sudden movements of popular caprice? 'For if thou altogether holdeth thy peace at this time, then shall there enlargement and deliverance arise to Israel from another place; but thou and thy Father's house shall be destroyed: and who knoweth whether thou art come into authority, for such a time as this?' It can never be expected, indeed, that a Rationalistic religion will want supporters, when unchecked scope is given to that lawlessness of the human will, which not even the strongest coercion could master. Yet there is a majesty in truth, which is strong enough finally to prevail. Especially when such an appeal addresses itself to the young, whose truthfulness is guaranteed by the independence of their age, as well as by the hereditary integrity of our nation.

For the principles which have been set before you will come into collision not now only nor once, but during those long years, when it will be yours to guide the public sentiment, and give utterance to the public voice. Provide yourselves then, I beseech you, with true principles of action, that when you have entered upon the arena of middle life, you may not be compelled to rescind your judgment, and retrace your steps. You think not that such principles are to be gained only by intellectual culture, or that to admit the irrefragable conclusions of logic is an Evangelical belief. Among the most telling arguments against Sacramental grace is the experience of ungodly men, who having sinned against it by riot in their youth, sin against it by incredulity in their age. For with our moral as with our intellectual opportunities, those who are the last to use are commonly the first to disparage them. Who so ready to undervalue that incomparable discipline, which the poets, historians, and philosophers of ancient time supply to the understanding, as those whose self-will or idleness has shrunk from sustaining it? Nor is it unnatural that men should desire to charge their defects upon their circumstances, rather than on themselves. Especially is this the case in the things of the Spirit: for what argument so sways with men as their own consciousness, and what so probable, therefore, as that ungodliness should engender unbelief? Inquire why men deny Sacramental grace, you will find the common reason to be that they have themselves misused it. Having cut themselves off from Christ's presence by deadly sins, and impatient of so tedious a mode of reconcilement as confession, repentance, and amendment, they seek some shorter road of approach to God. And such they fancy themselves to possess in that excitement of feeling, which brings them into natural relation with their Maker. And they forget that the thing which they despise is the Mediation of Christ, and His true presence with His people. For these depend on that coming in the flesh, which has its effect through those Sacramental ordinances which they have slighted. Thus do they shut their eyes to the true Sun of righteousness, and walk in the light of their fire, and of the sparks which they have kindled.

So close is the alliance between a pure life and a right creed. Would you be fitted then to engage safely in the contentions of the world; to maintain the ancient institutions of your country, and to vindicate the real dignity of man, your present self-denial, purity, and faith, must be the true husbandry which will precede so honourable an harvest. Do not wait for a new place, or fresh associates, or a riper age; but live *now* in purity of heart, if you would not lose the power of appreciating truth in time to come. For truth comes only from that Infinite Source, whose presence must be anticipated by grace in this life, if we should possess His full fruition in life everlasting.

NEWMAN WAS born in London in 1801. He was the eldest son of a banker who turned brewer when the family bank failed. His mother came from a Huguenot family. He was brought up in the Church of England, and educated in a private school at Ealing, but fell under Evangelical influence before going up to Trinity College, Oxford, from which he passed to become a fellow of Oriel in 1822. He was ordained deacon in 1824, priest a year later. He was successively curate at St Clement's, and then vicar of the University church of St Mary's, Oxford, from 1828.

At Oriel Newman had become friendly with Froude and Pusey, and under the influence particularly of the former his mind moved gradually away from Evangelical attitudes, although in 1828 Froude could still write half-jokingly to Keble that 'I would give a few odd pence if he were not a heretic!' In 1832 Newman accompanied Froude on a voyage to Italy which the latter had undertaken for reasons of health; during it they visited Wiseman in Rome. On the way back Newman wrote 'Lead, Kindly Light' (which he never meant to be sung as a congregational hymn) and most of the rest of his slender output of verse. He fell dangerously ill with a fever, but recovered from it convinced that he would not yet die: 'I have a work to do in England.'

It is from Newman's return, in 1833, and the preaching of Keble's sermon on National Apostasy soon after, that the Oxford Movement dates. In the words of Dean Church, it was 'Keble who inspired, Froude who gave the impetus and Newman who took up the work.' Newman certainly threw himself into the task of recalling the Church of England to her Catholic heritage. He wrote twenty-six of the ninety *Tracts for the Times* himself, and there is an attractive remembrance of his riding on horseback, in the early days of the ferment they caused, from parsonage to parsonage, distributing bundles of them to bewildered vicars who all at once found themselves bidden to 'magnify their office', read the Fathers and study to secure a firm grasp of the doctrine and discipline of the Church in case of disestablishment. Dean Church says: 'The ring of those early tracts was something very different from anything of the kind yet known in England. They were clear, brief, stern appeals to conscience and reason . . . . They were like the short, sharp, rapid utterances of men in danger and pressing emergency.'[1]

Froude's death in 1836 was a serious loss to Newman. He

pushed himself the harder to work—defending his thesis of the *via media*, which is to say the notion that the Church of England held an intermediate position between the excesses of Romanism on the one hand and Protestantism on the other, and that this position was blessedly consonant with the orthodoxy of the early Church. It was a pleasant theory on paper—but that was how Newman came eventually to discard it, as a 'paper theory'.

Throughout this period Newman preached regularly at four o'clock in the afternoon in St Mary's. Where the tracts were provocative, the sermons were superb expositions of doctrine. Where the tracts were brilliant, the sermons were quiet but inspired. As Dean Church comments: 'Without the sermons, the Movement would never have been what it was. . . . While men were reading the Tracts they were hearing the sermons.' And again, 'The sermons created a moral atmosphere in which men judged the questions in debate.'

This may be seen as one of Newman's two bequests to his century, and our own, outwith the context of Tractarianism—that he was an apostle to the mind of the times, giving men new terms in which they could understand the divine deposit of truth in the Christian faith. His second bequest, apparent especially since the Second Vatican Council, over which many felt his spirit to brood, is in the way his life serves an ecumenical purpose beyond itself—without Newman, the Church of England might not today have the hold she has on the faith preached from her pulpits by Donne and Andrewes; without Newman, the Church of Rome might not be the credible force in intellectual life which she became again for Englishmen in the latter half of the nineteenth century. Newman reminded the English Church of her heart, and encouraged the Roman Church to speak her mind. *How* he did this is best followed in his major writings, amongst which the eight volumes of *Parochial and Plain Sermons* (1834-42) certainly rank.

Returning to the 1830s, when these sermons were first preached, it is instructive to listen to the way their impact was described by a contemporary who had himself no reason to be in a mind to like them, being a Presbyterian:

Each separate sentence, or at least each short paragraph, was spoken rapidly, but with great clearness of intonation, and then, at its close, there was a pause lasting for nearly half a minute; and then another rapidly and clearly spoken sentence, followed by another pause. . . . The most remarkable thing about the service was the beauty, the silver intonation of Mr. Newman's voice as he read the Lessons. . . . The tone of voice in which his sermons were spoken, once you grew accustomed to it, sounded like a fine strain of unearthly music.[2]

Also, we have the witness of Matthew Arnold:

> Who could resist the charm of that spiritual apparition, gliding in the dim afternoon light through the aisles of St. Mary's, rising into the pulpit and then in the most entrancing of voices breaking the silence with words and thoughts which were a religious music—subtle, sweet, mournful. Happy the man who in that susceptible season of youth hears such voices. They are a possession to him for ever.

In 1838 Newman became editor of the *British Critic*, the most important Anglo-Catholic journal of its day, but about the same time his study of the monophysite heresy first raised in his mind a doubt as to whether the Anglican position was tenable on the principles of ecclesiastical authority which he had accepted. Three years later he published Tract 90, a Catholic interpretation of the Thirty-Nine Articles of the English Church, which suggests that their negations were not directed against the creed of Roman Catholics, but only against popular excesses. For this he was censured by the University authorities, and by his own bishop, who imposed silence upon him. Newman withdrew to the hamlet of Littlemore, part of his parish, where he refurbished a stable and some outhouses and began with a few friends a life of prayer and fasting on semi-monastic lines. He was, as he later described it, 'on his deathbed as regards membership of the Anglican Church'. At this time he published a formal retraction of the hard things he had said against Rome—and the extent of his spiritual development is to be gauged from the fact that as a young man he had held the Pope to be Anti-Christ, while Froude and other Anglicans untouched by Evangelicalism had never been able to understand the seriousness of this opinion.

Newman resigned the incumbency of St Mary's on 18 September 1843, preaching a few days later, in Littlemore church, the sermon on *The Parting of Friends* included here. It was his last sermon as a priest of the English Church. For two years he continued his withdrawn life of prayer and fasting, remaining in lay communion with the Church of his birth. Then, in the course of completing his *Essay on the Development of Christian Doctrine*, on 9 October 1845, he was received into the Roman Catholic Church by Father Dominic Barberi, an Italian Passionist, later canonized.

Newman was forty-five years a member of the Church of England. He was to be a member of the Church of Rome for another forty-five. Encouraged by Wiseman, he went to Rome, where he was ordained priest on Trinity Sunday, 1847. A visit to the Oratory of St Philip Neri at Santa Croce gave him his bearings, and when he came back he established at Birmingham the first Oratory in England. A controversy with Charles Kingsley, who had written that 'Truth for its own sake has never been a virtue with the Roman clergy' and added that 'Father Newman informs us that it need not, and on the whole ought not to be', led to the writing of *Apologia pro Vita Sua* (1864), a spiritual autobiography, which earned Newman the respect of people of all religious persuasions and none. His other masterpiece from this period is the *Essay in Aid of a Grammar of Assent* (1870), an analysis of the phenomenology of faith. Newman's later years were passed at the Birmingham Oratory. In 1879 he was created a cardinal, travelling to Rome to receive the honour from Leo XIII, but being allowed to continue to live in his Oratory thereafter. He suffered an illness in 1888 and was weakened by several falls. He celebrated his last mass on Christmas Day 1889, and died in 1890. His body rests in the burial ground of the Oratian Fathers amid the Lickey Hills.

NOTES
1. R. W. Church, *The Oxford Movement*, 1891, p. 98.
2. J. C. Shairp, *Studies in Poetry and Philosophy*, 2nd ed., 1872, pp.247, 249.

BIBLIOGRAPHY
Parochial and Plain Sermons, 8 vols., 1834-43.
Sermons, Chiefly on the Theory of Religious Belief, Preached before the University of Oxford, 1843.
Sermons on Subjects of the Day, 1843.
An Essay on the Development of Christian Doctrine, 1845.
Discourses to Mixed Congregations, 1849.
Sermons Preached on Various Occasions, 1857.
The Idea of a University, 1852-9.
Apologia pro Vita Sua, 1864.
An Essay in Aid of a Grammar of Assent, 1870.

PEACE IN BELIEVING
Isaiah 6:3.
And one cried unto another, and said, Holy, Holy, Holy, is the Lord of Hosts.

THIS WAS preached on 26 May 1839 in St Mary's, Oxford, as one of Newman's four o'clock sermons. It was then printed as the last sermon, number xxv, in volume six of *Parochial and Plain Sermons*. Its occasion was Trinity Sunday, and it represents Newman at his best on that subject. Yet it is rather of the doctrine than of the priest that we are led to think, for as Dean Church wrote generally of Newman's sermons in St Mary's: 'They made men think of the thing which the preacher spoke of, and not of the sermon or the preacher.' This applies especially to *Peace in Believing*. As C. S. Dessain has said in one of the better books about Newman:

> The last sermon in the sixth volume of *Parochial Sermons*, 'Peace in believing,' is perhaps the most perfect outline in English of the Revelation the Father has made through His Son and His Spirit. Here is no arid speculation, but the richness of revealed truth, and we are enabled to *realise* the doctrine of the Incarnation.[1]

The sermon should be related to others close to it in spirit: the one in the fourth volume on *Watching*, the one in the sixth on *The Incarnate Son, a Sufferer and Sacrifice*, and in the same volume the sermon entitled *The Cross of Christ the Measure of the World*—in which, as Dessain says, 'Newman shows the Crucifixion of the Son of God as the key to the Christian interpretation of life.' There is a very arresting passage in the sermon on the Passion:

> Now I bid you to consider that that Face, so ruthlessly smitten, was the Face of God Himself; the Brows bloody with the thorns, the sacred Body exposed to view and lacerated with the scourge, the Hands nailed to the Cross, and, afterwards, the Side pierced with the spear; it was the Blood, and the sacred Flesh, and the Hands, and the Temples, and the Side, and the Feet of God Himself, which the frenzied multitude then gazed upon. This is so fearful a thought, that *when the mind first masters it, surely it will be difficult to think of anything else....* [my italics][2]

Compare also Newman's mature thinking about the Holy Trinity in the *Grammar of Assent* (pages 125 ff.), where he insists that it is a reality of revealed religion upon which our own life may be built. In this sermon, *Peace in Believing*, the dogma comes alive in the mind so vividly that one may wonder if there is any other writing in English where it has been better apprehended by the intelligence.

It is a sentence from this sermon that Matthew Arnold recalls in *Discourses in America* (1885):

Forty years ago Newman was in the very prime of life; he was close at hand to us at Oxford; he was preaching in St. Mary's pulpit every Sunday; he seemed about to transform and renew what was for us the most national and natural institution in the world, the Church of England. . . . I seem to hear him still saying:

'After the fever of life; after wearinesses and sicknesses; fightings and despondings, languor and fretfulness; struggling and failing, struggling and succeeding; after all the changes and chances of this troubled unhealthy state, at length comes death, at length the white throne of God, at length the Beatific Vision.'

NOTES

1. C. S. Dessain, *John Henry Newman*, 1966, p. 51. Dessain presents the case for Newman. A more critical view is to be found in Henri Bremond's *The Mystery of Newman* (trans. H. C. Corrance, 1907).
2. J. H. Newman, *Parochial and Plain Sermons*, VI, p. 74 .

EVERY LORD's day is a day of rest, but this, perhaps, more than any. It commemorates, not an act of God, however gracious and glorious, but His own unspeakable perfections and adorable mysteriousness. It is a day especially sacred to peace. Our Lord left His peace with us when He went away; 'Peace I leave with you; My peace I give unto you: not as the world giveth, give I unto you' (John xiv. 27); and He said He would send them a Comforter, who should give them peace. Last week we commemorated that Comforter's coming; and to-day, we commemorate in an especial way the gift He brought with Him, in that great doctrine which is its emblem and its means. 'These things have I spoken unto you, that in Me ye might have peace: in the world ye shall have tribulation' (John xvi. 33). Christ here says, that instead of this world's troubles, He gives His disciples peace; and, accordingly, in to-day's Collect, we pray that we may be kept in the faith of the Eternal Trinity in Unity, *and* be 'defended from all adversities,' for in keeping that faith we are kept from trouble.

Hence, too, in the blessing which Moses told the priests to pronounce over the children of Israel, God's Name is put upon them, and that three times, in order to bless and keep them, to make His face shine on them, and to give them peace. And hence again, in our own solemn form of blessing, with which we end our public service, we impart to the people 'the peace of God, which passeth all understanding,' and 'the blessing of the Father, the Son, and the Holy Ghost.'

God is the God of peace, and in giving us peace He does but give Himself, He does but manifest Himself to us; for His presence is peace. Hence our Lord, in the same discourse in which He promised His disciples peace, promised also, that 'He would come and manifest Himself unto them,' that 'He and His Father would come to them, and make Their abode with them' (John xiv. 21, 23). Peace is His everlasting state; in this world of space and time He has wrought and acted; but from everlasting it was not so. For six days He wrought, and then He rested according to that rest which was His eternal state; yet not so rested, as not in one sense to 'work hitherto,' in mercy and in judgment, towards that world which He had created. And more especially, when He sent His Only-begotten Son into the world, and that most Gracious and All-pitiful Son, our Lord, condescended to come to us, both He and His Father wrought with a mighty hand; and They vouchsafed the Holy Ghost, the Comforter, and He also wrought wonderfully, and works hitherto. Certainly the whole economy of redemption is a series of great and continued works; but still they all tend to rest and peace, as at the first. They began out of rest, and they end in rest. They end in that eternal state out of which they began. The Son was from eternity in the bosom of the Father, as His dearly-beloved and Only-begotten. He loved Him before the foundation of the world. He had glory with Him before the world was. He was in the Father, and the Father in Him. None knew the Son but the Father, nor the Father but the Son. 'In the beginning was the Word, and the Word was with God, and the Word was God.' He was 'the Brightness of God's glory and the express Image of His Person;' and in this unspeakable Unity of Father and Son, was the Spirit also, as being the Spirit of the Father, and the Spirit of the Son; the Spirit of Both at once, not separate from them, yet distinct, so that they were Three Persons, One God, from everlasting.

Thus was it, we are told, from everlasting;—before the heavens and the earth were made, before man fell or Angels rebelled, before the sons of God were formed in the morning of creation, yea, before there were Seraphim to veil their faces before Him and cry 'Holy,' He existed without ministers, without attendants, without court and kingdom, without manifested glory, without any thing but Himself; He His own Temple, His own infinite rest, His own supreme bliss, from eternity. O wonderful mystery! O the depth of His majesty! O deep things which the Spirit only knoweth! Wonderful and strange to creatures who grovel on this earth, as we, that He, the All-powerful, the All-wise, the All-good, the All-glorious, should for an eternity, for years without end, or rather, apart from time, which is but one of His creatures, that He should have dwelt without those through whom He might be powerful, in whom He might be wise, towards whom He might be good, by whom He might be glorified. O wonderful, that all His deep and infinite attributes should have been without manifestation! O wonderful thought! and withal, O thought comfortable to us worms of the earth, as often as we feel in ourselves and see in others gifts which have no exercise, and powers which are quiescent! He, the All-powerful God, rested from eternity, and did not work; and yet, why *not* rest, wonderful though it be, seeing He was so blessed in Himself? why should *He* seek external objects to know, to love, and to commune with, who was all-sufficient in Himself? How could He need fellows, as though He were a man, when He was not solitary, but had ever with Him

His Only-begotten Word in whom He delighted, whom He loved ineffably, and the Eternal Spirit, the very bond of love and peace, dwelling in and dwelt in by Father and Son? Rather how was it that He ever began to create, who had a Son without beginning and without imperfection, whom He could love with a perfect love? What exceeding exuberance of goodness was it that *He* should deign at length to surround Himself with creation, who had need of nothing, and to change His everlasting silence for the course of Providence and the conflict of good and evil! I say nothing of the apostasies against Him, the rebellions and blasphemies which men and devils have committed. I say nothing of that unutterable region of woe, the prison of the impenitent, which is to last to eternity, coeval with Himself henceforth, as if in rivalry of His blissful heaven. I say nothing of this, for God cannot be touched with evil; and all the sins of those reprobate souls cannot impair His everlasting felicity. But, I ask, how was it that He who needed nothing, who was all in all, who had infinite Equals in the Son and the Spirit, who were One with Him, how was it that He created His Saints, but from simple love of them from eternity? Why should He make man in the Image of God, whose Image already was the Son, All-perfect, All-exact, without variableness, without defect, by a natural propriety and unity of substance? And when man fell, why did He not abandon or annihilate the whole race, and create others? why did He go so far as to begin a fresh and more wonderful dispensation towards us, and, as He had wrought marvellously in Providence, work marvellously also in grace, even sending His Eternal Son to take on Him our fallen nature, and to purify and renew it by His union with it, but that, infinite as was His own blessedness, and the Son's perfection, and man's unprofitableness, yet, in His loving-kindness, He determined that unprofitable man should be a partaker of the Son's perfection and His own blessedness?

And thus it was that, as He had made man in the beginning so also He redeemed him; and the history of this redemption we have been tracing for the last six months in our sacred Services. We have gone through in our memory the whole course of that Dispensation of active providences, which God, in order to our redemption, has superinduced upon His eternal and infinite repose. First, we commemorated the approach of Christ, in the weeks of Advent; then His birth, of the Blessed Mary, after a miraculous conception, at Christmas; then His circumcision; His manifestation to the wise men; His baptism and beginning of miracles;

His presentation in the Temple; His fasting and temptation in the wilderness, in Lent; His agony in the garden; His betrayal; His mocking and scourging; His cross and passion; His burial; His resurrection; His forty days' converse with His disciples after it; then His Ascension; and, lastly, the coming of the Holy Ghost in His stead to remain with the Church unto the end,—unto the end of the world; for so long is the Almighty Comforter to remain with us. And thus, in commemorating the Spirit's gracious office during the past week, we were brought, in our series of representations, to the end of all things; and now what is left but to commemorate what will follow after the end?—the return of the everlasting reign of God, the infinite peace and blissful perfection of the Father, the Son, and the Holy Ghost, differing indeed from what it once was by the fruits of creation and redemption, but not differing in the supreme blessedness, the ineffable mutual love, the abyss of holiness in which the Three Persons of the Eternal Trinity dwell. He, then, is the subject of this day's celebration,—the God of love, of holiness, of blessedness; in whose presence is fulness of joy and pleasures for evermore; who is what He ever was, and has brought us sinners to that which He ever was. He did not bring into being peace and love as part of His creation, but He was Himself peace and love from eternity, and He blesses us by making us partakers of Himself, through the Son, by the Spirit, and He so works in His temporal dispensations that He may bring us to that which is eternal.

And hence, in Scripture, the promises of eternity and security go together; for where time is not, there vicissitude also is away. 'The eternal God is thy refuge,' says Moses, before his death, 'and underneath are the everlasting arms: and He shall thrust out the enemy from before thee, and shall say, Destroy them; Israel then shall dwell in safety alone.' And again, 'Thou wilt keep him in perfect peace, whose mind is stayed on Thee, because he trusteth in Thee. Trust ye in the Lord for ever; for in the Lord Jehovah is everlasting strength.' And again, 'Thus saith the High and Lofty One that inhabiteth eternity. . . . I dwell in the high and holy place, with him also that is of a contrite and humble spirit, to revive the spirit of the humble, and to revive the heart of the contrite ones. . . . I create the fruit of the lips; peace, peace to him that is afar off, and to him that is near.' And, in like manner, our Lord and Saviour is prophesied of as being 'the *Everlasting* Father, the Prince of *peace*.' And again, speaking more especially of what He has done for us, 'The work of righteousness shall be *peace*; and the effect of righteousness, quietness and *assurance for ever*' (Deut. xxxiii. 27, 28; Isa. xxvi. 3, 4; lvii. 15, 19; ix. 6; xxxii. 17).

As then we have for many weeks commemorated the economy by which righteousness was restored to us, which took place in time, so from this day forth do we bring before our minds the infinite perfections of Almighty God, and our hope hereafter of seeing and enjoying them. Hitherto we have celebrated His great works; henceforth we magnify Himself. Now, for twenty-five weeks we represent in figure what is to be hereafter. We enter into our rest, by entering in with Him who, having wrought and suffered, has opened the kingdom of heaven to all believers. For half a year we stand still, as if occupied solely in adoring Him, and, with the Seraphim in the text, crying, 'Holy, Holy, Holy,' continually. All God's providences, all God's dealings with us, all His judgments, mercies, warnings, deliverances, tend to peace and repose as their ultimate issue. All our troubles and pleasures here, all our anxieties, fears, doubts, difficulties, hopes, encouragements, afflictions, losses, attainments, tend this one way. After Christmas, Easter, and Whitsuntide, comes Trinity Sunday, and the weeks that follow; and in like manner, after our soul's anxious travail; after the birth of the Spirit; after trial and temptation; after sorrow and pain; after daily dyings to the world; after daily risings unto holiness; at length comes that 'rest which remaineth unto the people of God.' After the fever of life; after wearinesses and sicknesses; fightings and despondings; languor and fretfulness; struggling and failing, struggling and succeeding; after all the changes and chances of this troubled unhealthy state, at length comes death, at length the White Throne of God, at length the Beatific Vision. After restlessness comes rest, peace, joy;—our eternal portion, if we be worthy;—the sight of the Blessed Three, the Holy One; the Three that bear witness in heaven; in light unapproachable; in glory without spot or blemish; in power without 'variableness, or shadow of turning.' The Father God, the Son God, and the Holy Ghost God; the Father Lord, the Son Lord, and the Holy Ghost Lord; the Father uncreate, the Son uncreate, and the Holy Ghost uncreate; the Father incomprehensible, the Son incomprehensible, and the Holy Ghost incomprehensible. For there is one Person of the Father, another of the Son, and another of the Holy Ghost; and such as the Father is, such is the Son, and such is the Holy Ghost; and yet there are not three Gods, nor three Lords, nor three incomprehensibles, nor three uncreated; but one God, one Lord, one un-created, and one incomprehensible.

Let us, then, use with thankfulness the subject of this day's Festival, and the Creed of St. Athanasius, as a means of peace, till it is given us, if we attain thereto, to see the face of God in heaven. What the Beatific Vision will then impart, the contemplation of revealed mysteries gives us as in a figure. The doctrine of the Blessed Trinity has been made the subject of especial contention among the professed followers of Christ. It has brought a sword upon earth, but it was intended to bring peace. And it does bring peace to those who humbly receive it in faith. Let us beg of God to bless it to us to its right uses, that it may not be an occasion of strife, but of worship; not of division, but of unity; not of jealousy, but of love. Let us devoutly approach Him of whom it speaks, with the confession of our lips and of our hearts. Let us look forward to the time when this world will have passed away and all its delusions; and when we, when every one born of woman, must either be in heaven or in hell. Let us desire to hide ourselves under the shadow of His wings. Let us beg Him to give us an understanding heart, and that love of Him which is the instinct of the new creature, and the breath of spiritual life. Let us pray Him to give us the spirit of obedience, of true dutifulness; an honest spirit, earnestly set to do His will, with no secret ends, no selfish designs of our own, no preferences of the creature to the Creator, but open, clear, conscientious, and loyal. So will He vouchsafe, as time goes on, to take up His abode in us; the Spirit of Truth, whom the world cannot receive, will dwell in us, and be in us, and Christ 'will love us, and will manifest Himself to us,' and 'the Father will love us, and They will come unto us, and make Their abode with us.' And when at length the inevitable hour comes, we shall be able meekly to surrender our souls, our sinful yet redeemed souls, in much weakness and trembling, with much self-reproach and deep confession, yet in firm faith, and in cheerful hope, and in calm love, to God the Father, God the Son, God the Holy Ghost; the Blessed Three, the Holy One; Three Persons, One God; our Creator, our Redeemer, our Sanctifier, our Judge.

THE THEORY OF DEVELOPMENTS IN RELIGIOUS DOCTRINE

Luke 2:19.

But Mary kept all these things, and pondered them in her heart.

THIS IS sermon xv in *Sermons, Chiefly on the Theory of Religious Belief, Preached before the University of Oxford*. It was first preached in St Mary's on the Feast of the Purification of Our Lady, also called Candlemas, 1843, and must have been the last sermon which Newman preached before the University, as he resigned his living at St Mary's in September of the same year. It is one of the finest of Newman's sermons preached before the University, and as the sermons delivered in those circumstances represent in his own reckoning his best work—'I must say I think they are as a whole, the best things I have written, and I cannot believe they are not Catholic and will not be useful', he wrote a year or two after his reception into the Roman Church—it may be as well to look closely at this specimen of them.

The first thing to be noticed is that Newman was sensitive to the problem of adjusting his style to his audience and to the circumstances in which he was required to preach. The university sermons have a strong intellectual content and a manner of address which befits a man talking to his equals; the sermons in *Parochial and Plain* are more suitable to the tender enquiring minds of undergraduates; those preached in the church at Littlemore are simpler, shorter, direct in their emotional appeal. I have tried to represent Newman in this volume by one sermon of each of the three kinds—in each case as good an example of its kind as I could find.

The Theory of Developments in Religious Doctrines is itself an important document in its relevance to two of Newman's master works—the *Essay on the Development of Christian Doctrine* (1845), and the *Essay in Aid of a Grammar of Assent* (1870). The relevance consists in his insisting (as he writes in the introduction to the *Essay on the Development of Christian Doctrine*) on Christianity *having its home in the world*—so that 'to know what it is, we must seek it in the world, and hear the world's witness of it'. Newman had by the time of this writing reached a point, far developed from his own early Evangelicalism, where he regarded 'the Incarnation [as] the central aspect of Christianity'. From this he goes on to an understanding of the importance of what in his essay he calls 'the sacramental, the hierarchical, and the ascetic'. The sermon can be perceived to be dealing deep down, as do most of the university sermons, with the relationship between faith and reason, with a recognition of the limitations of the intellect in its quest for absolute truth, and with the connection between conscience and the act of *assent* to that truth—conscience being regarded as the prime organ of religious apprehension.

Newman first began to ponder these matters when he read Butler—referred to interestingly in the course of the sermon before us. His mature reflections upon them are to be found in the *Grammar of Assent*. The second and third sections of the *Essay on the Development of Christian Doctrine* will be found especially apt for this sermon—in so far as they argue for the probability of developments in Christianity, of a developing *authority* in Christianity, and examine the character of the evidence for this. Newman's suggestion of a theory of religious *evolution* in this sermon, extended in the *Essay*, is remarkable. It came fourteen years before Darwin thought he saw such a process adumbrated in the world of objects—Newman, incidentally, found no difficulty in accepting *The Origin of Species*, so long as the idea of evolution was conceived to be theistic, or not exclusive of the theistic. The coherent development of Christian thought might in itself be considered both an unusual philosophical phenomenon and a proof of its divine guidance.

LITTLE IS told us in Scripture concerning the Blessed Virgin, but there is one grace in which the Evangelists make her the pattern, in a few simple sentences,—of Faith. Zacharias questioned the Angel's message, but 'Mary said, Behold the handmaid of the Lord; be it unto me according to thy word.' Accordingly Elisabeth, speaking with an apparent allusion to the contrast thus exhibited between her own highly-favoured husband, righteous Zacharias, and the still more highly-favoured Mary, said, on receiving her salutation, 'Blessed art thou among women, and blessed is the fruit of thy womb; Blessed is she that believed, for there shall be a performance of those things which were told her from the Lord.'

2. But Mary's faith did not end in a mere acquiescence in Divine providences and revelations: as the text informs us, she 'pondered' them. When the shepherds came, and told of the vision of Angels which they had seen at the time of the Nativity, and how one of them announced that the Infant in her arms was 'the Saviour, which is Christ the Lord,' while others did but wonder, 'Mary kept all these things, and pondered them in her heart.' Again, when her Son and Saviour had come to the age of twelve years, and had left her for awhile for His Father's service, and had been found, to her surprise, in the Temple, amid the doctors, both hearing them and asking them questions, and had, on her addressing Him, vouchsafed to justify His conduct, we are told, 'His mother kept all these sayings in her heart.' And accordingly, at the marriage-feast in Cana, her faith anticipated His first miracle, and she said to the servants, 'Whatsoever He saith unto you, do it.'

3. Thus St. Mary is our pattern of Faith, both in the reception and in the study of Divine Truth. She does not think it enough to accept, she dwells upon it; not enough to possess, she uses it; not enough to assent, she developes it; not enough to submit the Reason, she reasons upon it; not indeed reasoning first, and believing afterwards, with Zacharias, yet first believing without reasoning, next from love and reverence, reasoning after believing. And thus she symbolizes to us, not only the faith of the unlearned, but of the doctors of the Church also, who have to investigate, and weigh, and define, as well as to profess the Gospel; to draw the line between truth and heresy; to anticipate or remedy the various aberrations of wrong reason; to combat pride and recklessness with their own arms; and thus to triumph over the sophist and the innovator.

4. If, then, on a Day dedicated to such high contemplations as the Feast which we are now celebrating, it is allowable to occupy the thoughts with a subject not of a devotional or practical nature, it will be some relief of the omission to select one in which St. Mary at least will be our example,—the use of Reason in investigating the doctrines of Faith; a subject, indeed, far fitter for a volume than for the most extended notice which can here be given to it; but one which cannot be passed over altogether in silence, in any attempt at determining the relation of Faith to Reason.

5. The overthrow of the wisdom of the world was one of the earliest, as well as the noblest of the triumphs of the Church; after the pattern of her Divine Master, who took His place among the doctors before He preached His new Kingdom, or opposed Himself to the world's power. St. Paul, the learned Pharisee, was the first fruits of that gifted company, in whom the pride of science is seen prostrated before the foolishness of preaching. From his day to this the Cross has enlisted under its banner all those great endowments of mind, which in former times had been expended on vanities, or dissipated in doubt and speculation. Nor was it long before the schools of heathenism took the alarm, and manifested an unavailing jealousy of the new doctrine, which was robbing them of their most hopeful disciples. They had hitherto taken for granted that the natural home of the Intellect was the Garden or the Porch; and it reversed their very first principles to be called on to confess, what yet they would not deny, that a Superstition, as they considered it, was attracting to itself all the energy, the keenness, the originality, and the eloquence of the age. But these aggressions upon heathenism were only the beginning of the Church's conquests; in the course of time the whole mind of the world, as I may say, was absorbed into the philosophy of the Cross, as the element in which it lived, and the form upon which it was moulded. And how many centuries did this endure, and what vast ruins still remain of its dominion! In the capitals of Christendom the high cathedral and the perpetual choir still witness to the victory of Faith over the world's power. To see its triumph over the world's wisdom, we must enter those solemn cemeteries in which are stored the relics and the monuments of ancient Faith—our libraries. Look along their shelves, and every name you read there is, in one sense or other, a trophy set up in record of the victories of Faith. How many long lives,

what high aims, what single-minded devotion, what intense contemplation, what fervent prayer, what deep erudition, what untiring diligence, what toilsome conflicts has it taken to establish its supremacy! This has been the object which has given meaning to the life of Saints, and which is the subject-matter of their history. For this they have given up the comforts of earth and the charities of home, and surrendered themselves to an austere rule, nay, even to confessorship and persecution, if so be they could make some small offering, or do some casual service, or provide some additional safeguard towards the great work which was in progress. This has been the origin of controversies, long and various, yes, and the occasion of much infirmity, the test of much hidden perverseness, and the subject of much bitterness and tumult. The world has been moved in consequence of it, populations excited, leagues and alliances formed, kingdoms lost and won: and even zeal, when excessive, evinced a sense of its preciousness; nay, even rebellions in some sort did homage to it, as insurgents imply the actual sovereignty of the power which they are assailing. Meanwhile the work went on, and at length a large fabric of divinity was reared, irregular in its structure, and diverse in its style, as beseemed the slow growth of centuries; nay, anomalous in its details, from the peculiarities of individuals, or the interference of strangers, but still, on the whole, the development of an idea, and like itself, and unlike any thing else, its most widely-separated parts having relations with each other, and betokening a common origin.

6. Let us quit this survey of the general system, and descend to the history of the formation of any Catholic dogma. What a remarkable sight it is, as almost all unprejudiced persons will admit, to trace the course of the controversy, from its first disorders to its exact and determinate issue. Full of deep interest, to see how the great idea takes hold of a thousand minds by its living force, and will not be ruled or stinted, but is 'like a burning fire,' as the Prophet speaks, 'shut up' within them, till they are 'weary of forbearing, and cannot stay,' and grows in them, and at length is born through them, perhaps in a long course of years, and even successive generations; so that the doctrine may rather be said to use the minds of Christians, than to be used by them. Wonderful it is to see with what effort, hesitation, suspense, interruption,—with how many swayings to the right and to the left—with how many reverses, yet with what certainty of advance, with what precision in its march, and with what ultimate completeness,

292

it has been evolved; till the whole truth 'self-balanced on its centre hung,' part answering to part, one, absolute, integral, indissoluble, while the world lasts! Wonderful, to see how heresy has
but thrown that idea into fresh forms, and drawn out from it
farther developments, with an exuberance which exceeded all
questioning, and a harmony which baffled all criticism, like
Him, its Divine Author, who, when put on trial by the Evil One,
was but fortified by the assault, and is ever justified in His
sayings, and overcomes when he is judged.

7. And this world of thought is the expansion of a few words,
uttered, as if casually, by the fishermen of Galilee. Here is another
topic which belongs more especially to that part of the subject
to which I propose to confine myself. Reason has not only submitted, it has ministered to Faith; it has illustrated its documents;
it has raised illiterate peasants into philosophers and divines; it
has elicited a meaning from their words which their immediate
hearers little suspected. Stranger surely is it that St. John should
be a theologian, than that St. Peter should be a prince. This is a
phenomenon proper to the Gospel, and a note of divinity. Its
half sentences, its overflowings of language, admit of development; they have a life in them which shows itself in progress; a
truth, which has the token of consistency; a reality, which is
fruitful in resources; a depth, which extends into mystery: for
they are representations of what is actual, and has a definite lo-
cation and necessary bearings and a meaning in the great system
of things, and a harmony in what it is, and a compatibility in
what it involves. What form of Paganism can furnish a parallel?
What philosopher has left his words to posterity as a talent which
could be put to usury, as a mine which could be wrought? Here,
too, is the badge of heresy; its dogmas are unfruitful; it has no
theology; so far forth as it is heresy, it has none. Deduct its remnant of Catholic theology, and what remains? Polemics, explanations, protests. It turns to Biblical Criticism, or to the Evidences of Religion, for want of a province. Its *formulae* end in themselves, without development, because they are words; they are
barren, because they are dead. If they had life, they would increase and multiply; or, if they do live and bear fruit, it is but as
'sin, when it is finished, bringeth forth death.' It developes into
dissolution; but it creates nothing, it tends to no system, its re-
sultant dogma is but the denial of all dogmas, any theology, under
the Gospel. No wonder it denies what it cannot attain.

8. Heresy denies to the Church what is wanting in itself. Here,

then, we are brought to the subject to which I wish to give attention. It need not surely formally be proved that this disparagement of doctrinal statements, and in particular of those relating to the Holy Trinity and Incarnation, is especially prevalent in our times. There is a suspicion widely abroad,—felt, too, perhaps, by many who are unwilling to confess it,—that the development of ideas and formation of dogmas is a mere abuse of Reason, which, when it attempted such sacred subjects, went beyond its powers, and could do nothing more than multiply words without meaning, and deductions which come to nothing. The conclusion follows, that such an attempt does but lead to mischievous controversy, from that discordance of doctrinal opinions, which is its immediate consequence; that there is, in truth, no necessary or proper connexion between inward religious belief and scientific expositions; and that charity, as well as good sense, is best consulted by reducing creeds to the number of private opinions, which, if individuals will hold for themselves, at least they have no right to impose upon others.

9. It is my purpose, then, in what follows, to investigate the connexion between Faith and Dogmatic Confession, as far as relates to the sacred doctrines which were just now mentioned, and to show the office of the Reason in reference to it; and, in doing so, I shall make as little allusion as may be to erroneous views on the subject, which have been mentioned only for the sake of perspicuity; following rather the course which the discussion may take, and pursuing those issues on which it naturally opens. Nor am I here in any way concerned with the question, who is the legitimate framer and judge of these dogmatic inferences under the Gospel, or if there be any. Whether the Church is infallible, or the individual, or the first ages, or none of these, is not the point here, but the theory of developments itself.

10. Theological dogmas are propositions expressive of the judgments which the mind forms, or the impressions which it receives, of Revealed Truth. Revelation sets before it certain supernatural facts and actions, beings and principles; these make a certain impression or image upon it; and this impression spontaneously, or even necessarily, becomes the subject of reflection on the part of the mind itself, which proceeds to investigate it, and to draw it forth in successive and distinct sentences. Thus the Catholic doctrine of Original Sin, or of Sin after Baptism, or of the Eucharist, or of Justification, is but the expression of the inward belief of Catholics on these several points, formed upon an

analysis of that belief. Such, too, are the high doctrines with which I am especially concerned.

11. Now, here I observe, first of all, that, naturally as the inward idea of divine truth, such as has been described, passes into explicit form by the activity of our reflective powers, still such an actual delineation is not essential to its genuineness and perfection. A peasant may have such a true impression, yet be unable to give any intelligible account of it, as will easily be understood. But what is remarkable at first sight is this, that there is good reason for saying that the impression made upon the mind need not even be recognized by the parties possessing it. It is no proof that persons are not possessed, because they are not conscious, of an idea. Nothing is of more frequent occurrence, whether in things sensible or intellectual, than the existence of such unperceived impressions. What do we mean when we say, that certain persons do not know themselves, but that they are ruled by views, feelings, prejudices, objects which they do not recognize? How common is it to be exhilarated or depressed, we do not recollect why, though we are aware that something has been told us, or has happened, good or bad, which accounts for our feeling, could we recall it! What is memory itself, but a vast magazine of such dormant, but present and excitable ideas? Or consider, when persons would trace the history of their own opinions in past years, how baffled they are in the attempt to fix the date of this or that conviction, their system of thought having been all the while in continual, gradual, tranquil expansion; so that it were as easy to follow the growth of the fruit of the earth, 'first the blade, then the ear, after that the full corn in the ear,' as to chronicle changes, which involved no abrupt revolution, or reaction, or fickleness of mind, but have been the birth of an idea, the development, in explicit form, of what was already latent within it. Or, again, critical disquisitions are often written about the idea which this or that poet might have in his mind in certain of his compositions and characters; and we call such analysis the philosophy of poetry, not implying thereby of necessity that the author wrote upon a theory in his actual delineation, or knew what he was doing; but that, in matter of fact, he was possessed, ruled, guided by an unconscious idea. Moreover, it is a question whether that strange and painful feeling of unreality, which religious men experience from time to time, when nothing seems true, or good, or right, or profitable, when Faith seems a name, and duty a mockery, and all endeavours to

do right, absurd and hopeless, and all things forlorn and dreary, as if religion were wiped out from the world, may not be the direct effect of the temporary obscuration of some master vision, which unconsciously supplies the mind with spiritual life and peace.

12. Or, to take another class of instances which are to the point so far as this, that at least they are real impressions, even though they be not influential. How common is what is called vacant vision, when objects meet the eye, without any effort of the judgment to measure or locate them; and that absence of mind, which recollects minutes afterwards the occurrence of some sound, the striking of the hour, or the question of a companion, which passed unheeded at the time it took place! How, again, happens it in dreams, that we suddenly pass from one state of feeling, or one assemblage of circumstances to another, without any surprise at the incongruity, except that, while we are impressed first in this way, then in that, we take no active cognizance of the impression? And this, perhaps, is the life of inferior animals, a sort of continuous dream, impressions without reflections; such, too, seems to be the first life of infants; nay, in heaven itself, such may be the high existence of some exalted orders of blessed spirits, as the Seraphim, who are said to be, not Knowledge, but all Love.

13. Now, it is important to insist on this circumstance, because it suggests the reality and permanence of inward knowledge, as distinct from explicit confession. The absence, or partial absence, or incompleteness of dogmatic statements is no proof of the absence of impressions or implicit judgments, in the mind of the Church. Even centuries might pass without the formal expression of a truth, which had been all along the secret life of millions of faithful souls. Thus, not till the thirteenth century was there any direct and distinct avowal, on the part of the Church, of the numerical Unity of the Divine Nature, which the language of some of the principal Greek fathers, *prima facie*, though not really, denies. Again, the doctrine of the Double Procession was no Catholic dogma in the first ages, though it was more or less clearly stated by individual Fathers; yet, if it is now to be received, as surely it must be, as part of the Creed, it was really held every where from the beginning, and therefore, in a measure, held as a mere religious impression, and perhaps an unconscious one.

14. But, further, if the ideas may be latent in the Christian

296

mind, by which it is animated and formed, it is less wonderful that they should be difficult to elicit and define; and of this difficulty we have abundant proof in the history whether of the Church, or of individuals. Surely it is not at all wonderful, that, when individuals attempt to analyze their own belief, they should find the task arduous in the extreme, if not altogether beyond them; or, again, a work of many years; or, again, that they should shrink from the true developments, if offered to them, as foreign to their thoughts. This may be illustrated in a variety of ways.

15. It will often happen, perhaps from the nature of things, that it is impossible to master and express an idea in a short space of time. As to individuals, sometimes they find they cannot do so at all; at length, perhaps, they recognize, in some writer they meet, with the very account of their own thoughts, which they desiderate; and then they say, that 'here is what they have felt all along, and wanted to say, but could not,' or 'what they have ever maintained, only better expressed.' Again, how many men are burdened with an idea, which haunts them through a great part of their lives, and of which only at length, with much trouble, do they dispossess themselves? I suppose most of us have felt at times the irritation, and that for a long period, of thoughts and views which we felt, and felt to be true, only dimly showing themselves, or flitting before us; which at length we understood must not be forced, but must have their way, and would, if it were so ordered, come to light in their own time. The life of some men, and those not the least eminent among divines and philosophers, has centred in the development of one idea; nay, perhaps has been too short for the process. Again, how frequently it happens, that, on first hearing a doctrine propounded, a man hesitates, first acknowledges, then disowns it; then says that he has always held it, but finds fault with the mode in which it is presented to him, accusing it of paradox or over-refinement; that is, he cannot at the moment analyze his own opinions, and does not know whether he holds the doctrine or not, from the difficulty of mastering his thoughts.

16. Another characteristic, as I have said, of dogmatic statements, is the difficulty of recognising them, even when attained, as the true representation of our meaning. This happens for many reasons; sometimes, from the faint hold we have of the impression itself, whether its nature be good or bad, so that we shrink from principles in substance, which we acknowledge in influence. Many a man, for instance, is acting on utilitarian principles, who

is shocked at them in set treatises, and disowns them. Again, in sacred subjects, the very circumstance that a dogma professes to be a direct contemplation, and, if so be, a definition of what is infinite and eternal, is painful to serious minds. Moreover, from the hypothesis, it is the representation of an idea in a medium not native to it, not as originally conceived, but, as it were, in projection; no wonder, then, that, though there be an intimate correspondence, part by part, between the impression and the dogma, yet there should be an harshness in the outline of the latter; as, for instance, a want of harmonious proportion; and yet this is unavoidable, from the infirmities of our intellectual powers.

17. Again, another similar peculiarity in developments in general, is the great remoteness of the separate results of a common idea, or rather at first sight the absence of any connexion. Thus it often happens that party spirit is imputed to persons, merely because they agree with one another in certain points of opinion and conduct, which are thought too minute, distant, and various, in the large field of religious doctrine and discipline, to proceed from any but an external influence and a positive rule; whereas an insight into the wonderfully expansive power and penetrating virtue of theological or philosophical ideas would have shown, that what is apparently arbitrary in rival or in kindred schools of thought, is after all rigidly determined by the original hypothesis. The remark has been made, for instance, that rarely have persons maintained the sleep of the soul before the Resurrection, without falling into more grievous errors; again, those who deny the Lutheran doctrine of Justification, commonly have tendencies towards a ceremonial religion; again, it is a serious fact that Protestantism has at various times unexpectedly developed into an allowance or vindication of polygamy; and heretics in general, however opposed in tenets, are found to have an inexplicable sympathy for each other, and never wake up from their ordinary torpor, but to exchange courtesies and meditate coalitions. One other remark is in point here, and relates to the length to which statements run, though, before we attempted them, we fancied our idea could be expressed in one or two sentences. Explanations grow under our hands, in spite of our effort at compression. Such, too, is the contrast between conversation and epistolary correspondence. We speak our meaning with little trouble; our voice, manner, and half words completing it for us; but in writing, when details must be drawn out, and misapprehensions anticipated, we seem never to be rid of the responsibility of our task.

This being the case, it is surprising that the Creeds are so short, not surprising that they need a comment.

18. The difficulty, then, and hazard of developing doctrines implicitly received, must be fully allowed; and this is often made a ground for inferring that they have no proper developments at all; that there is no natural connexion between certain dogmas and certain impressions; and that theological science is a matter of time, and place, and accident, though inward belief is ever and every where one and the same. But surely the instinct of every Christian revolts from such a position; for the very first impulse of his faith is to try to express itself about the 'great sight' which is vouchsafed to it; and this seems to argue that a science there is, whether the mind is equal to its discovery or no. And, indeed, what science is open to every chance inquirer? which is not recondite in its principles? which requires not special gifts of mind for its just formation? All subject-matters admit of true theories and false, and the false are no prejudice to the true. Why should this class of ideas be different from all other? Principles of philosophy, physics, ethics, politics, taste, admit both of implicit reception and explicit statement; why should not the ideas, which are the secret life of the Christian, be recognized also as fixed and definite in themselves, and as capable of scientific analysis? Why should not there be that real connexion between science and its subject-matter in religion, which exists in other departments of thought? No one would deny that the philosophy of Zeno or Pythagoras was the exponent of a certain mode of viewing things; or would affirm that Platonist and Epicurean acted on one and the same idea of nature, life, and duty, and meant the same thing, though they verbally differed, merely because a Plato or an Epicurus was needed to detect the abstruse elements of thought, out of which each philosophy was eventually constructed. A man surely may be a Peripatetic or an Academic in his feelings, views, aims, and acts, who never heard the names. Granting, then, extreme cases, when individuals who would analyze their views of religion are thrown entirely upon their own reason, and find that reason unequal to the task, this will be no argument against a general, natural, and ordinary correspondence between the dogma and the inward idea. Surely, if Almighty God is ever one and the same, and is revealed to us as one and the same, the true inward impression of Him, made on the recipient of the revelation, must be one and the same; and, since human nature proceeds upon fixed laws, the statement

of that impression must be one and the same, so that we may as well say that there are two Gods as two Creeds. And considering the strong feelings and energetic acts and severe sufferings which age after age have been involved in the maintenance of the Catholic dogmas, it is surely a very shallow philosophy to account such maintenance a mere contest about words, and a very abject philosophy to attribute it to mere party spirit, or to personal rivalry, or to ambition, or to covetousness.

19. Reasonable, however, as is this view of doctrinal developments in general, it cannot be denied that those which relate to the Objects of Faith, of which I am particularly speaking, have a character of their own, and must be considered separately. Let us, then, consider how the case stands, as regards the sacred doctrines of the Trinity and the Incarnation.

20. The Apostle said to the Athenians, 'Whom ye ignorantly worship, Him declare I unto you;' and the mind which is habituated to the thought of God, of Christ, of the Holy Spirit, naturally turns, as I have said, with a devout curiosity to the contemplation of the Object of its adoration, and begins to form statements concerning Him before it knows whither, or how far, it will be carried. One proposition necessarily leads to another, and a second to a third; then some limitation is required; and the combination of these opposites occasions some fresh evolutions from the original idea, which indeed can never be said to be entirely exhausted. This process is its development, and results in a series, or rather body of dogmatic statements, till what was at first an impression on the Imagination has become a system or creed in the Reason.

21. Now such impressions are obviously individual and complete above other theological ideas, *because* they are the impressions of Objects. Ideas and their developments are commonly not identical, the development being but the carrying out of the idea into its consequences. Thus the doctrine of Penance may be called a development of the doctrine of Baptism, yet still is a distinct doctrine; whereas the developments in the doctrine of the Holy Trinity and the Incarnation are mere portions of the original impression, and modes of representing it. As God is one, so the impression which He gives us of Himself is one; it is not a thing of parts; it is not a system; nor is it any thing imperfect, and needing a counterpart. It is the vision of an object. When we pray, we pray, not to an assemblage of notions, or to a creed,

but to One Individual Being; and when we speak of Him we speak of a Person, not of a Law or a Manifestation. This being the case, all our attempts to delineate our impression of Him go to bring out one idea, not two or three or four; not a philosophy, but an individual idea in its own separate aspects.

22. This may be fitly compared to the impressions made on us through the senses. Material objects are whole, and individual; and the impressions which they make on the mind, by means of the senses, are of a corresponding nature, complex and manifold in their relations and bearings, but considered in themselves integral and one. And in like manner the ideas which we are granted of Divine Objects under the Gospel, from the nature of the case and because they are ideas, answer to the Originals so far as this, that they are whole, indivisible, substantial, and may be called real, as being images of what is real. Objects which are conveyed to us through the senses, stand out in our minds, as I may say, with dimensions and aspects and influences various, and all of these consistent with one another, and many of them beyond our memory or even knowledge, while we contemplate the objects themselves; thus forcing on us a persuasion of their reality from the spontaneous congruity and coincidence of these accompaniments, as if they could not be creations of our minds, but were the images of external and independent beings. This of course will take place in the case of the sacred ideas which are the objects of our faith. Religious men, according to their measure, have an idea or vision of the Blessed Trinity in Unity, of the Son Incarnate and of His Presence, not as a number of qualities, attributes, and actions, not as the subject of a number of propositions, but as one, and individual, and independent of words, as an impression conveyed through the senses.

23. Particular propositions, then, which are used to express portions of the great idea vouchsafed to us, can never really be confused with the idea itself, which all such propositions taken together can but reach, and cannot exceed. As definitions are not intended to go beyond their subject, but to be adequate to it, so the dogmatic statements of the Divine Nature used in our confessions, however multiplied, cannot say more than is implied in the original idea, considered in its completeness, without the risk of heresy. Creeds and dogmas live in the one idea which they are designed to express, and which alone is substantive; and are necessary only because the human mind cannot reflect upon it, except piecemeal, cannot use it in its oneness and entireness,

nor without resolving it into a series of aspects and relations. And in matter of fact these expressions are never equivalent to it; we are able, indeed, to define the creations of our own minds, for they are what we make them and nothing else; but it were as easy to create what is real as to define it; and thus the Catholic dogmas are, after all, but symbols of a Divine fact, which, far from being compassed by those very propositions, would not be exhausted, nor fathomed, by a thousand.

24. Now of such sacred ideas and their attendant expressions, I observe: —

(1.) First, that an impression of this intimate kind seems to be what Scripture means by 'knowledge.' 'This is life eternal,' says our Saviour, 'that they might know Thee the only True God, and Jesus Christ whom Thou hast sent.' In like manner St. Paul speaks of willingly losing all things, 'for the excellency of the knowledge of Christ Jesus;' and St. Peter of 'the knowledge of Him who hath called us to glory and virtue' (John xvii. 3; Phil. iii. 8; 2 Pet. i. 3). Knowledge is the possession of those living ideas of sacred things, from which alone change of heart or conduct can proceed. This awful vision is what Scripture seems to designate by the phrases 'Christ in us,' 'Christ dwelling in us by faith,' 'Christ formed in us,' and 'Christ manifesting Himself unto us.' And though it is faint and doubtful in some minds, and distinct in others, as some remote object in the twilight or in the day, this arises from the circumstances of the particular mind, and does not interfere with the perfection of the gift itself.

25. (2.) This leads me next, however, to observe, that these religious impressions differ from those of material objects, in the mode in which they are made. The senses are direct, immediate, and ordinary informants, and act spontaneously without any will or effort on our part; but no such faculties have been given us, as far as we know, for realizing the Objects of Faith. It is true that inspiration may be a gift of this kind to those who have been favoured with it; nor would it be safe to deny to the illuminating grace of Baptism a power, at least of putting the mind into a capacity for receiving impressions; but the former of these is not ordinary, and both are supernatural. The secondary and intelligible means by which we receive the impression of Divine Verities, are, for instance, the habitual and devout perusal of Scripture, which gradually acts upon the mind; again, the gradual influence of intercourse with those who are in themselves in possession of the sacred ideas; again, the study of Dogmatic

Theology, which is our present subject; again, a continual round of devotion; or again, sometimes, in minds both fitly disposed and apprehensive, the almost instantaneous operation of a keen faith. This obvious distinction follows between sensible and religious ideas, that we put the latter into language in order to fix, teach, and transmit them, but not the former. No one defines a material object by way of conveying to us what we know so much better by the senses, but we form creeds as a chief mode of perpetuating the impression.

26. (3.) Further, I observe, that though the Christian mind reasons out a series of dogmatic statements, one from another, this it has ever done, and always must do, not from those statements taken in themselves, as logical propositions, but as being itself enlightened and (as if) inhabited by that sacred impression which is prior to them, which acts as a regulating principle, ever present, upon the reasoning, and without which no one has any warrant to reason at all. Such sentences as 'the Word was God,' or 'the Only-begotten Son who is in the bosom of the Father,' or 'the Word was made flesh,' or 'the Holy Ghost which proceedeth from the Father,' are not a mere letter which we may handle by the rules of art at our own will, but august tokens of most simple, ineffable, adorable facts, embraced, enshrined according to its measure in the believing mind. For though the development of an idea is a deduction of proposition from proposition, these propositions are ever formed in and round the idea itself (so to speak), and are in fact one and all only aspects of it. Moreover, this will account both for the mode of arguing from particular texts or single words of Scripture, practised by the early Fathers, and for their fearless decision in practising it; for the great Object of Faith on which they lived both enabled them to appropriate to itself particular passages of Scripture, and became to them a safeguard against heretical deductions from them. Also, it will account for the charge of weak reasoning, commonly brought against those Fathers; for never do we seem so illogical to others as when we are arguing under the continual influence of impressions to which they are insensible.

27. (4.) Again, it must of course be remembered, as I have just implied, (though as being an historical matter it hardly concerns us here), that Revelation itself has provided in Scripture the main outlines and also large details of the dogmatic system. Inspiration has superseded the exercise of human Reason in great measure, and left it but the comparatively easy task of finishing

the sacred work. The question, indeed, at first sight occurs, why such inspired statements are not enough without further developments; but in truth, when Reason has once been put on the investigation, it cannot stop till it has finished it; one dogma creates another, by the same right by which it was itself created; the Scripture statements are sanctions as well as informants in the inquiry; they begin and they do not exhaust.

28. (5.) Scripture, I say, begins a series of developments which it does not finish; that is to say, in other words, it is a mistake to look for every separate proposition of the Catholic doctrine in Scripture. This is plain from what has gone before. For instance, the Athanasian Creed professes to lay down the right faith, which we must hold on its most sacred subjects, in order to be saved. This must mean that there is one view concerning the Holy Trinity, or concerning the Incarnation, which is true, and distinct from all others; one definite, consistent, entire view, which cannot be mistaken, not contained in any certain number of propositions, but held as a view by the believing mind, and not held, but denied by Arians, Sabellians, Tritheists, Nestorians, Monophysites, Socinians, and other heretics. That idea is not enlarged, if propositions are added, nor impaired if they are withdrawn: if they are added, this is with a view of conveying that one integral view, not of amplifying it. That view does not depend on such propositions: it does not consist in them; they are but specimens and indications of it. And they may be multiplied without limit. They are necessary, but not needful to it, being but portions or aspects of that previous impression which has at length come under the cognizance of Reason and the terminology of science. The question, then, is not whether this or that proposition of the Catholic doctrine is *in terminis* in Scripture, unless we would be slaves to the letter, but whether that one view of the Mystery, of which all such are the exponents, be not there; a view which would be some other view, and not itself, if any one of such propositions, if any one of a number of similar propositions, were not true. These propositions imply each other, as being parts of one whole; so that to deny one is to deny all, and to invalidate one is to deface and destroy the view itself. One thing alone has to be impressed on us by Scripture, the Catholic idea, and in it they all are included. To object, then, to the number of propositions, upon which an anathema is placed, is altogether to mistake their use; for their multiplication is not intended to enforce many things, but to express one,—

304

to form within us that one impression concerning Almighty God, as the ruling principle of our minds, and that, whether we can fully recognize our own possession of it or no. And surely it is no paradox to say that such ruling ideas may exert a most powerful influence, at least in their various aspects, on our moral character, and on the whole man: as no one would deny in the case of belief or disbelief of a Supreme Being.

29. (6.) And here we see the ordinary mistake of doctrinal innovators, viz. to go away with this or that proposition of the Creed, instead of embracing that one idea which all of them together are meant to convey; it being almost a definition of heresy, that it fastens on some one statement as if the whole truth, to the denial of all others, and as the basis of a new faith; erring rather in what it rejects, than in what it maintains: though, in truth, if the mind deliberately rejects any portion of the doctrine, this is a proof that it does not really hold even that very statement for the sake of which it rejects the others. Realizing is the very life of true developments; it is peculiar to the Church, and the justification of her definitions.

30. Enough has now been said on the distinction, yet connexion, between the implicit knowledge and the explicit confession of the Divine Objects of Faith, as they are revealed to us under the Gospel. An objection, however, remains, which cannot be satisfactorily treated in a few words. And what is worse than prolixity, the discussion may bear with it some appearance of unnecessary or even wanton refinement; unless, indeed, it is thrown into the form of controversy, a worse evil. Let it suffice to say, that my wish is, not to discover difficulties in any subject, but to solve them.

31. It may be asked, then, whether the mistake of words and names for things is not incurred by orthodox as well as heretics, in dogmatizing at all about the 'secret things which belong unto the Lord our God,' inasmuch as the idea of a supernatural object must itself be supernatural, and since no such ideas are claimed by ordinary Christians, no knowledge of Divine Verities is possible to them. How should any thing of this world convey ideas which are beyond and above this world? How can teaching and intercourse, how can human words, how can earthly images, convey to the mind an idea of the Invisible? They cannot rise above themselves. They can suggest no idea but what is resolvable into ideas natural and earthly. The words 'Person,'

'Substance,' 'Consubstantial,' 'Generation,' 'Procession,' 'Incarnation,' 'Taking of the manhood into God,' and the like, have either a very abject and human meaning, or none at all. In other words, there is no such inward view of these doctrines, distinct from the dogmatic language used to express them, as was just now supposed. The metaphors by which they are signified are not mere symbols of ideas which exist independently of them, but their meaning is coincident and identical with the ideas. When, indeed, we have knowledge of a thing from other sources, then the metaphors we may apply to it are but accidental appendages to that knowledge; whereas our ideas of Divine things are just coextensive with the figures by which we express them, neither more nor less, and without them are not; and when we draw inferences from those figures, we are not illustrating one existing idea, but drawing mere logical inferences. We speak, indeed, of material objects freely, because our senses reveal them to us apart from our words; but as to these ideas about heavenly things, we learn them from words, yet (it seems) we are to say what we, without words, conceive of them, as if words could convey what they do not contain. It follows that our anathemas, our controversies, our struggles, our sufferings, are merely about the poor ideas conveyed to us in certain figures of speech.

32. Some obvious remarks suggest themselves in answer to this representation. First, it is difficult to determine what divine grace may not do for us, if not in immediately implanting new ideas, yet in refining and elevating those which we gain through natural informants. If, as we all acknowledge, grace renews our moral feelings, yet through outward means, if it opens upon us new ideas about virtue and goodness and heroism and heavenly peace, it does not appear why, in a certain sense, it may not impart ideas concerning the nature of God. Again, the various terms and figures which are used in the doctrine of the Holy Trinity or of the Incarnation, surely may by their combination create ideas which will be altogether new, though they are still of an earthly character. And further, when it is said that such figures convey no knowledge of the Divine Nature itself, beyond those figures, whatever they are, it should be considered whether our senses can be proved to suggest any real idea of matter. All that we know, strictly speaking, is the existence of the impressions our senses make on us; and yet we scruple not to speak as if they conveyed to us the knowledge of material substances. Let, then, the Catholic dogmas, as such, be freely

admitted to convey no true idea of Almighty God, but only an earthly one, gained from earthly figures, provided it be allowed, on the other hand, that the senses do not convey to us any true idea of matter, but only an idea commensurate with sensible impressions.

33. Nor is there any reason why this should not be fully granted. Still there may be a certain correspondence between the idea, though earthly, and its heavenly archetype, such, that that idea belongs to the archetype, in a sense in which no other earthly idea belongs to it, as being the nearest approach to it which our present state allows. Indeed Scripture itself intimates the earthly nature of our present ideas of Sacred Objects, when it speaks of our now 'seeing in a glass *darkly*, but then face to face;' and it has ever been the doctrine of divines that the Beatific Vision, or true sight of Almighty God, is reserved for the world to come. Meanwhile we are allowed such an approximation to the truth as earthly images and figures may supply to us.

34. It must not be supposed that this is the only case in which we are obliged to receive information needful to us, through the medium of our existing ideas, and consequently with but a vague apprehension of its subject-matter. Children, who are made our pattern in Scripture, are taught, by an accomodation, on the part of their teachers, to their immature faculties and their scanty vocabulary. To answer their questions in the language which we should use towards grown men, would be simply to mislead them, if they could construe it at all. We must dispense and 'divide' the word of truth, if we would not have it changed, as far as they are concerned, into a word of falsehood; for what is short of truth in the letter may be to them the most perfect truth, that is, the nearest approach to truth, compatible with their condition. The case is the same as regards those who have any natural defect or deprivation which cuts them off from the circle of ideas common to mankind in general. To speak to a blind man of light and colours, in terms proper to those phenomena, would be to mock him; we must use other media of information accomodated to his circumstances, according to the well-known instance in which his own account of scarlet was to liken it to the sound of a trumpet. And so again, as regards savages, or the ignorant, or weak, or narrow-minded, our representations and arguments must take a certain form, if they are to gain admission into their minds at all, and to reach them. Again, what impediments do the diversities of language place in the way of

communicating ideas! Language is a sort of analysis of thought; and, since ideas are infinite, and infinitely combined, and infinitely modified, whereas language is a method definite and limited, and confined to an arbitrary selection of a certain number of these innumerable materials, it were idle to expect that the courses of thought marked out in one language should, except in their great outlines and main centres, correspond to those of another. Multitudes of ideas expressed in the one do not even enter into the other, and can only be conveyed by some economy or accommodation, by circumlocutions, phrases, limiting words, figures, or some bold and happy expedient. And sometimes, from the continual demand, foreign words become naturalized. Again, the difficulty is extreme, as all persons know, of leading certain individuals (to use a familiar phrase) to understand one another; their habits of thought turning apparently on points of mutual repulsion. Now this is always in a measure traceable to moral diversities between the parties; still, in many cases, it arises mainly from difference in the principle on which they have divided and subdivided that world of ideas, which comes before them both. They seem ever to be dodging each other, and need a common measure or economy to mediate between them.

35. Fables, again, are economies or accommodations, being truths and principles cast into that form in which they will be most vividly recognized; as in the well-known instance attributed to Menenius Agrippa. Again, mythical representations, at least in their better form, may be considered facts or narratives, untrue, but like the truth, intended to bring out the action of some principle, point of character, and the like. For instance, the tradition that St. Ignatius was the child whom our Lord took in His arms, may be unfounded; but it realizes to us his special relation to Christ and His Apostles, with a keenness peculiar to itself. The same remark may be made upon certain narratives of martyrdoms, or of the details of such narratives, or of certain alleged miracles, or heroic acts, or speeches, all which are the spontaneous produce of religious feeling under imperfect knowledge. If the alleged facts did not occur, they ought to have occurred (if I may so speak); they are such as might have occurred, and would have occurred, under circumstances; and they belong to the parties to whom they are attributed, potentially, if not actually; or the like of them did occur; or occurred to others similarly circumstanced, though not to those very persons. Many a theory or view of things, on which an institution is founded,

308

or a party held together, is of the same kind. Many an argument, used by zealous and earnest men, has this economical character, being not the very ground on which they act, (for they continue in the same course, though it be refuted,) yet, in a certain sense, a representation of it, a proximate description of their feelings in the shape of argument, on which they can rest, to which they can recur when perplexed, and appeal when questioned. Now, in this reference to accommodation or economy in human affairs, I do not meddle with the question of casuistry, viz. which of such artifices, as they may be called, are innocent, or where the line is to be drawn. That some are immoral, common sense tells us; but it is enough for my purpose, if some are necessary, as the same common sense will allow; and then the very necessity of the use will account for the abuse and perversion.

36. Even between man and man, then, constituted, as men are, alike, various distinct instruments, keys, or *calculi* of thought obtain, on which their ideas and arguments shape themselves respectively, and which we must use, if we would reach them. The cogitative method, as it may be called, of one man is notoriously very different from that of another; of the lawyer from that of the soldier, of the rich from that of the poor. The territory of thought is portioned out in a hundred different ways. Abstractions, generalizations, definitions, propositions, all are framed on distinct standards; and if this is found in matters of this world between man and man, surely much more must it exist between the ideas of men, and the thoughts, ways, and works of God.

37. One of the obvious instances of this contrariety is seen in the classifications we make of the subjects of the animal or vegetable kingdoms. Here a very intelligible order has been observed by the Creator Himself; still one of which we have not, after all, the key. We are obliged to frame one of our own; and when we apply it, we find that it will not exactly answer the Divine idea of arrangement, as it discovers itself to us; there being phenomena which we cannot locate, or which, upon our system of division, are anomalies in the general harmony of the Creation.

38. Mathematical science will afford us a more extended illustration of this distinction between supernatural and eternal laws, and our attempts to represent them, that is, our economies. Various methods or *calculi* have been adopted to embody those immutable principles and dispositions of which the science treats, which are really independent of any, yet cannot be contemplated or pursued without one or other of them. The first of these

instruments of investigation employs the medium of extension; the second, that of number; the third, that of motion; the fourth proceeds on a more subtle hypothesis, that of increase. These methods are very distinct from each other, at least the geometrical and the differential; yet they are, one and all, analyses, more or less perfect, of those same necessary truths, for which we have not a name, of which we have no idea, except in the terms of such economical representations. They are all developments of one and the same range of ideas; they are all instruments of discovery as to those ideas. They stand for real things, and we can reason with them, though they be but symbols, as if they were the things themselves, for which they stand. Yet none of them carries out the lines of truth to their limits; first, one stops in the analysis, then another; like some calculating tables which answer for a thousand times, and miss in the thousand and first. While they answer, we can use them just as if they were the realities which they represent, and without thinking of those realities; but at length our instrument of discovery issues in some great impossibility or contradiction, or what we call in religion, a mystery. It has run its length; and by its failure shows that all along it has been but an expedient for practical purposes, not a true analysis or adequate image of those recondite laws which are investigated by means of it. It has never fathomed their depth, because it now fails to measure their course. At the same time, no one, because it cannot do every thing, would refuse to use it within the range in which it will act; no one would say that it was a system of empty symbols, though it be but a shadow of the unseen. Though we use it with caution, still we use it, as being the nearest approximation to the truth which our condition admits.

39. Let us take another instance, of an outward and earthly form, or economy, under which great wonders unknown seem to be typified; I mean musical sounds, as they are exhibited most perfectly in instrumental harmony. There are seven notes in the scale; make them fourteen; yet what a slender outfit for so vast an enterprise! What science brings so much out of so little? Out of what poor elements does some great master in it create his new world! Shall we say that all this exuberant inventiveness is a mere ingenuity or trick of art, like some game or fashion of the day, without reality, without meaning? We may do so; and then, perhaps, we shall also account the science of theology to be a matter of words; yet, as there is a divinity in

the theology of the Church, which those who feel cannot communicate, so is there also in the wonderful creation of sublimity and beauty of which I am speaking. To many men the very names which the science employs are utterly incomprehensible. To speak of an idea or a subject seems to be fanciful or trifling, to speak of the views which it opens upon us to be childish extravagance; yet is it possible that that inexhaustible evolution and disposition of notes, so rich yet so simple, so intricate yet so regulated, so various yet so majestic, should be a mere sound, which is gone and perishes? Can it be that those mysterious stirrings of heart, and keen emotions, and strange yearnings after we know not what, and awful impressions from we know not whence, should be wrought in us by what is unsubstantial, and comes and goes, and begins and ends in itself? It is not so; it cannot be. No; they have escaped from some higher sphere; they are the outpourings of eternal harmony in the medium of created sound; they are echoes from our Home; they are the voice of Angels, or the Magnificat of Saints, or the living laws of Divine Governance, or the Divine Attributes; something are they besides themselves, which we cannot compass, which we cannot utter,— though mortal man, and he perhaps not otherwise distinguished above his fellows, has the gift of eliciting them.

40. So much on the subject of musical sound; but what if the whole series of impressions, made on us through the senses, be, as I have already hinted, but a Divine economy suited to our need, and the token of realities distinct from themselves, and such as might be revealed to us, nay, more perfectly, by other senses, different from our existing ones as they from each other? What if the properties of matter, as we conceive of them, are merely relative to us, so that facts and events, which seem impossible when predicated concerning it in terms of those impressions, are impossible only in those terms, not in themselves,— impossible only because of the imperfection of the idea, which, in consequence of those impressions, we have conceived of material substances? If so, it would follow that the laws of physics, as we consider them, are themselves but generalizations of economical exhibitions, inferences from figure and shadow, and not more real than the phenomena from which they are drawn. Scripture, for instance, says that the sun moves and the earth is stationary; and science, that the earth moves, and the sun is comparatively at rest. How can we determine which of these opposite statements is the very truth, till we know what motion

311

is? If our idea of motion be but an accidental result of our present senses, neither proposition is true, and both are true; neither true philosophically, both true for certain practical purposes in the system in which they are respectively found; and physical science will have no better meaning when it says that the earth moves, than plane astronomy when it says that the earth is still.

41. And should any one fear lest thoughts such as these should tend to a dreary and hopeless scepticism, let him take into account the Being and Providence of God, the Merciful and True; and he will at once be relieved of his anxiety. All is dreary till we believe, what our hearts tell us, that we are subjects of His Governance; nothing is dreary, all inspires hope and trust, directly we understand that we are under His hand, and that whatever comes to us is from Him, as a method of discipline and guidance. What is it to us whether the knowledge He gives us be greater or less, if it be He who gives it? What is it to us, whether it be exact or vague, if He bids us to trust it? What have we to care whether we are or are not given to divide substance from shadow, if He is training us heavenwards by means of either? Why should we vex ourselves to find whether our deductions are philosophical or no, provided they are religious? If our senses supply the media by which we are put on trial, by which we are all brought together, and hold intercourse with each other, and are disciplined and are taught, and enabled to benefit others, it is enough. We have an instinct within us, impelling us, we have external necessity forcing us, to trust our senses, and we may leave the question of their substantial truth for another world, 'till the day break, and the shadow flee away.' And what is true of reliance on our senses, is true of all the information which it has pleased God to vouchsafe to us, whether in nature or in grace.

42. Instances, then, such as these, will be found both to sober and to encourage us in our theological studies,—to impress us with a profound sense of our ignorance of Divine Verities, when we know most; yet to hinder us from relinquishing their contemplation, though we know so little. On the one hand, it would appear that even the most subtle questions of the schools may have a real meaning, as the most intricate *formulae* in analytics; and, since we cannot tell how far our instrument of thought reaches in the process of investigation, and at what point it fails us, no questions may safely be despised. 'Whether God was any where before creation?' 'whether He knows all creatures in

Himself?' 'whether the blessed see all things possible and future in Him?' 'whether relation is the form of the Divine Persons?' 'in what sense the Holy Spirit is Divine Love?' these, and a multitude of others, far more minute and remote, are all sacred from their subject.

43. On the other hand, it must be recollected that not even the Catholic reasonings and conclusions, as contained in Confessions, and most thoroughly received by us, are worthy of the Divine Verities which they represent, but are the truth only in as full a measure as our minds can admit it; the truth as far as they go, and under the conditions of thought which human feebleness imposes. It is true that God is without beginning, if eternity may worthily be considered to imply succession; in every place, if He who is a Spirit can have relations with space. It is right to speak of His Being and Attributes, if He be not rather super-essential; it is true to say that He is wise or powerful, if we may consider Him as other than the most simple Unity. He is truly Three, if He is truly One; He is truly One, if the idea of Him falls under earthly number. He has a triple Personality, in the sense in which the Infinite can be understood to have Personality at all. If we know any thing of Him,—if we may speak of Him in any way,—if we may emerge from Atheism or Pantheism into religious faith,—if we would have any saving hope, any life of truth and holiness within us,—this only do we know, with this only confession, we must begin and end our worship—that the Father is the One God, the Son the One God, and the Holy Ghost the One God; and that the Father is not the Son, the Son not the Holy Ghost, and the Holy Ghost not the Father.

44. The fault, then, which we must guard against in receiving such Divine intimations, is the ambition of being wiser than what is written; of employing the Reason, not in carrying out what is told us, but in impugning it; not in support, but in prejudice of Faith. Brilliant as are such exhibitions of its powers, they bear no fruit. Reason can but ascertain the profound difficulties of our condition, it cannot remove them; it has no work, it makes no beginning, it does but continually fall back, till it is content to be a little child, and to follow where Faith guides it.

45. What remains, then, but to make our prayer to the Gracious and Merciful God, the Father of Lights, that in all our exercises of Reason, His gift, we may thus use it,—as He would have us, in the obedience of Faith, with a view to His glory,

313

with an aim at His Truth, in dutiful submission to His will, for the comfort of His elect, for the edification of Holy Jerusalem, His Church, and in recollection of His own solemn warning, 'Every idle word that men shall speak, they shall give account thereof in the day of judgment; for by thy words thou shalt be justified, and by thy words thou shalt be condemned.'

The Parting of Friends

Psalms 104:23.

Man goeth forth to his work and to his labour until the evening.

THIS WAS preached on 25 September 1843, in the church at Littlemore, and first published as sermon xxvi in *Sermons on Subjects of the Day*. It was Newman's last sermon as an Anglican.

The occasion was also the anniversary of the dedication of the church, and the building was bright with flowers—although to Newman's friends these seemed to deck it as if for a funeral. Pusey celebrated the Eucharist—noting afterwards that he 'could hardly help mingling sorrow even with that Feast'.

Newman takes for his text the same words he had used in preaching his first sermon as an Anglican, eighteen years before. He speaks sensitively of partings in Holy Scripture, especially Christ's parting words to Jerusalem (Luke 19: 41, 42), and continues, 'A lesson, surely, and a warning to us all, in every place where He puts His Name, to the end of time. . . .' The description of Christ eating the Passover with His disciples before His Passion is notable for Newman's understanding of the humanity of the Son of God. Newman's own anguish, his fasts and meditations and setbacks, his withdrawal from the world, his silent deliberation upon the meaning of the adversities which his work had met, all these combine to strengthen his grasp of the mystery of the Cross. The sermon has a rare pathos.

A Presbyterian, looking back on *The Parting of Friends*, and what it foretold of the end of Newman's priesthood in the English Church, wrote later of the 'aching blank, the awful pause' which fell when 'that voice had ceased and we knew that we should hear it no more. It was as when, to one kneeling by night, in the silence of some vast cathedral, the great bell tolling solemnly overhead has suddenly gone still. . . . Since then many voices of powerful teachers may have been heard, but none that ever penetrated the soul like his.'[1]

Formally, Newman is dealing most of the time in imagery from the language of prophecy about Jerusalem, but no one can fail to see the real object of his thoughts, as he apostrophizes the English Church, asking in sorrow, 'O my mother, whence is this unto thee, that thou hast good things poured upon thee and canst not keep them, and bearest children, yet darest not own them? why has thou not the skill to use their services, nor the heart to rejoice in their love?' The whole sermon is solidly based

315

upon Scriptural incidents and in particular the grief of Christ over Jerusalem, yet it is below the surface one of the most autobiographical and emotional things which Newman wrote—and he was a man of much restraint.

NOTE

1. J. C. Shairp, *Studies in Poetry and Philosophy*, 1886, pp. 255-6.

WHEN THE Son of Man, the First-born of the creation of God, came to the evening of His mortal life, He parted with His disciples at a feast. He had borne 'the burden and heat of the day;' yet, when 'wearied with His journey,' He had but stopped at the well's side, and asked a draught of water for His thirst; for He had 'meat to eat which' others 'knew not of.' His meat was 'to do the will of Him that sent Him, and to finish His work;' 'I must work the works of Him that sent Me,' said He, 'while it is day; the night cometh, when no man can work' (John iv. 6. 34; ix. 4). Thus passed the season of His ministry; and if at any time He feasted with Pharisee and publican, it was in order that He might do the work of God more strenuously. But 'when the even was come He sat down with the Twelve.' 'And He said unto them, With desire have I desired to eat this Passover with you, before I suffer' (Matt. xxvi. 20). He was about to suffer more than man had ever suffered or shall suffer. But there is nothing gloomy, churlish, violent, or selfish in His grief; it is tender, affectionate, social. He calls His friends around Him, though He was as Job among the ashes; He bids them stay by Him, and see Him suffer; He desires their sympathy; He takes refuge in their love. He first feasted them, and sung a hymn with them, and washed their feet; and when His long trial began, He beheld them and kept them in His presence, till they in terror shrank from it. Yet, on St. Mary and St. John, His Virgin Mother and His Virgin Disciple, who remained, His eyes still rested; and in St. Peter, who was denying Him in the distance, His sudden glance wrought a deep repentance. O wonderful pattern, the type of all trial and of all duty under it, while the Church endures.

We indeed to-day have no need of so high a lesson and so august a comfort. We have no pain, no grief which calls for it; yet, considering it has been brought before us in this morning's service, we are naturally drawn to think of it, though it be infinitely above us, under certain circumstances of this season and the present time. For now are the shades of evening falling upon the earth, and the year's labour is coming to its end. In Septuagesima the labourers were sent into the vineyard; in Sexagesima the sower went forth to sow;—that time is over; 'the harvest is passed, the summer is ended' (Jer. viii. 20), the vintage is gathered. We have kept the Ember-days for the fruits of the earth, in self-abasement, as being unworthy even of the least of God's mercies; and now we are offering up of its corn and wine as a propitiation, and are eating and drinking of them with thanksgiving.

'All things come of Thee, and of Thine own have we given Thee' (1 Chron. xxix. 14). If we have had the rain in its season, and the sun shining in its strength, and the fertile ground, it is of Thee. We give back to Thee what came from Thee. 'When Thou givest it them, they gather it, and when Thou openest Thy hand, they are filled with good. When Thou hidest Thy face, they are troubled; when Thou takest away their breath, they die, and are turned again to their dust. When Thou lettest Thy breath go forth, they shall be made, and Thou shalt renew the face of the earth' (Ps. civ. 28-30). He gives, He takes away. 'Shall we receive good at the hand of God, and shall we not receive evil?' (Job ii. 10.) May He not 'do what He will with His own' (Matt. xx. 15)? May not His sun set as it has risen? and must it not set, if it is to rise again? and must not darkness come first, if there is ever to be morning? and must not the sky be blacker, before it can be brighter? And cannot He, who can do all things, cause a light to arise even in the darkness? 'I have thought upon Thy Name, O Lord, in the night season, and have kept Thy Law;' 'Thou also shalt light my candle, the Lord my God shall make my darkness to be light;' or as the Prophet speaks, 'At the evening time it shall be light' (Zech. xiv. 7).

'All things come of Thee,' says holy David, 'for we are strangers before Thee and sojourners, as were all our fathers; our days on the earth are as a shadow, and there is none abiding' (1 Chron. xxix. 15). All is vanity, vanity of vanities, and vexation of spirit. 'What profit hath a man of all his labour which he taketh under the sun? One generation passeth away, and another generation cometh; but the earth abideth for ever; the sun also ariseth, and the sun goeth down; . . . all things are full of labour, man cannot utter it; . . . that which is crooked cannot be made straight, and that which is wanting cannot be numbered' (Eccles. i. 3-15). 'To every thing there is a season, and a time to every purpose under heaven; a time to be born and a time to die; a time to plant and a time to pluck up that which is planted; a time to kill and a time to heal; a time to break down and a time to build up; . . . a time to get and a time to lose; a time to keep and a time to cast away' (Eccles. iii. 1-6). And time, and matter, and motion, and force, and the will of man, how vain are they all, except as instruments of the grace of God, blessing them and working with them! How vain are all our pains, our thought, our care, unless God uses them, unless God has inspired them! how worse than fruitless are they, unless directed to His glory, and given back to the Giver!

'Of Thine own have we given Thee,' says the royal Psalmist, after he had collected materials for the Temple. Because 'the work was great,' and 'the palace, not for man, but for the Lord God,' therefore he 'prepared with all his might for the house of his God,' gold, and silver, and brass, and iron, and wood, 'onyx stones, and stones to be set, glistering stones, and of divers colours, and all manner of precious stones, and marble stones in abundance' (1 Chron. xxix. 1, 2. 9). And 'the people rejoice, for that they offered willingly; . . . and David the king also rejoiced with great joy.' We too, at this season, year by year, have been allowed in our measure, according to our work and our faith, to rejoice in God's Presence, for this sacred building which He has given us to worship Him in. It was a glad time when we first met here,—many of us now present recollect it; nor did our rejoicing cease, but was renewed every autumn, as the day came round. It has been 'a day of gladness and feasting, and a good day, and of sending portions one to another' (Esther ix. 19). We have kept the feast heretofore with merry hearts; we have kept it seven full years unto 'a perfect end;' now let us keep it, even though in haste, and with bitter herbs, and with loins girded, and with a staff in our hand, as they who have 'no continuing city, but seek one to come' (Heb. xiii. 14).

So was it with Jacob, when with his staff he passed over that Jordan. He too kept feast before he set out upon his dreary way. He received his father's blessing, and then was sent afar; he left his mother, never to see her face or hear her voice again. He parted with all that his heart loved, and turned his face towards a strange land. He went with the doubt, whether he should have bread to eat, or raiment to put on. He came to 'the people of the East,' and served a hard master twenty years. 'In the day the drought consumed him, and the frost by night; and his sleep departed from his eyes' (Gen. xxxi. 40). O little did he think, when father and mother had forsaken him, and at Bethel he lay down to sleep on the desolate ground, because the sun was set and even had come, that there was the house of God and the gate of heaven, that the Lord was in that place, and would thence go forward with him whithersoever he went, till He brought him back to that river in 'two bands,' who was then crossing it forlorn and solitary!

So had it been with Ishmael; though the feast was not to him a blessing, yet he feasted in his father's tent, and then was sent

319

away. That tender father, who, when a son was promised him of Sarah, cried out to his Almighty Protector, 'O that Ishmael might live before Thee!' (Gen. xvii. 18)—he it was, who, under a divine direction, the day after the feast, 'rose up early in the morning, and took bread, and a bottle of water, and gave it unto Hagar, putting it on her shoulder, and the child, and sent her away. And she departed, and wandered in the wilderness of Beersheba' (Gen. xxi. 14). And little thought that fierce child, when for feasting came thirst and weariness and wandering in the desert, that this was not the end of Ishmael, but the beginning. And little did Hagar read his coming fortunes, when 'the water was spent in the bottle, and she cast the child under one of the shrubs, and she went and sat her down over against him a good way off; . . . for she said, Let me not see the death of the child. And she sat over against him, and lift up her voice, and wept.'

So had it been with Naomi, though she was not quitting, but returning to her home, and going, not to a land of famine, but of plenty. In a time of distress, she had left her country, and found friends and made relatives among the enemies of her people. And when her husband and her children died, Moabitish women, who had once been the stumbling-block of Israel, became the support and comfort of her widowhood. Time had been when, at the call of the daughters of Moab, the chosen people had partaken their sacrifices, and 'bowed down to their gods. And Israel joined himself unto Baal-peor, and the anger of the Lord was kindled against Israel.' Centuries had since passed away, and now of Moabites was Naomi mother; and to their land had she given her heart, when the call of duty summoned her back to Bethlehem. 'She had heard in the country of Moab, how that the Lord had visited His people in giving them bread. Wherefore she went forth out of the place where she was, and her two daughters-in-law with her, and they went on the way to return unto the land of Judah' (Ruth i. 6-8. 14, 15).

Forlorn widow, great was the struggle in her bosom, whether shall she do?—leave behind her the two heathen women, in widowhood and weakness like herself, her sole stay, the shadows of departed blessings? or shall she selfishly take them as fellow-sufferers, who could not be protectors? Shall she seek sympathy where she cannot gain help? shall she deprive them of a home, when she has none to supply? So she said, 'Go, return each to her mother's house: the Lord deal kindly with you, as ye have dealt with the dead and with me!' Perplexed Naomi, torn with contrary feelings; which tried her the more,—Orpah who left her, or Ruth who remained? Orpah who was a pain, or Ruth who was a charge? 'They lifted up their voice and wept again; and Orpah kissed her mother-in-law, but Ruth clave unto her. And she said, Behold, thy sister-in-law is gone back unto her people and unto her gods; return thou after thy sister-in-law. And Ruth said, Entreat me not to leave thee, or to return from following after thee: for whither thou goest, I will go; and where thou lodgest, I will lodge: thy people shall be my people, and thy God my God. Where thou diest, will I die, and there will I be buried; the Lord do so to me, and more also, if aught but death part thee and me' (Ruth i. 14-17).

Orpah kissed Naomi, and went back to the world. There was sorrow in the parting, but Naomi's sorrow was more for Orpah's sake than for her own. Pain there would be, but it was the pain of a wound, not the yearning regret of love. It was the pain we feel when friends disappoint us, and fall in our esteem. That kiss of Orpah was no loving token; it was but the hollow profession of those who use smooth words, that they may part company with us with least trouble and discomfort to themselves. Orpah's tears were but the dregs of affection; she clasped her mother-in-law once for all, that she might not cleave to her. Far different were the tears, far different the embrace, which passed between those two religious friends recorded in the book which follows, who loved each other with a true love unfeigned, but whose lives ran in different courses. If Naomi's grief was great when Orpah kissed her, what was David's when he saw the last of him, whose 'soul had from the first been knit with his soul,' so that 'he loved him as his own soul' (1 Sam. xviii. 1-3)? 'I am distressed for thee, my brother Jonathan,' he says; 'very pleasant hast thou been unto me; thy love to me was wonderful, passing the love of women' (2 Sam. i. 26). What woe was upon that 'young man,' 'of a beautiful countenance and goodly to look to,' and 'cunning in playing, and a mighty valiant man, and a man of war, and prudent in matters' (1 Sam. xvi. 12. 18); when his devoted affectionate loyal friend, whom these good gifts have gained, looked upon him for the last time! O hard destiny, except that the All-merciful so willed it, that such companions might not walk in the house of God as friends! David must flee to the wilderness, Jonathan must pine in his father's hall; Jonathan must share that stern father's death in battle, and David must ascend the vacant throne. Yet they made a covenant on parting: 'Thou shalt not only,' said Jonathan, 'while yet I live, show me the kindness of the Lord, that I die not; but also thou shalt not cut off thy kindness from my house for ever; no, not when the Lord hath cut off the enemies of David, every one from the face of the earth. . . . And Jonathan caused David to swear again, because he loved him, for he loved him as he loved his own soul.' And then, while David hid himself, Jonathan made trial of Saul, how he felt disposed to David; and when he found that 'it was determined of his father to slay David,' he 'arose from the table in fierce anger, and did eat no meat the second day of the month; for he was grieved for David, because his father had done him shame.' Then in the morning he went out into the field, where David lay, and the last meeting took place between the two. 'David arose out of a place toward the south, and fell on his face to the ground, and bowed himself three times; and they kissed one another, and wept one with another, till David exceeded. And Jonathan said to David, Go in peace, forasmuch as we have sworn both of us in the Name of the Lord, saying, The Lord be between me and thee, and between my seed and thy seed for ever. And he arose and departed; and Jonathan went into the city' (1 Sam. xx. 14-42).

David's affection was given to a single heart; but there is another spoken of in Scripture, who had a thousand friends and loved each as his own soul, and seemed to live a thousand lives in them, and died a thousand deaths when he must quit them: that great Apostle, whose very heart was broken when his brethren wept; who 'lived if they stood fast in the Lord;' who 'was glad when he was weak and they were strong;' and who was 'willing to have imparted unto them his own soul, because they were dear unto him' (Acts xxi. 21, 22. 1 Thess. ii. 8; iii. 8. 2 Cor. xiii. 9). Yet we read of his bidding farewell to whole Churches, never to see them again. At one time, to the little ones of the flock; 'When we had accomplished those days,' says the Evangelist, 'we departed, and went our way, . . . with wives and children, till we were out of the city; and we kneeled down on the shore and prayed. And when we had taken our leave one of another, we took ship, and they returned home again.' At another time, to the rulers of the Church: 'And now behold,' he says to them, 'I know that ye all, among whom I have gone preaching the kingdom of God, shall see my face no more. Wherefore, I take you to record this day, that I am pure from the blood of all men, for I have not shunned to declare unto you all the counsel of God. . . . I have coveted no man's silver, or gold, or apparel; . . . I have showed you all things, how that so labouring he ought to support the weak; and to remember the words of the Lord Jesus, how he said, It is more blessed to give than to receive.' And then, when he had finished, 'he kneeled down, and prayed with them all. And they all wept sore, and fell on Paul's neck, and kissed him; sorrowing most of all for the words which he spake, that they should see his face no more. And they accompanied him unto the ship' (Acts xxi. 5, 6; xx. 25-27, 33, 35, 36-38).

There was another time, when he took leave of his 'own son in the faith,' Timothy, in words more calm, and still more impressive, when his end was nigh: 'I am now ready to be offered,' he says, 'and the time of my departure is at hand. I have fought a good fight, I have finished my course, I have kept the faith. Henceforth there is laid up for me a crown of righteousness, which the Lord, the Righteous Judge, shall give me at that day' (2 Tim. iv. 6-8).

And what are all these instances but memorials and tokens of the Son of Man, when His work and His labour were coming to an end? Like Jacob, like Ishmael, like Elisha, like the Evangelist whose day is just passed, He kept feast before His departure; and, like David, He was persecuted by the rulers in Israel; and, like Naomi, He was deserted by His friends; and, like Ishmael, He cried out, 'I thirst' in a barren and dry land; and at length, like Jacob, He went to sleep with a stone for His pillow, in the evening. And, like St. Paul, He had 'finished the work which God gave Him to do,' and had 'witnessed a good confession;' and, beyond St. Paul, 'the Prince of this world had come, and had nothing in Him' (1 Tim. vi. 13. John xiv. 30). 'He was in the world, and the world was made by Him, and the world knew Him not. He came unto His own, and His own received Him not' (John i. 10, 11). Heavily did he leave, tenderly did he mourn over the country and city which rejected Him. 'When He was come near, He beheld the city, and wept over it, saying, If thou hadst known, even thou, at least in this thy day, the things which belong unto thy peace! but now they are hid from thine eyes.' And again: 'O Jerusalem, Jerusalem, which killest thy prophets, and stonest them that are sent unto thee, how often would I have gathered thy children together, as a hen doth gather her brood under her wings, and ye would not! Behold, your house is left unto you desolate' (Luke xix. 41, 42; xiii. 34, 35).

A lesson surely, and a warning to us all, in every place where He puts His Name, to the end of time; lest we be cold towards His gifts, or unbelieving towards His word, or jealous of His workings, or heartless towards His mercies. . . . O mother of saints! O school of the wise! O nurse of the heroic! of whom went forth, in whom have dwelt, memorable names of old, to spread the truth abroad, or to cherish and illustrate it at home! O thou, from whom surrounding nations lit their lamps! O virgin of Israel! wherefore dost thou now sit on the ground and keep silence, like one of the foolish women who were without oil on the coming of the Bridegroom? Where is now the ruler in Sion, and the doctor in the Temple, and the ascetic on Carmel, and the herald in the wilderness, and the preacher in the market-place? where are thy 'effectual fervent prayers,' offered in secret, and thy alms and good works coming up as a memorial before God? How is it, O once holy place, that 'the land mourneth, for the corn is wasted, the new wine is dried up, the oil languisheth, . . . because joy is withered away from the sons of men?' 'Alas for the day! . . . how do the beasts groan! the herds of cattle are perplexed, because they have no pasture, yea, the flocks of sheep are made desolate.' 'Lebanon is ashamed and hewn down; Sharon is like a wilderness, and Bashon and Carmel shake off their fruits' (Joel i. 10-18. Isa. xxxiii. 9). O my mother, whence is this unto thee, that thou hast good things poured upon thee and canst not keep them, and bearest children, yet darest not own them? why hast thou not the skill to use their services, nor the heart to rejoice in their love? how is it that whatever is generous in purpose, and tender or deep in devotion, thy flower and thy promise, falls from thy bosom and finds no home within thine arms? Who hath put this note upon thee, to have 'a miscarrying womb, and dry breasts,' to be strange to thine own flesh, and thine eye cruel towards thy little ones? Thine own offspring, the fruit of thy womb, who love thee and would toil for thee, thou dost gaze upon with fear, as though a portent, or thou dost loathe as an offence;—at best thou dost but endure, as if they had no claim but on thy patience, self-possession, and vigilance, to be rid of them as easily as thou mayest. Thou makest them 'stand all the day idle,' as the very condition of thy bearing with them; or thou biddest them be gone, where they will be more welcome; or thou sellest them for nought to the stranger that passes by. And what wilt thou do in the end thereof?. . .

Scripture is a refuge in any trouble; only let us be on our

guard against seeming to use it further than is fitting, or doing more than sheltering ourselves under its shadow. Let us use it according to our measure. It is far higher and wider than our need; and its language veils our feelings while it gives expression to them. It is sacred and heavenly; and it restrains and purifies, while it sanctions them.

And now, my brethren, 'bless God, praise Him and magnify Him, and praise Him for the things which He hath done unto you in the sight of all that live. It is good to praise God, and exalt His Name, and honourably to show forth the works of God; therefore be not slack to praise Him.' 'All the works of the Lord are good; and He will give every needful thing in due season; so that a man cannot say, This is worse than that; for in time they shall all be well approved. And therefore praise ye the Lord with the whole heart and mouth, and bless the Name of the Lord' (Tob. xxi. 6. Eccles. xxxix. 33-35).

'Leave off from wrath, and let go displeasure; flee from evil, and do the thing that is good.' 'Do that which is good, and no evil shall touch you.' 'Go your way; eat your bread with joy, and drink your wine with a merry heart, for God now accepteth your works; let your garments be always white, and let your head lack no ointment' (Ps. xxxvii. 8. 27; Tob. xii. 7; Eccles. ix. 7, 8).

And, O my brethren, O kind and affectionate hearts, O loving friends, should you know any one whose lot it has been, by writing or by word of mouth, in some degree to help you thus to act; if he has ever told you what you knew about yourselves, or what you did not know; has read to you your wants or feelings, and comforted you by the very reading; has made you feel that there was a higher life than this daily one, and a brighter world than that you see; or encouraged you, or sobered you, or opened a way to the inquiring, or soothed the perplexed; if what he has said or done has ever made you take interest in him, and feel well inclined towards him; remember such a one in time to come, though you hear him not, and pray for him, that in all things he may know God's will, and at all times he may be ready to fulfil it.